# Introduction to Human Resource Management

# Introduction to Human Resource Management

## Ashly Pinnington

Senior Lecturer in Human Resource Management,
University of Queensland

## Tony Edwards

Lecturer in Industrial Relations, Warwick Business School,
University of Warwick

OXFORD
UNIVERSITY PRESS

# OXFORD

UNIVERSITY PRESS

Great Clarendon Street, Oxford OX2 6DP

Oxford University Press is a department of the University of Oxford.
It furthers the University's objective of excellence in research, scholarship,
and education by publishing worldwide in

Oxford  New York

Athens  Auckland  Bangkok  Bogotá  Buenos Aires  Calcutta
Cape Town  Chennai  Dar es Salaam  Delhi  Florence  Hong Kong  Istanbul
Karachi  Kuala Lumpur  Madrid  Melbourne  Mexico City  Mumbai
Nairobi  Paris  São Paulo  Singapore  Taipei  Tokyo  Toronto  Warsaw

with associated companies in  Berlin  Ibadan

Oxford is a registered trade mark of Oxford University Press
in the UK and in certain other countries

Published in the United States
by Oxford University Press Inc., New York

© Ashly Pinnington and Tony Edwards 2000

The moral rights of the author have been asserted
Database right Oxford University Press (maker)

First published 2000

British Library Cataloguing in Publication Data

Data available

Library of Congress Cataloging in Publication Data

Data available

ISBN 0-19-877543-1

1 3 5 7 9 10 8 6 4 2

Typeset in OUP Swift and OUP Argo
by RefineCatch Limited, Bungay, Suffolk
Printed in Great Britain by
Bookcraft Ltd., Midsomer Norton, Somerset.

# Foreword

THE aim of this book is to introduce human resource management (HRM) and to do so in a way that is both challenging and rewarding. As a textbook it presents ideas that have both academic and practical relevance and has been designed to stimulate critical discussion and learning. We explore the issues of the way people are managed in organizations from different analytical perspectives—HRM and industrial relations. The chapters in this book give voice to these different perspectives without trying to force them into an identical view of the world. Both authors have a strong interest in human resources and the workplace, but rather than write on the subject through one authoritative voice, we present the debate on HRM through two voices. We have written the book together as objectively as each perspective permits. While we have both made a contribution to each chapter, Ashly Pinnington has been chiefly responsible for the chapters on definitions (Chapter 1) and managing human resources (Chapters 5 to 9) and Tony Edwards for the chapters on the context of HRM (Chapters 2 to 4) and internationalization (Chapter 10).

This book offers a comprehensive introduction to key concepts and practices in HRM. We have written with the assumption that the textbook will be used for learning through both individual study and discussion. It is intended primarily for undergraduate students interested in how people are managed at work but is also suitable for postgraduates who are new to the subject, particularly MBA students seeking an introduction to core or specialist modules in HRM. *Introduction to Human Resource Management* presents the fundamental concepts and issues of what is a comparatively young subject. Through reading it, you will come to understand more about how employees have been managed in the past and how they are currently managed, and you will be encouraged to investigate ways that people may be better managed in the future.

Chapter 1 explores definitions of HRM by introducing and reviewing competing HRM models. The next three chapters consider the wider environment that HRM functions within: Chapter 2 assesses the environment's influence on strategy, Chapter 3 examines the specific influence of the legal regulation of employment on HRM, and Chapter 4 discusses the implications of HRM for trade unions, combining a brief overview of the history of trade-unionism with an analysis of current developments.

The next five chapters concentrate on the policy and practice of managing human resources in work organizations. Chapter 5 on employee resourcing and careers covers issues concerning how employees are moved into, through, and out of organizations and examines how changes in resourcing have influenced careers. Chapter 6 on motivating employees examines old and new theories of how people are motivated at work. Chapter 7 on rewards and performance management concentrates on the 'extrinsic' factors of motivation and discusses new approaches to rewarding employees. Chapter 8 on learning and development overviews training and development in organizations and discusses innovative approaches to learning. Chapter 9 deals specifically with concepts of organizational change and advice on management practice in implementing change. Chapter 10 examines the relationship between internationalization and human resource management and, finally, the brief conclusion to the book reviews some of its primary themes and considers the future of HRM.

The book's ten main chapters are well suited for use in one semester or in term modules comprising ten or more lecture sessions and with this in mind the book has deliberately been kept concise. It provides the main points for an introduction to the subject, promoting active learning and debate without being overly detailed. The dialogue between HRM and industrial-relations perspectives across the chapters is lively and we hope that you will enjoy it, share our enthusiasm for the issues presented, and benefit by learning from a study and debate on human resource management.

Finally, a brief note about the way the book is structured. Each chapter contains an *Introduction* and *Summary* to help you maintain your orientation and review main points; suggestions for Further Reading for those who wish to know more about some of the main topics covered; *Study Questions* designed to let you engage with the material and absorb it more thoroughly by relating the concepts to the real world and to your own experiences; and *Notes* providing full references for the chapter. At the beginning of the book there are lists of *Figures* and *Tables* to help you when you wish to refer to these illustrations independently of reading the text. Similarly, the *Index* at the back of the book will help you quickly locate mentions of authors, companies, and specific subjects when you want to refer to them in future studies. You will also find a complete *Bibliography* at the end of the book, as well as a *Dictionary of Terms*. The *Case Studies* (Chapters 2–10) are based on real organizations and experiences; those in Chapters 5–10 were reported to the authors by general managers, human resource managers, and other employees in the organizations concerned.

# Acknowledgements

OUR thanks to Gail Prosser for copy editing preliminary drafts of the chapters. Grateful acknowledgement to Peugeot Training and Development for performance appraisal materials and to undergraduate and postgraduate students of London Business School, University of Warwick, University of Exeter, Coventry University, Henley Management College, and ICPE University of Ljubljana for feedback on draft chapters and case studies.

# Contents

# Figures

# Tables

# Part I

# Definitions

# Chapter 1
# What is HRM?

## Chapter Contents

Introduction

1 **North American and British Models of HRM**
Soft HRM
*The Harvard model, Beer et al. (US)*
*Guest (UK)*
Hard HRM
*The Michigan model, Fombrun et al. (US)*

2 **Industrial Relations Perspectives on HRM**
*Kochan's framework for labour relations (US)*
*Storey on HRM v. personnel management (UK)*

3 **The Influence of Japanese Management Practices**
*Oliver and Wilkinson*

4 **The European Environment of HRM**
*Brewster and Bournois*

Summary
Study Questions
Further Reading
Notes

# Introduction

H UMAN Resource Management (HRM) is a new way of thinking about how people should be managed as employees in the workplace. (A brief history of how the employer–employee relationship was handled before HRM is depicted in the timeline (Box 1.1).) In much the same way as there are different roads to success, HRM is not one theory but an evolving set of competing theories. HRM, as a tradition of thought on managing people, is most commonly traced back to seminal works written by American academics in the early 1980s. These American and American-inspired theories, or models, of HRM are sometimes subdivided under two schools of thought, 'hard' HRM and 'soft' HRM. Both of these schools will be discussed in this chapter. In essence, hard HRM focuses on managing and controlling employees so as to achieve the organization's strategic goals, whilst soft HRM gives more recognition to the needs of employees and the importance of their commitment to the organization.

In the employment relationship, employees contract their labour in exchange for various types of rewards from employers. Whether they are working full time or part time, employees seek to obtain from the employer what they consider to be equitable terms and conditions of employment. At the minimum, most employees expect to be managed and treated fairly. Indeed, as levels of education become higher, a greater proportion of the population world-wide expect more than this: they seek a range of intrinsic rewards such as job satisfaction, a degree of challenge, a sense of career progression, and satisfying relationships with co-workers. HRM has been proposed both as a way to meet these expectations and as a more effective way of managing employees, although there is considerable disagreement as to how far HRM can be implemented.

Advocates of HRM have presented it as having a role to play in both the private and public sectors. In the private sector, if the employer fails to manage the human resource well enough to compete successfully in the market-place, then ultimately the business will fail. The company may decline slowly where competition is weak or it may become rapidly bankrupt where competition is strong. The public sector, likewise, has an interest in effective management of employees, and the standards and quality of public-sector services are highly dependent on employees' motivation, skills, and service orientation. HRM, therefore, is about effective management of the employment relationship and applies to management activity in all organizational settings, even unpaid and voluntary work.

The remainder of this chapter is an overview of several different theories and approaches to HRM; subsequent chapters explore the application of HRM principles and practices in organizations today. The theories covered in the following sections come from some of the best-known North American and British writers on HRM and include the 'soft' and 'hard' distinction, industrial relations perspectives, and a European model of HRM. The influence of Japanese management practices on HRM is also

BOX 1.1
## UK Personnel Management/HRM Timeline

**1800s**
Some paternalist employers such as the Rowntree and Leverhulme families strongly concerned about the welfare of the workforce; health and education, for example, were seen as part of their responsibility. But employees' welfare primarily the concern of outside institutions and individuals, particularly the church, charities, and welfare workers.

**1900–38**
Formation and consolidation of personnel management as a professional body. Introduction of more systematic record keeping and management of the human resource. Role of 'looking after' workers, previously the domain of women, develops respectability at the higher levels of responsibility as 'man's work'.

**1939–45**
Intervention by national government in regulating employment and schemes for sustaining and improving morale in the workplace. Restrictions over trade union activity.

**1946–59**
Post-Second World War reconstruction. In 1946, Institute of Labour changes its name to the Institute of Personnel Management (IPM). Growth of collective bargaining. Unemployment low. Personnel management as manpower planning.

**1960–78**
Personnel management led by skilled industrial relations negotiators. Period of trade union militancy and industrial relations unrest. Increased government legislation on employment matters and growing unemployment.

**1979–89**
Introduction and development of human resource management as an ideology and a prescription for managing the employment relationship. Unemployment around three million. Government legislation curtailing the freedoms and powers of trade unions.

**1990–99**
In 1994, the Institute of Personnel Management (IPM) and Institute of Training and Development (ITD) merge to form the Institute of Personnel and Development (IPD). Human Resource Management becomes more consolidated as an orthodoxy, although many organizations still use the older term of 'personnel management' and very few apply HRM policies coherently or consistently.

introduced, because the Japanese methods have been so strongly influential in prompting Western executives and academics to reflect on how businesses are run by comparing how human resources are managed in the East with how they are managed in the West.

# 1 North American and British Models of HRM

## Soft HRM

### The Harvard Model, Beer *et al.* (US)

HRM was launched as a course in 1981 at Harvard Business School. It was the first new course in Harvard's core curriculum to be introduced for nearly twenty years. It was established because there was widespread feeling among Harvard's faculty that new developments in the fields of organizational behaviour, organizational development, personnel administration, and labour relations were best represented in a new course. In 1985, Richard Walton published an article in the *Harvard Business Review* called 'From Control to Commitment in the Workplace', which popularized soft HRM as a distinctive approach to managing human resources. His argument was that effective HRM depends not on strategies for controlling employees but on strategies for winning employees' commitment. The Harvard model, first put forward in 1984 by Michael Beer *et al.* in the book *Managing Human Assets*, takes a soft HRM perspective similar to that of Walton and was devised primarily to inform general managers of improved ways of managing people. The model recommends that general managers must hold greater responsibility for HRM. How to get general managers more involved in HRM has been a major preoccupation for organizations in the 1980s and 1990s and so we now consider Beer's model in more detail rather than Walton's which concentrates on the mutual concerns of employers and employees.

The Harvard model proposes that many of the diverse personnel and labour relations activities can be dealt with under four human resource (HR) categories: employee influence, human resource flow, reward systems, and work systems.[1] These are general issues that managers must attend to regardless of whether the organization is unionized or not, whatever management style is applied, and whether it is a growing or declining business.

*Employee influence* is the question of how much responsibility, authority, and power is voluntarily delegated by management and to whom. One of the critical questions here is, if management share their influence, to what extent does this create compatibility (the word the authors used is 'congruence') of interests between management and groups of employees? The assumption the authors make is that any influence employees have should be compatible with management's purpose and priorities. *Human resource flow* concerns managing the flow of people into, through, and out of the organization. This means making decisions on recruitment and selection, promotion, termination of employment, and related issues of job security, career development, advancement, and fair treatment. Managers and personnel specialists, according to the Harvard model, must work together to ensure that the organization has an appropriate flow of people to meet its strategic requirements.

*Reward systems* regulate how employees are extrinsically and intrinsically rewarded for their work. Extrinsic rewards are tangible pay and benefits: pay, overtime pay, bonuses, profit sharing, pensions, holiday entitlement, health insurance, and other benefits, such as flexible working hours. Intrinsic rewards are intangible benefits and are said to strongly influence employees' motivation, job satisfaction, and organizational commitment. Intrinsic rewards are rewards from the work itself, such as sense of purpose, achievement, challenge, involvement, self-confidence, self-esteem, and satisfaction. The Harvard model recommends that employees should be highly involved in the design of an organization's reward systems but observes that final decisions, besides meeting employees' needs, must be consistent with the overall business strategy, management philosophy, and other HRM policies. *Work systems* are the ways in which people, information, activities, and technology are arranged, at all levels of the organization, so that work can be performed efficiently and effectively.

Policies in these four areas must be designed and applied in a coherent manner because, Beer and his co-authors argue, HRM is considerably less likely to be effective where policies are disjointed, made up of odd combinations of past practices, and are *ad hoc* responses to outside pressures. The four policy areas must satisfy the many stakeholders of the enterprise—for example, shareholders, employees, customers, suppliers, communities, trade unions, trade associations, and government. Employees are major stakeholders of the enterprise and it is the responsibility of managers to establish systems that promote employee influence. Some people would say that managers do not consider enough how to facilitate employee influence; indeed, Beer *et al.* claim that, of the four issues discussed, employee influence is the central feature of an HR system, as illustrated in the triangle in Fig. 1.1.

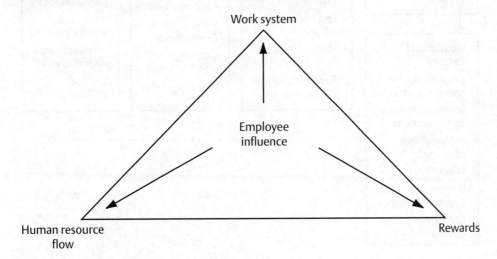

**Figure 1.1 Human resource system**

A further recommendation of the Harvard model is that, when making HRM policy decisions, managers should consider the 'four Cs': commitment, competence, congruence (compatibility), and cost-effectiveness. That is, managers should ask to what extent the policies they implement will: enhance the *commitment* of people to their work and the organization; attract, retain, and develop people with the needed *competence*; sustain *congruence* (compatibility) between management and employees; and be *cost-effective* in terms of wages, employee turnover, and risk of employee dissatisfaction.

The authors' conceptual overview of HRM is represented diagrammatically as a 'map of the HRM territory' (see Fig. 1.2). They propose that HRM is closely connected with both the external environment and the internal organization. Their model of the territory of HRM shows that stakeholder interests and 'situational factors' (the factors that make up the context in which a business must operate) are interlinked with HRM policy choices, which in turn lead to HR outcomes. These outcomes have long-term consequences that have a feedback effect on stakeholder interests and 'situational factors', and so on. The main stakeholder interests are: shareholders, management, employee groups, government, the community, and unions. The situational factors are: workforce characteristics, business strategy and conditions, management

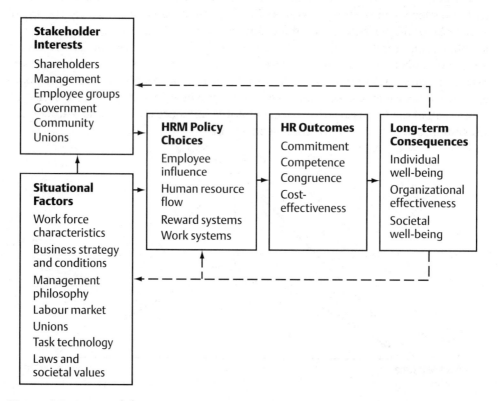

**Figure 1.2  A map of the HRM territory**

philosophy, labour markets, unions, task technology, and laws and societal values. The long-term consequences of HR outcomes are considered under three main headings: individual well-being, organizational effectiveness, and societal well-being.

The Harvard model is soft HRM because it concentrates attention on outcomes for people, especially their well-being and organizational commitment. It does not rank business performance or one of the stakeholder interests—for example, shareholders —as being inherently superior to other legitimate interests, such as the community or unions. Organizational effectiveness is represented in the Harvard model as a critical long-term consequence of HR outcomes, but alongside the equally important consequences of individual and societal well-being. An organization putting this model into practice would therefore aim to ensure that its employees were involved in their work and able to participate in decision making. HRM policies would be developed and implemented to meet employees' needs for influence, but within the limitation of having to be consistent with the overall business strategy and management philosophy.

## Guest (UK)

A second soft HRM model came from David Guest in 1987.[2] Guest argued that HRM in the UK should be about designing policies and practices to achieve four main outcomes: strategic integration (planning/implementation); high employee commitment to the organization; high workforce flexibility and adaptability; and a high-quality workforce. Strategic integration means ensuring that the organization's business plans are implemented through appropriately designed HR policies and practices. Companies have been criticized for treating HRM and strategy separately, therefore failing to combine HRM with the business strategy.

He proposed that these four HRM outcomes will lead to the desirable organizational outcomes of high job performance, stronger problem solving, greater change consistent with strategic goals, and improved cost-effectiveness, while also reducing employee turnover, absences, and grievances. However, Guest warned that these outcomes will be achieved only if an organization has a coherent strategy of HRM policies fully integrated into the business strategy and supported by all levels of line management.

Guest's model is similar to the Harvard but has seven HR policy categories instead of four (see Fig. 1.3). Four of Guest's categories are broadly the same as Beer's Harvard categories. Where Beer has *human resource flow*, Guest has *manpower flow* and *recruitment, selection, and socialization*; both models have *reward systems* as a category; and what Beer calls *work systems* Guest calls *organizational and job design*. Guest's three other categories are: policy formulation and management of change; employee appraisal, training, and development; and communication systems.

*Policy formulation and management of change* means establishing HR policy to explicitly identify the nature of the change required in a business and manage the process of change. *Employee appraisal, training, and development* involve both informally and formally evaluating employee performance and the need for training and development. Once these have been evaluated, policies must be in place to ensure that timely and appropriate training and employee development occur. *Communication systems* are the various processes and media that the organization uses to encourage two-way flows of

## Policies for identifying human resource and organizational outcomes

| Policies | Human resource outcomes | Organizational outcomes |
| --- | --- | --- |
| Organizational and job design | | High job performance |
| Policy formulation and implementation/management of change | Strategic planning/ implementation | High problem-solving |
| Recruitment, selection and socialization | Commitment | Successful change |
| Appraisal, training and development | Flexibility/adaptability | Low turnover |
| Manpower flows— through, up and out of the organization | | Low absence |
| Reward systems | Quality | Low grievance level |
| Communication systems | | High cost-effectiveness i.e. full utilization of human resources |

### Figure 1.3 Guest's model of HRM

*Source*: Guest, D. E., 'Human Resource Management and Industrial Relations', *Journal of Management Studies* (1987), 24, 5, September, pp. 503–21, Table 11, p. 516.

information between management and employees. Typically, these systems use bottom-up and top-down methods: a bottom-up method might be, for example, an employee suggestion scheme, and a top-down method might be a quarterly newsletter on the business performance of the organization.

Guest's model has been criticized for presenting an ideal and for assuming unrealistic conditions for practising HRM.[3] Guest himself reported ten years later, in 1997, that whilst considerably more research data on HRM in organizations had been gathered, the link between the adoption of HRM policies and high performance remains somewhat elusive. He described progress in the UK towards HRM as being somewhat slow and 'crab-like'. British trade unions, he wrote, have started to become more positive about HRM and will work more openly and productively with management; however, many senior managers still retain a short-term perspective on their businesses. The result is that many HR initiatives appear to employees to be management fads rather than a genuine long-term commitment to the organization and its people.

Guest's model constitutes soft HRM for the same reasons that the Harvard model does: both give strong recognition to the needs of employees (for example, motivation and development) in the running of the organization. Also, both are committed to employees' needs as long as the measures taken to meet those needs remain consistent with the strategy of the organization and management aims. Guest claims his model is more straightforward than the Harvard model, which maps the territory of HRM, because he simply prescribes that improved implementation of just seven HR policies will result in better HR outcomes.

# Hard HRM

## The Michigan Model, Fombrun *et al.* (US)

In the same year (1984) that Beer *et al.* published *Managing Human Assets*, Fombrun, Tichy, and Devanna published *Strategic Human Resource Management*.[4] This book proposed a different model of HRM, frequently referred to as the Michigan School because one of its main proponents was an academic from the University of Michigan's Graduate School of Business Administration,[5] although the ideas were generated in partnership with researchers from two other well-known American universities, Wharton and Columbia. The British academic, John Storey, describes this model as 'hard' HRM because it emphasizes treating employees as a means to achieving the organization's strategy, as a resource that is used in a calculative and purely rational manner. Hard HRM focuses more than soft HRM does on using people as resources and as a means towards the competitive success of the organization.[6]

It is easy to be overly simplistic when evaluating Fombrun, Tichy, and Devanna's approach to HRM. On the one hand, there are those who dismiss it for being inhuman; on the other, there are those who proclaim it to be just common sense and the only route to business success. Arguably, the strength *and* the major limitation of their approach is that it focuses on the organization and how it can best rationally respond to its external environment. Focusing on the level of the organization has the advantage of drawing attention to aspects partly under the control of management, such as formal strategy, structure, and preferred culture. On the other hand, attending to the organizational level may lead managers to assume that, through organizational strategy, structure, and HR systems, they have more power than they really have to change individuals and influence the external environment.

Hard HRM assumes that increasing productivity will continue to be management's principal reason for improving HRM; while this is a major factor in many private- and public-sector organizations, it clearly is not the only one. Fombrun *et al.* argue that conditions of the external environment—for example, heightened competition and market uncertainty—necessitate 'strategic' HRM, that is, HRM designed to achieve the strategies, or goals, of the organization.

The authors proposed a framework for strategic HRM that assumes the needs of the firm are paramount.[7] They said organizations exist to accomplish a mission or achieve objectives and that strategic management involves consideration of three interconnected issues. First, the mission and strategy must be considered because these are an organization's reason for being. Second, the organization's structure, personnel requirements, and tasks, must be formally laid out, including systems of accounting and communications. Third, HR systems need to be established and maintained because, as the authors state, 'people are recruited and developed to do jobs defined by the organization's formal structure: their performance must be monitored and rewards allocated to maintain productivity'.[8]

The Michigan model observes that different business strategies and related organization structures can lead to contrasting styles of HRM in activities such as selection, appraisal, rewards, and development.[9] For example, a single-product company with a traditional functional structure (that is, structured according to the various functions of the business—finance, accounting, marketing, sales, production and operations, personnel, etc.) will select its people on the basis of their expertise in the specific functions. Appraisal of employee performance will be largely informal and administered via personal contact; the reward system will vary unsystematically across the functions and employee development will be limited primarily to the functional area in which the employee works. On the other hand, a company with a multi-divisional structure and a strategy for product diversification may have a very different system of HRM. Selection would be systematic and according to both functional experience and general management ability. The appraisal system would be formal and impersonal based on quantitative criteria such as productivity and return on investment and on qualitative, subjective judgements about individual performance. The reward system would systematically reward contribution to the diversification strategy, and bonuses would likely be paid according to achievement of profitability targets. Employee development would be more complex and systematic than it would be in a company with a single-product strategy. In the multi-divisional company, employees are accustomed to being periodically transferred to different functions and areas of business. Individual development would be cross-divisional, cross-subsidiary, and corporate.

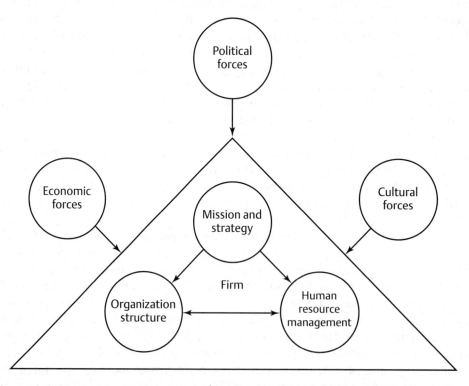

**Figure 1.4 Strategic management and environmental pressures**

*Source: Strategic Human Resource Management* by C. J. Fombrun, N. M. Tichy, and M. A. Devanna (Fig. 3.1, p. 35), copyright © 1984 John Wiley & Sons. Reprinted by permission of John Wiley & Sons, Inc.

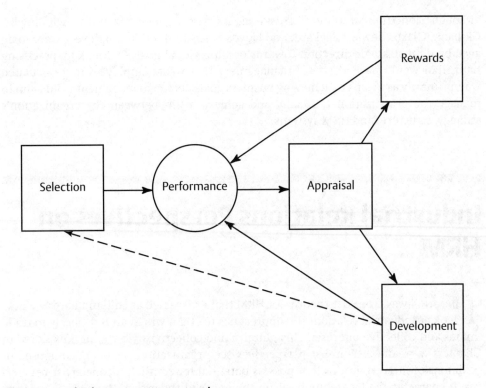

## Figure 1.5 The human resource cycle

*Source*: *Strategic Human Resource Management* by C. J. Fombrun, N. M. Tichy, and M. A. Devanna (Fig. 3.2, p. 41), copyright © 1984 John Wiley & Sons. Reprinted by permission of John Wiley & Sons, Inc.

The Michigan model represents the external and internal factors of HRM as a triangle (see Fig. 1.4). Once management have decided how the mission and business strategy, organization structure, and HRM are to be organized and integrated—and assuming it is an appropriate response to political, economic, and cultural forces —then they can begin to design the human resource system in more detail.

Finally, the Michigan model argues that within HRM there is a human resource cycle affecting individual and organizational performance (see Fig. 1.5). It describes the four functions of this cycle as follows:

Performance is a function of all the human resource components: *selecting* people who are best able to perform the jobs defined by the structure, *appraising* their performance to facilitate the equitable distribution of rewards, motivating employees by linking *rewards* to high levels of performance, and *developing* employees to enhance their current performance at work as well as to prepare them to perform in positions they may hold in the future.[10]

The Michigan model is hard HRM because it is based on strategic control, organizational structure, and systems for managing people. It acknowledges the central importance of motivating and rewarding people, but concentrates most on managing human assets to achieve strategic goals. Subsequent empirical research has not produced evidence of organizations systematically and consistently practising hard HRM, although a longitudinal study (by Truss *et al.*, 1997) of large organizations (including BT, Citibank, Glaxo, Hewlett Packard, and Lloyds Bank) found that employees were managed by tight strategic direction towards organizational goals. A company practising hard HRM would have a style of management that treats employees in a calculated way, primarily as means to achieving business goals. Its top management would aim to manage the organization rationally and achieve a 'fit' between the organization's strategy, structure, and HRM systems.

# 2   Industrial Relations Perspectives on HRM

T URNING away from the theories of HRM that are classed as soft and hard, we now look at industrial relations (IR) approaches to HRM, which attend closely to trade unions and collective interests. This pluralist and collectivist viewpoint is explored in Chapters 2, 3, and 4. Pluralist perspectives see organizations as being composed of coalitions of interest groups that possess potential for conflict. A collectivist perspective is characterized by an emphasis on the needs of the group, the opposite of individualism. In this section we look at an influential framework for analysing industrial relations that promotes partnership between unions, employers, and government, and at a checklist, written by Storey, for investigating points of difference between HRM and traditional personnel management.

### Kochan's Framework for Labour Relations (US)

One of the most common criticisms of hard HRM is that it focuses exclusively on the organization and its needs while ignoring the wider environment in which all organizations operate. Hard HRM is also criticized for having a managerialist orientation and for assuming a 'unitarist' perspective—this means that employees' needs and interests are ultimately subservient to the needs of the organization as dictated by management. Thomas Kochan is known for being critical of unitarist approaches to HRM and he proposed a framework for analysing industrial relations that addresses the need for transformation of the employment relationship at the level of society more than at the level of the organization.

Kochan, Katz, and McKersie proposed in their 1994 book, *The Transformation of American Industrial Relations*, that the future of American industrial relations will be decided by the strategic choices of business, labour, and the government.[11] Kochan *et al.* acknowledged the diversity of American IR practices but concluded that four broad patterns, or 'scenarios', of evolution are nevertheless observable.

Scenario 1 proposes a 'continuation of current trends', characterized by the continuing decline of private-sector unionization; stabilized and comparatively high public-sector unionization; increased technological change and contracting out of services previously provided in-house (often known as 'outsourcing') as management aim to reduce the influence and scope of unions; and generally reduced innovation in HRM practices. Scenario 1 envisages a widening gap between those companies that are pursuing a highly skilled workforce, teamwork, and other human resource innovations on the one hand and companies that are downsizing, cost cutting, and generally taking a reactive stance to employee relations on the other. A variant of this is Scenario 2, 'labour law reform', in which all of the conditions of Scenario 1 apply but at a slower rate of change. Political leaders will encourage reforms to reduce the influence of union labour in the belief that they are responsible for many of the problems in the management–union relationship.

Scenario 3, 'diffusion of labour-management innovations', argues that if reforms are combined with broader innovation in bargaining relationships between management and unions, particularly in companies that are partially unionized, then management commitment to HRM issues may be strengthened. Scenario 4, 'new organizing strategies', predicts fundamental change in IR, with a transformation of the relationship between business, labour, and government, brought about by new approaches to HRM developing in the growing occupations and industries. The authors warn, though, that this scenario is the least likely to occur (although it is probably the most interesting one to contemplate!).

All four future scenarios assume IR outcomes are determined by a continuously evolving pattern of environmental pressures and organizational responses. The progress of IR unfurls over time as a result of choices made by labour, management, and government. Kochan *et al.* believed that the general trend in IR towards a weaker role for unions as portrayed in their four scenarios reflects the 'deep-seated resistance towards unions that historically has been embedded in the belief system of US managers'.[12]

Kochan's framework was based on analysing trends in labour relations in the US and the scenarios extrapolate from them the different possible future outcomes for US business and society. It assumes that there is greater potential for innovation in HRM in the twenty-first century than there was in the twentieth century, although the transformation of labour relations is not something that has happened yet, either in the USA or the UK. We now consider a checklist for analysing HRM and IR that was specifically developed to identify the extent of change from traditional personnel management and IR towards HRM.

## Storey on HRM v. Personnel Management (UK)

John Storey proposed that HRM can be understood in four different ways. First, it can be viewed as another word for personnel management, as simply breathing new life into old ideas and ways of working by changing the jargon. Second, it can signal a more integrated use of personnel-management policies and practices. Storey cited the Michigan model of strategic HRM as an example of this second view, commenting that performance in that model is affected by a cycle of HR interventions that are sequential managerial tasks; therefore, it is arguably a more integrated use of personnel management. A third use of the term 'HRM', Storey said, is to signal a more business-oriented and business-integrated approach to the management of labour. The 'levers' of HRM (selection, rewards, etc.) are pulled in integration with one another so that the system is in line with the business strategy. Storey noted the Beer/Harvard model as being exemplary of this approach but criticized it for being too general in contrast to a fourth position, that of Richard Walton, which argues that HRM is a unique and distinct approach to employee commitment via policies of mutuality (as in mutual goals, influence, respect, rewards, and responsibility).[13]

Storey quoted work by Karen Legge that underlines three important differences between HRM and personnel management.[14] HRM more strongly emphasizes development of the management team, strategic integration of business management and people management, and the management of organizational culture. Storey took this further in his 'twenty-five-item checklist' (see Fig. 1.6). This table of differences is frequently quoted in textbooks and HRM teaching, but it must be remembered that the points are meant to highlight an idealized view of the range of opinion Storey encountered in his research interviews with managers. He conducted case research on fifteen British organizations from the automotive, public sector, electrical and mechanical, and process industries and found that HRM was being applied piecemeal by managers rather than adopted as a coherent approach.[15] His points of difference provide a stereotypical but helpful means for describing different perspectives on HRM and personnel management/IR.

Storey's 'ideal description' of personnel management/IR is a clear picture of traditional personnel management supportive of the co-existence of management and unions. Here personnel management operates under collective bargaining arrangements in which unions have sufficient power that management has to negotiate and work with them. Each of the twenty-five points marks a contrast between personnel management and HRM. For example, point 6, 'the nature of relations', under the 'beliefs and assumptions' dimension, asserts that HRM admits only one legitimate interest to which all should adhere (a 'unitarist' orientation), while personnel management assumes there to be many legitimate interests in the organization (a 'pluralist' orientation).

The twenty-five points can be used as a framework to assess an organization's approach to human resource management. To date, however, most British companies have tended to concentrate on one or two areas of HR policy and practice, such as teamwork and employee involvement, rather than integrating a range of initiatives.[16]

# 3 The Influence of Japanese Management Practices

WE now turn to Japanese management practices and examine their influence in Britain as an alternative approach to HRM. It has been said that HR

| Dimension | Personnel and IR | HRM |
|---|---|---|
| *Beliefs and assumptions* | | |
| 1 Contract | Careful delineation of written contracts | Aim to go 'beyond contract' |
| 2 Rules | Importance of devising clear rules/ mutuality | 'Can do' outlook: impatience with 'rule' |
| 3 Guide to management action | Procedures/consistency control | 'Business need'/flexibility/ commitment |
| 4 Behaviour referent | Norms/custom and practice | Values/mission |
| 5 Managerial task *vis-à-vis* labour | Monitoring | Nurturing |
| 6 Nature of relations | Pluralist | Unitarist |
| 7 Conflict | Institutionalized | De-emphasized |
| 8 Standardization | High (e.g. 'parity' an issue) | Low (e.g. 'parity' not seen as relevant) |
| *Strategic aspects* | | |
| 9 Key relations | Labour–management | Business–customer |
| 10 Initiatives | Piecemeal | Integrated |
| 11 Corporate plan | Marginal to | Central to |
| 12 Speed of decisions | Slow | Fast |
| *Line management* | | |
| 13 Management role | Transactional | Transformational leadership |
| 14 Key managers | Personnel/IR specialists | General/business/line managers |
| 15 Prized management skills | Negotiation | Facilitation |
| *Key levers* | | |
| 16 Foci of attention for interventions | Personnel procedures | Wide-ranging cultural, structural and personnel strategies |
| 17 Selection | Separate, marginal task | Integrated, key task |
| 18 Pay | Job evaluation: multiple, fixed grades | Performance-related: few if any grades |
| 19 Conditions | Separately negotiated | Harmonization |
| 20 Labour–management | Collective bargaining contracts | Towards individual contracts |
| 21 Thrust of relations with stewards | Regularized through facilities and training | Marginalized (with exception of some bargaining for change models) |
| 22 Communication | Restricted flow/indirect | Increased flow/direct |
| 23 Job design | Division of labour | Teamwork |
| 24 Conflict handling | Reach temporary truces | Manage climate and culture |
| 25 Training and development | Controlled access to courses | Learning companies |

## Figure 1.6 Storey's twenty-five-item checklist

*Source*: *Human Resource Management: A Critical Text*, J. Storey, 1995, Routledge, Table 1.1, p. 10. An earlier version of this checklist appeared in J. Storey, *Developments in the Management of Human Resources*, 1992, Blackwell, as figure 2.2, p. 35. 'Twenty-seven points of difference'.

initiatives are integrated to a greater extent, both with each other and with the business strategy, in Japanese-managed organizations than they are in British-managed organizations.

## Oliver and Wilkinson

Oliver and Wilkinson offer an interpretation of HRM in the UK, chiefly relating to the manufacturing industries, based on what they call 'the Japanization of British industry'.[17] By 'Japanization' they mean two things: one, an evolving process during the 1980s and 1990s of emulation of Japanese manufacturing methods; and, two, increasing Japanese direct investment in Western economies.

Oliver and Wilkinson concluded from their research that Japanese production methods are based on the successful management of high-dependency relationships.[18] In Japan, the economy is organized in a different manner to the West. Japanese managers are accustomed to high-dependency relationships and to working within a group of organizations that have long-term business relationships. This sense of mutual dependency is reflected in Japan at the level of government, where top business leaders are willing to seek consensus on how competitive business strategies should serve the national interest, and at the level of the organization, where relationships between company unions and management are less adversarial.

In contrast, UK businesses have tended to act independently and in competition with one another. Oliver and Wilkinson observed that the stumbling block to long-term change in people management and manufacturing methods lies in the difficulty UK managers have both culturally and practically in coping with greater dependency between organizations, unions, suppliers, and government.[19] The traditional approach to employment by government in the UK has been to minimize regulation of employers' interests and influence the employment relationship only so far as it concerns basic rights and legal codes of practice. Longer-term supplier partnerships and supplier reduction programmes are comparatively new phenomena in the UK. Historically, the customary way of managing suppliers has been to keep them at arm's length and to bargain on price, which in Oliver and Wilkinson's terms constitutes a 'low-dependency relationship'.[20]

The Japanese economy grew very suddenly from 2% of the world's GDP in 1967 to 10% in 1987, prompting many countries to examine the causes of Japan's success. Comparative studies of Japanese corporations and corporations in other countries revealed remarkable differences in productivity and quality[21] and distinct methods of manufacturing and people management. Oliver and Wilkinson argue that developed Western countries can successfully adopt Japanese production methods, but only where an organization is able to control and work within a wider, supportive environment:

Japanization is not simply a matter of implementing total quality control and just-in-time (JIT) production processes—it entails the adoption of particular work practices and personnel and industrial relations systems as well, and the whole package of change is most likely to succeed where the organization has some degree of control over its external environment.[22]

Oliver and Wilkinson noted some similarities in practice between the USA and Japan towards unions, one example being the tendency of Japanese start-up companies in the UK to adopt a strategy of union avoidance. Unions are recognized by these Japanese companies in traditional manufacturing regions where there is pressure to work with them, but in regions with less of a collective union tradition (for example, Livingston, Telford, Worcester, and Northampton) they are not. UK attitudes towards Japanese management practices vary from being very supportive and seeing them as the solution to British industry's problems[23] to seeing them as entailing work intensification, heightened control, and greater profits exclusively for the suppliers of capital.[24]

Whatever one's viewpoint, there is little doubt that HR practices associated with Japanese management methods, such as thorough selection procedures, single-status conditions for all employees in the workplace (sometimes symbolized by a common work uniform), systematic performance appraisal, and innovations in pay and rewards, have been influential not only in the UK but in many countries in Europe, to which the last section of this chapter will now turn.

# 4 The European Environment of HRM

R ECENTLY, interest has grown in the possibility of there being a model of HRM which is distinctly European. The model of the European environment of HRM, first produced in 1991 by Chris Brewster and François Bournois, emphasizes the cultural, legal, and market contexts of human resource strategy and practice.[25] Brewster says that he prefers Thomas Kochan's framework of IR (discussed above), which, he contends, is a more comprehensive view of the range of social factors influencing HRM than other models, such as soft and hard HRM. He also proposes that the model of the European environment of HRM is partly a response to dissatisfaction with American HRM.[26] The anti-unionism of the American approach to HRM has been more consistent in US national culture than in some countries within Europe which have shown greater willingness, during some periods of their history, to work within a social partnership.

### Brewster and Bournois (1991)

In the Brewster and Bournois model, HR strategy is only partly subservient to corporate strategy because HRM is influenced by behaviour and performance from both inside and outside the organization. The organization and its human resource strategies and practices interact with the environment and, at the same time, are part of it. The model shows that HRM policy and practice are not exclusively an organization's choice but are also influenced by the wider environment, particularly the national culture and the industry sector the organization operates in (see Fig. 1.7).

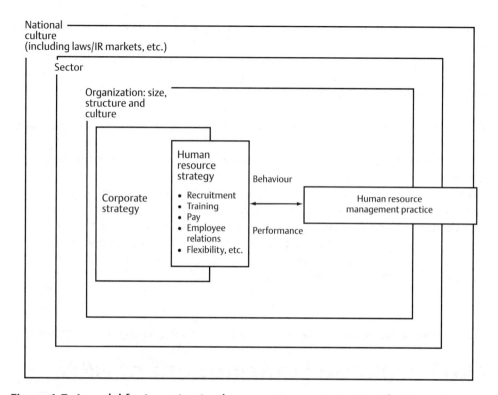

**Figure 1.7  A model for investigating human resource strategies: the European environment**

*Source*: Brewster and Hegewisch (1994), *Policy and Practice in European Human Resource Management* (1994) Routledge, Figure 1.1, p. 6. Adapted from C. Brewster and F. Bournois (1991), 'A European Perspective on Human Resource Management', *Personnel Review*, 20, 6, pp. 4–13.

In 1995 Brewster reported the results of a survey[27] covering fourteen European countries in which three regional clusters corresponding to level of socio-economic development were found: a Latin cluster (Spain, Italy, France); a Central European cluster (Central European countries plus the UK and Ireland); and a Nordic cluster (Norway, Sweden, Denmark). Brewster proposed that the survey shows Latin countries to be at the lowest stage of socio-economic development, the UK and Ireland next, then continental Central European countries, and finally Nordic countries at the top of the development scale.[28] The Latin culture, at the lowest stage of development, according to Brewster, is characterized by an oral culture and political structures that create docile attitudes towards authority, whereas the culture of the highest stage—that of the Nordic countries—displays a widespread collective orientation to management, extensive consultation between employers and workers, documented strategies, and (perhaps this conclusion is to be expected from an HRM researcher) substantial and authoritative HRM departments.

Despite the tendency of the national cultures to cluster into three regional groups, Brewster found some trends common across most European countries. Pay determination, according to the evidence of the survey, is becoming increasingly decentralized, and flexible pay systems are becoming more common. Flexible working practices are increasing in European countries (for example, atypical working; annualized hours; and temporary, casual, and fixed-term contracts). There is, unfortunately, also continuity in lack of equal opportunities in so far as, at senior management level, women and ethnic minorities are still under-represented. However, other opportunities vary much more by country. For example, in Greece and Spain, where women are a third of the workforce, there is very limited childcare provision, but in Sweden and France the provision is more extensive. Training investment is on the increase overall in the whole of Europe, particularly for managerial and professional staff, but the level of government intervention varies greatly by country.[29] The role of the HR function was also found to vary according to country, HR enjoying the greatest representation at board level in Spain and France, where 70–80% of organizations have an HR director (thus contradicting, on this point, Brewster's ranking of the Latin cluster as the least developed), and somewhat less in the UK, where fewer than 50% of organizations have an HR director.

European employment differs from employment in other parts of the world in that it is comparatively more unionized, and unions play a wider role in society and the workplace in European countries than they do in many other countries. Brewster attributes some of the persistence of unions in Europe to their official recognition, as social partners, within the European Union. So, what is the model of the European environment of HRM? Essentially, it has similarities with Kochan's framework in that both accommodate partnership between unions, employers, and government. The European model assumes that national culture shapes HRM practices and that the culture of countries within Europe are, despite their differences, more positive overall towards social partnership than is US culture. In summary, however, the European environment of HRM does not indicate a distinctive move away from personnel management; rather what's happening in Europe is a complex mix of continuation of traditional personnel management and change towards HRM.

# Summary

THE US and UK models of soft HRM and the US model of hard HRM discussed in this chapter propose ways of better managing human resources. They are a mixture of the old and the new and cover many of the areas of traditional personnel management—for example, recruitment and selection, appraisal, rewards, and training and development. Both hard and soft HRM share a concern for matching the organization's strategic needs.

In sum, the hard face of HRM emphasizes the 'quantitative, calculative, and business strategic aspects of managing the headcount resource in as "rational" a way as for any other economic factor' while the soft face emphasizes 'communication, motivation and leadership'.[30]

Guest's model of soft HRM emphasizes the new by predicting the HRM factors that lead to desirable outcomes for people and organizations. These models of hard and soft HRM provide different perspectives, but all are unitarist; that is, they assume that management represents the main legitimate interest in a business, and that employees' interests are largely aligned with those of managers.

Japanese management practices also are unitarist but operate by expecting a more stable and interdependent relationship among large global Japanese corporations, and between these corporations and their networks of long-term suppliers. The environmental factors an organization must deal with strongly influence policy and practice, particularly the national government and, in the case of Japanese companies, the special characteristics of the organization of Japanese industry. Oliver and Wilkinson assert that the Japanese approach can be adopted in other countries, such as the UK, if the organization can sustain sufficient control over its environment.

Brewster and Bournois' model assumes the organization and its HRM are strongly constrained by wider social forces, particularly national characteristics. Their model of the European environment of HRM draws attention to the significant role played by national culture in shaping HRM. It accords a positive role to social partnership between unions, employers, and government. Kochan's framework shares a similar emphasis on the significance of national characteristics and acknowledges the importance of partnership with unions. However, it is not as optimistic as the Brewster model, perceiving there to be less likelihood of progress in social partnership because of US employers' traditional suspicion of unions. The Kochan IR framework nevertheless differs from the other US and UK models of HRM by prescribing that a stronger partnership should exist between unions, employers, and government. Kochan's framework does not advocate HRM from a unitarist viewpoint but assumes a pluralist perspective that acknowledges a long-term role for unions working in partnership with employers and government as the most effective means of reconciling their differences.

We should make a brief diversion here to mention that this chapter has not reviewed radical theories of HRM[31] and IR, with the result that all of the models covered are normative, meaning that they don't fundamentally question the values of the society they exist in.[32] Watson's radical definition of personnel management serves as an excellent illustration of a radical theory:

Personnel management is concerned with assisting those who run work organisations to meet their purposes through the obtaining of the work efforts of human beings, the exploitation of those efforts and the dispensing with of those efforts when they are no longer required. Concern may be shown with human welfare, justice or satisfaction but only insofar as this is necessary for controlling interests to be met and, then, always at least cost.[33]

HRM has also been strongly criticized by some academics for being a vacuous rhetoric, the ambiguity of which hides a harsher market reality of employees' labour becoming increasingly a commodity.[34] Karen Legge has proposed that HRM as a philosophy is essentially a hyping of the theory and practice of personnel management and that it has the purpose of obscuring the realities of change. A radical perspective argues that heightened competition, recession, and socio-politico-economic changes associated with pursuit of the 'enterprise culture' (during the Conservative govern-ments of Margaret Thatcher and John Major) have presented employers and managers with both constraints and opportunities (as will be discussed in the next three chap-ters). Legge claims that their response has been largely pragmatic and, further, some managers, HR practitioners, and academics have sought to justify these changes to the employment relationship under the banner of progressive HRM.[35]

Returning now to sum up the models of HRM outlined in this chapter: all of them recommend change in the way that human resources are managed, although they differ in their estimates of its likelihood. Most see change as desirable but very dif-ficult to obtain on a large scale. Guest's model of soft HRM prescribed how manage-ment and employees should organize their work and behave in their jobs in order to achieve high organizational performance, but ten years after creating the model, he could not provide substantial evidence of its working in reality, although he remains highly committed to the possibility of a link between investment in HRM and com-pany profitability.[36] Storey's model focuses on change by revealing differences of approach between HRM and traditional personnel management. Storey presents HRM as having the potential eventually to supersede personnel management, although he expresses strong doubt about the empirical evidence for extensive change having occurred in the UK during the 1980s. The Michigan model of strategic HRM is arguably the closest to traditional personnel management in non-union settings. It is consistent with Kochan's criticism of US employers by not being supportive of partnership with unions or tolerant of pluralist employee interests.

Three common elements of all of these models are unitarism, the need for man-agement to adopt a strategic approach, and ensuring organizations achieve new social goals. To a greater or lesser extent, all make the assumption that management's inter-ests are the most legitimate ones in the running of the business. All advise that HRM ultimately must fit the competitive environment, and a prerequisite of this is that organizations be less *ad hoc* in their management decision making and more strategic. Finally, all predict that HRM innovations will be in the long-term social interest of employees, employers, and the nation. These three elements of HRM—the unitarist, the strategic, and the social—will be referred to throughout the remainder of this book.

The next part of the book, Chapters 2, 3, and 4, analyse in detail the environment that organizations are operating in today. The environmental factors highlighted must be considered by any organization planning to adopt an HRM approach.

# Study Questions

1   Examine the timeline at the beginning of this chapter illustrating the history of how employees have been managed since the 1800s. Based on this history, what continuities and what changes do you think there will be in the way the employer–employee relationship is handled over the next fifty years?

2   Analyse Kochan's framework and explain how it differs from soft and hard HRM models.

3   Clarify with others each of Storey's twenty-five points of difference between HRM and personnel management/industrial relations.

4   Assess the adequacy of Brewster and Bournois' model in explaining HRM in European countries.

5   Select a case study of an organization and assess its HRM policy and practice using two models of your choice.

# Further Reading

Bratton, J. and Gold, J., *Human Resource Management: Theory and Practice*, 2nd edn, (London: Macmillan, 1999), chapter 1, pp. 3–36.

Beer, M., Spector, B., Lawrence, P. R., Quinn Mills, D., and Walton, R. E., *Managing Human Assets: The Ground Breaking Harvard Business School Program* (NY: The Free Press, 1984).

Kochan, T. A. and Osterman, P., *The Mutual Gains Enterprise: Forging a Winning Partnership among Labor, Management and Government* (Boston, MASS: Harvard Business School Press, 1994).

Keenoy, T., 'HRM: Rhetoric, Reality and Contradiction', *International Journal of Human Resource Management* (1990), 1, 3, pp. 363–384.

# Notes

1.  Beer, M., Spector, B., Lawrence, P. R., Quinn Mills, D., Walton, R. E., *Managing Human Assets* (New York: The Free Press, 1984). Beer, M. and Spector, B., 'Corporate wide

transformations in human resource management', in R. E. Walton and P. R. Lawrence (eds.), *Human Resource Management — Trends and Challenges* (Boston, Harvard Business School Press, 1985). It should be noted that the actual term 'soft HRM' was coined later by John Storey in 1988.

2. Guest, D. E., 'Human Resource Management and Industrial Relations', *Journal of Management Studies* (1987), 24, 5, pp. 503–21. Truss *et al.* (1997) (full publication details provided in bibliography at end of book) argue that Guest's model actually combines hard and soft HRM, the primary hard element being strategic integration.

3. Bratton, J. and Gold, J., *Human Resource Management: Theory and Practice* (Basingstoke: Macmillan, 1994), pp. 23–6; Keenoy, T., 'HRM: Rhetoric, Reality and Contradiction', *International Journal of Human Resource Management* (1990), 1, 3, pp. 363–84; Keenoy, T., 'HRM: a case of the wolf in sheep's clothing?', *Personnel Review* (1990), 19, 2, pp. 3–9.

4. Fombrun, C. J., Tichy, N. M., and Devanna, M. A., *Strategic Human Resource Management* (New York: John Wiley & Sons, 1984).

5. Legge, K., *Human Resource Management: Rhetorics and Realities* (Basingstoke: Macmillan, 1995).

6. Storey, J., 'Developments in the management of human resources: an interim report', *Warwick Papers in International Relations* (University of Warwick, November, 1987); Storey, J., *Developments in the Management of Human Resources* (Oxford: Blackwell, 1992); Beardwell, I. and Holden, L., *Human Resource Management: A Contemporary Perspective*, 2nd edn (London: Financial Times, Pitman Publishing, 1997).

7. Devanna, M. A., Fombrun, C. J., and Tichy, N. M., 'A Framework for Strategic Human Resource Management', in C. J. Fombrun, N. M. Tichy and M. A. Devanna, *Strategic Human Resource Management* (New York: John Wiley & Sons, 1984), pp. 33–51.

8. Ibid., p. 34.

9. Fombrun *et al.* (pp. 36–9) developed their concept of HRM through discussion of some of the well-known literature on management style, organizational structure, and strategy, notably Mayo (1993), Chandler (1962), and Galbraith and Nathanson (1978) (full publication details provided in bibliography).

10. Devanna *et al.*, 'A Framework for Strategic Human Resource Management', p. 41.

11. Kochan, T. A., Katz, H. C., and McKersie, R. B., *The Transformation of American Industrial Relations* (New York: Basic Books, 1986; second edition published in New York by Cornell University Press in 1994). In the second edition, the authors argued that wide-scale change and concerted effort by business, labour, and government were more likely than they had been when they wrote the first edition.

12. Kochan, Katz, and McKersie, *The Transformation of American Industrial Relations*, 2nd edn. (New York: Cornell University Press, 1994), p. 14.

13. Walton, R. E., 'From control to commitment in the workplace', *Harvard Business Review* (1985), 63, 2, pp. 77–84; Walton, R. E. 'Towards a Strategy of Eliciting Employee Commitment Based on Policies of Mutuality', in R. E. Walton and P. R. Lawrence (eds.), *Human Resource Management — Trends and Challenges* (Boston, MA: Harvard Business School Press, 1985), pp. 35–65.

14. Legge, K., 'Human Resource Management — A Critical Analysis', in J. Storey (ed.), *New Perspectives on Human Resource Management* (London: Routledge, 1989), pp. 19–40.

15. Storey, J., *Developments in the Management of Human Resources* (Oxford: Blackwell, 1992). Figure 2.2 in Storey (1992) was entitled 'Twenty-seven points of difference'. However, in Storey (1995) it was reproduced as Table 1.1 'The twenty-five-item checklist'. We have adopted the later version.

16. Storey, J., *New Perspectives on Human Resource Management*, 2nd edn. (London: Routledge, 1991); Storey, J., *Developments in the Management of Human Resources* (Oxford: Blackwell, 1992); Storey, J., *Human Resource Management: a Critical Text* (London: Routledge, 1995).

17. Oliver, N. and Wilkinson, B., *The Japanization of British Industry* (Oxford: Blackwell, 1988); Oliver, N. and Wilkinson, B., *The Japanization of British Industry: New Developments in the 1990s* (Oxford: Blackwell, 1992).

18. Oliver and Wilkinson, *The Japanization of British Industry: New Developments in the 1990s*, pp. 82–8; Ouchi, W., *Theory Z* (Reading, MA: Addison-Wesley, 1981).

19. Oliver and Wilkinson, *The Japanization of British Industry: New Developments in the 1990s*, pp. 316–43; Pinder, C. C., 'Valence-Instrumentality-Expectancy Theory'; in V. H. Vroom, Porter, L. W., and Lawler, E. E. III, *Managerial Attitudes and Performance* (Homewood, IL: Irwin-Dorsey, 1968).

20. Oliver and Wilkinson, *The Japanization of British Industry: New Developments in the 1990s*, pp. 323–5.

21. Womack, J. P., Jones, D. T. and Roos, D., *The Machine that Changed the World: The Triumph of Lean Production* (New York: Rawson, Macmillan, 1990).

22. Oliver and Wilkinson, *The Japanization of British Industry: New Developments in the 1990s*, p. 18.

23. Wickens, P. D., *The Road to Nissan* (London: Macmillan, 1987).

24. Garrahan, P. and Stewart, P., *The Nissan Enigma: Flexibility at Work in a Local Economy* (London: Mansell, 1992).

25. Brewster, C. and Bournois, F., 'A European Perspective on Human Resource Management', *Personnel Review* (1991), 20, 6, pp. 4–13.

26. Brewster, C. and Hegewisch, A., *Policy and Practice in European Human Resource Management* (London: Routledge, 1994), p. 6; Guest, D. E., 'Human Resource Management and the American Dream', *Journal of Management Studies* (1990), 27, 4, pp. 378–97; Brewster, C., HRM: the European Dimension, in J. Storey (ed.), *Human Resource Management: A Critical Text* (London: Routledge, 1995) pp. 309–31; Leat, M., *Human Resource Issues of the European Union* (London: Financial Times, Pitman Publishing, 1998).

27. Brewster and Hegewisch, *Policy and Practice*.

28. Brewster said his empirical survey found a Latin country cluster similar to that first reported by Filella (1991), p. 3 (full publication details provided in bibliography). (Brewster, C., 'HRM: The European Dimension', in J. Storey (ed.), *Human Resource Management: A Critical Text* (London: Routledge, 1995), pp. 309–31.)

29. Bournois, F., *La Gestion des Cadres en Europe* (Personnel Management in Europe) (Paris: Editions Eyrolles, 1991); Sparrow and Hiltrop, J.-M., *European Human Resource Management Transition* (Hemel Hempstead: Prentice-Hall, 1994).

30. Storey, J. and Sisson, K., *Managing Human Resources and Industrial Relations* (Buckingham: Open University Press, 1993), p. 17.

31. Burrell, G. and Morgan, G., *Sociological Paradigms and Organizational Analysis* (London: Heinemann, 1979).

32. Legge, K., 'HRM: rhetoric, reality and hidden agendas', in J. Storey (ed.), *Human Resource Management: A Critical Text* (London: Routledge, 1995), pp. 33–59; Legge, K., *Human Resource Management: Rhetorics and Realities* (Basingstoke: Macmillan, 1995); Hope-Hailey, V., Gratton, L., McGovern, P., Stiles, P. and Truss, C., 'A Chameleon Function? HRM in the 90s', *Human Resource Management Journal* (1997), 7, 2, pp. 5–18.

33. Watson, T. J., *Management, Organization and Employment Strategy: New Directions in Theory and Practice* (London: Routledge and Kegan Paul, 1986), p. 176.

34. Keenoy, T., 'HRM: Rhetoric, Reality and Contradiction', *International Journal of Human Resource Management* (1990), 1, 3, pp. 363–84; Keenoy, T., 'HRM: A Case of the Wolf in Sheep's Clothing?, *Personnel Review* (1990), 19, 2, pp. 3–9; Keenoy, T. and Anthony, P., 'Human Resource Management: Metaphor, Meaning and Morality', in P. Blyton and P. Turnbull (eds.), *Reassessing Human Resource Management* (London: Sage, 1992).

35.  Legge, K., 'HRM: Rhetoric, Reality and Hidden Agendas', in J. Storey (ed.), *Human Resource Management: A Critical Text* (London: Routledge, 1995), pp. 33–59.

36.  Guest, *People Management*, 4, 24, 10 December 1998, p. 14. ' "The message is clear", said David Guest, professor of psychology at Birkbeck College, London, who has led research for the IPD [Institute of Personnel and Development] on the psychological contract. "We're beginning to get the kind of evidence that shows a link between investing in human resources management and improvement in the bottom line." '

# Part II

# Context

# Chapter 2

# The Environment of HRM

## Chapter Contents

# Introduction

I N the first chapter, we saw that HRM has grown in popularity during the 1980s and 1990s. This growth has coincided with profound changes that have been taking place in the economic and political context in which firms trade. One consequence of these changes has been that competitive pressures on firms have grown. This in part stems from the fact that firms are increasingly competing on an international rather than solely national basis and in part from moves made by national governments to promote greater competition. In this changing context, HRM has appeared to be very attractive to managers because it promises to provide a 'solution' to these competitive pressures.

This period has also been characterized by a decline in the influence of trade unions. This decline owes much to structural change in labour markets, particularly the decline of industries in which unions were traditionally strong. It has also been caused by government reforms in some countries, notably Britain, designed to restrict union power and restore managerial prerogative. The result has been that managers face less organized opposition to proposed organizational changes. Thus while greater competitive pressures have made HRM one attractive option, the greater power of management within organizations has made the implementation of this option easier. This chapter investigates the nature of these changes and whether a coherent move towards HRM, in which the workforce is managed in a strategic way, is indeed the likely response to them by managers in British organizations.

# 1 Features of the Economic and Political Environment

## Internationalization

D URING the last two decades of the twentieth century competition between firms has become increasingly internationalized. There are a number of sources of this development. First, international trade of goods and services takes place more intensively and in a wider range of industries than hitherto; Freeman notes that the ratio of international trade to GDP more than doubled in most advanced countries between 1960 and 1990.[1] A principal reason for this is the gradual reduction in barriers to trade through the successive rounds of the General Agreement on Tariffs and Trade (GATT) talks, which have reduced or abolished import quotas and tariffs globally. Similar developments have occurred within regions of the world—the Single European Market (SEM), the North American Free Trade Agreement (NAFTA), and the Association of South-East Asian Nations (ASEAN). Technological changes have also facilitated the growth of international trade, particularly in the service sector, largely because they have reduced the need for the provider of services to be located geographically close to the purchaser. For example, the data entry for the booking of tickets for airlines worldwide is commonly carried out in South-east Asia, the information being transferred electronically.

Second, whereas for much of the post-war period the dominant manufacturing nations were in Western Europe and North America, in recent years a third block has been added to that list, Asia. Competition from Asian firms, often producing at much lower costs than their European and American counterparts, has intensified competitive pressures in the world economy. Consequently, the share of world markets accounted for by Asian countries has risen substantially, a contributory factor to the decline of industries such as shipbuilding in Western economies. For example, in the USA imports from developing countries as a proportion of GDP tripled between 1960 and 1990.

Third, multinational companies, defined as those which operate in more than one country, have increased their share of output, employment, and investment in almost all economies. Thus domestic producers have not only seen the pressures of overseas competition rise through international trade but also have seen overseas competitors setting up operations in their own countries, resulting in an increasing proportion of national output being controlled by foreign-owned companies.[2] In addition, developments in international transport have enabled multinational companies (MNCs) to stratify their production across borders and exert considerable control from the headquarters. For example, many MNCs have attempted to create a cadre of global managers who travel regularly across sites, forging closer relations between different parts of the multinational. The rise of foreign direct investment by MNCs is shown in Table 2.1.

**TABLE 2.1**
**The stock of foreign direct investment (billions of US dollars)**

| Year  | 1967 | 1973 | 1980 | 1988 | 1997 |
|-------|------|------|------|------|------|
| Total | 112  | 211  | 551  | 1141 | 3456 |

*Source*: United Nations, *World Investment Report*, 1998, New York: UN Statistics used with the permission of the United Nations Conference on Trade and Development, Geneva.

# The Reform of the Public Sector

While internationalization has increased competitive pressures on private-sector organizations, public-sector organizations have also experienced greater competition.

This is particularly so in the UK, where successive Conservative governments in the 1980s and 1990s saw the public sector as being saddled with weak and ineffectual management and strong trade unions. A central part of the reform process was to privatize many of the nationalized industries through floating the companies on the stock market. Thus British Telecom, British Airways, British Gas, the electricity and water companies, British Rail, British Steel, and the mines as well as many others were all sold off to the private sector and the management of these companies were subsequently answerable to shareholders rather than the government. Of the large trading companies that were under nationalized ownership at the beginning of the 1980s only the Post Office remains state-owned. Relatedly, many of these privatized firms that used to be monopolies have been broken up and subjected to competition as well as being freed from restrictions that prevented them from diversifying into different industries and investing abroad. The effects on labour management have been marked: trade unions were increasingly marginalized and issues such as training and recruitment were made subject to severe cost pressures and consequently are now dealt with in a more *ad hoc* manner.[3] Perhaps most notably, employment levels fell sharply both in the run-up to privatization and in the years afterwards. For example, the workforce in British Telecom has almost halved since privatization from 240,000 in 1984 to 127,000 in 1997, while the workforce in British Steel fell dramatically in the years prior to privatization from 166,000 in 1980 to 54,000 at the time of privatization in 1988 and the fall has continued since.

The reform of the public sector was also achieved through introducing market pressures into those public services that were not privatized. Compulsory Competitive Tendering (CCT) in health and local authorities obliged public-sector management to put out to tender certain ancillary services. This meant that private firms were able to submit bids for the carrying out of activities such as cleaning, laundry, and catering in hospitals and refuse collection in local authorities, and that managers were obliged to accept the lowest bid. Moreover, schools and hospitals were encouraged to 'opt out' of local authority control, compete with one another, and manage their own budgets. The consequences of CCT and opting out in the public services were similar to those of privatization: employment levels fell, the position of trade unions was weakened, and it became more difficult for managers to plan ahead on issues such as training.[4]

What lay behind these changes was the government's view of the role of the state, which owed much to the rise of the 'New Right'. A key part of this ideology was that state intervention in the economy is rarely beneficial, for three reasons: first, the absence of the profit motive in the public sector leads to lower levels of efficiency; second, government spending 'crowds out' more efficient private-sector activity; and, third, regulations by governments impose costs on firms that lower their competitiveness. Thus it became an aim of the Conservatives to reduce the amount of government spending as a proportion of national output (GDP). In fact, this aim was thwarted by higher welfare spending, partly as a result of unemployment and partly because of growing inequality of pay. Nevertheless, while the overall size of state activity did not fall, the role of the state changed considerably. Privatization and 'marketization', as we have seen, were key elements; so too was deregulation of the labour market.

# Deregulation of the Labour Market

The government's view of the labour market was that it was unable to respond quickly and flexibly enough to market forces. This 'inflexibility' was caused partly because trade unions were too strong and partly because employment protection legislation prevented employers from being able to adjust the number of people they employ and the terms and conditions under which they are employed. The result was that firms were often saddled with wages held above their 'free market' level, retaining people they did not need but were unable to lay off. In the long term, the government argued, this reduced the competitiveness of British firms and raised unemployment. This view was vividly expressed in the work of Hanson and Mather, who argued strongly for deregulation of the labour market.[5]

Government policies concerning labour market regulation in the 1980s and 1990s aimed to remove these rigidities. The legal basis on which trade unions operated was undermined in a number of ways. Three examples illustrate this: first, trade unions were made liable for damages caused to one employer when they organized industrial action that related to a dispute with a different employer (secondary action); second, the statutory procedure by which unions had a legal right to be recognized by an employer was abolished; and, third, the practice known as the 'closed shop', in which employees were obliged to join a union, was made unlawful.[6] Unquestionably, these and other changes weakened trade unions, making it more difficult for them to organize industrial action, gain recognition from employers, and enforce membership amongst a workforce. (This is a theme to which we will return in Chapter 4.)

The second plank of deregulation was concerned with weakening the employment protection legislation that had grown up in the 1960s and 1970s. In the main this related to unfair dismissal legislation, which had been introduced in order to place limits on the ability of employers to fire their employees. The system was changed in a number of ways, three of which are illustrated here: first, the qualifying period of continuous service with an employer required to bring an unfair dismissal case was raised from six months to two years; second, the burden of proof was removed from the employer and became 'neutral'; third, employees bringing a case were required to lodge a deposit with the tribunal in order to deter 'frivolous' cases being brought.[7] A key consequence of these changes was that legal restrictions on employers' ability to lay off workers were weakened.

These deregulatory measures were taken at a time when the labour market was experiencing other profound changes. Of great significance was the structural change in the labour market, resulting in a rapid and substantial shift in the nature of jobs available. In particular, the number of jobs in manufacturing declined sharply, from around 35% of the workforce in 1980 to around 20% in 1997. In this period there were significant increases in the proportion of women in the workforce and in the number of part-time workers; half of all employees are now female and a quarter of all employees are part-timers.[8]

## Unemployment

Also of great significance were the persistently high levels of unemployment that characterized this period. For most of the post-war period, unemployment had tended to be about 2–3% of the workforce; it began to rise in the mid-1970s and then sharply in the early 1980s. Since then it has fluctuated according to the economic cycle but has never got close to the levels of the 1950s and 1960s: in 1998 unemployment amounted to 6% of the workforce but it has averaged around 10% during the last two decades of the twentieth century.[9] This has had enormous social repercussions as well as causing personal distress for those involved. In addition, high levels of unemployment strengthen the hand of employers in dealing with their workforces, largely because the pool of available labour that employers can draw upon makes employees wary of taking any action which antagonizes management. Thus it becomes easier for employers to push through organizational changes.

# 2 Management in British Firms: A Strategic Response?

## Evidence of the Take-up of HRM

CHANGES in the environmental context during the 1980s and 1990s appear not only to have made HRM an attractive response to greater competitive pressures but also to have made it easier to implement. What evidence, then, is there that organizations in Britain have moved towards adopting HRM? In this section we attempt to answer this question in terms of the three major features that the various models of HRM have in common, as established in the summary of Chapter 1: a strategic approach, unitarism, and new social goals. To recap these features, first, they all emphasize the importance of managing the workforce in a 'strategic' way, insisting that policies and practices concerning the management of people should be consistent with the long-term business strategy of the organization. Second, all of the models are essentially unitarist in that they stress the common interests between managers and employees and have little to say about differences of interest and tensions between these groups. Indeed, Storey argues that models of HRM 'de-emphasize' the potential for conflict within organizations.[10] Third, following from these two points, HRM's advocates envisage benefits for employees as well as for management where HRM is adopted. In particular, some advocates have stressed the advantages in terms of improved job security and working relationships, greater involvement in decision making, rewards based on performance, and better training and development. Making an overall assessment of the extent to which British organizations have changed in this direction is bound to be a problematic task. None the less, a review of the evidence gathered from surveys and case studies does provide some revealing indicators.

On the face of it, there has been considerable change in British organizations, implying that HRM has taken root in a significant way. It is now commonplace to hear managers of large corporations talking about the need to manage their labour in a more strategic way; many routinely refer to people as 'the organization's most important asset' and argue that getting the most out of the workforce is likely to provide the competitive edge for the firm. The rhetoric of senior managers is often clearly unitarist, including talk of the need to develop a sense of shared goals and greater trust between management and workforces. Managers also often stress the benefits to employees of the HRM-style initiatives that they adopt. For example, it is often claimed that practices such as teamworking empower people to make decisions without having to refer upwards to their manager and that the commitment to training allows employees to ensure that their skills are maximized, while performance-related pay provides rewards for people according to their performance.

The Workplace Employee Relations Surveys (conducted in 1980, 1984, 1990, and 1998) provide empirical support for the assertion that some of this HRM rhetoric is linked to actual adoption of HRM-style practices. The 1998 survey, based on information from 2,000 establishments, shows a high prevalence of employee involvement and communication practices. For example, in relation to communication between managers and employees, in 61% of the surveyed establishments there is a system of team briefing for groups of employees, while 42% operate 'problem-solving groups'. Moreover, practices designed to develop a sense of teamwork and to remove symbolic divides between different categories of employees within organizations also appear to be widespread: in 65% of the establishments most employees work in formally designated teams and 41% are characterized by 'single status' arrangements for managers and non-managerial employees.[11]

This picture is consistent with that gathered from case studies. In his research into fifteen 'mainstream' organizations in Britain, Storey found an extensive take-up of HRM-style approaches, which is consistent with evidence from other case studies.[12] A case study of a large engineering project management company appears to provide further evidence of a preference for tighter strategic control. In this company HR became more integrated with the business strategy than it was previously, and the HR function was given responsibility for determining the allocation of human resources to projects which in the past had primarily been the role of engineering managers. Also, in an unusual innovation for the HR function, it became responsible for monitoring part of corporate and divisional performance, particularly cost containment within project pre-planning and operations.[13] Case studies of the management practices of inward investors from countries such as the USA and Japan also appear to demonstrate a more strategic approach. Companies such as Nissan and IBM have been seen as exemplars of a more strategic approach to the management of labour, based around creating a high-trust working environment, facilitating the involvement of employees in decision making, and 'upskilling' the workforce. US and Japanese companies have also preferred to export their management style and their approach to industrial relations and trade unions. US firms tend to favour non-unionized or minimal union involvement and Japanese firms, whenever possible, tend to pursue a single-union deal emphasizing a non-adversarial and unitarist role.[14]

Many organizations, in addition to inward investors, have reduced the traditional role of British trade unions by refusing to negotiate over issues such as staffing levels and, in some cases, by 'de-recognizing' unions altogether. As we will see in Chapter 4, the proportion of workplaces with one or more recognized unions has fallen from around two-thirds to less than one-half in the last fifteen years.[15] Moreover, union membership has declined substantially over the last two decades of the twentieth century, from 55% in 1979 to 30% in 1998, the longest continuous fall on record. Organized industrial action, moreover, is now lower than it has been for generations.[16] One interpretation of this trend is that the move towards more unitarist managerial attitudes, an important part of the ideology of HRM, has led firms to minimize the role of trade unions.

Further evidence of the take-up of HRM stems from the positive signs of an increase in Britain's provision of training and evidence of improved institutional arrangements linked to employers' business goals. The national institutional arrangements for stimulating training have been under continual reform during the 1980s and 1990s and there have been some significant developments suggesting a tentative move away from the *ad hoc*, *laissez-faire* tradition of British systems of education and training. In higher education there has been a substantial growth in business teaching by business schools and in specialist courses tailored to business issues for students studying science and technical subjects, especially engineering. Also, the launch of the Modern Apprenticeship scheme, underwritten by local TECs and ITOs (now called National Training Organizations), offered just under 115,000 places between 1995–7 and there are some positive signs that it may arrest the terminal decline since the 1960s of UK apprenticeship training positions.[17] The extent to which firms in Britain are investing in employee development must be a key test of whether people are managed in a more strategic way than hitherto. There are some grounds for optimism here since there appears to have been some growth in the amount of training carried out by firms in Britain. The proportion of employers' labour costs accounted for by expenditure on training rose from 0.3% in 1981 to 0.5% in 1988. In addition, more people appear to have received job-related training, much of it centring around employees obtaining NVQs.[18] An evaluation of the Investors in People Standard found some evidence that organizations holding the award are adopting a more systematic process for adjusting training and development to business strategy.[19] In the manufacturing sector, the most commonly applied training and development practices in the 1990s are individual development stimulated by appraisal, competence-based training, training-needs analysis, and management development, all suggesting that some HR practices are taking hold.[20] There are grounds, therefore, for claiming that HRM is becoming established in Britain. However, careful analysis of the implementation of new practices demonstrates that the adoption of HRM has not lived up to the claims of its advocates. We now turn to examining the evidence for the three common features of HRM models: a strategic approach, unitarism, and new social goals.

First, to what extent can these initiatives be seen as a strategic and coherent response to changes in the environment? Overall, the evidence does not point to a coherent take-up of strategic HRM in British firms. Indeed, the picture is one of a rather selective, piecemeal, and *ad hoc* implementation of the policies and practices we associate with HRM. A mass of evidence demonstrates that the implementation of new-style HRM practices in UK firms has not been 'strategic'.[21] This evidence, gathered from surveys and case studies, concerns the adoption of both the 'soft' aspects of HRM, emphasizing commitment, motivation, and training in order to achieve a highly committed and adaptable workforce, and the 'hard' aspects, stressing the need to manage the workforce in as cost-efficient a way as possible. The picture emerging from this evidence, based on a great diversity of practice in British companies, is that 'while there is considerably more evidence for the "hard" than for the "soft" version, most British managements are being nowhere as "strategic" as many commentators have claimed'.[22]

For example, one of the central findings of the two Company Level Industrial Relations Surveys (CLIRS) conducted at Warwick University, in 1985 and 1992, illustrates the relative absence of strategic behaviour that firms exhibit in the management of their workforces.[23] In both surveys, respondents at headquarters level of the firms in the survey, all of which employed at least 1,000 people in at least two sites, were asked whether the firm had a clear policy concerning the management of employees. The presence of such a policy would appear to be a prerequisite for a strategic approach. However, the findings suggest that there was very little evidence of a clear, strategic approach; despite the vast majority of respondents claiming that there was such a policy, when asked to describe it many were unable to do so at all or were able to do so in only vague terms. Moreover, even in those cases where a detailed response was given, this policy appeared to be at odds with other responses to particular aspects of management style. Storey was anxious to stress that, despite the range of initiatives being taken in his case studies, 'most cases failed to show much in the way of an integrated approach to employment management, and still less was there evidence of strategic integration with the corporate plan'.[24] Rather, managers appeared to have experimented with these 'new' practices in an essentially opportunistic and pragmatic way. Indeed, in the international perspective, British firms have not gone as far as their counterparts in Europe in implementing practices in the area of employee involvement, a key aspect of HRM: a manufacturing company survey in 1994 found that the country lagged behind world-wide best practice in the employee involvement practices of quality circles, suggestion schemes, and attitude surveys, with a third or less of manufacturing firms making full use of these.[25]

Recent research into HRM in several large companies in Britain (BT, Chelsea & Westminster Trust, Citibank, Glaxo Pharmaceuticals, Hewlett Packard, Kraft Jacobs Suchard, Lloyds Bank, and W. H. Smith) found that, while the principles of soft HRM were espoused in organizations, the organizational commitment to them was high only in Hewlett Packard. Moreover, actual business practice was more concerned with the tight strategic control associated with hard HRM.[26] The research did find some evidence of stronger linkages between business strategy and HR strategy but concluded that the role of the HR function had been reduced following the devolution of responsibility for many HR issues to line management. Thus the HR function tended to provide routine personnel services, advice, and consultancy for line management; these line managers had little institutional incentive to prioritize long-term issues of people management because it was not an activity that contributed to career success.[27]

Second, how far has employer ideology become more unitarist? If HRM has become firmly embedded in British organizations then we might expect firms to have made a clear attempt to move away from accepting trade unions as legitimate representatives of employees. The evidence on union recognition by firms, reviewed above, appears at first sight to be consistent with this. However, to interpret the decline in union recognition as being caused by a change in managerial ideology would be to miss the point. In part, this is because unitarism has always been evident amongst British management: while some managers, particularly those in the personnel function, have appeared to exhibit pluralist beliefs in general and an acceptance of trade unions in particular, others have been more clearly unitarist and have been hostile to trade unions. Thus managers exhibiting unitarist beliefs is scarcely a new phenomenon. Seeing the decline in union recognition as being caused by a resurgence of unitarism also ignores the fact that many organizations, including a clear majority of large ones, continue to accept trade unions and formally bargain with them to set pay and conditions. This is particularly the case for those firms that have introduced HRM-style practices. Only very rarely is it the case that de-recognition has been carried out as part of a deliberate policy change in the management of people. Collective bargaining continued to operate in the majority of those firms that had implemented HRM practices, so that team briefings and problem-solving groups coexisted with, rather than replaced, unionized channels of communication. Arguably, this indicates a continuing pluralist element to management style. Of course, it might be the case that managers hoped that introducing new channels for communicating with the workforce would eventually bypass the trade union institution, leading to unions fading away or, as some have put it, 'withering on the vine'. But even this view, according to Storey, attributes a more strategic aspect to managerial behaviour than was in fact the case.[28] The decline in union recognition, therefore, should not be interpreted as evidence of a significant shift in managerial ideology towards HRM.

Third, to what degree have employees benefited from the introduction of HRM-style practices? There are good reasons for questioning the extent to which this is the case. While the increase in the amount of training appears to be a genuine gain for employees, there are serious concerns amongst many academics about the quality of much of it. Furthermore, employers are tending to structurally disadvantage some segments of the workforce so that training opportunities in Britain are not as good for the 'peripheral' worker as they are for the full-time member of the workforce. This shows that the benefits of HRM are less likely to extend beyond core employees because organizations are failing to invest in the long-term future of the growing number of peripheral employees. A five-year comparison study (1990–5) of training opportunities for employees on part-time and on short-term, full-time contracts of employment found a growing proportion of the flexible workforce were not getting work-related training.[29]

Moreover, the impact of organizational restructuring and greater emphasis on numerical flexibility have generally not delivered benefits for employees or created a more equitable relationship. Organizational downsizing affects the psychological contract between employee and employer by substantially altering expectations, with the general result that many of the retained employees experience a lack of career development and feel a greater amount of job insecurity.[30] A study of managers in a downsized and delayered privatized electricity company found that because career prospects were perceived to be far worse than they were prior to privatization, people were not intrinsically motivated by lateral mobility and were seeking to obtain more extrinsic satisfaction from their level of pay and more intrinsic motivation through professional work achievements.[31]

The evidence on the operation of performance-related pay (PRP) has also disappointed the advocates of HRM. A study during 1995 of PRP in six NHS trusts found that it raised levels of motivation for a minority of managers, but the majority felt that the scheme's rewards for superior performance were not high enough to motivate increased effort.[32] Similar conclusions followed a study of PRP in a study of three financial services organizations (a bank, a building society, and an insurance company) where employees generally felt that performance pay at around 2% of total pay was 'much ado about nothing'.[33] Other evidence suggests that, far from motivating employees, PRP has tended to create a sense of injustice and dissatisfaction. In particular, many employees perceive the criteria by which their performance is assessed to be unfair.[34]

Practices designed to increase employee involvement and consultation also appear to have had mixed results. New quality initiatives, involving greater employee involvement, were widespread in companies during the 1980s, first, in the form of Quality Circles and Statistical Process Control and later, during the 1990s, Total Quality Management (TQM) and Business Process Redesign (BPR). A survey found that quality programmes were extremely common in the financial services industry with initiatives implemented in over 90% of banks, building societies, and insurance companies. Unfortunately for advocates of quality management, not all of these initiatives have had the effect that was intended: a study of TQM and BPR in a major UK retail bank, for example, found that staff had actually become more cynical about their effectiveness and benefit to employees.[35] It has been argued that positive HR outcomes from programmes such as TQM and BPR will only be realized when management show better appreciation of the downside of work intensification—stress, excessive control, and employment insecurity—and concentrate more consistently on realizing the potential creativity and empowerment of the workforce.[36] Another study of TQM and BPR programmes in two British manufacturing firms (named best practice companies by the Department of Trade and Industry) revealed similar problems, these change initiatives being overshadowed by redundancies and cost-cutting activities during the recession of the early 1990s.[37] More generally, while such initiatives appear to offer greater scope for employees to voice their opinions and to be informed of important developments within the organization, many writers have questioned the extent to which employees are genuinely able to influence key decisions.

In other areas, too, there is not much evidence that HRM has been particularly effective as a means of obtaining social progress. For example, with regard to sex discrimination in the workplace, Dickens argues convincingly that HRM has reinforced existing gender inequalities (see Chapter 3).[38] Similarly, there is evidence for age discrimination taking place through British employers' HR flow policies. Greater employee outflow over recent years, especially through redundancy and early retirement, has reduced the proportion of older people in full-time employment. In 1975, 84% of British males aged 60–64 were economically active; by 1994, the proportion had reduced to 49%, of which approximately 5% were registered unemployed, with the result that in the five years before eligibility for UK state pension only four in ten males were actually working.[39] Employers' HR policies and practices, therefore, do not appear to have benefited older employees:

'Only a small minority of UK organizations have begun to recognize this group's right to equal employment opportunities and, among those with written statements, very few display any depth of commitment to its implementation.'[40]

To conclude this section on the take-up of HRM, there are good reasons for questioning the extent to which HRM has been implemented strategically, has been caused by a shift in managerial ideology, and has benefited employees. Indeed, a range of sources of evidence testify to the large number of firms in Britain that show no inclination of taking the 'high road' to competitive success apparent in models of HRM. On the contrary, a large number appear to be characterized by low productivity and compete on the basis of low cost rather than high quality. For employees in these firms the picture is scarcely the optimistic one painted by advocates of HRM: Sisson has characterized a firm which offers low rates of pay, little in the way of training, and few rights to involvement or representation as a 'bleak house'.[41] Overall, the evidence indicates that a strategic approach to the management of employees is far rarer than many advocates of HRM suggest. Rather, contemporary developments are best seen as being caused by managers responding to the political context and business conditions by asserting their control in an essentially pragmatic and *ad hoc* fashion. Why has the take-up of HRM occurred in such a piecemeal fashion? What factors have made it difficult for firms to take a more long-term, strategic approach?

# 3    Explaining the Lack of Strategic HRM

T HE explanation for the limited and pragmatic take-up of HRM in part arises out of differences of interest within organizations. Writers such as Pettigrew and Mintzberg[42] emphasize the inevitability of individuals and groups having divergent aims and priorities, which results in strategy emerging 'more from a pragmatic process of bodging, learning, and compromise than from a rational series of grand leaps forward'.[43] From this perspective, then, strategies emerge as a result of continual readjustments arrived at through political activity between different organizational actors. The differences of interest between the organizational actors inherently limit the extent to which organizations exhibit strategic behaviour. In this scenario, it is hardly surprising if managers fail to implement a coherent package of the practices associated with HRM (this issue is developed in Chapter 9). Compounding these limitations to the implementation of strategic HRM are elements of the general business environment that also serve to make strategic behaviour difficult to achieve. Two of these, the financial and training systems, are reviewed in the following subsections.

## The Financial System

The financial system in Britain is one factor that makes a strategic approach difficult. In Britain banks are highly centralized and dominated by the concerns of the London HQ, making the relationship between banks and firms distant and remote, with little close personal contact between the managers and owners of firms and those responsible for lending in the banks. In addition, bank lending is generally short-term in nature. This is mainly because banks are concerned with maintaining high levels of liquidity; that is, they are able to recall loans they have made at short notice in order to meet the possible recall of their deposits. A key influence over banks in this respect is the Bank of England, which is responsible for the stability of the banking system and sees liquidity as a way in which the dangers of the collapse of banks can be minimized. The banks obtain liquidity through borrowing on the short-term money markets in the City to meet their own demands for cash. A key consequence of this short-term borrowing is that a high proportion of their lending is also short-term in nature, often through overdrafts rather than long-term loans, with rates of interest being relatively high. In 1992, 60% of bank lending by the NatWest (excluding mortgages) was for less than a year and under 20% was for more than five years; in contrast, half of the lending by Deutsche Bank, Germany's largest bank, is for more than four years. More generally, 58% of all lending to small and medium-sized firms is in the form of overdrafts, which are short-term in nature; the comparable figures for Germany, France, and Italy are 14%, 31%, and 35%, respectively.[44] Long-term investments, and a 'strategic' approach to the management of labour, are more difficult in British firms as a result.

The problem of short-term bank lending is made worse by the lack of commitment from financial backers in the British financial system. Shareholdings can be easily bought and sold on the stock market and, crucially, there are few restrictions on takeovers. Thus one firm can gain control of another if it can persuade enough of the existing shareholders to sell their shares, and they do this primarily through offering to buy the shares at a price above the existing market price. Takeovers can be a threat to senior managers in the targeted firms because the successful bidder often replaces them following takeover. Fending off the threat of hostile takeover, therefore, becomes a preoccupation in many firms. Some writers see this pressure acting as a disciplining mechanism on managers, forcing them to manage as efficiently as possible; others see it leading to managerial behaviour being more short-term in nature.

A growing body of evidence indicates that takeovers rarely serve to improve efficiency. Franks and Mayer show that the profitability of companies that are subject to takeover bids is no worse than that of comparable firms that have not been involved in a takeover.[45] This indicates that takeovers do not act as a mechanism by which managerial failure is rectified. Even more importantly, merged companies frequently fail to deliver the expected benefits and, indeed, more commonly perform worse than they did before the merger: one recent study found that 'acquisitions have a systematic detrimental impact on company performance'.[46] The implications of this evidence are particularly serious when one considers the recent wave of mergers and acquisitions in the UK economy.

Arguably of even more significance than performance in firms which have merged is how the threat of takeover affects managerial behaviour in firms potentially the subject of a merger. Where managers perceive takeover to be a threat to their own position it is likely that they will pursue a course of action designed to make takeover more difficult. One way they can do this is by distributing a large proportion of profits in the form of dividends to shareholders rather than investing in research and development, new plant and machinery, or training, thereby creating loyalty amongst these shareholders and making them less likely to sell their shareholdings to a bidder. Table 2.2 shows that dividend payments to shareholders are much higher in the UK than in

TABLE 2.2

## Dividend yields in the G7 countries, 1993

| | | | |
|---|---|---|---|
| UK | 3.9 | Italy | 2.2 |
| France | 2.9 | Germany | 2.1 |
| USA | 2.8 | Japan | 0.8 |
| Canada | 2.6 | | |

*Note*: Dividend yields measure dividend payments in relation to equity values rather than current profits

*Source*: Institute for Public Policy Research, Commission on Public Policy and British Business (1997) *Promoting Prosperity: A Business Agenda for Britain*, published by Vintage.

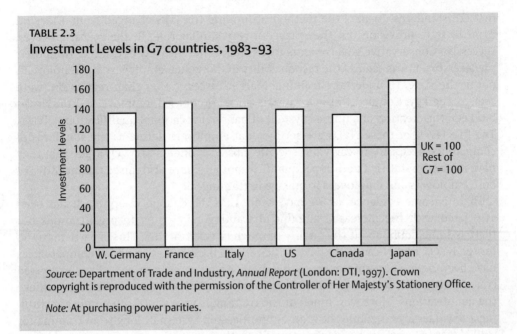

**TABLE 2.3**
**Investment Levels in G7 countries, 1983–93**

*Source:* Department of Trade and Industry, *Annual Report* (London: DTI, 1997). Crown copyright is reproduced with the permission of the Controller of Her Majesty's Stationery Office.

*Note:* At purchasing power parities.

other large, developed economies, while Table 2.3 shows that investment levels are comparably lower. As well as paying high dividends, managers can also make takeover more difficult by maintaining high levels of profitability in the short term in order to ensure the share price is high enough to make a bid expensive and, therefore, more difficult.

Pressures from the financial institutions, therefore, have pushed companies into making higher dividend payments than do their counterparts in other countries and have forced them into concentrating primarily on immediate profit growth. This has made it more difficult for British firms to compete in industries that require long-term investments; hence, the relative absence of British-owned firms in the automotive and electrical sectors. More generally, pressures from financial institutions have contributed to the relative decline of the British economy, leading to slow output growth and low levels of investment. Such a climate is hardly conducive to the implementation of strategic HRM.

## The Training System

If the financial system makes a 'strategic' approach difficult, so too does the skill level of the workforce in Britain. In the period 1980–2000 there has been a transformation in the institutions and structures that constitute the training system in Britain. During the 1960s a series of Industrial Training Boards (ITBs) were created, consisting of employer and trade union representatives. They had the power to issue a levy on all firms within a sector to fund grants to companies whose training plans met ITB standards. In 1973 the method of funding the ITBs changed from a levy on firms to state provision but they played a very similar role. In the 1980s, however, successive Conservative governments took a very different view of training from their predecessors. It was seen as the responsibility of individual employers and employees, not of the state, to undertake training. Market forces, rather than regulation, were seen as the key. Coupled to the emphasis on market-based, employer-led initiatives has been the creation of a unified system of national vocational qualifications (NVQs). The five levels of these NVQs are set by what employers define as the standards of competence necessary to carry out specific jobs. Proponents of NVQs argue that they have raised the status of vocational qualifications and have also raised the incentive of both employers and employees to engage in training.

There is some evidence, as we have seen, that the change in approach has been associated with the increased amount of training happening in organizations but there is some doubt about the quality of much of this training. This is particularly so for the NVQs; some academics have criticized the narrow way in which competencies have been defined by employers, while many employers themselves have expressed concern about the lack of general educational standards required in order to achieve the qualifications. Moreover, much of the training is very short, often only constituting a few days a year, while the craft apprenticeship system of long-term training for skilled manual workers has declined significantly.[47]

The market-based system in Britain contrasts with the emphasis in many European countries on legislative support for training and the involvement of trade unions in its provision. In Germany, for example, the 'dual' system of vocational training combines on-the-job training for three to four days a week with one to two days a week at a vocational training college. The administration of this system is carried out by a number of interested parties: national and regional governments, chambers of industry, employers, and unions. It has been argued that this collaboration has meant that solutions arrived at jointly promote commitment from different groups, reducing disputes and tensions between them.[48] In France, a national system of apprenticeships is funded partly by the state and partly by a special tax on employers. In addition, a separate law forces employers to spend at least 1.2% of their total pay-bill on training; in fact, on average they spend 2.8%.[49]

All the available evidence testifies to the differences between the skill levels of the workforce in Britain and those of workforces in other large developed economies. Gross value added per person hour in manufacturing is about 25% higher in France and 33% higher in Germany than it is in Britain.[50] The skills gap is most acute at the level of intermediate skills, largely those that were previously achieved through apprenticeships. In services, too, skill levels are considerably lower in Britain than in Germany and France.[51]

A key consequence of this relative skills gap is that a strategic approach to the management of labour involving the development of the skills of the workforce is more difficult for UK firms than it is for their counterparts in other countries. This is in part because the skill level of workers at the point of recruitment is lower, meaning that individual employers must bear significant costs in bringing their employees up to the required level. Moreover, in the market-based system, with its absence of a

TABLE 2.4
**Productivity in UK manufacturing relative to the rest of the G7, 1993**

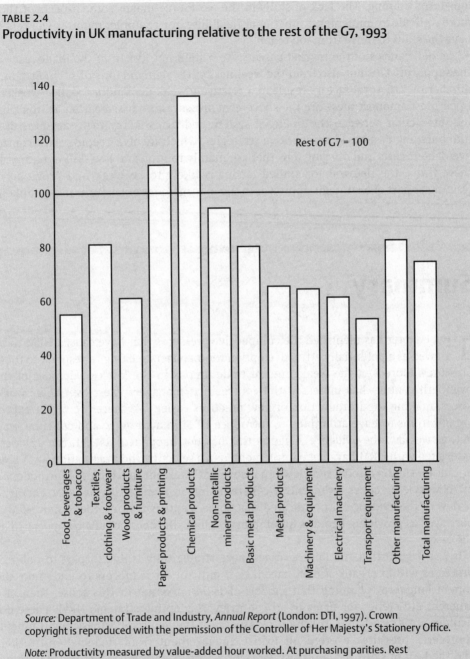

Rest of G7 = 100

*Source:* Department of Trade and Industry, *Annual Report* (London: DTI, 1997). Crown copyright is reproduced with the permission of the Controller of Her Majesty's Stationery Office.

*Note:* Productivity measured by value-added hour worked. At purchasing parities. Rest of G7 excludes Italy.

training levy or of state provision, the temptation exists for individual employers to poach trained workers from other firms rather than carry out training themselves. Hence, the danger of poaching acts as a disincentive to employers to invest in long-term training. The lack of skills in the workforce makes some aspects of HRM more difficult to implement; functional flexibility, for example, requires workers to have the skills to move from job to job.

The deficiencies of the market-based system stem not just from the inadequacy of the supply of skills but also from the weakness of the demand for skills.[52] In Britain, a number of structural factors result in a relatively weak demand for skilled workers. Uppermost amongst these are the short-term pressures discussed earlier arising from the interaction between the financial system and firms. Many firms are pressured into pursuing cost-based competitive strategies, which involve keeping tight control over labour costs and offering jobs that are mainly routine and low-skill in nature. In these firms, the demand for skilled labour is likely to be weak and provision of training as part of a strategic approach to the management of labour is most unlikely.

# Summary

THIS chapter has identified the competitive pressures that have caused HRM to be viewed as a potentially attractive option for managers seeking to respond to these pressures. Moreover, the weakening of trade unions in the last two decades of the twentieth century has increased the control that managers exert over their workforces, making the introduction of new practices easier. We therefore might expect organizations to have attempted to introduce HRM in a strategic and coherent way, but, as we saw, the evidence suggests this has not happened. Rather, the practices associated with HRM have been implemented in a selective and pragmatic way. A note of caution should also be struck when assessing the extent to which the introduction of HRM-style practices represents a coherent shift in managerial ideology. Finally, a review of the evidence also indicated that some scepticism is in order when HRM is portrayed as providing benefits for employees since this does not always appear to be the case.

It was argued that the failure to act more strategically is due in part to political processes within organizations that make it difficult for managers to undertake the sort of long-term planning that models of HRM advocate. In this sense, there are inherent difficulties for firms in all countries in adopting strategic HRM. These difficulties are exacerbated in Britain by aspects of the general business environment; short-term pressures exerted on British management from financial institutions and the lack of skills in the British workforce were identified as factors inhibiting a strategic approach to managing workforces. This is not to say that there has been no take-up of HRM; indeed, Storey identified a 'remarkable array of initiatives' that were in keeping with models of HRM in the organizations he studied.[53] Rather, this chapter has attempted to show that it is not surprising that these initiatives are rarely implemented as part of a strategic, coherent approach.

BOX 2.1
## Case Study—Unemployment and Wage Flexibility

A key debate within the European Union in the 1990s concerned the desirability of wage flexibility as a way of reducing unemployment. Joblessness in the mid-1990s had risen to historically high levels in many European countries, especially when compared to other developed economies (see Table 2.5). One explanation commonly advanced to account for this is that labour markets in Europe are saddled with 'inflexibilities'; strong trade unions, legal support for collective bargaining, minimum wages, and employment protection laws all prevent employers from adjusting terms and conditions to match fluctuations in demand. In contrast, in the USA unions and legal regulation of employment are much weaker and, hence, there is a much greater degree of 'wage flexibility'. Proponents of free markets argue that this flexibility has been a major factor in the employment growth in the USA in the 1980s and 1990s and explains why unemployment is much lower there than it is in Europe.

TABLE 2.5
### International comparisons of unemployment (% of labour force), 1996

| Korea | 2.0 | Germany | 9.0 |
|---|---|---|---|
| Japan | 3.4 | Canada | 9.7 |
| USA | 5.4 | Sweden | 10.0 |
| UK | 8.2 | Italy | 12.0 |
| Australia | 8.6 | France | 12.3 |

*Source*: Bamber, G., Ross, P., and Whitehouse, G., 'Employment Relations and Labour Market Indicators in Ten Industrialised Market Economies: Comparative Statistics', *International Journal of Human Resource Management* (1998), 9, 2, pp. 401-35

In keeping with this view, the Conservative governments of the 1980s and 1990s consistently argued that European economies were over-regulated and that an effective cure for unemployment was to deregulate labour markets. The election of Tony Blair's Labour Party in May 1997 did not fundamentally change this—Blair went out of his way after the election to call for greater flexibility in Europe. Is wage flexibility, then, a panacea for European unemployment?

Richard Freeman, in an article in the *Oxford Review of Economic Policy*, argues that the extent to which wage flexibility is responsible for employment growth in the USA is exaggerated.[54] The real earnings of the lowest-paid workers in the USA have fallen sharply as a result of wage flexibility; between 1979 and 1993 the hourly earnings of men with less than twelve years of schooling dropped by 27%; despite this, however, the work opportunities for low-paid workers fell during this period. This, according to Freeman, is because employment levels are determined to a much greater degree by the nature of demand than by the cost of labour; 'despite large pay-cut induced movements down the demand curve for the less-skilled, demand shifts dominated changes in employment, so that falling wages were associated with falling work'.

Furthermore, Freeman argues that wage flexibility has been associated with very high social costs. The fall in the wages of those at the bottom of the income distribution meant that inequality grew substantially; estimates put the growth in inequality at 28% in the period 1979 to 1993. The fact that this rise was brought about principally through lower wages at the bottom end of the income distribution rather than higher wages for those at the top has meant that poverty has grown substantially. This was felt particularly amongst young families; the proportion of American children in families below the official poverty level increased from 14.2% in 1973 to 21.1% in 1991.

Wage flexibility was a major factor not only in the rise in inequality but also in the rise in crime. A number of studies link individuals' labour market experience to their propensity to be involved in crime. Freeman argues that the decline in real earnings for young, less-educated men was mirrored by a rise in criminal activity among this group. The last three decades have seen an enormous rise in the prison population in the USA, fivefold since 1970. This rise is concentrated among those groups that are most likely to be unemployed in Europe—young, less-educated men. In 1993, 1.9% of the American male population of working age were in prison and a further 4.7% were either on probation or parole and were, therefore, 'under supervision of the criminal justice system'. It would appear that US-style wage flexibility has not been the unqualified success that many portray it as.

*Case Study Activity*

If you were appointed as an adviser to the British government, what would you tell them about the merits of using wage flexibility to cure unemployment?

# Study Questions

1 In what ways has economic activity become more internationalized and how has this affected British firms?

2 Imagine that you are a manager in a recently privatized firm: what practical changes to your work is privatization likely to bring?

3 How have changes to employment law increased the ability of managers to push through organizational change?

4 Imagine that you are a manager in a British firm which is rumoured to be in danger of being taken over: how could you protect the firm from takeover and why might this not involve pursuing strategic HRM?

5 Why do British firms invest less in training their workforces than do their counterparts in France and Germany?

# Further Reading

Blyton, P. and Turnbull, P., *The Dynamics of Employee Relations* (Basingstoke: Macmillan, 1998).

Legge, K., *Human Resource Management: Rhetorics and Realities* (Basingstoke: Macmillan, 1995).

Sisson, K. and Marginson, P., 'Management: Systems, Structures and Strategy', in P. Edwards, (ed.), *Industrial Relations: Theory and Practice in Britain* (Oxford: Blackwell, 1995).

Storey, J. and Sisson, K., *Managing Human Resources and Industrial Relations* (Buckingham: Open University Press, 1993), chapter 3, pp. 52–79.

# Notes

1. Freeman, R., 'Does Globalisation Threaten Low-Skilled Western Workers?', in J. Philpott (ed.), *Working for Full Employment* (London: Routledge, 1997).

2. United Nations, *World Investment Report*, (New York, United Nations, 1998).

3. Colling, T. and Ferner, A., 'Privatization and Marketization', in P. Edwards (ed.), *Industrial Relations: Theory and Practice in Britain* (Oxford: Blackwell, 1995).

4. Colling, T. and Ferner, A., 'Privatization and Marketization', in P. Edwards (ed.), *Industrial Relations: Theory and Practice in Britain* (Oxford: Blackwell, 1995).

5. Hanson, C. and Mather, G., *Striking Out Strikes* (London: IEA, 1988).

6. Dickens, L. and Hall, M., 'The State: Labour Law and Industrial Relations', in P. Edwards (ed.), *Industrial Relations: Theory and Practice in Britain* (Oxford: Blackwell, 1995).

7. Hepple, R., 'The Rise and Fall of Unfair Dismissal', in W. McCarthy (ed.), *Legal Intervention in Industrial Relations: Gains and Losses* (Oxford: Blackwell, 1992).

8. Office for National Statistics, *Labour Market Trends* (London: ONS, 1998).

9. Ibid.

10. Storey, J., *Developments in the Management of Human Resources* (Oxford: Blackwell, 1992).

11. Cully, M., Woodland, S., O'Reilly, A., Dix, G., Millward, N., Bryson, A., and Forth, J., *The 1998 Workplace Employee Relations Survey: First Findings* (London: Department of Trade and Industry, 1998).

12. Storey, J., *Developments in the Management of Human Resources* (Oxford: Blackwell, 1992).

13. Clark, I., 'Competitive Pressures and Engineering Process Plant Contracting', *Human Resource Management Journal* (1998), 8, 2, pp. 14–28 (see pp. 26–7).

14. Ferner, A., 'Country of Origin Effects and HRM in Multinational Companies', *Human Resource Management Journal* (1997), 7, 1, pp. 19–37.

15. Cully, M., Woodland, S., O'Reilly, A., Dix, G., Millward, N., Bryson, A., and Forth, J., *The 1998 Workplace Employee Relations Survey: First Findings* (London: Department of Trade and Industry, 1998).

16. Office for National Statistics, *Labour Market Trends* (London: ONS, 1998).

17. Gospel, H., 'The Revival of Apprenticeship Training in Britain?', *British Journal of Industrial Relations*, (1998), 36, 3, September, pp. 435–57 (see p. 452).

18. Keep, E. and Rainbird, H., 'Training', in P. Edwards (ed.), *Industrial Relations: Theory and Practice in Britain* (Oxford: Blackwell, 1995).

19. Alberga, T., Tyson, S., and Parsons, D., 'An Evaluation of the Investors in People Standard', *Human Resource Management Journal* (1997), 7, 2, p. 4.

20. Poole, M., and Jenkins, G., 'Developments in Human Resource Management in Manufacturing in Modern Britain', *International Journal of Human Resource Management* (1997), 8, 6, December, pp. 841–56 (see p. 848).

21. Blyton, P. and Turnbull, P. (eds.), *Reassessing Human Resource Management* (London: Sage, 1992); Legge, K., *Human Resource Management: Rhetorics and Realities* (London: Macmillan, 1995); Millward, N., *The New Industrial Relations?* (London: PSI, 1994); Storey, J., *Developments in the Management of Human Resources* (Oxford: Blackwell, 1992); Sisson, K., 'In Search of HRM', *British Journal of Industrial Relations* (1993), 31, 2, 201–10.

22. Sisson, K. and Marginson, P., 'Management: Systems, Structures and Strategy', in P. Edwards, (ed.), *Industrial Relations: Theory and Practice in Britain* (Oxford: Blackwell, 1995).

23. Marginson, P., Edwards, P., Martin, R., Purcell, J. and Sisson, K., *Beyond the Workplace: Managing Industrial Relations in the Multi-Establishment Enterprise* (Oxford: Blackwell, 1988); Marginson, P., Armstrong, P., Edwards, P., Purcell, J. with Hubbard, N., 'The Control of Industrial Relations in Large Companies: An Initial Analysis of the Second Company Level Industrial Relations Survey', *Warwick Papers in Industrial Relations*, No. 45, December 1993.

24. Storey, J. and Sisson, L., *Managing Human Resources and Industrial Relations* (Buckingham: Open University Press, 1993).

25. Poole and Jenkins, 'Developments in Human Resource Management', p. 845.

26. Truss, C., Gratton, L., Hope-Hailey, V., McGovern, P. and Stiles, P., 'Soft and Hard Models of Human Resource Management: A Reappraisal', *Journal of Management Studies* (1997), 34, 1, January, pp. 53–73 (see p. 64).

27. McGovern, P., Gratton, L., Hope-Hailey, V., and Stiles, P. 'Human Resource Management on the Line?', *Human Resource Management Journal* (1997), 7, 4, pp. 12–29 (see p. 26); Hall, L. and Torrington, D., 'Letting Go or Holding On—The Devolution of Operational Personnel Activities', *Human Resource Management Journal* (1998), 8, 1, pp. 41–55 (see pp. 51–2).

28. Storey, J., *Developments in the Management of Human Resources* (Oxford: Blackwell, 1992).

29. Arulampalam, W. and Booth, A. L., 'Training and Labour Market Flexibility: Is there a Trade-off?', *British Journal of Industrial Relations* (1998), 36, 4, December, pp. 521–36 (see p. 521).

30. Martin, G., Staines, H., and Pate, J., 'Linking Job Security and Career Development in a New Psychological Contract', *Human Resource Management Journal* (1998), 8, 3, pp. 20–40 (see p. 37).

31. Ebadan, G. and Winstanley, D., 'Downsizing, Delayering and Careers—The Survivor's Perspective', *Human Resource Management Journal* (1997), 7, 1, pp. 79–91 (see pp. 88–9).

32. Dowling, B. and Richardson, R., 'Evaluating Performance-Related Pay for Managers in the National Health Service', *International Journal of Human Resource Management* (1997), 8, 3, June, pp. 348–66 (see p. 357).

33. Lewis, P., 'Managing Performance-Related Pay based on Evidence from the Financial Services Sector', *Human Resource Management Journal* (1998), 8, 2, pp. 66–77 (see p. 76).

34. Gilman, M., *Performance Related Pay in Practice: Organization and Effect* (PhD Thesis: University of Warwick, 1998).

35. Knights, D. and McCabe, D., 'How Would You Measure Something Like That?: Quality in a Retail Bank', *Journal of Management Studies* (1997), 34, 3, May, pp. 371–88 (see p. 382).

36. Knights, D. and McCabe, D., 'The Times they are a Changin'? Transformative Organizational Innovations in Financial Services in the UK', *International Journal of Human Resource Management* (1998), 9, 1, February, pp. 168–84 (see p. 184).

37. De Cock, C. and Hipkin, I., 'TQM and BPR: Beyond the Beyond Myth', *Journal of Management Studies* (1997), 34, 5, September, pp. 659–75 (see pp. 666–7).

38. Dickens, L., 'What HRM Means for Gender Equality', *Human Resource Management Journal* (1998), 8, 1, pp. 23–40.

39. Lyon, P., Hallier, J. and Glover, I., 'Divestment or Investment? The Contradiction of HRM in Relation to Older Employees', *Human Resource Management Journal* (1998), 8, 1, pp. 56–66 (see p. 56).

40. Taylor, P. and Walker, A., 'Policies and Practices Towards Older Workers: A Framework For Comparative Research', *Human Resource Management Journal* (1998), 8, 3, p. 4.

41. Sisson, K., 'In Search of HRM', *British Journal of Industrial Relations* (1993), 31, 2, 201–10.

42. Pettigrew, A., *The Politics of Organisational Decision Making* (London: Tavistock, 1973); Mintzberg, H., 'Crafting Strategy', *Harvard Business Review* (1987), July–August, pp. 65–75.

43. Whittington, R., *What is Strategy—and Does it Matter?* (London: Routledge, 1993).

44. Hutton, W., *The State We're In* (London: Jonathan Cape, 1996).

45. Franks, J. and Mayer, C., 'Do Hostile Takeovers Improve Performance?', *Business Strategy Review* (1996), 7, 4, pp. 1–6.

46. Dickerson, A., Gibson, H., and Tsakalotos, E., *The Impact of Acquisitions on Company Performance: Evidence from a Large Panel of UK Firms* (Canterbury: University Press, 1995).

47. Keep, E. and Rainbird, H., 'Training', in P. Edwards (ed.), *Industrial Relations: Theory and Practice in Britain* (Oxford: Blackwell, 1995).

48. European Industrial Relations Review, 'West Germany. The Dual Training System', No. 195, April, 1990.

49. Industrial Relations Review and Report, 'Recruitment and Training Abroad. The Labour Market in France', No. 500, November 1991.

50. Department of Trade and Industry, *Annual Report*, (London: DTI, 1997).

51. Jarvis, V. and Prais, S., 'Two Nations of Shopkeepers: Training for Retailing in Britain and France', *National Institute Economic Review*, May 1989, 58–74.

52. Keep, E. and Mayhew, K., 'Training Policy for Competitiveness', in H. Metcalf, (ed.), *Future Skill Demand and Supply* (London: PSI, 1995).

53. Storey, J., *Developments in the Management of Human Resources* (Oxford: Blackwell, 1992).

54. Freeman, R., 'The Limits to Wage Flexibility in Curing Unemployment', *Oxford Review of Economic Policy* (1995), 11, 1, pp. 63–72.

# Chapter 3
# Employment Law

## Chapter Contents

# Introduction

To understand the role of the law in the employment relationship it is helpful to distinguish between three different types of employment regulation: unilateral, joint, and legal. In the first of these, management determine the key elements of the relationship between the employer and employee without interference from an external body. Hence, unilateral regulation involves, for example, management alone setting terms and conditions, specifying the tasks employees are expected to perform, and carrying out any disciplinary action. In joint regulation, on the other hand, management negotiate with a representative of the workforce, normally a trade union. Pay determination is perhaps the main focus of joint regulation, but unions may also exert influence over job demarcations (the boundaries between jobs) and may have shaped the nature of disciplinary procedures. The final type, legal regulation, concerns the way the law shapes the conduct of the employment relationship in, for example, restricting management's ability to hire and fire and to discriminate against particular groups.

It is clear that the take-up of HRM has been primarily at the instigation of management: models of HRM, as we have seen, stress the importance of managers acting strategically, while the evidence on the take-up of HRM demonstrates that it is management, rather than employees or their representatives, who initiate the implementation of HRM practices.[1] In other words, the introduction of practices associated with HRM in recent years is a product of unilateral regulation. This has coincided with a decline in the strength and coverage of trade unions, as we will see in Chapter 4, resulting in a weakening of joint regulation. This chapter focuses on the nature of legal regulation, examining the ways in which legislation shapes aspects of the employment relationship, how this has changed in recent years, and how this relates to interest in HRM.

# 1 The Emergence of Statutory Employment Rights

Until relatively recently the British system of industrial relations (IR) was characterized as being 'voluntarist'. A key element of this 'voluntarism' is the relative absence of legal regulation; aspects of the employment relationship were generally left to the 'voluntary' negotiation of management and trade unions, or to management unilaterally, to determine. Where collective agreements were made these were not, and still are not, legally binding; that is, there is nothing in law that prevents either party from breaking a collective agreement (so long as it does not contravene individual contracts of employment). Moreover, successive governments for most of the twentieth century did not seek to use legal intervention in IR in order to give employees legal rights on issues such as minimum wages or maximum working hours. This is not to say that the law played no part in regulating employment nor that employees had no legal rights, but what is clear is that for most of the twentieth century individual employment rights in Britain were far weaker than in most European countries.[2]

During the 1960s and particularly the 1970s, however, the tradition of voluntarism was eroded. One element of the change was the use of legislation to restrict the actions of trade unions, in particular by making it more difficult for them to organize industrial action (this is expanded upon in Chapter 4). The other element in the change from voluntarism to greater legal intervention was the creation of a set of legal rights for individual employees. These statutory rights, which supplemented any rights individuals possessed in their contracts of employment, are the subject we concentrate on in this chapter.

Individual employment rights emerged in two broad areas. First, legislation sought to provide employees with a degree of protection against dismissal. This initially took the form of the Redundancy Payments Act of 1965, which obliged employers to pay compensation to employees who were made redundant. The rationale for this was to provide some recognition of past service and to ease the onset of technological and other changes by inducing employees more readily to accept the loss of their jobs. In fact, the statutory payments do not apply to all workers; those with less than two years' continuous service are excluded. Moreover, the payments, which vary according to age, weekly pay, and length of service, are generally modest. The impact of the Act, consequently, has been limited, and the impact on job security has been negligible.[3]

Arguably of greater impact on job security has been the unfair dismissal legislation, first contained in the Industrial Relations Act of 1971. The primary aim of this legislation was to restrict the grounds on which employers could dismiss employees. As well as protecting employees, the Act was intended to promote good personnel management by inducing employers to set up disciplinary procedures in order to minimize the likelihood of a dismissal being seen as unfair by the legal system. These procedures commonly involve a system of spoken and written warnings and often clearly state at what stage personnel and senior managers should become involved. Those devising the legislation hoped that such procedures would reduce the amount of industrial action over dismissals by providing an alternative system through which contested dismissals could be challenged.[4]

Whether a dismissal is fair or unfair is determined by the so-called 'two-stage test'. The first stage is to establish whether the reason for dismissal is one of the five 'fair' reasons specified in the legislation: capability, conduct, redundancy, complying with a statutory requirement, or 'some other substantial reason'. The last of these is vague but has been interpreted to include dismissals arising from business reorganizations, pressure to dismiss from a third party, and personality conflicts.[5] If the tribunal decides that the dismissal was not for one of these reasons then it is automatically deemed unfair and the employee wins the case. If, on the other hand, it is seen as being for a fair reason then the tribunal considers the second stage, whether dismissal was a 'reasonable' action for the employer to take. If the use of dismissal is deemed to have fallen within the 'range of reasonable responses' that an employer might take, then the dismissal is seen as fair; if not, then the employee wins the case.[6]

The second broad area of individual employment rights concerns discrimination against women and ethnic minorities. The Sex Discrimination Act (SDA) of 1975 outlaws discrimination on grounds of gender or marital status in employment. The Act distinguished between direct and indirect discrimination: the former involves a requirement or condition being applied differently to men and women so as to disadvantage women; the latter involves a requirement or condition (that is not necessary for the job) being applied equally to men and women but in such a way as to make it more difficult for women to comply (whether this was the intention or not). Two examples illustrate the distinction:

*Direct discrimination*—the refusal to offer a woman a job in London when it is learnt that her husband is due to be transferred to Leeds in six months' time. This is direct discrimination because it is based on an assumption that married women will always follow their husbands.

*Indirect discrimination*—a 35-year-old woman is told by an employer that she cannot be considered for a post because they are looking for someone under the age of 30. This is indirect discrimination because the condition that an applicant be under 30 is such that the proportion of women who can comply with it is considerably smaller than the proportion of men who can comply with it, as the responsibilities of childbearing and -minding fall disproportionately on women.[7]

Thus the legislation outlaws both overt and more subtle forms of discrimination. There are some grounds, however, on which it is justifiable for an employer to specify whether a man or a woman is required. These relate to where there is a genuine occupational qualification for the employee to be of a particular gender and include: the nature of the job calling for a particular gender for reasons of physiology (for example, models) or authenticity in dramatic performance (for example, actors); the job needing to be done by a member of one sex to preserve decency or privacy (for example, security staff frisking customers); and the job involving supervision and attention of a single-sex group in a hospital, prison, or old people's home.[8]

The other major legislation designed to prevent discrimination against women was the Equal Pay Act (EPA) 1970, which provides for equal pay and conditions for women when doing work that is the same as, or similar to, work done by a man and where work performed by women in one job is shown to be of 'equal value' to that performed by men under the same employer. In order to prove that her work is of equal value to that of men, a woman must show that the work is comparable in the demands it places on her in terms of criteria such as effort levels and the skills required.[9]

The Race Relations Act (RRA) 1976 provided similar rights for members of racial groups to those given to women by the SDA. The legislation defines a racial group by reference to one or more of the following: colour, race, nationality (including citizenship), or ethnic or national origins. Again, the concepts of direct and indirect discrimination were established to outlaw discrimination in employment on the grounds of race.[10]

Accompanying this legislation was the creation of specific institutions through which these rights could be enforced. Uppermost amongst these were industrial tribunals (ITs), which act as specialist employment courts and hear cases brought by individual employees. The panel of the ITs, comprising an employer representative, a trade unionist, and a legal expert, hear the case from both parties, who may hire legal representation but do not have to. The hearings are generally held within roughly twelve weeks of the application's first being lodged with the IT and are normally over within a day. While the ITs have not entirely achieved their aims of being cheap, accessible, speedy, informal, and able to utilize expertise, they compare favourably to the ordinary courts on these criteria.[11] In fact, the majority of the cases brought do not reach the ITs: many are settled through conciliation by the official body, ACAS (Advisory, Conciliation and Arbitration Service), whose responsibility it is to try to settle such disputes; others are dropped by the employee; and in other cases the employer concedes the case before it reaches a tribunal (see Table 3.6).

There are also two specific agencies that were created to help enforce the legislation, the Equal Opportunities Commission (EOC) and the Commission for Racial Equality (CRE). Both the EOC and the CRE have the power to support individuals in bringing a claim as well as to initiate proceedings with respect to discriminatory advertising and persistent discrimination.[12] They also both have investigative and campaigning roles. It has been argued that the existence of these bodies has raised awareness of the laws concerning equality and also lent to them greater authority than they otherwise would possess.[13]

During the 1980s and 1990s individual employment rights have been subject to conflicting forces. Domestically, the Conservative governments in office between 1979 and 1997 saw the legislation as imposing costs and risks on firms, thereby harming their competitiveness. Realizing the political dangers in abolishing this body of legislation altogether, the Conservatives set about attempting to weaken it instead in a number of ways. For example, the qualifying period for entitlement to claim unfair dismissal was raised from six months to two years, reducing the number of employees covered, and the burden of proving the reasonableness of a dismissal was removed from the employer and became 'neutral', making it more difficult for an employee to win a case.[14]

Internationally, however, the influence of the EU helped strengthen employment rights. The UK government were obliged by the European Union to introduce the Sex Discrimination Act of 1986 in order to strengthen the equal value legislation, following cases in which the court found Britain to be in breach of European law. The EU influence also forced the government to improve pregnancy and maternity leave rights. More recently, the signing by the new Labour government of the Social Chapter, a European Union initiative designed to provide a floor of basic employment rights across Europe, will have the effect of strengthening the European influence, particularly in relation to the rights of part-time workers, who are, of course, disproportionately female.

TABLE 3.1

## Legislation on individual employment rights

| Year | Act | Impact |
|------|-----|--------|
| 1965 | Redundancy Payments Act | Provided limited redundancy pay |
| 1970 | Equal Pay Act | Provided equal pay for work of 'equal value' |
| 1971 | Industrial Relations Act | Provided the right to claim unfair dismissal |
| 1975 | Sex Discrimination Act | Outlawed discrimination on grounds of sex |
| 1976 | Race Relations Act | Outlawed discrimination on grounds of race |
| 1978 | Employment Protection (Consolidation) Act | Consolidated and extended existing employment rights |
| 1979 | Unfair Dismissal Order | Raised qualifying period for entitlement to unfair dismissal to one year |
| 1985 | Unfair Dismissal Order | Raised qualifying period for entitlement to unfair dismissal to two years |
| 1986 | Sex Discrimination Act | Coverage of sex discrimination legislation extended * |
| 1986 | Wages Act | Scope and function of Wages Councils reduced |
| 1989 | Employment Act | Equal access for men and women to training * |
| 1993 | Trade Union Reform and Employment Rights Act | Pregnancy & maternity rights improved * Wages Councils abolished |
| 1995 | Disability Discrimination Act | Establishes limited legal protection for the disabled |
| 1997 | Incorporation of the Social Chapter | Affects parental leave, rights for part-timers, 'European Works Councils' |
| 1998 | 'Fairness at Work' White Paper | Recommends strengthening of unfair dismissal, including lowering qualifying period to one year and increasing payments |

* signifies legislative change prompted by EU

*Source*: Adapted from Dickens, L. and Hall, M., 'The State: Labour Law and Industrial Relations' in P. Edwards (ed.), *Industrial Relations: Theory and Practice in Britain* (Oxford: Blackwell, 1995).

# 2 The Impact of Individual Employment Legislation

THESE legislative attempts to provide job security and outlaw discrimination have undoubtedly had some impact. The unfair dismissal legislation has placed limits on the ability of employers to sack people, ensuring that an employer has a 'fair' reason for doing so and has acted 'reasonably'. It is generally agreed that the legislation has made employers more careful in dismissing people, while employees who are victims of unfair dismissal now have the opportunity for legal redress, either through being reinstated or receiving some compensation. Therefore, it would appear that employees have a higher level of job security than they would have in the absence of the legislation.

However, it is also clear that the legislation has fallen some way short of providing genuine job security. This is demonstrated in a number of ways. Only a small proportion of cases brought are ultimately successful at an industrial tribunal (see Table 3.6). This fact alone does not necessarily mean that the legislation has failed to provide job security, since the legislation may have deterred employers from dismissing people 'unfairly'. Other statistics, however, cast doubt on there being a deterrent effect. Despite the legislation's being based on an assumption that reinstatement is the 'primary' remedy for cases of unfair dismissal, only 1.6% of cases won by the employee result in an order for the employee to be reinstated (although in a small number of others the employer offers to do this rather than pay compensation).[15] This is partly because tribunals have been wary of recommending reinstatement but also because, even when they do, such an order is not legally binding on an employer. Moreover, the compensation payments are too low to provide a significant deterrent to employers. The median payment to employees winning unfair dismissal cases at ITs in 1995–6 was £2,499, down by 24% from the previous year.[16] This median award constitutes an average of only eight and a half weeks' pay.

The limited impact of the legislation also arises out of tribunals' interpretation of key terms. The term 'some other substantial reason' has been interpreted so broadly as to make it easier for employers to pass the first stage of the two-stage test (establishing that the reason for dismissal was a 'fair' reason); Hepple argues that it has been interpreted to include almost anything that is not trivial or 'unworthy'.[17] Similarly, the way that tribunals interpret the second stage, the 'reasonableness' test, has also tended to make it easier for employers to pass: in a series of rulings, the tribunals (and appeal courts) have redefined the second stage of the test concerning reasonableness, weakening the original interpretation. Overall, therefore, the unfair dismissal legislation appears not to have significantly constrained managerial action. Indeed, it has been argued that it has added a legitimacy to managerial action and has, therefore, acted to reinforce the managerial prerogative.[18]

The anti-discrimination legislation has undoubtedly had some impact. In a number of ways the labour market position of women has improved since the 1970s. In 1971 women constituted 38% of employees in the UK; in 1997 the figure reached 45% (see Table 3.2). Furthermore, the difference in pay between men and women in full-time employment (the gender pay gap) has narrowed: while women earned 63% of the earnings of men in 1970, this figure had risen to 74% in 1996 (see Table 3.3). Women have gradually become more successful in entering certain high-profile jobs that had previously been the preserve of men, as illustrated by the rise in the number of female MPs in the 1997 general election.

However, it is clear that women continue to suffer from a disadvantaged position in the labour market in comparison to men. Women are disproportionately employed in the so-called 'atypical' workforce of part-timers, temporary workers, and homeworkers. The jobs the members of this workforce perform are not only generally low-paid but also tend to have less favourable fringe benefits, such as bonus schemes and overtime payments, than do full-time, 'standard' jobs. Moreover, the labour market

TABLE 3.2
## Female participation in the labour market (thousands), 1997

| Labour Market Participation | All | Male | Female |
| --- | --- | --- | --- |
| Total | 26,279 | 55.3% | 44.7% |
| Full-timers | 19,727 | 67.2% | 32.8% |
| Part-timers | 6,544 | 19.4% | 80.6% |

*Source*: Office for National Statistics, *Labour Market Trends* (London: ONS, 1998). Crown copyright 1998.

TABLE 3.3
## The gender pay gap, 1997

| Pay gap—Gross weekly earnings of full-time employees (£ per week) | | | |
| --- | --- | --- | --- |
| | All | Male | Female | Pay gap |
| Mean | 342 | 378 | 274 | 72.5% |
| Median | 295 | 325 | 236 | 72.6% |

| Pay gap—Gross weekly earnings of all employees (£ per hour) | | | |
| --- | --- | --- | --- |
| | All | Male | Female | Pay gap |
| Mean | 7.58 | 8.63 | 6.39 | 74.0% |
| Median | 6.22 | 7.14 | 5.31 | 74.4% |

*Source*: Office for National Statistics, *Labour Market Trends* (London: ONS, 1998). Crown copyright 1998.

continues to be characterized by industrial segregation: women are disproportionately located in distribution, hotels and catering, and in health and education and are much less likely to be employed in the primary sector or in manufacturing, communications, and construction (see Table 3.4). There is also continued occupational segregation: managerial and professional posts are still overwhelmingly filled by men, whereas clerical and sales jobs are largely filled by women (see Table 3.5). Furthermore, while the pay gap narrowed initially following the introduction of equal-pay legislation, it now appears to be stable. A similar position emerges when we examine the position of ethnic minorities. Ethnic minority groups appear to be in a disadvantaged position within the labour market, with this disadvantage being most marked for black workers. Black workers are disproportionately located in unskilled or only partly-skilled jobs and earn less than other groups earn. Most notably, the rates of unemployment are much higher among ethnic minority groups than among whites: in 1997 the rate of unemployment amongst ethnic minority men as a whole was twice that for white men, while the rate for black men was almost three times as high. While

## TABLE 3.4
### Proportion of employees in each occupation who are female, 1997

| Occupation | % female | Occupation | % female |
|---|---|---|---|
| Craft and related | 9 | Associate professional and technical | 49 |
| Plant and machine operators | 19 | Sales | 65 |
| Managers and administrators | 33 | Personal and protective | 68 |
| Professional | 40 | Clerical and secretarial | 75 |
| Other occupations | 48 | | |

*Source*: Office for National Statistics, *Labour Market Trends* (London: ONS, 1998). Crown copyright 1998.

## TABLE 3.5
### Proportion of employees in each industry who are female, 1997

| Industry | % female | Industry | % female |
|---|---|---|---|
| Construction | 9.5 | Banking and finance | 44.9 |
| Energy and water | 20.7 | Distribution, hotels, and catering | 51.7 |
| Transport and communication | 24.3 | Other services | 53.6 |
| Agriculture and fishing | 25.6 | Public administration, education, and health | 69.5 |
| Manufacturing | 26.8 | | |

*Source*: Office for National Statistics, *Labour Market Trends* (London: ONS, 1998). Crown copyright 1998.

economists differ over the extent to which the pay gap in particular, and the disadvantaged position of women and ethnic minority groups in general, is caused by discrimination, most agree that a proportion of it is due to discriminatory practices by employers.[19]

Clearly, legislation has gone only part of the way to removing discrimination. Dickens argues that in the area of sex discrimination this is because of, first, weaknesses in the provisions, procedures, and institutions contained in and created by the legislation and, second, the underlying assumptions on which the legislation is based.[20] Concerning the former, the number of cases brought under the SDA and EPA is low: in 1995–6 there were 3,677 and 694 claims a year, respectively, compared with 38,557 for unfair dismissal. The proportion of these that are successful is also low—the majority of cases (over 80% for both the SDA and the EPA) were disposed of or dropped before reaching a tribunal in 1995–6, while less than 6% were ultimately successful at a tribunal (see Table 3.6). Thus the legislation appears to be little-used and used with little success. The interpretation of the law by the judiciary, moreover, has not been sympathetic to the aims of the legislation, particularly concerning the concept of indirect discrimination and when it is 'justifiable'. The weakness of the institutions designed to support the legislation has compounded the situation, particularly the limited legal role and insufficient funding of the EOC and CRE.

Turning now to consider the underlying assumptions on which the legislation is based, there are three sources of weakness, as identified by Dickens.[21] The concept of equality contained in the legislation is based on formal, procedural equality of opportunity rather than on equality of outcome. It has been argued that 'the liberal equality of opportunity approach has great problems accommodating structural sources of social capacities and skills and hence the structural sources of social inequality'.[22] The legislation is also based on seeing the 'male as the standard', in that equality is seen in terms of 'norms set by and for men'. For example, the requirement by employers that employees perform some duties after normal working hours is

TABLE 3.6
## Cases brought to industrial tribunals, 1995–6

| | Total number of cases | Settled by ACAS | Withdrawn | Successful at hearing | Dismissed at hearing | Disposed of otherwise |
|---|---|---|---|---|---|---|
| Unfair dismissal | 38,557 | 38.1% | 29.9% | 11.2% | 18.3% | 2.5% |
| Equal pay | 694 | 18.4% | 65.7% | 5.2% | 6.6% | 4.0% |
| Race discrimination | 1,737 | 23.3% | 37.8% | 6.3% | 26.1% | 6.6% |
| Sex discrimination | 3,677 | 39.8% | 41.0% | 5.9% | 9.7% | 3.6% |

*Source*: Office for National Statistics, *Labour Market Trends* (London: ONS, 1998). Crown copyright 1998.

accepted by the judiciary as normal practice, despite it generally being more difficult for women to work long hours because they are much more likely than men to bear childcare and other domestic responsibilities. Dickens also criticizes the perception of discrimination contained in the legislation, which fails to see any role for the law in removing institutional discrimination but, rather, concentrates on individuals seeking compensation for specific acts of discrimination.[23] Thus the legislation does not permit a collective approach to issues that by their nature affect a group of employees, such as the nature of a pay structure. Similar problems have been found with the race legislation.

# 3  HRM and Employment Legislation

THIS section examines two related issues. The first is how the nature of employment law in general places constraints on managers seeking to introduce HRM and how deregulation in the 1980s and 1990s in particular has eased these constraints. The second is whether the introduction of HRM makes legal regulation less necessary than it has been in the past.

As noted earlier in this chapter as well as in Chapter 2, the labour market was significantly deregulated during the 1980s and most of the 1990s. One area of deregulation was related to unfair dismissal: as we have seen, the law was altered to take away the right to claim unfair dismissal for many and to make it more difficult for those who retained the right to win a case. Other important deregulatory measures were taken in this period. The legal basis on which trade unions operate was attacked; in particular, the grounds on which unions could retain 'immunity' from prosecution following industrial action were narrowed. The Wages Councils, which had set minimum rates of pay for workers in many poorly-paid industries, were abolished. Similarly, the Fair Wages Resolution, which protected public-sector workers from being undercut by private-sector operators, was abolished, paving the way for the introduction of compulsory competitive tendering.

In this tidal wave of deregulatory measures, the anti-discrimination legislation escaped almost unscathed. Indeed, it was even strengthened marginally as a result of the 1986 Sex Discrimination Act. This is largely because of the influence of the European Union: the British government was bound by the rulings of the European Court of Justice, which repeatedly found the UK to be in breach of European law with respect to equality issues.[24] This European influence was minimized wherever possible, however, through a 'grudging, minimalist approach to compliance with Europe',[25] by opposing new European directives, and by opting out of the Social Chapter altogether.

The result of the deregulation has unquestionably been to strengthen the managerial prerogative, or what in this chapter has been termed 'unilateral regulation'. A key consequence is that management can more easily introduce organizational changes such as HRM. In other words, in the 1980s and 1990s the introduction of HRM has been facilitated by the weakening of legal (and joint) regulation. It has been argued, moreover, that the introduction of HRM reduces the need for legal regulation. In a context of a new breed of 'enlightened' managers following employee-friendly HRM policies, there is no longer a rationale, so the argument goes, for legislation providing for employment rights.[26] How justified is such a view?

We will examine this question in relation to the two main areas of employment rights considered in this chapter. First, has HRM provided greater job security, undermining the rationale for the unfair dismissal legislation? The rhetoric of HRM stresses the benefits to both managers and employees to be gained from an HRM approach. Greater job security is one of these benefits, arising in part out of the improved organizational performance that results from HRM, leading managers to recruit rather than lay off workers. It also arises out of HRM's emphasis on training to achieve a quality workforce, giving management an incentive to retain employees in whose skills they have invested. Such a view is based on the 'soft' dimension of HRM, emphasizing people-centred policies designed to develop a committed, resourceful workforce.

However, as we have seen, the empirical evidence of HRM in practice suggests that there has been much more emphasis on the hard than the soft dimensions in UK organizations (see Chapter 2). It is the hard dimension that stresses the need to manage labour in as 'rational' a way as any other factor of production and that has led to associations being made between HRM and 'numerical' flexibility and 'downsizing'. In this context, therefore, the rosy scenario for employees envisaged by the advocates of hard and soft HRM is not realized. Crucially, the emphasis on hard HRM would appear to reduce rather than increase job security. The rationale for legal intervention to protect job security looks stronger, rather than weaker, in this context.

With regard to the second area of employment rights considered in this chapter, those relating to equality, it can also be argued that HRM reduces the need for legal intervention. As Dickens notes, models of HRM often see 'equal opportunities' as a key personnel policy.[27] More generally, advocates of HRM argue that it leads to an emphasis on valuing and developing employees as an organization's 'most important asset' and that it follows from this that management in HRM organizations will seek to nurture those workers whose potential has been most overlooked in the past. The implication, then, is that management will have a clear incentive to promote equality issues. This view is also known as the 'business case' for equal opportunities.

However, Dickens argues that this view is highly problematic because of its failure to see that much of the language of HRM is itself gendered.[28] That is, the elements of HRM affect men and women differently, perpetuating rather than challenging gender inequality. Evidence on the way performance-related pay (PRP) operates, for example, suggests that the rewards of this practice go disproportionately to men.[29] PRP schemes, moreover, simultaneously undermine job evaluation schemes, which have been important mechanisms in promoting equal pay. In addition, employee 'commitment', seen by Guest as one of the goals of HRM,[30] is often constructed in such a way as to make it easier for men than for women to demonstrate this quality. For example, working after hours is commonly seen as a key element of being committed and, as stated earlier, this is more difficult for women, who disproportionately bear the responsibilities of domestic work, notably childcare. Moreover, Dickens argues, devolution of personnel responsibilities from personnel specialists to line managers, another characteristic of HRM, is also detrimental to equality. This is partly because those with expertise in equality issues are no longer handling recruitment, pay, and so on. It is also because devolution of personnel policies is part of a wider trend towards the creation of decentralized units operating under short-term accounting controls, which, the evidence suggests, are more likely to sideline the equality agenda. From this point of view, therefore, the rise of HRM does not appear to weaken the case for legal intervention to promote equality.

# Summary

THIS chapter has reviewed the nature and development of legal regulation of the employment relationship. It has been argued that the 'voluntarist' nature of the system that characterized British industrial relations for much of the twentieth century has been severely eroded over the last three decades. This has taken the form of legal restrictions on trade union action and the emergence of legal rights of individual employees, particularly in the field of job security and anti-discrimination. These rights continue to exist, albeit in a somewhat weaker form, despite the deregulatory measures passed by successive Conservative administrations in the 1980s and 1990s. At first sight, the legislation on individual employment rights appears to present significant constraints on employers. However, it has been shown that these constraints are not in reality that significant: the law is seldom used by employees and, when it is used, it has tended to be guided by employers' interests. Hence, the creation of individual employment rights has had the paradoxical effect of legitimizing managerial prerogative. The chapter ended by reviewing the argument that new-style HRM renders employment protection legislation redundant; this view was rejected.

What future developments are likely concerning the legal framework for employment? The election of the Labour Party in May 1997 has led to two key developments that promise to deliver a modest strengthening of employment rights. The new government committed itself to domestic legislation to improve employees' rights concerning unfair dismissal and within a year had produced a White Paper, entitled 'Fairness at Work', which proposed significant changes to unfair-dismissal law: the qualifying period required to be able to claim unfair dismissal at a tribunal is to be reduced from two years to one and the maximum payment for compensation to employees who win a case at a tribunal will be substantially lifted to £50,000. (The White Paper's provisions relating to union rights are dealt with in Chapter 4). The second important step that the new government took was to sign the Social Chapter. The Social Chapter was created as part of the Maastricht Treaty in 1991 but the previous Conservative government, fiercely opposed to the idea of European regulation over employment issues, had secured an 'opt-out' for the UK. The move by the new government has had an immediate impact—UK directives relating to the creation of 'European Works Councils' in multinational companies, to parental leave, and to equal rights for part-timers have so far been passed under the Social Chapter. However, the impact is likely to grow as more directives are passed, and equal rights between men and women is one issue particularly likely to be addressed, as this is one of the five priority areas of the Social Chapter.

---

BOX 3.1

## Case Study—Speech Therapists

Pamela Enderby is an experienced speech therapist in the National Health Service in the UK. The profession of speech therapy is very heavily dominated by females, in contrast to comparable professions, such as clinical psychology, which is male-dominated. Professor Enderby viewed the lower rates of pay that speech therapists receive in comparison to psychologists as discriminatory. As a result, in 1986 Professor Enderby launched a case under the Equal Pay legislation, claiming that her work was of 'equal value' to that of psychologists and that therefore she should receive the same rate of pay. She was supported in the case by MSF, the union representing speech therapists.

In April 1997 the union claimed victory on behalf of Professor Enderby. In an out-of-court settlement, the Department of Health agreed to the demands of the union that Enderby and a second female speech therapist, Lesley Cogher, should be paid the same as male psychologists and should also receive back pay to compensate for the shortfall in earnings in previous years. The case has implications for the other 1,500 speech therapists in the NHS and, more generally, the NHS may well re-examine its payment structures for other groups of staff to ensure that they do not fall foul of the legislation. Roger Kline, the national secretary of MSF, claimed that 'the case is a momentous one. It has implications for women staff throughout the NHS and other industries. It is a landmark decision and is the biggest single breakthrough on equal pay for women for many years.'[31]

At first sight, the case would appear to show how effective the equal pay legislation has been in bringing about 'equal pay for work of equal value'. However, the case has highlighted two key weaknesses in the workings of the legislation. First, it took eleven years for the case to be resolved. The case has been subject to numerous appeals and counter-appeals. A key point came in 1993 when Enderby won an appeal at the European Court of Justice that she had suffered indirect discrimination, at which point the case was referred back to the industrial tribunal. However, another four years of appeals and delays followed before the claim was eventually settled. Given the nature of the legal hurdles and delays involved in bringing such a claim, it is hardly surprising that so few equal pay cases are brought and that even fewer are successful.

Second, even after the eleven-year saga, no legal precedent was set by the case. This is in part because the NHS management conceded the case before a judgement was reached, no legal precedent was set and, therefore, other speech therapists have to pursue their own claims. This problem is compounded by another aspect of the law on discrimination, which is that the law sees discrimination as occurring in individual acts and so does not permit a group case for all 1,500 speech therapists to be brought. Consequently, other individual speech therapists have to pursue their own cases before payment structures are regraded for everyone. Moreover, many speech therapists have been discouraged by their employers from taking a claim themselves through fixed budgets; that is to say, there will be job cuts if they do so.

*Case Study Activity*

Discuss whether the law on equal pay for work of equal value needs to be reformed. If so, how?

# Study Questions

1. Imagine that you were a personnel manager in a firm when the unfair dismissal legislation was first introduced. How would you be affected? And what might you do differently following the introduction of the legislation?

2. Why did successive Conservative governments in the 1980s and 1990s seek to weaken individual employment rights?

3. Why has the unfair dismissal and redundancy legislation not provided job security in the way that some had hoped?

4. The Equal Pay and Sex Discrimination Acts have been in place for more than twenty years, so why do men continue to be paid more than women?

5. Imagine that you are a human resources manager and have to report to your boss on the implications of the unfair dismissal legislation being strengthened. Would you tell him or her that the organization had anything to fear?

# Further Reading

Deakin and Morris, *Labour Law* (London: Butterworths, 1998).

Dickens, L. and Hall, M., 'The State: Labour Law and Industrial Relations', in P. Edwards (ed.), *Industrial Relations: Theory and Practice in Britain* (Oxford: Blackwell, 1995).

Hepple, R., 'Unfair Dismissal', in W. McCarthy (ed.), *Legal Intervention in Industrial Relations: Gains and Losses* (Oxford: Blackwell, 1992).

Pitt, G., *Employment Law* (London: Sweet and Maxwell, 1995).

# Notes

1. Storey, J., *Developments in the Management of Human Resources* (Oxford: Blackwell, 1992).

2. Hyman, R., 'The Historical Evolution of British Industrial Relations', in P. Edwards (ed.), *Industrial Relations: Theory and Practice in Britain* (Oxford: Blackwell, 1995).

3. Anderman, S., 'Unfair Dismissal and Redundancy', in R. Lewis (ed.), *Labour Law in Britain* (Oxford: Blackwell, 1986).

4. Dickens, L., Jones, M., Weekes, B., and Hart, M., *Dismissed: A Study of Unfair Dismissal and the Industrial Tribunal System* (Oxford: Blackwell, 1985).

5. Hepple, R., 'Unfair Dismissal', in W. McCarthy (ed.), *Legal Intervention in Industrial Relations: Gains and Losses* (Oxford: Blackwell, 1992).

6. Pitt, G., *Employment Law* (London: Sweet and Maxwell, 1995).

7. Grewal, H., *A Guide to the Sex Discrimination Act* (London: Macdonald, 1990).

8. Ibid.

9. Ibid.

10. Pitt, G., *Employment Law* (London: Sweet and Maxwell, 1995).

11. Dickens, L., 'Comparative Systems of Unjust Dismissal: The British Case', *Annals of the American Academy of Political and Social Sciences* (November 1994).

12. Pitt, G., *Employment Law* (London: Sweet and Maxwell, 1995).

13. Dickens, L., 'Comparative Systems of Unjust Dismissal: The British Case', *Annals of the American Academy of Political and Social Sciences* (November, 1994).

14. Hepple, R., 'Unfair Dismissal', in W. McCarthy (ed.), *Legal Intervention in Industrial Relations: Gains and Losses* (Oxford: Blackwell, 1992).

15. Office for National Statistics, *Labour Market Trends* (London: ONS, 1998).

16. Ibid.

17. Hepple, R., 'Unfair Dismissal', in W. McCarthy (ed.), *Legal Intervention in Industrial Relations: Gains and Losses* (Oxford: Blackwell, 1992).

18. Dickens, L., 'Comparative Systems of Unjust Dismissal: The British Case', *Annals of the American Academy of Political and Social Sciences* (November, 1994); Hepple, R., 'Unfair Dismissal'.

19. Dickens, L., 'Anti-discrimination Legislation: Exploring and Examining the Impact on Women's Employment', in W. McCarthy (ed.), *Legal Intervention in Industrial Relations: Gains and Losses* (Oxford: Blackwell, 1992).

20. Ibid.

21. Ibid.

22. Ibid., p. 125.

23. Ibid.

24. Colling, T. and Dickens, L., 'Selling the Case for Gender Equality: Deregulation and Equality Bargaining', *British Journal of Industrial Relations* (1998), 36, 3, pp. 389–411.

25. Ibid., p. 392.

26. See, for example, Department of Employment, 'Employment for the 1990s', Cm 540 (London: HMSO, 1989).

27. Dickens, L., 'What HRM Means for Gender Equality', *Human Resource Management Journal* (1998), 8, 1, pp. 23–40.

28. Ibid.

29. Bratton, J. and Gold, J., *Human Resource Management: Theory and Practice* (London: Macmillan, 1994), p. 219.

30. Guest, D. E., 'Human Resource Management and Industrial Relations', *Journal of Management Studies* (1987), 24, 5, pp. 503–21.

31. 'NHS warns on funding after equal pay case', *Financial Times*, 5 April 1997.

# Chapter 4

# Trade Unions and Industrial Relations

## Chapter Contents

Introduction

# Introduction

O NE of the leading writers on industrial relations defined it as the 'study of the rules governing employment'.[1] Edwards defines these rules as follows:

A rule is a social institution involving two or more parties which may have its basis in law, a written collective agreement, an unwritten agreement, a unilateral decree or merely an understanding that has the force of custom. In non-union settings, as much as in union ones, rules determine rates of pay, hours of work, job descriptions and many other aspects of employment. [Industrial relations] is thus about ways in which the employment relationship is regulated.[2]

The first set of rules identified above, those that originate in law, can be thought of as legal regulation. The second, those that arise out of negotiated agreements (written or unwritten) between employers and trade unions, can be thought of as joint regulation. The third set of rules, those that are imposed by an employer, can be thought of as unilateral regulation. Pay levels, for example, can be regulated by any of the three mechanisms identified above: the law may set pay levels for some groups of workers through a minimum wage; negotiations between management and trade unions may determine levels of pay for other groups; and for the rest pay will be determined by management alone. These three different types of regulation of the employment relationship were introduced in Chapter 2 and are central to this chapter in its analysis of developments in industrial relations.

The main elements of HRM have been identified in earlier chapters, particularly Chapter 1. We have seen how it is essentially unitarist in its approach in that it stresses common interests between employers and employees and, relatedly, that it stresses individualist as opposed to collectivist values. In the main models of HRM it is rare to find attention being paid to the potential for conflict and its management in the employment relationship; indeed, Storey argues that conflict is 'de-emphasized' in models of HRM.[3] Consequently, in these models there is a big question mark over the role of trade unions, and hence joint regulation, since one of the major reasons why managers may be willing to recognize a trade union is in order to assist in the management of conflict.[4] Where a firm pursues HRM, which assumes that the interests of managers and the workforce are aligned, then the usefulness of having a trade union to represent the interests of employees and negotiate with management on their behalf is likely to be questioned by management. This managerial antipathy to unions is likely to be compounded where management is attempting to generate individualistic values in the organization. Unions in this situation, representing essentially collectivist values, may be seen by management as outdated and increasingly inappropriate for an ever more competitive environment. Indeed, as we will see later in this chapter, there is some evidence that during the 1980s and 1990s many firms have sought to limit the role of unions or to do away with them altogether.

Moreover, many of the specific practices associated with HRM may pose a threat to traditional management–trade union relations. One element of HRM is the emphasis on direct communication between managers and employees; it is direct in that the two groups meet face to face. In contrast, indirect communication takes place via a representative of the workforce. The emphasis on direct communication can be a threat to unions—many unionists have feared that their role in communicating with the workforce is bypassed. Performance-related pay schemes are another example of a practice that may threaten the traditional role of unions since they involve an element of pay being determined by individuals' performance. Thus, the role of trade unions in determining pay rates for groups of workers is potentially undermined.

This chapter investigates the implications of HRM for trade unions in particular and industrial relations more generally. It will focus on contemporary developments in British industrial relations, such as the decline of unionization and the decentralization of collective bargaining. At first sight, these changes over the last two decades of the twentieth century appear to support the view that, in an age where HRM has been seen by many as a panacea for managerial problems, companies have sought to reduce the role of unions as part of a concerted and coherent shift in the way they manage their workforces. Further, it could be that HRM has meant that employees see less need to join a union as they are increasingly satisfied with the way they are managed under this new approach.

This view is called into question in this chapter: it will be argued that changes in British industrial relations have not been primarily caused by HRM policies implemented by employers. Rather, it is argued that the changes are due to two other factors. First, the changes can be seen as a reassertion of unilateral regulation by employers who have taken advantage of changes in the political and economic environment to take greater control of industrial relations. Second, the changes are also due to structural change within the economy: the areas where trade unions were well established, such as engineering, mining, and docks, have declined while unions have experienced greater difficulties recruiting and organizing in the industries that have taken their place, such as tourism and financial services. We begin with an analysis of the historical development of British industrial relations.

# 1 The History of British Industrial Relations

I N the international context, one of the most distinctive aspects of British industrial relations (IR) is the tradition of 'voluntarism', which refers to the general absence of statutory regulation of the employment relationship. In other words, legal regulation of the employment relationship has traditionally been very limited. Rather, the relationship was largely regulated by the 'voluntary' agreement of management and trade unions or through management actions alone. In part the tradition of voluntarism arose out of the suspicion that trade unions had for the law, fearing that legal regulation would work to the benefit of employers.

Some of the legacies of the voluntarist system can still be seen today. In Britain, there is not, and has never been, any positive right in law for employees to take strike action: employees can be dismissed by their employer if they do so, since they are in breach of their contract of employment (though future legislation looks set to change this by entitling employees to unfair dismissal rights if they are sacked for taking lawful industrial action). Furthermore, as noted in Chapter 3, a collective agreement resulting from negotiations between management and trade unions is not legally binding in the UK; either party is entitled in law to ignore aspects of the agreement if they so wish (as long as in doing so they do not contravene individual contracts of employment). A further example of the back seat that the law takes in regulating employment issues in the UK is the absence of any legal provisions for forcing employers to consult with their workforce, apart from on specific issues such as redundancies.

In many European countries the law has traditionally played a much greater role in regulating the employment relationship.[5] In most European countries employees taking strike action cannot be dismissed for doing so while collective agreements signed by management and trade unions are legally binding. Moreover, legal provisions exist in many European countries forcing employers in workplaces above a certain size to set up works councils in order to consult and negotiate with employee representatives if their employees so wish.

In the UK, historically, unilateral regulation of employment was the dominant form of regulation. British employers after the industrial revolution were reluctant to give up their prerogative over issues at the workplace, such as pay levels and the organization of work. Their power to do this was always contested, of course, but employees generally lacked the ability to challenge the prerogative of employers. Writing about employers in the nineteenth century, Hyman argues that 'many of the new factory entrepreneurs imposed the "barrack-line discipline" of which Marx wrote; some of the leading coal-owners were notorious for their autocratic treatment of labour; the railways were managed on military lines; and so on'.[6] In this period employees thought to be seeking to organize resistance to management control by forming 'combinations' were sacked, imprisoned, or even deported to Australia. Thus, during most of the last century and the first part of this one, employers were hostile to trade unions.

During the twentieth century, and particularly in the period after the Second World War, two developments occurred that made it more difficult for employers to exclude unions. First, union membership grew steadily: the proportion of the workforce in a union (union density) grew from 13.1% in 1900 to a peak of 53.4% in 1979.[7] Second, and related to the first point, the legal context, while remaining essentially voluntarist, became more favourable to trade unions. This followed the gradual introduction of universal suffrage for men through the nineteenth century and for women in the early twentieth century and debates in Parliament about labour's right to organize and bargain with employers. Significantly, in the 1906 Trades Disputes Act unions were granted immunity from prosecution by their employers for damages arising from industrial action. Up until this point, unions could be sued by an employer for damages for lost business resulting from industrial action, thereby making it almost impossible for unions to call any action without risking bankruptcy. Thus, the combined effect of these twin developments—the growth in union membership and the more favourable legal climate—was that an increasing proportion of firms established formal recognition of one or more unions and conducted negotiations with them, primarily over pay. Thus, joint regulation of employment through collective bargaining grew in importance while unilateral regulation declined.

Having accepted the inevitability of granting unions recognition, private-sector employers sought to bargain with unions in such a way as to minimize the impact on the workplace. Many employers tried to do this through joining together with other employers for the purposes of bargaining. This became known as multi-employer bargaining: under this system, negotiations take place between representatives of a group of employers, often covering an entire industry, and officials from the trade union or unions concerned. The Engineering Employers' Federation (EEF), for example, for years conducted negotiations with their trade unions to set pay rates for all employees in the industry. In the public sector, which was greatly expanded following the series of nationalizations of key industries and the setting up of the National Health Service in the immediate post-war period, the state as employer sought to encourage unionization. Collective bargaining arrangements were established at national level in most areas of the public sector and successive governments supported, or at least accepted, these arrangements.

For unions, multi-employer bargaining had the attraction of being able to establish a 'rate for the job' and also encouraged employees to identify with their occupation rather than the particular company for which they worked.[8] For employers, however, it is not so readily apparent why they should have wished to engage in multi-employer bargaining. The rationale for their doing so at the time was basically twofold. First, employers, who were keen to retain their prerogative at the workplace on issues such as the organization of work, saw multi-employer bargaining as a way of neutralizing the union's influence at the workplace. While the union would influence issues that affected all plants, such as pay levels, it would be difficult for them to influence those issues that are specific to individual plants, such as the organization of work. Thus, multi-employer bargaining was a way in which 'unions could be kept out of the plant'.[9] Second, firms facing relatively strong unions risked being 'picked off' one by one if they negotiated separately with the unions. This was a particular concern for small firms operating in industries in which labour costs made up a large proportion of total costs and were, therefore, an important element of competition. For management in these firms, multi-employer bargaining had the advantage of setting wage rates across the industry—if the union(s) secured an increase in pay, employers knew that this applied to all other firms. In this way, multi-employer bargaining 'took wages out of competition'.[10]

In the immediate post-war years multi-employer bargaining determined the pay and conditions of the overwhelming majority of employees.[11] This arrangement gradually came under strain, however. In a situation where unemployment was low, as was the case in the 1950s and 1960s, firms facing recruitment problems were willing to pay above the nationally agreed rate set by multi-employer bargaining in order to attract the sufficient quantity and quality of labour. Union representatives at plant level, known as shop stewards, could see in this situation the potential for securing advances for their members and, consequently, sought to negotiate with management at plant level to this effect. Thus, formal multi-employer agreements were supplemented by informal plant-level agreements.

Indeed, this was the main finding of the Donovan Commission, which was set up in the mid-1960s to investigate the state of British IR. They began their report with the famous statement: 'There are two systems of industrial relations in Britain today.'[12] The two systems referred to were the formal and informal negotiations described above. At plant level they found that unions—through their representatives at this level, the shop stewards—exerted considerable influence over a range of issues, including pay levels and the organization of work. Many of the outcomes of this bargaining were not subject to formal agreement but rather became part of 'custom and practice'. The Commission argued for a move away from multi-employer bargaining, which was increasingly ineffective at setting pay levels, and for a formalization of plant-level bargaining in order to bring greater 'order' to IR at the workplace.

During the 1970s the Conservative government of Edward Heath, influenced to some extent by the Donovan report, sought to break with the tradition of voluntarism in order to bring about reform of what it saw as the informality and disorder of IR. In the Industrial Relations Act of 1971 the government introduced wide-ranging legal changes, including making collective agreements legally binding and introducing heavy financial penalties on unions responsible for 'unfair industrial practices'.[13] The Act was a fiasco: unions refused to co-operate with the main provisions and employers, too, were reluctant to use their new legal powers. When the Conservatives were defeated in 1974, a defeat which owed much to the political embarrassment inflicted by a dispute with coal miners, the new Labour administration repealed the Act. The tradition of voluntarism was now partially broken, despite the failure of the Act, as legislation giving employees certain rights, such as the right to claim unfair dismissal and the right not to be sexually or racially discriminated against, was introduced throughout the decade.

The Labour government's approach to dealing with trade unions was strongly influenced by the prevailing economic conditions. A sharp rise in the price of oil in the mid-1970s created inflationary pressures across the Western world, while in Britain this exacerbated the domestic inflation created by an economy that was growing at an unsustainable rate. Inevitably, inflation rose sharply, peaking at 24% in 1976. The government's response was to seek to control pay levels, especially in the public sector, through an incomes policy agreed with trade unions. The policy succeeded in delivering wage restraint for a short time, inflation began to fall, and the economic situation briefly began to improve.

The incomes policy, however, came under pressure from unions, which were anxious to end the wage restraint it entailed, and it collapsed in 1978, leading to the notorious 'Winter of Discontent', in which there were numerous strikes over pay. Labour were turned out of office in May 1979, a date that was to become a watershed in British IR. The Conservatives, led by Margaret Thatcher, promised to reverse decades of relative economic decline by weakening trade unions and allowing managers to establish greater control.

It is possible from the above history to draw out the main elements of British IR at the beginning of the 1980s. Joint regulation of employment was the dominant form of regulation over pay: in 1980, 70% of employees had their pay determined by collective bargaining.[14] The form this joint regulation took had shifted in the post-war period away from the multi-employer level towards the single-employer level: for a majority of those employees who had their pay determined by collective bargaining, single-employer bargaining was the most important level. Shop stewards were prevalent and influential; they were to be found in the majority of workplaces in manufacturing and the public sector.[15] Moreover, many organizations had taken steps to formalize IR through establishing disputes and grievance procedures, which often allowed unions the right to represent individuals. Unions at the end of the 1970s wielded considerable political influence and, indeed, had played a part in the downfall of the two previous governments. Those on the right described the state of industrial relations as constituting 'the British disease', in that British firms were saddled with high wages and inflexible working practices, and advocated reforms to bring about a restoration of the managerial prerogative. This was what was to happen in the 1980s.

# 2  Changes in Industrial Relations in the 1980s

T HERE is little doubt that profound changes took place in British IR in the 1980s. The most obvious and important change was the weakening of union influence over employers or, in other words, of joint regulation. Perhaps the most well-documented aspect of this change was the decline in union membership, which experienced the longest continuous fall on record, declining in every year since 1979 (see Table 4.1). At the beginning of the 1980s, more than twelve and a half million people in Britain belonged to a trade union; by 1996 this had fallen to just under eight million. As a

TABLE 4.1

**Union membership and labour force density in the UK, 1979–96**

| Year | Aggregate Membership (Thousands) | Labour Force Density (%) | Year | Aggregate Membership (Thousands) | Labour Force Density (%) |
|------|------|------|------|------|------|
| 1979 | 13,289 | 53 | 1988 | 10,376 | 40 |
| 1980 | 12,947 | 52 | 1989 | 10,158 | 39 |
| 1981 | 12,106 | 51 | 1990 | 9,947 | 38 |
| 1982 | 11,593 | 48 | 1991 | 9,585 | 37 |
| 1983 | 11,236 | 46 | 1992 | 9,048 | 36 |
| 1984 | 10,994 | 44 | 1993 | 8,700 | 35 |
| 1985 | 10,821 | 43 | 1994 | 8,278 | 33 |
| 1986 | 10,539 | 41 | 1995 | 8,091 | 32 |
| 1987 | 10,475 | 41 | 1996 | 7,935 | 31 |

*Source*: Office for National Statistics, *Labour Market Trends* (London: ONS, 1998). Crown copyright 1998.

proportion of the total labour force, the fall was from just over half of those in the workforce in 1979 to just under a third in the middle of the 1990s. This has had a detrimental impact on unions' finances, since most of their revenue comes from the subscriptions of their members, and has also reduced their bargaining power with management.

Related to the decline in union membership is the decline, or contraction, of collective bargaining during this period. There are a number of elements to this contraction. The proportion of workplaces in which management formally recognized a union for the purposes of negotiations over terms and conditions (union recognition) fell from 66% in 1984 to 45% in 1997 (see Table 4.2). This fall was steepest in the manufacturing industry—the sector in which unions were well entrenched for much of the post war years. A different way of measuring the contraction of collective bargaining is to examine the proportion of employees whose pay was determined by collective bargaining (bargaining coverage), which had fallen to 36% by 1997.[16]

Not only did collective bargaining contract in these ways, but also, where it remained, there were several qualitative changes. Perhaps most important amongst these is that fewer issues are now subject to negotiation compared with the number at the beginning of the 1980s. Where joint regulation remained, the scope of this regulation narrowed so that more issues were determined unilaterally by management. The aspect of the employment relationship that most commonly fell out of the scope of bargaining was staffing levels: as Millward *et al.* put it, 'employment levels and closely related issues were the ones that management most commonly succeeded in removing from the bargaining agenda'.[17]

The other key change in the nature of collective bargaining, where it remained, was a further decentralization in terms of the level at which bargaining took place, continuing the trend of the 1960s and 1970s away from multi-employer bargaining

TABLE 4.2

**Union recognition and coverage in Britain, 1984–97**

| Year | Recognition (% of workplaces) |
| --- | --- |
| 1984 | 66 |
| 1990 | 53 |
| 1997 | 45 |

*Source:* Cully, M., Woodlands, S., O'Reilly, A., Dix, G., Millward, N., Bryson, A., and Forth, J., *The 1998 Workplace Employee Relations Survey: First Findings* (London; Department of Trade and Industry, 1998). Crown copyright is reproduced with the permission of the Controller of Her Majesty's Stationery Office.

towards single-employer bargaining. One study of trends in the level of bargaining suggests that by 1990 as few as one in every ten workers had their pay determined by multi-employer bargaining, down from three in every ten in 1980 and from six in every ten in 1950 (see Table 4.3). This can largely be explained by looking back to the rationale for employers undertaking multi-employer bargaining in the first place. The first incentive for managers to conduct union negotiations jointly with other employers was to try to 'keep the union out of the plant'; as we have seen, they were largely unsuccessful in attempting to do this in the 1960s and 1970s, thereby weakening this rationale. Moreover, as unions became much weaker in the 1980s the consequences of dealing with unions at the plant level were much less threatening for management. The second incentive, the attempt to 'take wages out of competition', was also undermined by the increasing degree to which competition was becoming international. In many industries, firms in the UK competed with those in other countries that were obviously not party to British collective bargaining, thereby limiting the degree to which wages could be taken out of competition.

It is clear that the developments in the 1980s, which have continued into the 1990s, have meant that the role of joint regulation has declined while unilateral regulation has increased. At first sight, these changes appear to be consistent with the view that management in UK firms have sought to reduce the role of trade unions and collective bargaining as part of a shift towards an individualistic HRM approach. This view is lent further support by the evidence reviewed in previous chapters that there has been a growth in practices associated with HRM, such as performance-related pay schemes, quality circles, appraisal, and psychometric tests in recruitment. Are there really grounds for seeing the developments in the way firms deal with trade unions as evidence of a shift towards HRM? To what extent can these changes be put down to a coherent management attempt to reform workplace industrial relations?

TABLE 4.3

## The coverage of collective bargaining in the UK, 1950–90

| Extent and nature of collective bargaining | % of private sector employees covered | | | | |
| --- | --- | --- | --- | --- | --- |
| | 1950 | 1960 | 1970 | 1980 | 1990 |
| Pay not fixed by collective bargaining | 20 | 25 | 30 | 30 | 50 |
| Pay fixed by collective bargaining | 80 | 75 | 70 | 70 | 50 |
| Multi-employer | 60 | 45 | 35 | 30 | 10 |
| Single employer | 20 | 30 | 35 | 40 | 40 |

*Source*: Brown, W., Marginson, P., and Walsh, J., 'Management: Pay Determination and Collective Bargaining', in Edwards, P. (ed.), *Industrial Relations: Theory and Practice in Britain* (Oxford: Blackwell, 1995)

The interpretation that developments in IR have been caused by a management shift towards HRM would be highly misleading for two reasons. The first of these is that much of the change in how companies deal with unions has been brought about by the changing political, economic, and industrial context in which firms trade and not by a shift in management ideology along the lines of HRM. Politically, the Conservative government elected in 1979 with Thatcher as prime minister was committed to reducing union power, seeing this as one of the primary causes of Britain's relatively poor performance internationally. Consequently, the government, through numerous pieces of legislation between 1979 and 1997, restricted the ability of unions to take industrial action and regulated their internal affairs in a way that the law had not previously done. The government also reduced union influence in the public sector directly through such actions as the banning of trade unions at its intelligence centre (GCHQ) and withdrawing the negotiation rights for teachers. It is widely acknowledged that these actions played a part in the weakening of unions in this period.

Economically, the growth of international trade and overseas investments by multinational companies in the 1980s and 1990s increased the degree of international competition with UK firms. The gradual removal of trade barriers within the European Union made it easier for firms in one member state to trade in another. Perhaps of even more significance, however, was the emergence of many Asian countries as low-cost manufacturers of a variety of products. The pressure on firms in the UK to retain control over their labour costs grew and the ease with which unions could negotiate a wage increase, in the knowledge that the increase could be passed on to customers in the form of higher prices, declined. In this situation, there was more opposition to unions from management and less incentive for employees to join a union.

Industrially, the trend, evident in the 1960s and 1970s, of a decline in manufacturing industry and the growth of the service sector increased sharply at the beginning of the 1980s. The recession of 1979 to 1981 resulted in one million jobs being lost in manufacturing; in total, employment in manufacturing declined from 7.2 million jobs in 1979 to just under 4.0 million in 1998.[18] Union membership and power had historically been strongest in manufacturing industries, such as engineering, and so the traditional heartlands of union strength declined. The new jobs in the service sector came mainly in industries such as hotels and catering, where unions have always been weak. Furthermore, many of the new jobs were for part-timers and were filled by women; union membership has traditionally been lower among these two groups. Thus, rather like it has for many endangered species, the unions' natural habitat was disappearing.

These political, economic, and industrial developments were key influences on the nature of IR. Accordingly, they have created a very different context within which the employment relationship is conducted, presenting management with the possibility of rationalizing the role of trade unions or doing away with them altogether. Of course, where aspects of industrial relations changed in particular firms, management clearly had a role in bringing this about. However, it appears that managerial actions involved responding to and taking advantage of external developments rather than being driven by a change in ideology along the lines of HRM, something demonstrated in extensive case study research.[19]

The second reason for doubting the interpretation that developments in industrial relations have been caused by a managerial shift towards HRM is the nature of change. If this interpretation were correct, you would expect to find those firms that have moved away from having a recognized trade union and those which never had one to be those most active in pursuing HRM policies. That is, HRM would be most firmly established in non-union firms. In fact, the opposite is the case. As Sisson notes in reviewing the evidence from the most authoritative surveys of British industrial relations, the Workplace Industrial Relations Survey:

Other things being equal ... one might have expected that the most likely workplaces in which the evidence of HRM would be found would be those that are union free. This is where many of the practices originated in the USA. It is also where commentators have suggested that HRM might be found in its most developed state in the UK. In the event, the position is the exact opposite. It is union rather than the non-union workplaces that exhibit the fragments of HRM that are to be found.'[20]

This suggests that where firms have moved from joint regulation through collective bargaining to unilateral regulation the move has not been accompanied by the introduction of HRM practices. Thus, the changes in industrial relations can best be seen as an attempt by management to reassert their prerogative over issues that had previously been subject to union influence. In this respect, the developments we have witnessed should be seen as traditional responses by employers to developments in the context of IR that have presented them with a new range of opportunities rather than as part of a shift towards a new model of labour management such as HRM.

# 3   **Recent Developments**

T HE nature of government policy in the labour market in Britain in the last two decades of the twentieth century has been a central element of this chapter. Policy under successive Conservative governments was geared towards weakening joint and legal regulation in order to 'free-up' the labour market, making it more flexible. Thus, domestically, the law was used to restrict union activity, and the legislation granting rights to individual employees that grew up in the 1960s and 1970s was eroded. Moreover, under the Conservatives, Britain whenever possible resisted moves from the European Union designed to strengthen legal regulation; this is exemplified by the British opt-out of the Social Chapter, which was created and signed by all of the other member states at Maastricht in the Netherlands in 1991.

The election in May 1997 brought a change of government when Tony Blair's Labour party came to power. Labour has traditionally had very strong links with the trade unions and still receives around half of its funding from this source. Although Blair was anxious to seek to distance the party from close identification with the unions in the run-up to the election, party policy is still influenced to some extent by them. Thus one of the areas where the greatest differences between the Conservatives and Labour exists is in policy in the labour market. The change of government, therefore, has brought a significant, if not radical, shift in policy in this area both at home and in Europe.

At home, the proposal attracting most of the attention is to create a statutory right to recognition for trade unions. The White Paper of 1998, entitled 'Fairness at Work', proposes that if unions can secure 40% or more of the votes of the entire workforce in a firm (as opposed to just 40% of those voting) in a ballot on union recognition, then the management will be under a legal obligation formally to recognize the union for the purposes of collective bargaining. This will give unions a 'foot in the door' in companies where they have a high level of support but where management refuses to negotiate with them. It is unlikely, however, that the impact will be great; the 40% requirement will often be difficult to achieve where union membership is low and, even where it is achieved, the law provides only for the formal right to recognition and will not fundamentally shift the balance of power between management and union.

Other domestic legislation will also have a significant, though not enormous, impact. 'Fairness at Work' also proposed changes to unfair dismissal law: the qualifying period for entitlement to claim unfair dismissal will be lowered from two years to one; the ceiling on payments for compensation to individuals who win a case will be raised substantially, potentially allowing larger payments; and workers who are dismissed for taking lawful industrial action will become eligible to claim unfair dismissal. Separate legislation proposes the creating of a national minimum wage, the first time the UK has ever had a comprehensive minimum rate of pay. The Low Pay Commission, the body set up by the government to provide guidelines on how the minimum wage should operate, recommended the rate be set at £3.60 per hour. The government accepted this figure for workers over 21 but decided on a lower rate of £3.00 for those aged between 18 and 21 (rising to £3.20 after a year). These rates will affect approximately 1.5 million low-paid workers, but the unions were disappointed, having hoped for something in excess of £4.00.[21]

In Europe, Labour has reversed Conservative policy by signing up to the Social Chapter. As was mentioned in Chapter 2, this involves the directives agreed by member states in the employment area being applied to Britain. So far only two directives have been passed through the Chapter, concerning rights to parental leave and the creation of 'European Works Councils' in multinational companies. Arguably of greater importance than either of these two directives, however, will be the European Working Time Directive, which was passed via the Health and Safety arm of the EU rather than the Social Chapter. This directive creates a legal maximum of forty-eight working hours a week, averaged over a four-month period, although employees can choose to work longer if they wish and a number of groups are exempt. It also creates a right to four weeks' paid holiday—something that had not previously existed in the UK—and guaranteed rest periods.[22]

Individually, each of these legal changes will have only a modest impact. Taken together, however, they represent a significant change in government policy, marking the end of a long period of 'deregulation' with moves towards strengthening both legal and joint regulation. One suspects, however, that what will affect the positions of unions in Britain more than these legal changes are those economic and structural factors which this chapter has shown have played a large part in union decline in the 1980s and 1990s.

# Summary

T HIS chapter has reviewed the historical development of British IR, charting the growth in union membership and influence and the development of collective bargaining. The extent and significance of the changes in IR that have taken place since 1979 have also been established. It has been argued that these changes owe little to a widespread adoption of the ideology and practices associated with HRM and that, rather, they stem from a pragmatic reassertion of the managerial prerogative.

It is easy to see why managers see benefits in the weakening of unions and the contraction of collective bargaining. But what of the consequences for employees? The evidence suggests that the nature of IR in non-union firms rarely conforms to a picture of HRM involving enlightened managers seeking to generate commitment to the organization from employees, their relations being largely harmonious. There are, no doubt, examples of this, but it would seem that they are relatively few and far between. Research demonstrates a rather less attractive picture of life in non-union firms. Compared with unionized firms, non-union firms are characterized by a greater frequency of industrial accidents, dismissals, and compulsory redundancies and a lower incidence of procedures through which employees can air grievances, of structures for the dissemination of information to the workforce, and of employee representation.[23] In sum, the chapter has not sought to deny that HRM has taken root in a limited way in the UK. It does, however, reject the view that changes in IR over the last two decades of the twentieth century were caused by this development.

BOX 4.1

## Case Study—British Airways

The case of British Airways (BA) exemplifies the arguments developed in this chapter. During the 1970s, when the company was publicly owned, BA was affected by numerous instances of industrial action. Indeed in 1976–7 there was a stoppage on average once a week. Personnel managers spent much of their time 'fire-fighting'; that is, dealing with one dispute after another as they arose. During the period leading up to privatization (1987), management's approach changed significantly. A number of HRM policies were adopted that aimed to generate a much greater focus on customer service. This was known as the 'Putting People First' (PPF) scheme. Furthermore, the company sought to rationalize its relationships with its trade unions. During the 1980s this involved restricting the influence of unions over issues such as staffing levels; the company successfully shed almost 14,000 jobs between 1981 and 1983 as part of a cost-cutting exercise. Moreover, the 1997 strike of cabin crew resulted from the management's refusal to negotiate with the union over their proposed changes to terms and conditions. On the face of it, therefore, developments in the way people have been managed at BA are consistent with the view that management has sought to downplay the role of unions as part of a shift towards HRM.

Closer examination, however, reveals there to be irresolvable conflicts between the PPF scheme and the cost-cutting programmes. The redundancies of the early 1980s and, more recently, the proposed changes to pay and conditions in 1997 created deep tensions between management and the workforce, evident in accusations of intimidation by managers and threats to sue individual employees if they went on strike. This is hardly the harmonious atmosphere envisaged by advocates of HRM. In this context, the PPF programme was unlikely to has a lasting impact.

Moreover, there is little evidence that these changes have been pursued in a strategic way. Rather, managerial initiatives should best be seen as pragmatic responses to external pressures. The cost-cutting package of the early 1980s came at a time when unions were suddenly weakened following the recession and the election of the Conservative government, enabling management to push through the changes. The PPF, on the other hand, came at a time of falling unemployment when the company was anxious to recruit and retain staff. Thus managerial actions appear to have been guided by conditions in the product and labour markets. Privatization also influenced managerial priorities and actions. The period leading up to 1987 was one in which managers were anxious to increase profitability in order to make the sale of shares a success; hence, the cost-cutting of the early to mid-1980s. Now, as a privatized company, BA is under pressure to satisfy shareholders through dividend payments and rises in the share price; arguably, this has pressured management into the cost-cutting of the late 1990s.

At the time of writing, the IR climate at BA could at best be described as unsettled. In sum, there is clear evidence of management's seeking to marginalize trade unions, particularly the Transport and General, but little evidence that HRM practices have created a harmonious working environment.

*Sources*: Blyton, P. and Turnbull, P., *The Dynamics of Employee Relations* (London: Macmillan, 1993); Colling, T., 'Experiencing Turbulence: Competition, Strategic Choice and the

Management of Human Resources in British Airways', *Human Resource Management Journal* (1995), 5, 5, pp. 18–32; *Financial Times*, various issues.

*Case Study Activity*

Discuss what the experience of British Airways tells us about the ease with which managers can change the climate of industrial relations.

# Study Questions

1 What were the key aspects of 'voluntarism' and to what extent has it been eroded in recent decades?

2 You are a personnel manager at Tesco: what factors would you consider in deciding whether to recognize a union?

3 In what ways has collective bargaining declined in recent decades?

4 Why does HRM pose a question mark over the role of trade unions?

5 Imagine you are a practising personnel manager working in the services industry. Compare and contrast employment legislation since the 1997 election of the Labour government with that of the previous Conservative governments during 1979-97.

# Further Reading

Blyton, P. and Turnbull, P., *The Dynamics of Employee Relations* (London: Macmillan, 1993).

Edwards, P., (1995) 'The Employment Relationship', in P. Edwards, (ed.), *Industrial Relations: Theory and Practice in Britain* (Oxford: Blackwell, 1995).

—— Hall, M., Hyman, R., Marginson, P., Sisson, K., Waddington, J., and Winchester, D., 'Great Britain: From Partial Collectivism to Neo-Liberalism to Where?', in A. Ferner and R. Hyman (eds), *Changing Industrial Relations in Europe* (Oxford: Blackwell, 1998).

Guest, D., 'Trade Unions and HRM', in J. Storey, (ed.), *Human Resource Management: A Critical Text* (London: Routledge, 1995).

# Notes

1. Clegg, H., *The Changing System of Industrial Relations in Great Britain* (Oxford: Blackwell, 1979).

2. Edwards, P., 'The Employment Relationship', in P. Edwards, (ed.), *Industrial Relations: Theory and Practice in Britain* (Oxford: Blackwell, 1995), p. 5.

3. Storey, J., *Developments in the Management of Human Resources* (Oxford: Blackwell, 1992).

4. Guest, D., 'Trade Unions and HRM', in J. Storey (ed.), *Human Resource Management: A Critical Text* (London: Routledge, 1995).

5. Ferner, A. and Hyman, R., (eds), *Changing Industrial Relations in Europe* (Oxford: Blackwell, 1998).

6. Hyman, R., 'The Historical Development of British Industrial Relations', in P. Edwards, (ed.), *Industrial Relations: Theory and Practice in Britain* (Oxford: Blackwell, 1995).

7. Waddington, J. and Whitston, C., 'Trade Unions: Growth, Structure and Policy', in P. Edwards, (ed.), *Industrial Relations: Theory and Practice in Britain* (Oxford: Blackwell, 1995).

8. Brown, W., Marginson, P., and Walsh, J., 'Management: Pay Determination and Collective Bargaining', in P. Edwards, (ed.), *Industrial Relations: Theory and Practice in Britain* (Oxford: Blackwell, 1995).

9. Sisson, K., *The Management of Collective Bargaining: An International Comparison* (Oxford: Blackwell, 1987).

10. Brown, Marginson, and Walsh, 'Management: Pay Determination and Collective Bargaining'.

11. Ibid.

12. Donovan Commission, *Royal Commission on Trade Union and Employers Associations* (London: HMSO, 1968), p. 1.

13. Hyman, R., 'The Historical Development of British Industrial Relations', in P. Edwards, (ed.), *Industrial Relations: Theory and Practice in Britain* (Oxford: Blackwell, 1995).

14. Daniel, W. and Millward, N., *Workplace Industrial Relations in Britain* (London: Heinemann, 1983).

15. Terry, M., 'Trade Unions: Shop Stewards and the Workplace', in P. Edwards, (ed.), *Industrial Relations: Theory and Practice in Britain* (Oxford: Blackwell, 1995).

16. Office for National Statistics, *Labour Market Trends* (London: ONS, 1998).

17. Millward, N., Stevens, M., Smart, D. and Hawes, W., *Workplace Industrial Relations in Transition* (Aldershot: Dartmouth, 1992), p. 353.

18. Office for National Statistics, *Labour Market Trends* (London: ONS, 1998).

19. Blyton, P. and Turnbull, P. (eds), *Reassessing Human Resource Management* (London: Sage, 1992); Storey, J., *Developments in the Management of Human Resources* (Oxford: Blackwell, 1992).

20. Sisson, K., 'In Search of HRM', *British Journal of Industrial Relations* (1993), 31, 2, pp. 201–10.

21. *Financial Times*, 16 June 1998.

22. Hall, M. and Sisson, K., *Coming to Terms with the EU Working Time Directive* (London: IRS, 1997).

23. Millward, N., Stevens, M., Smart, D., and Hawes, W., *Workplace Industrial Relations in Transition* (Aldershot: Dartmouth, 1992).

# Part III

# Managing Human Resources

# Chapter 5

# Employee Resourcing and Careers

## Chapter Contents

# Introduction

H AVING assessed the extent of the take-up of HRM in the wider UK environment, we now turn in these next five chapters to examining more closely the HRM approach itself, beginning with employee resourcing and careers.

Employee resourcing, as an HR policy, aims to supply an organization with the right quality and number of people to achieve its strategy. Resourcing affects the perform-ance of the organization and has significant social consequences for the individual and society. Employee resourcing influences employees' skill development, their commitment to the organization, and their careers, and it has potential for positive and negative consequences on individuals' well-being. From the perspective of HRM, management should plan employee resourcing of the organization carefully because human resource planning is one way of integrating human resources with the requirements of the organization's strategy, although the evidence is that few organ-izations consistently use HR planning in practice.[1] Most models of HRM advocate improved policy and practice in employee resourcing; for example, Beer *et al.* proposed that general managers should become more proactive in employee resourcing by managing the 'flow' of human resources into, through, and out of the organization.[2] They advised that organizations should develop human resource flow policies, observ-ing that many exhibit human resource flow patterns but that management do not plan employee resourcing, thus failing to integrate it with business strategy.

This chapter looks at employee resourcing from three perspectives—individual, organizational, societal—and especially considers how resourcing policies and prac-tices influence people's careers. The three stages of HR flow—inflow, internal flow, and outflow—are also covered. The second of these, internal flow, which consists of actions that affect employees' work roles, promotion, career satisfaction, and development, is considered as part of the discussion on the individual perspective in Section 1. Inflow and outflow are considered on their own in Section 2 on managing human resource flow. The chapter concludes with a brief look at some of the tools and techniques of HR planning, previously known as manpower or personnel planning.

# 1  Three Perspectives on Human Resource Flow Policies

M ANAGING human resource flow strategically means determining a flow pattern that takes into account likely effects on employee commitment to the organization, the ability of the organization to adapt to changing circumstances, and the culture of the organization. Flow patterns have a profound impact on employees' security and careers, although the effect on employee commitment will be considered a higher priority from the soft HRM perspective (in which employee well-being is an important end in itself) than it is from the hard HRM perspective.[3] The pattern of human resource flow creates, sustains, or erodes the level of competence of the organization over time. More broadly, flow patterns influence the well-being of local communities and society by creating employment or resulting in unemployment. Looked at another way, human resource flow is a result of the management of flow policies, systems, and practices that, taken together, ought to be a viable strategic response to three areas: employees' individual needs (personal objectives and career plans), organizational requirements (business objectives, HR plans), and social institutions (government policy, legislation, education institutions, unions). Beer *et al.* represent human resource flow diagrammatically as shown in Fig. 5.1.

## The Individual Perspective – Careers

Before looking at how flow policies affect organizations and society we first consider how employee resourcing affects individuals. This section discusses internal flow from the perspective of the individual and his or her evolving concept of a career at work. Employees experience human resource flow through the way it affects their employment conditions and career development. Careers can be short or long and many people will change careers several times during their working life. Everett Hughes in 1937 defined careers as having both subjective and objective components.[4] Subjectively, individuals experience a sense of continuity of purpose and progression in skill or responsibility as they move through their careers. Often, people who feel their careers have been frustrated perceive that there could have been more development or change. In addition to the subjective sense of identity that can be gained from 'having a career', there is the objective view, by which one can plot the movement of the individual within the social order of the organization, for example, from shopfloor worker to supervisor to middle manager.

Advocates of soft HRM have argued that careers should not be treated as the sole preserve of managerial and professional employees, but should be seen as being important to everyone. Careers are closely connected with individuals' experience of

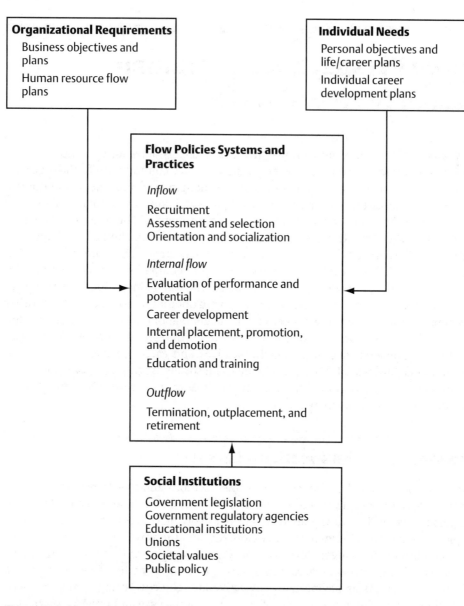

**Figure 5.1  Human resource flow**

*Source*: Based on ideas from J. Walker (1980) *Human Resource Planning*, New York: McGraw-Hill. Reprinted with the permission of The Free Press, a Division of Simon & Schuster, Inc., from *Managing Human Assets* by Michael Beer, Bert Spector, Paul R. Lawrence, D. Quinn Mills, Richard E. Walton. (Figure 4.3, p. 99). Copyright © 1984 by The Free Press.

home and work life, and change in either of these two critical areas can cause people to alter their role expectations and career goals. An employee's sense of career is something that develops over time and has varying psychological meaning as career aspirations and expectations are modified. For example, in a study of UK managers and professionals nearing retirement, 48% said that family and personal relationships were the most important thing to them at this stage of their life histories and careers.[5]

An individual's sense of identity is closely bound up with roles he or she plays at home and work. For example, a woman who is both an employee and a mother experiences conflicting demands on her time and energy that have to be managed daily. Success in performing her various roles will be affected by the relative importance that she and others attach to them. Our career preferences and choices are also affected by our personalities; in general, some individuals deeply value stability and security, while others place greater importance on novelty and change. Groups of people pass through similar phases of career expectation governed by common patterns of life history, the culture of organizations, and the norms of society. For instance, most young people in the initial stage of a career do not have the same family responsibilities that many older people have during their mid-life careers, when children and ageing parents are major domestic commitments.

Most people face obstacles and setbacks in their careers, and many employees, blue-collar and white-collar, change their jobs and even their occupations several times over their working lives. As people's experience of life changes over time, they adjust to some extent their concept of self and personal identity. There are some conventionally successful individuals whose careers progress relatively smoothly and develop in a linear and 'upwardly mobile' fashion. John Kotter's 1982 study of general managers in the US found common factors for success; it seems to be connected with achievement at an early age and major responsibility being attained before the individual is in his or her mid-thirties.[6] However, managerial careers in the 1980s and 1990s have been less stable and predictable in developed Western countries than they were in the period between 1950 and 1980. Fundamental changes in government policy, especially concerning privatization and deregulation (as discussed in Chapter 2), have combined with greater competitive pressures, causing many large corporate organizations to flatten or 'de-layer' their managerial hierarchies, to 'downsize', and to subcontract what are considered peripheral services. One consequence of the reduction in levels of the organizational hierarchy for employees is that, in both the public and private sector, there is less incentive to seek hierarchical promotion. There now exists in organizations less opportunity for promotion, social advancement, and higher status than was available in the past. Reduced promotion prospects have been accompanied by fewer permanent contracts of employment and more part-time and fixed-term contracts. Such changes in employment prospects mean that employees either adapt their idea of what constitutes a career or become dissatisfied when their career expectations are not met.

Career satisfaction is a result of an individual's identification with home and work roles, performing them successfully, and being able to meet new challenges. In the work context, individual career satisfaction partly depends on the organization's providing opportunities for employees to develop competences in a variety of roles.

Charles Handy draws attention to the fact that a range of roles faces employees, in addition to the specific job roles allocated in their individual job descriptions.[7] During daily interaction, employees act in different contexts as subordinate, peer, and superior.

Career dissatisfaction will often result when ambitious and high-performing individuals outgrow their job roles and seek new challenges but their organizations are unwilling or unable to respond by introducing new opportunities. Tension and conflict may also be created because individuals' career aspirations change over time and may eventually no longer match organizational requirements. Career crisis can result from such mismatches, or when work and home lives are in serious conflict, or when the individual's job does not suit his or her abilities and personality. Crisis, as Handy reminds us, can be caused as much by role underload as by role overload.[8] A severe career crisis will often lead to job change, and if the crisis is not managed proactively by the individual, it can result in damaging psychological experiences such as long-term depression, 'burn-out', or inability to hold down a job for a reasonable length of time.

To help explain individual career choice and success and failure in careers, Ed Schein introduced the influential concept of 'career anchors' in 1978.[9] These are self-perceived attributes, motives, attitudes, and values that shape individual careers. Schein lists the following six career anchors: managerial competence (interpersonal, analytical, emotional), technical-functional competence, security, creativity, autonomy, and independence. Schein claimed that if these career anchors were present in employees' work, then they would be more satisfied with their careers and more committed to the organization. To feel that they have managerial competence, employees must be able to interact effectively with other people, analyse situations clearly, and maintain a balanced emotional life. Technical-functional competence can be as broad as the skills of general management or as narrow as the specific competences of an engineer who maintains technical equipment. Schein's other career anchors, except for job security, assume an individualist orientation to work according to which an employee expects independence, creativity, and autonomy in, for example, determining tasks, prioritizing and scheduling work, and evaluating the results. A more collectivist orientation to work would list alternative career anchors such as contributing to the group's purpose, working as a member of a team, and decision making by consultation and consensus. Schein pointed out that good planning of HR flow policies and employee development is a prerequisite to the existence and healthy functioning of career anchors in an organization.

In the USA and the UK during the 1980s, it became more common for people to feel that stable careers no longer existed and that organizations were unable any longer to offer a job for life. In the mid-1990s, Herriot and Pemberton claimed that the very notion of career itself had fundamentally changed because the bargain between employer and employee that held in the 1960s and 1970s no longer applied.[10] Their research was concerned with managerial careers, although many of their points about the changing employment relationship apply to all employees in organizations where a contractual guarantee of lifelong employment and job security is no longer the norm. The authors say that the old deal has changed to a new deal.

**Old Deal**

| *You offered* | *Organization offered* |
|---|---|
| Loyalty—not leaving | Security of employment |
| Conformity—doing what you were asked | Promotion prospects |
| Commitment—going the extra mile | Training and development |
| Trust—they'll keep their promises | Care in trouble |

*Source:* Herriot and Pemberton, *New Deals: The Revolution in Managerial Careers* (1995).

The old deal was a relational contract whereby each party—employer and employee—learnt to trust one another over time. Loyalty and organizational commitment were high wherever this trust existed, to the extent that each party would go the extra mile, even where there was no extrinsic benefit (for example, financial gain) to be had. For example, in the banking industry, it was not unknown for employers to help the families of loyal, long-service employees who died suddenly by paying out a greater financial benefit than they were contractually obliged to render. Employees who were approaching retirement or who underperformed for significant periods of time would be accommodated and tolerated rather than summarily dismissed. On the employees' side, people have worked beyond contract, putting in long hours when necessary and forgoing offers of better jobs elsewhere or other benefits because of a sense of loyalty and commitment to the organization. People usually entered at the bottom and stayed with the organization throughout their careers. Blue-collar employees, graduates, and MBA students may have been hired at different entry levels. In general, older people were not asked to leave because legislation in the past made the costs of termination of employment prohibitive. Large corporations in Japan operated these systems, as did some companies in the West, such as Hewlett Packard and IBM, until the late 1980s. Lifelong employment systems became less common in the West during the 1990s than they had been in the 1960s and 1970s. They are becoming the preserve of smaller and smaller categories of workers, notably those in corporations in Japan, where there are signs that there, too, they are changing.

Increasing competitive pressures in general and change in national governments' policy faced by multinational and national organizations have both contributed to eroding the ability of employers to fulfil their side of the bargain under the terms of the old deal. Management style in the public sector has changed towards giving greater significance to value for money and towards facilitating private company services. In the 1990s, professionals in both the public and private sectors are expected to be more 'businesslike' when dealing with clients. In industrial research and development, employment for technicians and scientists has generally become less secure as employers more frequently replace experienced employees as they reach middle age with younger people.[11] The new deal, as proposed by Herriot and Pemberton, is a much more transactional relationship whereby each party weighs up the opportunities and costs of being in the relationship, adopting a short-term and less trusting attitude. The new deal is a less permanent psychological contract in which the two parties are unsure about what is being offered and what will be offered in the future.

**New Deal**

| *You offer* | *Organization offers* |
| --- | --- |
| Long hours | High pay |
| Added responsibility | Rewards for performance |
| Broader skills | A job |
| Tolerance of change and ambiguity | |

*Source:* Herriot and Pemberton, *New Deals: The Revolution in Managerial Careers* (1995).

Since the 1980s, many organizations, first in manufacturing and then in the service industries, have transformed the conditions of employment. In many instances, employees have perceived there to be two major sources of inequity during this change: procedural inequity in how new deals have been struck and distributive injustice in how rewards have been distributed. A prominent example of such inequity ocurred in 1994 when, after privatization of the utility British Gas, the chief executive, Cedric Brown, was awarded a 75% increase in salary to £475,000 a year; shortly afterwards, 2,600 showroom staff were warned that their salaries of £13,000 per annum were unrealistically high and redundancies could not be ruled out.[12]

The new deal, Herriot and Pemberton surmise, is a less happy relationship than the old deal. Unless it is managed better by both parties, they predict that the new deal will render organizations uncompetitive. They recommend that there be new, different deals to reflect the fact that organizations are no longer able to offer relational contracts and that employees want different things from their careers. They propose three main types of contracts that might better suit the new deal, for both parties: part-time contracts (with hours flexible to meet demand peaks), project contracts (with outcomes and completion dates specified but methods left open), and core contracts (with learning flexible to meet organizational change requirements, but some security and employability for core workers).

Herriot and Pemberton note that the flexibility of part-time contracts is proving especially suitable to the career aspirations of unskilled and semi-skilled female employees and to early retirees who wish to continue working, but not full-time. They add to this list a small but growing group of part-time managers, many who have been made redundant or who are unwilling to work in organizations that have significantly changed since they commenced their careers. The authors rename these part-time contracts 'lifestyle contracts' because they allow employees to more easily manage home and work responsibilities.

Project contracts are suited to people who are stimulated by careers with a technical focus, relatively unencumbered by organizational politics and the administrative duties typical of employment in the larger organization. This type of contract is named the 'autonomy contract' because it offers employees independence, challenge, and the opportunity to concentrate on an area of expertise. Finally, core contracts are suited to people who have a 'managerial competence' career anchor (as described above) and therefore find motivation and job satisfaction in developing the general skills of the core employee. Organizations have to develop their core employees continuously to remain competitive and innovative, and so this contract is termed the 'development contract.'

Herriot and Pemberton observe that each of these types of contract is prone to difficulties for employer and employee, especially because employers will be tempted to renege on even this new deal by exploiting part-time workers, over-controlling project workers, and failing to develop core workers. They recommend that both parties continually monitor and renegotiate the contracts. Their hope is that, in future new deals, individual employees will offer the capability to learn and clear added value, while organizations will offer employability, a flexible contract, and individualized rewards.[13]

From the perspective of HRM, effective human resource flow means matching individual career needs with organizational needs. This first section has shown that the employees' sense of career is dynamic and affected by a variety of factors, some within and others outside the individual's control. Herriot and Pemberton's concept of new deals in employment illustrates that employee resourcing in an organization is increasingly likely to be characterized by distinct agreements being applied to groups of people working under different contracts. Further, they warned that there are strong pressures on employers to act opportunistically in employee resourcing. New deals during the 1990s have tended to negotiate a no compulsory redundancy pledge from employers in return for concessions from the workforce normally in terms of an agreement on new flexible working practices. Britain's biggest bank, Lloyds-TSB, promises employees a job for life as long as they can prove they are flexible to change and agree to flexible working practices.[14]

## The Organizational Perspective — Four Cultures

Organizational culture establishes norms and expectations of how people should be treated and serve the needs of the organization. Culture affects employee resourcing by influencing the values and beliefs of owners, management, and other employees about which flow policies are appropriate. Research by Fons Trompenaars on culture illustrates the influence of organizational culture on employee resourcing. In 1993 Trompenaars proposed a framework for understanding cultural diversity in business.[15] He argued that cultural differences create four distinct corporate cultures, which he calls *family*, *Eiffel Tower*, *guided missile*, and *incubator*.

The *family culture* is dispersed amongst 'members of the family' (Trompenaars describes it as 'diffuse'), has parent figures in authority, is intuitive in its decision making, supports leadership from the top, and expects love and respect from its employees. HR flow policies are not clearly formalized and depend on decisions made by a few individuals at the top of the organization. Senior management will demand loyalty and in return employees will demand to be treated like members of the family; however, flow policies in this culture will often be ambiguous and to some extent depend on who is considered by those in authority to be part of the family.

The *Eiffel Tower culture* is bureaucratic and mechanistic, placing more emphasis on rational efficiency and analytical skills than the family culture does. People are treated as human resources and expected to follow organizational job descriptions, rules, and procedures. Flow policies in this culture are more likely to be formally laid down in writing. They are applied with a systematic logic that emphasizes hierarchical status, office, and function more than attending to individuals and their feelings. Emphasis will be on procedural fairness in the implementation of rules and on distributive justice according to principles of rational efficiency of the organization.

In the *guided missile culture*, work tasks are set as if they form part of a computer control system. This task-centred culture is tuned to altering its path according to feedback from the environment. The organization is structured by projects with clearly specified goals, and employees are expected to become specialists or experts in their area of responsibility. Flow policies are established to achieve the completion of tasks and projects. Loyalty to a project will be seen as more important than loyalty to the organization. Recruitment from the external labour market will be readily utilized when specialist expertise is lacking. Employees can expect to be managed by objectives and rewarded with performance-related pay. Promotion and development opportunities for the internal labour market will be based on previous project success, leading to high performers being offered assignments that are more challenging and entail more responsibility. A twin career track is consistent with this culture—one track for specialists, who don't want too much administrative responsibility, and one for general managers, who lose some of their technical currency to perform managerial duties.

The *incubator culture* is characterized by opportunity for personal growth and change. Relationships between employees are dynamic, energetic, and dispersed ('diffuse'). Management is by example and through enthusiasm with an emphasis on improvisation and joint creativity. Flow policies in this organization are unlikely to be clearly articulated, the tendency being for employees to be recruited and laid off according to workload. Where creativity attracts business, the organization will find it easy to recruit young and talented employees who seek the opportunity to work in a successful and creative environment. Where business is slack and employment vacancies exist on the external labour market, top management may formulate rudimentary flow policies in an effort to retain skilled and creative employees, and in readiness for an upturn in work.

Trompenaars's four cultures provide one explanation for why organizations do not have clearly defined human resource flow policies. A formulated, documented business strategy is likely to be present, at best, in two of the four organizational cultures, Eiffel Tower and guided missile, where there is an openness towards systematic methods. In the family and incubator cultures there is less interest in the accountability of top management and less preoccupation with decision making based on rational thinking. The belief system in these two cultures is more concerned with maintaining a sense of community based on loyalty and trust. In the family culture, loyalty is primarily to other family members, and in the incubator culture, trust comes about through shared work activity rather than loyalty being something owed to specific people. HR flow policies are therefore unlikely to be seen in these cultures as critical to running an organization.

Trompenaars's framework for organizational culture helps us understand why employee resourcing has not routinely applied HR flow policies in the past. As far as the more recent situation is concerned, there is evidence that some organizations have been developing a simpler rationale for HR flow policies. During the 1990s many large

US and UK organizations identified 'core competences', which were the skills deemed by top management to be critical for future success. From an organizational perspective, HR flow policies are designed to assist with the timely supply of the right quality of people to achieve an organization's strategy. Once core competences are identified, they can be used by HR managers as guidelines for improving policy and practice in employee resourcing with the aim of improving the strategic value of the human resource and the competitiveness of the company.[16] The remainder of this section reviews one recent and influential description of core competence.

Prahalad and Hamel analysed the success of Japanese corporations such as NEC, Canon, Honda, Sony, Yamaha, and Komatsu in comparison with the success of US organizations in cultivating and exploiting core competences to launch new, innovative products. They advised top management to think much more carefully about the relationship between competences and end products. In their 1990 *Harvard Business Review* article entitled 'The Core Competence of the Corporation', the authors use the analogy of a tree—the competences being the roots and the end products being the fruits.[17] Japanese corporations, the authors propose, have understood better than US organizations how product innovation draws upon core competences. For example, Canon's laser and colour copiers and laser imagers are the result of having exploited competences in precision mechanics, fine optics, and microelectronics.

Prahalad and Hamel describe how the US company GTE was well positioned in the early 1980s to become a major competitor in the fast-developing information and communication industry. It was active in telecommunications and its operations relied on competences in a variety of areas, for example, telephones, semiconductors, and packet switching systems. They observe that in 1980, GTE's sales were nearly $10 billion while the sales of the Japanese company NEC in the same year were $4 billion. But by 1988, GTE's sales had grown to only $16.5 billion while NEC's had grown to $22 billion. What had happened? GTE had decided to focus on core competences in telephone operations, defence, and lighting products. The company was organized into strategic business units (SBUs) and took the decision to divest its products and core competences in TVs and semiconductors, and entered into joint ventures in switching, transmission, and digital systems. Meanwhile, NEC grew as a world leader in semi-conductors and became a first-tier competitor in telecommunication products and computers. Through its core competences, NEC was able to bridge the gap between telecommunications and office automation and produce a range of information and communication products, for example, mobile telephones, fax machines, and laptop computers.

The implication of Prahalad and Hamel's analysis for employee resourcing is that multidivisional organizations must facilitate the building of core competences. These competences enable the corporation to develop and innovate by utilizing a variety of technologies and experiences from diverse product markets. HR flow that is restricted to developing products within separate, autonomous SBUs are less likely to engender core competences that in turn lead to creative development of new product markets. The authors propose that Japanese corporations have been much more successful than Western corporations have in nurturing distinctive competences because they facilitate learning in the organization across different product technologies.

The employee resourcing challenge for modern corporations, therefore, is to nurture core competences. They are the roots of success and cannot be assessed for their future usefulness on the basis of the current financial performance of product technologies within SBUs. Human resource flow policies that are based on a narrow portfolio investment analysis of SBU performance may be cost-effective in the short term, but can stifle an organization's vision of the future and may even damage its capability to innovate.

## The Societal Perspective—National Culture

The societal perspective on employee resourcing is discussed in this section through reference to recent research on HRM and theory of national culture by Hofstede.

Chapter 1 discussed Brewster and Bournois' model of the European environment of HRM and Brewster's report on a survey of HRM in Europe. In this report Brewster noted that there has been a trend in employee resourcing throughout Europe toward fewer 'standard' working contracts and more 'atypical working' (for example, part-time and short- and fixed-term contracts). As for what is happening specifically in the UK, Guest also reported that issuing fewer standard working contracts has become more common in some occupations, including HRM and personnel management.[18] More responsibility for HRM or personnel management has gone to line managers. Also, there has been an increase in the subcontracting of HR services and, in some organizations, devolvement of personnel management activity from central to local management. As was discussed in Chapter 2, subcontracting of services in the UK public sector has been strongly pursued, and there has been an increase in subcontracting in all major West European countries.[19]

A UK Labour Force Survey conducted in 1996 provides some evidence of change in working practices: 42% of temporary workers stated that they were working on a temporary contract because they could not find permanent employment. Between 1992 and 1996 there was a 30% increase in temporary working in the UK, resulting in 7% of the total workforce being engaged in temporary work. This sudden growth was a break from the previous stable trend (during the period 1984–91) of around 5% of the total workforce being in temporary employment.[20]

However, Guest, whose model of HRM was also discussed in Chapter 1, is somewhat cautious in evaluating the extent to which flexible working and new employment contracts have been applied in the UK organizations he researched. The evidence is that change in employment contracts has been less dramatic than some proponents of these working practices would lead us to believe. As Guest explains:

There has been a move towards more people who could be described as flexible workers in the UK. But the growth has been mainly in part-time workers, it has been restricted to a few industrial sectors such as retail and it is not an accelerating trend. The number of fixed-term contracts has grown but far less dramatically than we might expect.[21]

The work of the influential writer on culture Geert Hofstede further explains the influence of national culture on employee resourcing and HR flow policies. During the 1970s, Hofstede conducted a well-known study of national cultures.[22] He researched forty countries to determine empirically the differences in national culture, and he identified four dimensions that seemed to distinguish national cultures from each other: *power distance*, *uncertainty avoidance*, *individualism–collectivism*, and *masculinity*. He concluded that these four dimensions explain differences in the 'collective mental programming of people in different national cultures'.[23]

*Power distance* is the extent to which a society accepts an unequal distribution of power, high power distance societies accepting a large difference in status between superior and subordinate while low power distance societies expect the reverse. The Philippines and Mexico, for example, have high power distance, while Austria and Denmark have low power distance. *Uncertainty avoidance* is the degree to which a society attempts to avoid uncertainty in life through greater career stability, formal rules, intolerance of deviance, belief in absolute truth, and attainment of expertise. The cultures of Greece and Japan exhibit high uncertainty avoidance, while Singapore and Sweden have cultures with low avoidance. *Individualism–collectivism* is the degree to which a society is seen as being composed of individuals (an extreme example of individualism would be Margaret Thatcher's contentious political statement that there is no such thing as society only individuals), while collectivism is characterized by a tighter social framework in which individual identity is bound up with that of the group (family, clan, organization). The USA and Australia are high in individualism, while Pakistan and Thailand are high in collectivism. Finally, *masculinity* is the extent to which society favours the supposedly masculine values of assertiveness and acquisitiveness rather than the supposedly more feminine values of concern for people and quality of life. Japan and Australia are high in masculinity, while Scandinavian countries and the Netherlands are low.

HR flow policies can be strongly influenced by the national cultural assumptions within which the organization operates. Flow policies operating on the basis of high power distance will seek to sustain hierarchical status differences between employees. The idea that 'boss is boss' is less likely to offend people who accept high power distance, and they will not be surprised by decision making routinely based on position rather than expertise, nor by unequal access to information and development opportunities. Flow policies constructed to support a culture high in uncertainty avoidance place more emphasis on career stability and predictability of future job advancement. Training and development in this culture occurs in regular phases, particularly before promotion to a higher position. In highly individualist cultures, flow policies that promote rapid turnover of employees and frequent recruitment from the external labour market will seem more natural than they would in collectivist cultures, in which greater recognition is commonly given to the family, and employers are held more responsible for contributing to the maintenance of stable, local-community relationships. Organizations functioning in a masculine culture will believe it is natural when devising flow policies to place higher emphasis on concern for task than on concern for people.

Hofstede's four dimensions of national culture help to explain different styles of management and the variety of practice in HR flow policies. The dimensions have been used here to illustrate how national culture can affect flow policies, although it is clear that they have implications stretching widely into many other areas of HRM. To sum up this section on societal influences on human resource flow, the influences are complex, but there are common trends that must be understood if managers and employers are to create and implement HR policy effectively. Likewise, for employees, an insight into the influence of culture and society, combined with self-insight, will help them to manage their careers and adapt to situations confidently so as to sustain their individual effectiveness and psychological well-being.

# 2  Managing Human Resource Flow

H AVING looked at some of the issues and forces surrounding human resource flow policies, we now focus on HR flow itself and how it is managed in organizations. As internal flow has been covered in section 1 of this chapter, we focus here on inflow and outflow.

## Managing Inflow

Managing inflow chiefly concerns recruitment and selection, which are two separate but, obviously, linked processes. Recruitment is the process of attracting candidates for vacant jobs, and selection is the process of choosing the right person for the job from among a pool of candidates.[24] Recruitment and selection are an important part of achieving strategic goals and have significant impact on employment stability and employee turnover. In the past, managers have often avoided accurately informing recruits and longer-serving employees about the realities of their career prospects and likely progression within the organization with the result that many employees later become dissatisfied, having forged an ill-informed 'psychological contract' with their employer.

During the last two decades of the twentieth century, recruitment and selection systems have been used to stimulate organizational change.[25] Greater interest in the processes of selection has generally been accompanied by an increasing emphasis on the attitudes and behaviours of employees.[26] Organizations seeking to identify the best group of employees for achieving strategic change frequently specify the skills or competences they want.[27] Large organizations have introduced more assessment programmes for identifying employees with career potential that fits the business strategy. These programmes use biodata (individuals' life histories), psychometric testing (scientific measurement of personality and competences), and assessment centres (centres that administer structured tests and activities to assess employees' career potential and development needs, occupational psychologists often included amongst the assessors).[28] These new and more 'scientific' systems of selection and recruitment have led to new methodologies of evaluation and assessment, particularly the competence-based approach, which is applied to a wide range of jobs and has been used to describe managerial work that has become more 'outward-looking, market-focused and team-oriented'.[29] In 1990, for example, the National and Provincial Building Society decided to recruit and select present and potential job holders of key posts according to 'key post competences'. The new post-holders were expected to exhibit competence in achieving the key account-abilities of enterprise, customer care, and success; previously, employees had worked in a culture dominated by the values of sobriety, caution, loyalty, respect-ability, thrift, and stability.[30]

The competences of employees have become important criteria for selection and recruitment.[31] They are being used to identify people who can cope with the present and future challenges of work;[32] however, they are only one part of the process of achieving a more productive internal organization. In 1998, Paul Sparrow observed that Ford Motor Company and Lucas Industries made considerable improvements to the productivity of the workplace by attending more carefully to work organization and other factors influenced by management initiative.[33] Over a fifteen-year period, Ford reduced the number of workers needed to make a car per day from five to two. Lucas Industries' automotive manufacturing business reduced lead times from fifty-five days to twelve days.

Sparrow argues that with strategy, structure, and systems being changed to create new organizational design and with business processes such as just-in-time (JIT) and business process reengineering (BPR) being radically rethought, less importance is being attached to the 'person–job fit'. Greater interest is now being shown in indi-viduals' capacity to contribute to several fundamentally different business processes. Change in organization design, therefore, is having an impact on resourcing along with other HRM policies and practices. Selection and recruitment is now concerned with identifying people who can cope with a new organizational environment in which:

- employees are exposed to new sources of information and new networks of relationships;
- there are changes to the roles that employees are expected to play;
- managers think differently about the tasks that need to be done;
- required decision-making processes are altered;
- the timespans of discretion before the consequence of an inappropriate decision become known are altered;
- the criteria for effectiveness, such as the judgement and leadership capabilities needed by employees, are altered;
- there are shifts in the actual work content and business process flow;
- the choice of performance management criteria and measurement metrics is changing;
- there are changes to career aspirations, problems created by the natural inclination of people not to break the habits of their past and present roles, and significant shifts in their power, influence, and credibility.[34]

As new organizational design has tended to move away from bureaucratic and 'tall' (multi-layered), hierarchical structures, it has altered the design of jobs. Parker and

Wall identify five common features of the content of these new jobs.[35] First, operational knowledge has become more critical as the new systems require greater flexibility and faster adaptation to change in workflow and quicker error detection. Second, employees find their work is more reliant on others' performance because buffers in the system such as spare inventory, extra staff, supervisory management, and specialist inspectors have been removed. Third, the operations function has more contact with both internal and external customers, increasing the importance of controlling the costs of machine downtime and eliminating inefficiencies and bottlenecks in workflow. Fourth, greater employee discretion and responsibility require higher-order cognitive competences, such as decision making and problem solving. Fifth, more attention is being paid to employees' social competences, especially their ability to work both independently and unsupervised and, when required, as members of a team, co-operating and communicating effectively. However, there is a lack of evidence for selection systems focusing on team competences. In Chapter 2 we saw the finding of the Workplace Employee Relations Survey (1998) that in 65% of establishments employees are organized into formally designated teams, and it is worth noting that although companies use sophisticated methods for selecting people for individual jobs they rarely use similarly systematic approaches for teams. Michael West *et al.* argue that organizations should improve the profile of their teams through incorporating more systematic methods of competence-based selection.[36]

In the more specific context of graduate recruitment, graduates' ability to rate their own performance has been found to be a reliable predictor of success in the job. There is a difference in gender here, women being better than men at rating themselves accurately on their strengths and weaknesses.[37] A study of graduate selection in three European countries—Britain, Holland, and France—found highly significant differences in the various selection methods. The methods used included traditional interviews, criterion-referenced interviews (interviews linked to behavioural anchors), situational interviews, references, ability tests, personality tests, biodata, assessment centres, application forms, graphology (France and Netherlands only), and astrology (France and Netherlands only), and the authors of the research concluded that, similar to previous findings from research on management selection, while the more sophisticated techniques are being used in all three countries, some techniques with poor psychometric efficacy are still widespread.[38]

Research has shown that in the mid-1990s, in addition to neither adopting selection systems for teams nor favouring systems with strong psychometric efficacy, employers were not formulating plans for graduate recruitment that addressed the increased shortage of young recruits caused by the fall in birth rates since the 1970s.[39] There are many signs for an increased use of more selection tools during the last two decades of the twentieth century, but research by academics shows there is a lot more work to be done in making these systems more rigorous and in evaluating the effectiveness of different selection methods and the quality of assessors' judgements. Good selection and recruitment practice by an employer is also more likely to create a favourable impression of the organization, improving its ability to attract and retain people. Some estimates say that reaction to the selection process accounts for 15–20% of a candidate's decision on whether or not to accept a job offer.[40]

The remainder of this section on managing inflow provides some fundamental and practical guidelines on two commonly used methods of selection: face-to-face interviews and psychometric testing.

BOX 5.1
## Effective Interviewing

The structured interview, it should be remembered, is based on clearly identified competences that the candidate should possess to be successful in the job. The fundamental question then is which of the candidates meet the essential selection criteria. Time has to be allocated effectively and good rapport should be established to ensure that the candidates are all able to perform at their best. Maureen Guirdham has published guidelines for effective face-to-face interviewing, which are included in the example of a good-practice checklist shown below.[11]

*Interviewers' Checklist*
The following items would be rated on a scale of 1 (very poor) to 5 (excellent) for effectiveness.

Reception of candidates
Room arrangements
Introductory remarks created an open and businesslike climate
Candidates were able to talk informally before transition to selection interview
Chair described the job and the organization thoroughly
Interview plan
Established an easy and informal relationship
Did not plunge too quickly into demanding questions
Asked patient and unhurried interview questions
Interviewers appeared sincere and friendly
Interviewers encouraged candidate to talk
Asked open questions (i.e. many different answers might be given)
Asked closed questions (i.e. when appropriate and requiring definite categorical answers)
Asked probing questions (i.e. questions that follow up important issues and concerns)
Asked hypothetical questions (i.e. what candidates would do given specific circumstances)
Asked play-back questions (confirmed what the candidate was saying at critical junctures)
Prevented candidate from glossing over important facts/issues
Covered interview plan in enough detail
Time management
Analysed career of candidate
Analysed strengths
Analysed weaknesses
Identified behaviour patterns
Identified competences
Identified attitudes
Identified preferences
Maintained pace
Maintained direction
Avoided making unnecessary, early conclusions
Avoided leading questions

Avoided discriminating questions
Listening/talking ratio
Recorded candidate's answers
Encouraged candidate to ask questions towards the end of the interview
Ensured candidate had the information needed to decide whether to accept job or not
Made it clear what would happen next
Ended the interview on the right note
Had sufficient information on the interview to discuss all of the candidates thoroughly
Feedback given to candidates on their performance, after interview.

Line and HR managers need to be aware of good practice in interviewing, and training in this technique of selection is important.

The face-to-face interview will probably continue to be the most commonly used method of selection because it provides an opportunity for both parties to find out more about each other and decide whether or not they want to work together. Interviewing has the advantage over other methods in that it is flexible and, although time-consuming, uses fewer resources than do some other popular assessment methods. Its disadvantages are that many people have poor interviewing skills and often don't know it. Psychological studies have shown that people tend to be attracted to others they see as like themselves,[42] so interviewers may end up choosing the person they feel they have most in common with rather than the person who is best for the job. The unstructured interview is said to be little better than chance, although many recruiters would be surprised to be told that their own unstructured interviewing is no better than a shake of the dice! Research shows interviewing on its own to be an ineffective way of selecting the best performers; however, its validity is increased when combined with other assessment methods directly related to present and future job requirements. Structured selection methods and training in interviewing technique can improve the quality of selection decisions.

In addition to interviewing, psychometric tests have come to be used more frequently in the 1980s and 1990s as part of selection practice. Japanese corporations investing in Europe—for example, Toyota and Nissan—have been renowned for their rigorous, formal selection methods applied to all levels, including the shop-floor employee and office worker. The tests are not all new, and some early versions have been utilized within the military and the public sector for some jobs for over fifty years. A small industry has developed providing testing and assessment services, starting in the 1960s and 1970s in the USA and then in the UK. The use of assessment and development centres is now used in 50% of major British employing organizations, but, according to occupational psychologists and experts on assessment, unfortunately many practices are superficial, reducing the validity and reliability of these centres. Common problems are lack of assessor training and guidance, lack of rationale for links between the exercises and the dimensions assessed, inadequate time devoted to activities and assessment, and insufficient validation of assessment instruments.[43]

There are two main types of psychometric test: reasoning and personality. The reasoning tests assess qualities such as aptitude, cognitive skill, ability, and intelligence. Personality tests examine how individuals behave and react to different situations, producing a profile of their personality traits, preferences, and attitudes. Cattell's 16PF (sixteen personality factors), Saville and Holdsworth's OPQ (Occupational Personality Questionnaire), and the Myers–Briggs Type Indicators have been used widely. These tests ask a variety of questions about individuals' likes and preferences, and often several questions addressing the same personality variable will be scattered throughout the questionnaire. Some tests incorporate questions to assess possible bias, such as a social desirability bias, whereby individuals tend to give what they believe is the socially desirable response. Also, the scoring key and analysis can determine a candidate's consistency and reliability of response, for example, the extent to which the respondent answers similar questions the same way. Many of the questions are about basic values, attitudes, and preferences.

---

**BOX 5.2**

Gerald A. Cole lists some of the issues that must be considered before administering psychological tests.[44]

Is such a test appropriate in the circumstances and will it provide the information that we are looking for in a candidate?

Is a test to be used as an aid to short-listing or as an element in final selection?

How will test evidence be weighed in comparison with other elements of the selection process?

Is the test a fair one to use with the candidates in question, e.g. does it unfairly discriminate against ethnic minorities or women?

Should candidates be given an opportunity to prepare for the test beforehand?

Will candidates be given feedback on their test results?

How will confidentiality of test results be protected?

Should the test(s) be administered and/or analysed by the organization's own staff or by specialist consultants? (NB: The British Psychological Society will award a Certificate of Competence to staff who undertake relevant training and assessment.)

What steps should be taken to monitor the use of tests and to assess their value and effectiveness?

In addition to ensuring fair and due process in selection decisions as recommended by Cole, some academics and occupational psychologists have recommended maintaining a degree of healthy scepticism about the extent to which one can be rigorous in what is a process of exchange of information and negotiation between prospective employer and employee. On this point, Sue Newell and Chris Rice offer the following salutary caution: 'Selection decisions are outcomes of human interpretations, conflicts, confusions, guesses and rationalisations rather than clear pictures unambiguously traced out on an engineer's drawing board.'[45]

# Managing Outflow

Whether or not an organization is based in an economy such as Britain's, heavily influenced by short-term pressures created by the financial system, or in one such as Germany's, influenced by longer-term pressures, and whether it has an individualist or a collectivist culture, management in countries throughout the world at times find themselves under pressure to make reductions in the workforce. Early retirement and laying off low performers have been common methods of altering the age and competence profile of a workforce with the aim of reducing costs and retaining people believed to have an appropriate attitude to the changing work environment. Beer *et al.* observed that these outflow strategies are becoming more and more constrained by national employment legislation. There has been a rapid increase in legal action taken by individuals in the USA claiming unjustified discharge or discrimination. From their soft HRM perspective, Beer *et al.* therefore identify the central strategic dilemma of an organization as balancing employees' need for job security and employment rights with the organization's use of outflow as a means of cost reduction and renewal.[46] There follows a brief overview of the various ways of approaching outflow: lifelong employment, downward and lateral mobility, early retirement, and workforce reduction and redundancy.

Fewer companies offer lifelong employment in the 1990s. Even those employers that have made agreements with unions, such as Blue Circle, or have used lifelong employment for core workers as part of a strategy of 'sophisticated' human relations, such as IBM and Hewlett Packard, are prone to reassess individuals' job security according to individual and organizational performance. Sophisticated approaches to human relations are typical of the newer, non-unionized industries such as computers, electronics, and pharmaceuticals, in which employees are retained through a range of modern personnel management techniques and special incentives and rewards.[47] These sophisticated approaches are not, however, the general trend of the majority of non-unionized industries and their companies. Whether 'lifelong employment' really means lifelong employment is tested whenever there is a serious industry recession or exceptionally poor competitive performance. Some organizations, such as Ford and Rover, made lifelong employment commitments to core employees in the late 1980s and early 1990s in exchange for changed attitudes and flexibility of working practices and targets. Rover's 'lifelong' deal between management and unions in 1992, called the New Deal, has been accompanied by a general improvement in productivity and profitability with increased recruitment and shift work at some of the plants. There are signs, however, that significant problems with the New Deal are beginning to emerge, with the possibility that BMW may relocate UK-based Rover Group operations to countries where it is cheaper to operate.[48] The flexible-hours deal agreed at the end of 1998 between Rover management and unions, which reduced the working week to thirty-five hours with no overtime and no attendance bonuses in return for no compulsory redundancies, nevertheless has been predicted to become a more commonplace arrangement in the future.

The process of rationalization of human resources has been occurring over the last two decades of the twentieth century in most European countries and especially in the UK, with significant influence on employee resourcing, particularly hierarchical promotion and long-term job security. In manufacturing companies such as British Aerospace and GEC (for example, the GEC subsidiary company Marconi Instruments) and elsewhere—in the retail, banking, and insurance industries, for instance—the reduction in the number of layers in the hierarchy from top management to the most junior employee has been from between thirteen and twenty levels down to as few as three levels. Beer *et al.* argue that where a company emphasizes performance in the job over position in the status hierarchy, downward and lateral career movement (for example, a division manager may be asked to return to being head of a particular function or a sales manager may be requested to return to working in the field) will be easier to implement without causing fundamental loss of self-esteem.[49]

Early retirement at age 50 or 55 has been a common outflow strategy, often accompanied by compensation packages such as pension benefits similar to those normally received at retirement at age 60–65. For American companies in the 1980s, this was the most popular method of managing outflow in the attempt to revitalize their international competitiveness.[50] Since then, it has become a popular strategy for public-sector restructuring in many countries.

Severe reduction of the workforce often has damaging consequences for the local labour market. Managing outflow in this way is often emotionally charged for both management and employees. Local communities often suffer hardship and unrest until either new jobs become available within the organization or new business and industry develop in the region. In the UK, South Wales and north-east England are just two of the regions that suffered until new viable businesses and industries grew to replace the traditional manufacturing companies. Downsizing in manufacturing has had a negative effect on employment opportunities throughout many regions of Europe that were highly dependent on this and other old industries. Case study research on the practices of employment restructuring suggests that some variation exists in management style influenced by national culture: in four case organizations in Poland, managers generally adopted less harsh practices than their Western counterparts, but the researchers concluded that there would likely be a convergence towards Western practice.[51]

Managers who have been involved in major redundancy programmes have often found that the employees who are retained by the organization judge their employer as much by the way it treats the redundant and early-retired employees as by the way it treats them themselves. In the UK there are codes of good practice published by the Department of Trade and Industry for observing fair treatment and due process. The key to good practice in managing outflow is being able to maintain participative and open two-way communication and to resolve conflicts quickly and equitably. In some countries, much stricter procedural mechanisms have to be observed. For instance, in Germany there are much tighter institutional constraints and legislative requirements surrounding consultation with employees and their representatives than exist in the UK.[52]

Rationalization of organizations, particularly 'downsizing', has been found in both the USA and Europe to force people down transitional career paths on which they experience strong emotions such as shock, disbelief, betrayal, animosity, lowered morale, guilt, higher stress, and fears over job security.[53] Kets de Vries and Balazs studied rationalization in Europe and found it also has negative effects on managers, once the 'organizational memory' (the collective knowledge of the history of the organization) and crucial HR skills are disrupted.[54] Their research found that some employees adjusted to the change by downplaying its emotional significance and forming a more cynical psychological contract. Others adjusted less successfully and displayed more emotion, attempting to 'get even' by withdrawal or reduced involvement. However, it is not only in the area of compulsory redundancy that self-esteem, organizational commitment, job satisfaction, and work motivation can be strongly affected. Herriot recommends that managers and HR practitioners pay more attention to individual well-being during any type of career transition, and he provides examples of how change in organizations and jobs forces such transitions:

- redundancy, demotion, or the move to part-time employment can damage self-esteem, threaten identity (e.g. as breadwinner), and damage people's sense of agency;
- cross-functional moves can threaten professional identity, but conversely may add to self-esteem;
- promotions, role changes, and allocation to more prestigious projects may enhance self-esteem;
- promotions may, however, split work and home identity, since taking on a heavier workload may threaten one's identity as effective parent, spouse, or partner;
- the increased frequency of transitions may threaten the stability of our identity, since our capacity to incorporate the new roles into our notions of who we are may be stretched to the limit;
- our feeling of being in some sense in control of our lives can only be supported if we have a degree of choice about the whether, when, and what of transitions.[55]

How an organization manages HR outflow is a good indicator of its management style and culture. Managing outflow is a strong test of the skills and endurance of managers who are responsible for the process of making employees redundant, and for other means of moving people out of the organization. Invariably, one also has to take into account that what is acceptable practice will differ to an extent according to national culture. For example, in Korea local companies have a tradition of not encouraging 'inter-firm mobility' (the practice of employees with significant work experience leaving one company and joining a competitor), and a study of downsizing during the mid-1990s recession found that US multinational corporations offered part-time contracts while Korean firms prohibited such arrangements.[56] Unfortunately, some companies and individuals have been insensitive to the psychological damage the realities of outflow can cause employees, and it is a major responsibility of the HR function to ensure that these transitions are handled effectively for the benefit of both the organization and its employees.[57]

# 3   Human Resource Planning

T HERE is a range of quantitative methods available for HR planning and established statistical means of representing the inflow, internal flow, and outflow of human resources. New business strategies will demand new approaches to employee resourcing; for example, if a company acquires another company, it will have to identify those employees who are considered critical to the new organization and those who are considered to duplicate resources. And strategies for entry into new markets or areas of business often prompt the development of HR plans for retaining and developing select groups of employees.

Quantitative techniques for planning human resources have been available for nearly fifty years; however, research evidence suggests that utilization of HR planning techniques has been *ad hoc*.[58] The importance of HR planning in ensuring that the organization has the human resources to achieve its strategic goals has long been asserted and this figures plainly in the Institute of Personnel and Development's definition of HR planning:

The systematic and continuing process of analysing an organization's human resource needs under changing conditions and developing personnel policies appropriate to the longer-term effectiveness of the organization. It is an integral part of corporate planning and budgeting procedures since human resource costs and forecasts both affect and are affected by longer-term corporate plans.[59]

Storey and Sisson argue that increasing uncertainty about conditions in the external environment, combined with the traditional reluctance of UK managers to plan human resources, bodes ill for increased use of strategic rational planning.[60] They observe that most HR planning methods have three key components: identifying the demand for labour, identifying the supply of labour, and reconciling supply and demand. The reconciliation process should be consistent with the business strategy.

Armstrong provides a number of practical examples of strategies leading to different HR plans.[61] 'Acquisition strategies' require the forecasting of HR needs. 'Retention strategies' entail planning how to retain the people the organization wants to keep. 'Development strategies' (for example, multiskilling) involves describing how the skills and competences of employees will be increased to meet the needs of the organization. 'Utilization strategies' set targets for improving productivity and cost-effectiveness. 'Flexibility strategies' aim to develop more flexible working practices, and 'downsizing strategies' find ways that numbers of employees can be reduced. An example of a flexibility strategy is NatWest's launch in 1999 of new annualized-hours contracts to cover extended opening times without inflating the wages bill. The scheme covers 15,000 branch employees and means that employees work a set number of hours annually rather than a standard working day plus overtime.[62]

Practical tools for planning and measuring HR flow are available and can be useful for assessing HR performance by making industry comparisons or benchmarking with 'best practice' organizations. One such tool is manpower planning, which is used at both the national and organizational level. At the national level, it is primarily an activity of government and industry bodies. At the organizational level, it is essentially used to forecast workload and manpower. The techniques of manpower planning are numerical and include time series analysis (a quantitative method of measuring and representing how data varies over time), HR forecasts, and budgets.

Three common, organizational measures of HR flow are the turnover index, stability index, and survival rate. The turnover index measures wastage:

$$\frac{\text{Number of leavers in one year (or other specified period)}}{\text{Average number of employees during same period}} \times 100$$

The stability index measures the tendency for longer-serving employees to remain with the organization:

$$\frac{\text{Number with one year's service or more}}{\text{Number employed one year ago}} \times 100$$

The survival rate plots the distribution curve of losses from entry groups of employees on a graph, time on the x axis and percentage of leavers on the y axis.

John Bramham distinguishes manpower planning from human resource planning, saying:

Planning for human resources is more focused on culture, attitude and employee development, the argument being that when these are in place financial and technical control of numbers and costs naturally follows.[63]

However, this chapter has found little evidence that HRM reduces the need for manpower/HR planning; rather it suggests that management is missing the opportunity to implement HR planning and improve employees' understanding of their future role in the organization. Clearer policy on HR flow should, through management's making long-term commitments to employees' careers and development, increase employee trust, resulting in higher performance at work.[64] Managers will less likely succeed in their long-term strategic goals where HR planning is given over to serving solely short-term financial considerations.

Further, in the context of global business and, specifically, multinational corporations (MNCs), organizations should be more systematic and informed about international human resource management (IHRM). The recruitment and development of international managers is a key challenge facing MNCs and there is a recent and growing research literature on this topic. The failure rates of expatriate managers, for example, have been studied and there are differences between countries in the reasons for failure. In US and UK multinationals, 'inability of spouse to adjust' to a new country and culture is the number-one reason for managers failing to perform well, while in Japanese companies it is 'inability to cope with larger overseas responsibility'. MNCs need to take action on this and other relevant research to minimize the major causes of failure in resourcing and become more flexible to national differences and cultural preferences. There is also now more knowledge on the success factors for training and development, which MNCs have by and large neglected. They have preferred to develop home country national managers exclusively and neglect managers from other countries.

The literature on IHRM highlights three important lessons linking employee resourcing with employee development: do not simply export parent country training and development practices but adapt them; align development to the specific strategic needs in each country as well as the overall strategy of the firm; and encourage more transfers of managers between headquarters and other countries to develop management teams that have more global capabilities.[65]

# Summary

THREE perspectives on human resource policies—individual, organizational, and societal—have been discussed. Individuals' career progression and opportunities for development are reduced when there is little internal flow of human resources. Overall, there has been increased experimentation with different types of employment contract, sometimes known as 'new deals', which is one of the consequences of reduced collective-bargaining arrangements and a more individualized employment relationship. HR flow policies are influenced by the culture of the organization, and Trompenaars's four corporate cultures was introduced to illustrate how some cultures accommmodate formalized HR policy better than others. During the 1990s, managers in large organizations have talked about core competences as a rationale for determining HR flow. Prahalad and Hamel proposed that competences will flourish better where there is a long-term orientation towards the potential of the company's different markets and innovative technologies. National culture has an influence on HR flow policy and to illustrate this it was argued that there has been greater pressure towards social partnership between government, employers and unions in European countries than in the United States. Hofstede's four dimensions of national culture were discussed to explain how HR flow policies are influenced by the national cultural assumptions under which organizations operate.

Human resource policies were categorized into three areas—internal flow, inflow, and outflow—and it was argued that many organizations have been attempting to apply more systematic methods of recruitment and selection to improve the quality of internal flow, most notably through psychometric testing and competences. However, some organizations have been less effective in managing outflow, which is an area in which HR professionals should be more involved in managing the transitions. Finally, formal methods and techniques of HR planning were discussed in order to increase awareness of their availability and the fact that they have been underutilized.

BOX 5.3

## Case Study—Residential and Outdoor Education Centres in Mercia

The following case is an example of an organization that successfully achieved an ambitious development strategy under pressure of decreasing resources.

### 1991

In 1991, Mercia County Council directly supported two non-residential outdoor education centres and four residential centres. In addition, the county had recently bought in to residential training and development provision at two other centres. In its budget exercise of January 1992, the Education Committee set target savings of £125,000, with £5,000 to be saved in the first year (1992–3) and the remainder, £120,000, by the end of the second year (1993–4). This reduction in funding left a total of £133,000 to be deployed for the eight centres. The reductions were part of a broader package of spending cuts required by the County Council in 1992–4, designed to meet an increasingly tight standard spending assessment set by central government. The principle of local management of schools also required that an increasingly small proportion of the county's education budget could be retained centrally.

At the time, it was agreed that each of the centres had its own unique place in the overall pattern of provision. The two non-residential centres concentrated on adventure activities. The four residential centres were primarily for use by children from local schools. Two were converted primary schools in rural locations working with the 7–11 age group and each run by their own warden paid on teachers' salary terms and conditions. The other two residential centres were based in a National Park and were part-funded by it and managed by part-time support staff. The two centres that had been bought in to, for provision of training and development, were an arts-based residential centre at which a half-time County Council employee supported visiting groups and a coastal residential centre with good facilities for outdoor and environmental activities. This latter centre was in receipt of a grant rather than a subsidy.

Line management for the centre staff was not uniform. Patterns of usage for each centre were varied, as were occupancy rates, income, and the level of County Council support.

### 1996

Following release of the 1992–4 budget reduction of 47%, a strategic review of the centres took place. Key objectives were established by Council officers. These were published and circulated in 1992, and continued as objectives for the centres in 1996. The key objectives were:

- access would be maintained for educational groups from Mercia to all of the present centres;
- the curriculum offered would be maintained and developed;
- coherence of provision across all centres would be extended;
- centres would be encouraged to develop their own separate identities.

In addition, three secondary objectives were stated:

- centres would consider other sources of funding and income generation;
- proposals would be put forward only if considered achievable for managers;

- centres would be encouraged to move towards a position of self-financing whilst not losing sight of other values.

The following changes were made after widespread consultation and open meetings throughout the country:

A mission statement was developed and agreed. The centres were put in better communication and co-ordination with personnel management central services. Centres were asked to take on an increased range of user groups and extend the length of the season, where possible. Two wardens were made redundant and replaced by staff having a more administrative and managerial job role. The wardens' teaching responsibilities were partly replaced by the creation of part-time, peripatetic curriculum support for three of the centres. Overall, the centres were now managed by a more uniform line-management structure including properly co-ordinated marketing activity. The funding for each centre was reduced on the basis of an assessment of what cuts each could realistically bear. There was a substantial increase in charges and tighter management systems of expenditure were introduced. Centres were encouraged to engage in more active contact with management committees of local visiting groups.

In a previous Mercia County Council policy statement outdoor education was said to comprise outdoor pursuits, typically adventure activities such as canoeing, caving, and rock climbing; outdoor studies (for example, fieldwork for geography courses); and short-stay residential experience. Adult, youth, and community groups are increasing their usage of the centres for these purposes. And the Residential and Outdoor Education centres have continued to become more involved in helping schools with delivering aspects of the National Curriculum, ranging across the subject areas and including personal and social development.

The base budget in 1995/6 was £97,000 against income of £409,000. Seven out of the eight centres had increased usage in 1995, compared to usage in the three previous years.

*Case Study Activity*
Analyse and discuss how employee resourcing in particular and HRM in general changed in the Mercia outdoor education case.

# Study Questions

1   Discuss what, in your view, are the main issues for employee resourcing at the three levels of the individual, the organization, and society.

2   How have careers changed in organizations? Write a ten-point list of principles and an agenda for employer action on career management and development.

3   What is the role of organizational culture in employee resourcing?

4   What is the role of national culture in employee resourcing?

5   What are the main issues in managing outflow? What skills do managers need to develop for the effective management of outflow?

# Further Reading

Handy, C. J., *Understanding Organizations*, 4th edition, London: Penguin.

Herriot, P. and Pemberton C., *New Deals: The Revolution in Managerial Careers* (Chichester: John Wiley & Sons, 1995).

Kamoche, K., 'Strategic Human Resource Management within a Resource-Capability View of the Firm', *Journal of Management Studies* (1996), March, 33, 2, pp. 213–33.

Storey, J. and Sisson, K., *Managing Human Resources and Industrial Relations* (Milton Keynes: Open University Press, 1993), chapter 5, pp. 110–30.

# Notes

1. Rothwell, S., 'Human Resource Planning', in J. Storey (ed.), *Human Resource Management: A Critical Text* (London: Routledge, 1995), pp. 167–202; Evenden, R., 'The strategic management of recruitment and selection', in R. Harrison, *Human Resource Management: Issues and Strategies* (Wokingham, England: Addison-Wesley, 1993); Miller, E., 'Strategic Staffing', in C. Fombrun, N. M. Tichy and M. A. Devanna, *Strategic Human Resource Management* (New York: John Wiley & Sons, 1984).

2. Beer, M., Spector, B., Lawrence, P. R., Quinn Mills, D., and Walton, R. E., *Managing Human Assets: The Groundbreaking Harvard Business School Program* (New York: The Free Press, Macmillan, 1984), pp. 9 and 66–112.

3. Walton, R. E., 'Toward a Strategy of Eliciting Employee Commitment Based on Policies of Mutuality', in R. E. Walton and P. R. Lawrence (eds.), *Human Resource Management, Trends and Challenges* (Boston: Harvard Business School Press, 1985), 35–65. 'The new HRM model is composed of policies that promote mutuality—mutual goals, mutual influence, mutual respect, mutual rewards, mutual responsibility. The theory is that policies of mutuality will elicit commitment which in turn will yield both better economic performance and greater human development.'

4. Hughes, E. C., 'Institutional Office and the Person', *American Journal of Sociology* (1937), 43, pp. 404–13.

5. Curnow, B. and McLean, F. J., *Third Age Careers* (London: Gower Press, 1994).

6. Kotter, J. P., *The General Managers* (New York: Free Press, 1982).

7. Handy, C. J., *Understanding Organizations*, 4th edn. (London: Penguin, 1993).

8. Ibid.

9. Schein, E. H., *Career Dynamics: Matching Individual and Organisational Needs*, (Reading, MA: Addison-Wesley, 1978). Schein, E. H., 'How "career anchors" hold executives to their career paths', in R. Katz (ed.), *Managing Professionals in Innovative Organizations* (Cambridge, MA: Ballinger Publishing Company, Harper & Row, 1988), pp. 487–97.

10. Herriot, P. and Pemberton, C., *New Deals: The Revolution in Managerial Careers* (Chichester: John Wiley & Sons, 1995).

11. McGovern, P., *HRM, Technical Workers and the Multinational Corporation* (London: Routledge, 1998), pp. 136–45.

12. *Financial Times*, 15 and 16 December 1994 and 1 May 1996.

13. Herriot, P., 'The Management of Careers', in S. Tyson (ed.), *Strategic Prospects for HRM* (London: Institute of Personnel and Development, 1995), pp. 184–205 at p. 196; Hendry, C. and Jenkins, R., 'Psychological Contracts and New Deals', *Human Resource Management Journal* (1997), 7, 1, pp. 38–44.

14. *People Management*, 4, 19, 1 October 1998, p. 12

15. Trompenaars, F., *Riding the Waves of Culture* (London: Economist Books, 1993).

16. Kamoche, K., 'Strategic Human Resource Management Within A Resource-Capability View of the Firm', *Journal of Management Studies* (1996), March, 33, 2, pp. 213–33 (see p. 213).

17. Prahalad, C. and Hamel, G., 'The Core Competence of the Corporation', *Harvard Business Review* (1990), May–June, pp. 79–91.

18. Guest, D. E., 'Beyond HRM: Commitment and the Contract Culture', in P. Sparrow and M. Marchington (eds.), *Human Resource Management: The New Agenda* (London: Financial Times, Pitman Publishing, 1998), pp. 37–51.

19. Brewster, C., 'Flexible working in Europe: extent, growth and the challenge for HRM', in Sparrow and Marchington (eds.), *Human Resource Management: The New Agenda*, pp. 245–58.

20. UK Labour Force Survey, Spring 1996.

21. Guest, 'Beyond HRM', p. 46.

22. Hofstede, G., *Culture's Consequences: International Differences in Work Related Values* (Beverly Hills: Sage, 1980).

23. Ibid., p. 42.

24. Wright and Storey, 'Recruitment and selection', in I. Beardwell and L. Holden, *Human Resource Management: a Contemporary Perspective*, 2nd edn. (London: Financial Times, Pitman Publishing, 1997), pp. 210–76.

25. Iles, P. and Salaman, G., 'Recruitment, Selection and Assessment', in J. Storey (ed.), *Human Resource Management: A Critical Text* (London: Routledge, 1995), pp. 203–33.

26. Townley, B., 'Selection and Appraisal: Reconstituting "Social Relations"?', in Storey (ed.), *New Perspectives on Human Resource Management*.

27. Boam, R. and Sparrow, P., *Designing and Achieving Competency: A Competency-Based Approach to Developing People and Organizations* (Maidenhead: McGraw-Hill, 1992).

28. Robertson, I. T., Iles, P. A., Gratton, L., and Sharpley, D., 'The Psychological Impact of Selection Procedures on Candidates', *Human Relations* (1991), 44, 9, pp. 963–82; Baron, H. and Janman, K., 'Fairness in the Assessment Centre', in C. L. Cooper and I. T. Robertson, *International Review of Industrial and Organizational Psychology*, Vol. II (Chichester: John Wiley, 1996), pp. 61–114.

29. Iles and Salaman, 'Recruitment, Selection and Assessment', p. 208.

30. Ibid., p. 209.

31. Feltham, R., 'Using Competencies in Selection and Recruitment', in R. Boam and P. Sparrow, *Designing and Achieving Competency: A Competency-Based Approach to Developing People and Organizations* (Maidenhead: McGraw-Hill, 1992), pp. 89–103.

32. Ibid., p. xxi.

33. Sparrow, P., 'New Organisational Forms, Processes, Jobs and Psychological Contracts: Resolving the HRM Issues', in P. Sparrow and M. Marchington (eds.), *Human Resource Management: The New Agenda* (London: Financial Times, Pitman Publishing, 1998), pp. 117–41; Kandola, R. and Pearn, M., 'Identifying Competences', in R. Boam and P. Sparrow, *Designing and Achieving Competency: A Competency-Based Approach to Developing People and Organizations* (Maidenhead: McGraw-Hill, 1992).

34. Sparrow, 'New Organisational Forms, Processes, Jobs and Psychological Contracts', p. 120; Buchanan, D. A. 'Principles and practice in work design', in K. Sisson (ed.), *Personnel Management: A Comprehensive Guide to Theory and Practice in Britain*, 2nd edn. (Oxford: Blackwell, 1994).

35. Parker, S. K. and Wall, T. D., 'Job Design and Modern Manufacturing', in P. Warr (ed.), *Psychology and Work*, 4th edn. (London: Penguin, 1996).

36. West, M.A., Borrill, C.S., and Unsworth, K.L., 'Team effectiveness in organizations', in C. L. Cooper and I. T. Robertson (eds.), *International Review of Industrial and Organizational Psychology*, Vol. 13, (Chichester: John Wiley, 1998), pp. 1–48 at p. 32.

37. *People Management* (1999), 5, 1, 14 January, p. 15.

38. Hodgkinson, G. P. and Payne, R.L., Short research note: 'Graduate Selection in Three European Countries', *Journal of Occupational Organizational Psychology* (1998), 71, pp. 359–65 (see p. 361); Shackleton, V. and Newell, S., 'European management selection methods: A comparison of five countries', *International Journal of Selection and Assessment* (1994), 2, pp. 91–102.

39. Hodgkinson, G. P., Daley, N., and Payne, R. L., *International Journal of Manpower* (1995), 16, 8, pp. 59–76; Hodgkinson, G. P., Snell, S., Daley, N., and Payne, R. L., 'A Comparative Study of Knowledge of Changing Demographic Trends and the Importance of HRM Practices in Three European Countries', *International Journal of Selection and Assessment* (1996), 4, 4, October, pp. 184–94.

40. Fletcher, C., *People Management* (1998), 4, 23, 26 November, p. 40.

41. Guirdham, M., *Interpersonal Skills at Work* (London: Prentice Hall, 1990).

42. Hatch, M. J., *Organization Theory: Modern, Symbolic and Postmodern Perspectives* (Oxford: Oxford University Press, 1997), p. 228.

43. Fletcher, C. and Anderson, N., 'A superficial assessment', *People Management* (1998), 4, 10, 14 May, p. 44.

44. Cole, G. A., *Personnel Management*, 3rd edn. (London: DP Publications, 1993), pp. 210–11.

45. Newell, S. and Rice, C., 'Assessment, Selection and Evaluation: Problems and Pitfalls', pp. 129–65 in J. Leopold, L. Harris, and T. Watson, *Strategic Human Resourcing: Principles, Perspectives and Practices* (London: Financial Times, Pitman Publishing, 1999).

46. Beer, M., Spector, B., Lawrence, P. R., Quinn Mills, D., and Walton, R. E., *Managing Human Assets: The Groundbreaking Harvard Business School Program* (New York: The Free Press, Macmillan, 1984), pp. 129–65.

47. Purcell, J. and Gray, A., 'Corporate personnel departments and the management of industrial relations: two case studies in ambiguity', *Journal of Management Studies* (1986), 23, 2, pp. 205–23.

48. The instability of Rover's operations in the UK may become a recurring theme generally that threatens lifelong employment security. See the following: *The Times* (24 July 1998) p. 25, 'Rover threaten to close Longbridge', *The Daily Telegraph* (21 October 1998) p. 1; *People Management*, 4, 25, (24 December 1998), p. 10; *The Sunday Times* (14 March 1999), 'Labour offers £200m to Longbridge'.

49. Beer *et al.*, *Managing Human Assets*, p. 93.

50. Ibid.; Ference, T. P., Stoner, J. A. F., and Warren, K. E. 'Managing the career plateau' in R. Katz (ed.), *Managing Professionals in Innovative Organizations* (Cambridge, Mass. Ballinger Publishing Company, Harper and Row, 1988).

51. Redman, T. and Keithley, D., 'Downsizing goes East? Employment re-structuring in post-Socialist Poland', *International Journal of Human Resource Management* (1998), 9, 2, April, pp. 274–95, at p. 274.

52. Blyton, P. and Turnbull, P. (eds.), *Reassessing Human Resource Management* (London: Sage, 1992). See the British Steel case.

53. Sparrow, 'New Organisational Forms, Processes, Jobs and Psychological Contracts' (n. 33 above), p. 129.

54. Kets de Vries, M. F. R. and Balazs, K., 'The Downside of Downsizing', *Human Relations* (1997), 50, 1, pp. 11–50.

55. Herriot, P., 'The Role of the HRM Function in Building a New Proposition for Staff', in P. Sparrow and M. Marchington (eds.), *Human Resource Management: The New Agenda* (London: Financial Times, Pitman Publishing, 1998), pp. 106–16.

56. Feldman, D. C., and Kim, S., 'Acceptance of buyout offers in the face of downsizing: empirical evidence from the Korean electronics industry. Study of a major Korean electronics company', *International Journal of Human Resource Management* (1998), 9, 6, December, pp. 1008–25 (see p. 1008).

57. Doherty, N., 'Downsizing', S. Tyson (ed.), in *The Practice of Human Resource Strategy* (London: Financial Times, Pitman Publishing, 1997), pp. 27–40.

58. Rothwell, 'Human Resource Planning' (n. 1 above).

59. Institute of Personnel Management, *Statement on Human Resource Planning* (London: IPM, 1992).

60. Storey, J. and Sisson, K., *Managing Human Resources and Industrial Relations* (Milton Keynes: Open University Press, 1993).

61. Armstrong, M., *A Handbook of Personnel Management Practice*, 6th edn. (London: Kogan Page, 1996), p. 409.

62. *People Management*, 5, 2, 28 January 1999, p. 16

63. Bramham, J., *Human Resource Planning*, 2nd edn. (London: Institute of Personnel and Development, 1994), p. 164.

64. Schuler and Jackson subdivide human resource planning into 5 phases: (1) identify the key business issues; (2) determine the human resource implications; (3) develop human resource objectives and goals; (4) design and implement human resource policies, programs, and practices; (5) evaluate, revise, and refocus. Schuler, R. S. and Jackson, S. E., *Human Resource Management: Positioning for the 21st century*, 6th edn. (Minneapolis-St. Paul, MN: West Publishing Company, 1996), pp. 137–41.

65. Scullion, H., 'International HRM', in J. Storey (ed.), *Human Resource Management: a Critical Text* (London: Routledge, 1995), pp. 352–82 at p. 377; Hofstede, G., *Culture's Consequences: International Differences in Work Related Values* (Beverly Hills: Sage, 1980).

# Chapter 6
# Motivating Employees

## Chapter Contents

Introduction

# Introduction

T HE topic of this chapter, motivating employees, is linked to material in the following chapter on financial rewards, because paying employees is part of motivating them. However, we deal with employee motivation in depth in its own chapter because it is pivotal to the study of HRM and because different theories of what fundamentally motivates people at work underpin the various models of HRM. For example, as we saw in Chapter 1, soft HRM adopts an approach of development and commitment in addressing motivation, while hard HRM concentrates more on controlling and using people as a means to the organization's ends. Whatever their particular concept of HRM, its advocates claim it is an alternative approach to the traditional employment relationship, and therefore some understanding of the psychological theories of motivation will be helpful in evaluating HRM theory and practice. Motivation theory is significant to many social science disciplines and will help the reader determine how far HRM is capable of motivating employees in new ways that are distinct from past approaches. A basic understanding of what motivates and de-motivates employees is also a valuable underpinning to management practice. This chapter first covers motivating individuals and then motivating groups. The section on motivating groups discusses equity theory and two important theories of management motivation.

# 1 Motivating Individuals

T HIS section on motivating individuals gives an overview of several content theories and process theories of motivation. Content theories seek to explain *what* motivates employees; process theories explain *how* to motivate employees. Three content theories are described—Maslow's hierarchy of needs, McClelland's three basic needs, and Herzberg's motivators and hygiene factors—all of them 'need' theories, which means that they assume that individuals' motivation is driven by common and fundamental needs. Four process theories are then described: Latham and Locke's goal theory, Porter and Lawler's expectancy theory, Bandura's self-efficacy theory, and Hackman and Oldham's research on job design. At the end of this section, the limitations of content and process theories are discussed.

# Content Theories — What Motivates Employees

## Maslow's Hierarchy of Needs

Abraham Maslow's hierarchy of five basic needs—physiological needs (food, water, sleep, oxygen, warmth, and freedom from pain), safety, social belonging, esteem, and self-actualization—comprises lower- and higher-order needs.[1] Maslow claimed that as each level of need, starting with the lower-order needs, is gratified, we seek a higher-order need (see Fig. 6.1). We start by seeking to satisfy our physiological needs and when those are satiated, safety needs emerge, and so on. Social belonging, esteem, and self-actualization are growth needs—in other words, they are needed for growth beyond a basic level of existence. The two lower-order needs, physiological needs and safety, are deficiency needs. This means that if a deficiency arises at some point for whatever reason in the individual's supply of physiological necessities or feeling of physical safety, redressing this deficiency can temporarily become more important than fulfilling the higher-order needs. When all of the deficiency needs are again satisfied, the individual can again be motivated by growth needs, first seeking rewarding social relationships, then prestige, recognition, and achievement, and then the highest category of growth, self-actualization, which is the desire for self-fulfillment through personal development of one's potential. This can be expressed in many different ways, including maternally/paternally, occupationally, and artistically.

Maslow's theory has long had appeal partly because it appears to be so readily applicable to most situations; however, on close inspection the attractiveness of the theory is its vagueness and difficulty to disprove.[2] The distinction it makes between lower-order needs (physiological, safety) and higher-order needs (social, esteem, self-actualization) is one that has had intuitive appeal to students and business practi-

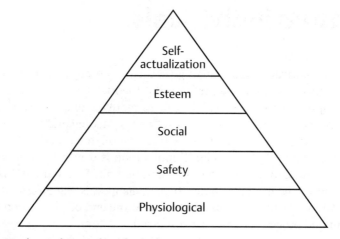

**Figure 6.1  Maslow's hierarchy of needs**

*Source: Organizational Behaviour: Concepts, Controversies, Applications* (Exhibit 5-2, p. 170) by Stephen Robbins, © 1998. Reprinted by permission of Prentice-Hall, Inc., Upper Saddle River, NJ.

tioners from different backgrounds and cultures partly because it is imprecise and open to a wide variety of interpretations.[3] Nevertheless, the hierarchy retains significance for business and management students by drawing attention to the prominent role of intrinsic motivation in ensuring that work is satisfying for employees.

## McClelland's Three Basic Needs

David McClelland's well-known theory of need motivation focuses on the needs of achievement, power, and affiliation.[4] People with a high need for achievement seek jobs and tasks in which they have personal responsibility and can obtain quick feedback on their progress and attainment. High achievers are moderate risk takers, preferring the odds of success to be even or in their favour. They are not motivated by success that can be put down to good luck, preferring outcomes that they believe are a consequence of their own achievements. People with a high need for power seek situations where they can have power and influence over others. They like to be in positions of status and authority and frequently will aim to increase their influence over others in preference to concentrating on effective work performance. Lastly, people with a high need for affiliation are motivated by being liked and accepted by others. They are most motivated in work situations where there is a high degree of co-operation and where greater priority is given to attaining mutual understanding among the group rather than to competition between individuals.

In summary: the achievement need is the drive to excel and to achieve according to standards set by both others and oneself; the need for power is the need to make others behave in ways they otherwise would not behave; and the need for affiliation is the desire for friendly interpersonal relationships. McClelland's research found that high achievers—who sought situations in which they gain personal responsibility, get feedback, and undertake moderate risks—were people who tend to be successful in entrepreneurial activities; however, they are not always the best general managers. It is the needs for power and affiliation, according to McClelland, that are related to managerial success, particularly in large organizations, the best general managers having a high need for power and a relatively low need for affiliation.

## Herzberg's Motivators and Hygiene Factors

In 1968, Frederick Herzberg published an article in the *Harvard Business Review* (*HBR*) that by 1987 had sold 1.2 million reprints, the largest sale of any article in *HBR*'s history. The article was republished in 1987 as an *HBR* Classic, entitled 'One More Time: How Do You Motivate Employees?'. Herzberg proposes that the key to motivating employees lies in job design and job enrichment. He argues that there has been a series of myths about motivation and cites nine personnel practices that in his view are failed past attempts to instil motivation.

Reducing the time spent at work, he says, will not motivate employees because motivated people seek more hours of work, not fewer. Increasing wages, or reducing them in an economic depression, does not motivate people either. Fringe benefits, he suggests, have become an expectation and are unlikely to motivate. People take for granted having to work only five days a week and for less than ten hours a day.

Furthermore, they see stock options and medical coverage as being almost a basic right of employment. Herzberg also criticizes human-relations teaching in the business schools and companies of his time, implying that managers have become soft and employees more awkward, so that they have to be told to do something three times rather than doing it after being asked only once, as they would have done in the past. He also suggests that sensitivity training, improving two-way communication between managers and employees, job participation, and employee counselling are all failed attempts at motivation.

In summary, past personnel initiatives have been unsuccessful because they do not reorganize the job. Only by doing this, Herzberg claims, will employees gain more of a sense of achievement, recognition, intrinsic satisfaction from work, responsibility, advancement, and personal learning and growth. Herzberg sees individuals as having two sets of basic needs. One set stems from the in-built drive to avoid pain and to satiate biological needs. The other set of needs is unique to human beings and is concerned with achievement, recognition for achievement, the work itself, responsibility, growth, and advancement. The first set of needs he calls hygiene factors, which are extrinsic to the work the employee does and include company policy and administration, supervision, interpersonal relationships, working conditions, salary, status, and security. The second set of needs comprise growth needs or motivating factors and are intrinsic to the work.

Herzberg's first article was based on twelve different research investigations that included in their samples low-level supervisors, professional women, agricultural administrators, men about to retire from management, hospital maintenance staff, manufacturing supervisors, nurses, food handlers, military officers, engineers, scientists, housekeepers, teachers, technicians, female assemblers, accountants, and foremen. In these studies, the employees were asked to describe positive and negative job events. Motivating factors (motivators) were found to be those that contributed to job satisfaction, and hygiene factors were those that, at best, meant employees would not be dissatisfied.

Herzberg criticized previous work on job design and enrichment for concentrating too greatly on horizontal job loading—loading employees with more tasks and more variety in their work—yet not including in the job any motivating factors that lead to an improved sense of achievement, recognition, responsibility, advancement, or growth over the longer term. Herzberg advises that organizations redesign their jobs so that they are more enriched with motivators. Jobs need to have vertical loading to be motivating (that is, any new component added to the job should build upward toward job satisfaction) and should be designed to make employees feel they have more responsibility and opportunity for growth.

Some of Herzberg's views are contentious and have been the subject of hot debate. His article bluntly recommends some very simple practices of management, for example:

The argument for job enrichment can be summed up quite simply: if you have employees on a job, use them. If you can't use them on the job, get rid of them, either via automation or by selecting someone with lesser ability. If you can't use them and you can't get rid of them, you will have a motivation problem.[5]

The 1987 *HBR* reprint concludes with a retrospective commentary on the original article, in which Herzberg defends his basic distinction between motivation factors and hygiene factors; however, he does suggest that the original article ignored the positive role played by organizational behaviourists[6] in reducing workplace tension, implying an admission that his article went too far in denigrating the positive contribution of management practice that is sensitive to human relations. He also presents further research evidence, found in a job-attitudes study conducted in six countries, supporting the importance of motivators. They were again found to be important in contributing to job satisfaction, while hygiene factors at best reduced the occurrence of job dissatisfaction.

Herzberg provides a model of job enrichment that is consistent with the recent focus on serving the customer and that highlights the contribution of learning and feeling in business performance. In the model, employees work closely together in serving clients and understanding and developing the product. Five ingredients are proposed as contributing to client- and product-focused learning and feeling: control over resources, self-scheduling, personal accountability, direct communication with authority, and direct feedback. Herzberg warns that personnel practices in the 1980s have become too focused on hygiene factors and serving the bottom line. He proposes that the work ethic and the quality-of-work-life movement have succumbed to what he says are the abstract and emotionless fields of finance and marketing. Job enrichment, he asserts, is still the key to designing work that motivates employees.

Content theories of motivation identify what motivates human beings. Two of the content theories discussed here, Maslow's and Herzberg's, assume, first, that needs can be subdivided into higher- and lower-order needs and, second, that healthy and well-adjusted individuals will aspire to the fulfilment of higher-order needs once lower-order needs have been adequately satisfied. All three of the content theories discussed maintain an individualist conception of motivation and subordinate social contribution and belonging to individual achievement and 'self-actualization'. These theories have been criticized for propounding a male-dominant perspective on motivation. They have been described as being too specific to the national culture in which they were developed[7] and for promoting a gender-specific view of reality that favours men by prioritizing motivation in the workplace above motivation in other contexts, such as home and family.[8]

# Process Theories—How to Motivate Employees

## Latham and Locke's Goal-directed Theory[9]

Latham and Locke in 1979 stated that the advantage of goal theory is that it has clear practical applications for managing and motivating people. They observe that most managers are not in a position to change people's personalities and the best they can do is to use incentives to direct employees' energies towards the goals of the organization. Money, they say, is the primary incentive, but there are many others, such as participation in decision making, job enrichment, behaviour modification (using structured systems of incentives to modify employees' behaviour), and organization development.

Latham and Locke reported on laboratory experiments showing that individuals who were given specific, challenging goals out-performed those who were given vague goals. These experiments also found that pay and performance feedback resulted in improved performance only where the feedback led the individuals to set themselves higher goals than they had before. The authors also reported studies they undertook to help supervisors improve the productivity of logging crews in North America. Giving logging crews specific production goals, such as the amount of wood to be felled and collected, was found to increase productivity—when it was combined with a supervisory presence on site. Crews left on their own without supervision tended to under-perform. When there was an atmosphere of trust between managers and subordinates, crews given the most demanding goals were found to out-perform others, having higher rates of productivity and lower rates of absenteeism, injury, and employee turnover.

Similar experiments by Latham and Locke with drivers loading trucks in a unionized US company found that when drivers set goals for attaining correct load capacity, large sums of money were saved for the company through reduction of waste. The researchers concluded that three steps should be followed to obtain the best results in goal setting. First, goals must be specific rather than vague; clear time-limits must be set for goal accomplishment; and goals should be challenging and reachable. Second, managers must ensure that employees accept and remain committed to the goals. This is best achieved when there is an atmosphere of trust between managers and subordinates and when a supportive supervisory style is used. Non-supportive supervisory styles were found not to motivate employees towards goal commitment. The third step is to give employees support in the form of adequate resources, money, equipment, time, and help. The authors' finding was that goal setting works best when it is combined with good managerial judgement and when both production goals and employee-development goals are attended to.

## Porter and Lawler's Expectancy Theory

Victor Vroom's book *Work and Motivation* is regarded by many as a landmark in the field of motivation.[10] His theory assumes that human behaviour is goal-directed and that work will be more motivating when it provides the opportunity for goal attainment and needs satisfaction. Vroom developed what is known as expectancy theory, in which motivation is a function of each individual's expectation that his or her behaviour will result in outcomes that have psychological value. It is predicted, according to expectancy theory, that individuals will behave in ways they think are likely to lead to rewards they value. Expectancy theory was developed to explain how individuals can be motivated when they have different values and priorities for rewards. The theory's recommendation for managers is that work should be designed so that effective performance leads to outcomes desired by employees. People will work hard if their labours achieve things they want, which can vary from extrinsic rewards such as a productivity bonus to intrinsic rewards such as the pleasure obtained purely from doing the task.

In 1968 Porter and Lawler devised a model of motivation based on Vroom's expectancy theory that has frequently been taught to managers.[11] The model describes a person's motivation as a function of three things: the attractiveness of the rewards, performance-to-reward expectancy, and effort-to-performance expectancy.

First, the perceived attractiveness of the rewards: motivation to exert effort is stimulated by the prospect of desired rewards. People must value the rewards in order to be motivated to perform. Rewards, as was first mentioned in Chapter 1, can be either intrinsic or extrinsic. Those who are motivated by intrinsic rewards, such as challenging job assignments, will be motivated by the work itself more than will people who are primarily motivated by extrinsic rewards, such as money.

Second, performance-to-reward expectancy: this is the employee's expectation that if the desired performance is achieved, then desired rewards will be obtained. For example, if the employee's pay is linked to the financial performance of the organization through a profit-sharing system and if the organization consistently makes low profits, then the profit-sharing element of the reward system will not be very motivating.

Third, effort-to-performance expectancy: employees will make the necessary effort only when they believe there is a reasonable probability of achieving the target performance. For example, when working in a small team, the individual may believe his or her effort is likely to have a direct effect on the group. However, when the same individual is asked to help improve the overall profits of the whole company, which employs many thousands, this person may feel that his or her contribution won't make a significant difference to the company results. The larger the group, the less any one person feels that individual effort will affect overall performance. Effort-to-performance expectancies are influenced by ability and perception of role: any individual must be adequately educated and trained to accomplish the necessary tasks and should have a perception of his or her role that is sufficiently consistent with the performance actually required.

Porter and Lawler's revised version of Vroom's expectancy theory model is shown in Fig. 6.2. The model recognizes that the perceived attractiveness of the extrinsic and intrinsic rewards offered by the organization will depend on how much employees value them. It says that effort-to-performance expectancies will be moderated by ability, traits, and perceptions of role, and the level of effort applied will depend on individuals' ability, training, and role perceptions. Performance-to-reward expectancies will in turn be moderated by a sense of equity and a perception that the rewards are allocated fairly. If employees believe some individuals or groups have obtained an unfair proportion of the rewards, then the aggrieved will be less satisfied and less motivated to perform to the level required in the future. The jagged line between performance and rewards on the diagram is there to show that motivation is a function of the performance–reward relationship. Two of the feedback loops depicted represent the reinforcement and increase of motivation. First, achieving the performance and obtaining the reward strengthen an individual's belief that a similar outcome will recur in future. Second, the satisfaction from the reward strengthens motivation by increasing the individual's valuation of the reward.

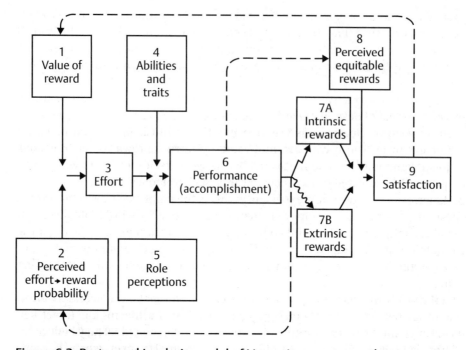

**Figure 6.2 Porter and Lawler's model of Vroom's expectancy theory**

*Source*: Pinder in Vroom and Deci (eds.), *Management and Motivation*, Harmondsworth: Penguin Books 1992, second edition, p. 98

The expectancy model does not include all of the factors that organizations must influence in order to motivate employees. Other important factors include the relationship between management and employees, development opportunities for employees, and meaningful work goals. Especially problematic for organizations has been sustaining a motivational link between rewards and performance. It is a complex link and it is often not easy to develop good measures of performance and to communicate the evaluation of individuals' performance in ways that are acceptable and motivating. Organizations frequently have difficulties in linking pay to performance. Trust must be sustained between management and employees, and the evaluation system for rewards has to be credible and visible if individuals are to be motivated. Otherwise, they will not believe that the extrinsic rewards promised will materialize upon delivery of effective performance.

### Bandura's Self-efficacy Theory

Albert Bandura's self-efficacy theory is often quoted in the management literature.[12] It proposes that the main influence over behavioural change and motivation is self-efficacy, which is the strength of belief an individual has in his or her ability to achieve outcomes through behaviour. Bandura cites previous research showing that positive reinforcement of behaviour does not persuade individuals to act in a similar manner in the future unless they believe the same actions will again be rewarded.[13] Bandura says that mastery and effective performance are more influenced by high self-efficacy than they are by previous track record.

His theory states that people have the capacity to exceed their previous performance or to perform worse than they did before by holding different expectations of their own efficacy. Expectations of what degree of personal mastery they can achieve will influence both the point at which they start relying on coping behaviours (behaviours that appear in order to help someone get through a specific situation) and how long they will persist with them. The individuals' expectations of their own efficacy are a major determinant of what activity they will choose to work at, the amount of effort they will expend, and the length of time they will spend dealing with stressful situations. Efficacy expectations differ from task to task and, of course, from individual to individual. For example, individuals may have efficacy expectations of either broad or narrow magnitude, generality, and strength. Magnitude is the extent to which they believe in being able to perform ever more complex tasks. Generality is the sense of being able to master a range of situations. Strength is the degree to which individuals will cope with setbacks and failure.

Bandura's self-efficacy theory is a theory of social learning, being concerned primarily with how individual learning is affected by social factors such as maintaining self-confidence and making comparisons between oneself and other people. It proposes that four major sources of information are used by individuals in creating their sense of personal efficacy: *performance accomplishment, vicarious experience, verbal persuasion,* and *physiological states. Performance accomplishment* (in other words, success) raises expectations of mastery, whilst repeated failure lowers them. Once self-efficacy has been established, it tends to generalize to other situations. If the sense of self-efficacy is low, the individual's performances may be debilitated by preoccupations with personal inadequacies. Improved self-efficacy enables the individual to transfer effective behaviours to a wider range of situations and tasks.

*Vicarious experience* includes the experiences people have of seeing others perform well, sometimes under adverse conditions. By comparing themselves with others, people gain a heightened sense of self-efficacy; by seeing that others can do it, they believe they can too. Bandura says that efficacy expectations created solely by modelling them on other people's behaviour, however, are weaker and more vulnerable to change than is the experience of successful performance by oneself.

*Verbal persuasion* is known to have an important influence on people's sense of self-efficacy. Individuals can be encouraged to believe they will succeed through suggestion and coaching. This persuasion must take place in conditions that allow improvement and effective performance to occur; otherwise, the persuaders will be discredited in the eyes of the individuals learning to achieve mastery if they fail to perform effectively due to unfavourable conditions.

The *physiological state* that affects self-efficacy is emotional arousal, high arousal usually debilitating performance. Increased levels of anxiety and fear will negatively influence individuals' sense of self-efficacy by provoking imagined threats that far exceed the actual threat of the situation. Self-efficacy is much more likely to improve where the individual feels that the successful performance was the result of skill rather than luck.

Bandura's theory of social learning helps to explain why some company training programmes spend considerable time motivating employees to hold a high sense of self-efficacy. Perhaps the most surprising and important assertion of self-efficacy theory is that perceived self-efficacy proves to be a better predictor of behaviour than does past performance.

## Hackman and Oldham on Job Design

Hackman and Oldham's research on job design follows in the tradition of expectancy theory with its assumption that individuals are motivated by outcomes that they value. It extends Porter and Lawler's work by identifying job characteristics likely to motivate individuals, although to different degrees according to their individual psychology and values. They argued in 1976, similar to Herzberg on job enrichment, that motivation is concerned with effective design of jobs and matching the correct people to the work required:

When people are well matched with their jobs, it rarely is necessary to force, coerce, bribe, or trick them into working hard and trying to perform the job well. Instead, they try to do well because it is rewarding and satisfying to do so.[14]

Hackman and Oldham recommend three conditions for internal motivation. First, the individual must have knowledge of the results of his or her work; otherwise, it will be difficult to be emotionally influenced by the outcomes. Second, the individual must experience responsibility for the results of work. People must be allowed to take initiative and feel pride in the results when they do well, and feel concern when goals are not achieved. Third, the individual must experience work as being meaningful. Hackman and Oldham say that when all three of these factors are present, strong internal work motivation will develop and is likely to persist. Their view is that motivation at work has more to do with the design of tasks and jobs than it has to do with individual dispositions.

The authors also propose five job characteristics that lead individuals to experience their work as being meaningful, possessing responsibility, and enabling knowledge of results. The five characteristics are *skill variety, task identity, task significance, autonomy,* and *feedback from the job.* The first three lead to experiencing work as meaningful; the fourth, autonomy, leads to experiencing responsibility for outcomes of the work; and the fifth leads to knowing the actual results of the work (see Fig. 6.3).

*Skill variety* is the number of different skills required to do the work. *Task identity* is the extent to which the job has an identifiable beginning and end with a visible outcome. In other words, people must feel that they are doing more than a mundane, pointless task. *Task significance* is the degree to which the job is felt to affect other people's lives. Hackman and Oldham observe that the three different task characteristics may occur at quite different levels and still be meaningful to any one individual. For example, two out of these three characteristics may be quite low and yet the task still be found to be motivating. For other employees, all three may have to be high before they will experience the work as meaningful. *Autonomy* is defined by the authors as 'the degree to which the job provides substantial freedom, independence, and discretion to the individual in scheduling the work and in determining the procedures

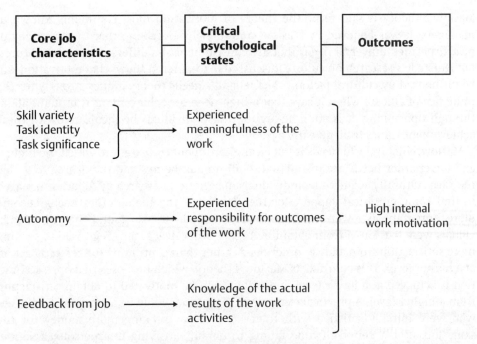

**Figure 6.3  Hackman and Oldham's job characteristics**

*Source:* J. Hackman and G. Oldham, *Work Redesign* (Figure 4.6, p. 90) © 1980 by Addison Wesley Publishing Co., Inc. Reprinted by Addison Wesley Longman.

to be used in carrying it out'.[15] As autonomy increases, individuals will feel more responsible for their work and also more accountable. Knowledge of results comes through *job feedback*, either from people or via machine. The feedback must be directly linked to the job the individual is doing. Individual differences are important in determining how each employee is motivated by his or her work. Three characteristics seem to be especially important: the level of knowledge and skill; the psychological need for growth and personal learning (some have stronger growth needs than others); and the degree to which the individual is satisfied with the work context. People who are not satisfied with their pay, job security, co-workers, and supervisors will not respond as positively to jobs designed to be motivating. It is commonly thought that when employees are demotivated and dissatisfied, they are less likely to provide a satisfactory service for customers. There is some research evidence to support this; for example, a survey of Sainsbury's employees' attitudes suggests that the more satisfied they are at work, the happier customers are with the service they receive.[16]

# Limitations of Content and Process Theories

Content and process theories of motivation can help managers understand how to better motivate their employees. The content theories, concentrating on what motivates people, show the importance of satisfying higher- and lower-order needs.

Maslow's theory is said to be the theory of motivation most commonly known to managers. It was believed by Maslow, and later by Herzberg, that the hierarchy of needs specified universal needs that are consistent across different national cultures, but Hofstede's research on culture (discussed in Chapter 5) shows that motivation will be influenced by cultural factors.[17] McClelland's needs theory argues strongly for the influence of culture when it says that a high need for achievement is brought about through upbringing. It is vital, he argues, that individuals be inculcated with these achievement values from an early age.

Maslow's hierarchy of needs is not clear, then, about the extent to which the higher- and lower-order needs are instinctual to all human beings and the degree to which they are culturally acquired by individuals in societies. Research by Alderfer managed to find some empirical support for the claim that the higher-order needs become more important as lower-order needs are satisfied. He also found that when individuals were frustrated from obtaining higher-order needs, they regressed to seeking more satisfaction from a lower-order need rather than continuing to seek satisfaction at a higher level. This contradicts Maslow's theory, which proposes that once satisfaction is achieved at a lower level, individuals will be motivated to obtain satisfaction from a higher level. A practical example of regression would be a group of employees who were initially satisfied with their level of pay seeking more money for the same job after a period of time failing to obtain satisfying interpersonal relationships within the workplace.[18] Salancik and Pfeffer observe that the overall research evidence supporting the hierarchy of needs is slight. The findings of research studies on the hierarchy can be explained by other theories that appear to be equally plausible to Maslow's explanation.[19] Nevertheless, despite these shortcomings, content theories—and especially Maslow's—remain the best-known to people in business.

Process theories of motivation, whether primarily concerned with job satisfaction, general motivation, or job design, tend to be formulated in terms of expectancy theory. The theory is helpful to managers in reminding them that they must take account of individual differences between employees. The reward system, to an extent, must be capable of catering for employees' different needs and perceptions. Expectancy theory shows that individuals make different evaluations of actions, goal achievement, and the connections between actions and rewards. Expectancy theory is, however, a complex needs-satisfaction model of motivation that has been criticized for its lack of simplicity in guiding management action.[20] Process theories, from the point of view of guiding managerial practice, have the advantage over content theories by explaining how people are motivated. However, managers have found it difficult to ascertain how to implement expectancy theory in their organizations, and have often been sceptical of the benefit gained from doing so. Hackman and Oldham's theory of job design is a useful version of expectancy theory because it prescribes five specific areas of work organization to which management should attend and to which they often can attend in practice. Their theory concentrates attention on designing jobs so that improved processes of individual motivation are more likely to result.

Content and process theories of motivation are helpful for gaining a better understanding of how individuals can be motivated. However, they have been criticized for the limited extent to which their principles can be applied in practice, for being biased towards Western individualist culture, and for presenting, usually implicitly, a male-dominated view of work and family. This last criticism concerning gender bias argues that these motivation theories adopt an essentially male perspective whenever they assert that relationships with others are fundamentally of lower order and of less value than individual achievement.[21] To end this section on a more general point, the theories that have been discussed so far highlight individual differences of motivation and do not accord much significance to the role of the group and environmental factors.

# 2  Motivating Groups

THIS second section reviews three theories that focus—more than those discussed so far—on the role played in motivation by the social group. It introduces equity, agency, and stewardship theories of motivation. Equity theory considers how an individual's motivation is influenced by his or her perception of the group. Agency and stewardship theories aim to explain what motivates groups, particularly management. They make assumptions about *how* managers should be motivated (process) on the basis of fundamentally different assumptions about human nature and *what* motivates management (content). The agency perspective is more consistent with hard HRM (controlling), and the stewardship perspective with soft HRM (employee commitment).

## Equity Theory

The equity theory of motivation aims to explain the way that employees agree a 'fair rate for the job'. Adams says that individuals compare what they contribute to the employment relationship and what they receive from it in return. Contributions include effort, skills, training, and seniority, while returns are pay, fringe benefits, recognition, status, and promotion. Employees compare their contributions and returns with those of other employees and, if dissatisfied by the comparison, will reduce their effort, seek a pay rise or promotion, or attempt to reconcile their dissatisfaction either by rationalizing the differences in contributions and returns between themselves and others as being fair or by selecting another reference group to compare themselves against.[22]

Equity theory demonstrates that individuals are concerned not only with the total reward package they get but how this compares with what others who are in a similar position receive. Empirical research on equity theory shows that employees are motivated by a sense of distributive justice; that is, employees are more motivated where they perceive rewards to be fairly distributed between people.

Adams studied how people responded to others' being paid more or less than themselves and found that they will do one of six things:

1. People will maximize returns that they value (because these are what are most important).
2. They will minimize contributions that require effort and change.
3. They will resist changes that are a strong challenge to their self-concept and self-esteem.
4. They will resist changing themselves more than they will resist reconsidering the equity of others' contributions and returns.
5. They will quit their jobs only when they perceive there to be a very high level of inequity and when they can find no other means of reducing the sense of unfairness. If the inequity is felt less strongly, absenteeism results.
6. Once the individual has established a sense of what is fair, this viewpoint becomes stable over time and part of the individual's sense of security.[23]

Jaques recommended that pay must pass the 'felt fair' principle. Employees have standards for what constitutes fair payment that are shared unconsciously among the work population of any given country. When an individual assesses his or her pay against that of another employee, that employee's pay must be in line with what is thought to be a fair rate for the job, and the individual must be perceived by others as capable of performing the job.[24] Armstrong observes that this 'felt fair' principle is one of the most common methods used for determining employee rewards.[25] The principle is applied in collective agreements, where they still exist, between management and trade unions at national, regional, and local levels of bargaining. It is also applied in negotiating an individual's rewards. The same basic principle applies in employment contracts, whatever the size of the business, although what is felt to be fair by employers and employees in a large *Times* 500 organization can be very different from what is felt to be fair in a small local business. What is felt fair will also differ by region and by country. It is common for employers to offer higher rates of pay in more prosperous areas. Employees who are doing the same job in the south-east of England will often expect to be paid more than those working in other regions where the cost of living is lower. Even in occupations where there are fixed national rates of pay, there may be extras, such as a London weighting allowance. At the country level, different expectations and customary practices will influence what is thought to be a fair reward. In Thailand, for example, large domestic companies automatically increase pay annually to match the rate of inflation. Torrington and Chee Huat examined some of the differences in human resource management that play an important role in determining employees' expectations in East Asian countries.[26] In Singapore, all employers are required to contribute to the Central Provident Fund, which is a mandatory saving scheme providing for retirement and medical benefits. Singaporean employees' contributions are high compared to contributions in other countries, and a worker coming to live in Singapore may take time to adjust to feeling that the higher contribution rates are fair.

# Two Theories of Management Motivation

Agency and stewardship theories are two contrasting views of what motivates management. Agency theory has hard HRM's emphasis on control and rewarding required behaviour, and stewardship theory has soft HRM's attention to employee commitment and influence.

Agency theory is an economic theory that has been widely used in management education and training within business schools. Agency theory predicts that owners (or 'principals') and managers (or 'agents') will behave differently in serving their own interests and that these will differ from each other: principals seek to maximize their wealth and managers follow their own interests, which will not always be consistent with principals' interests. The theory advises owners to 'incentivize' managers to serve the interests of owners' capital by rewarding and controlling the managers to pursue the owners' interests.

Gomez-Mejia and Balkin have criticized agency theory for being too managerialist and for recommending that managers treat employees as objects.[27] The theory is highly instrumentalist in that it views employees as a means to management's ends rather than as having legitimate ends of their own. Agency theory is, however, reasonably effective in explaining the differential reward systems found in the UK and USA for senior managers and other employees. In most organizations, managers receive higher pay than other employees do, and better fringe benefits, often enjoying privileged access to more company shares, larger profit-related payments, and higher performance bonuses. These differences in the reward system are in response to a range of factors; nevertheless they can be seen as empirical evidence supporting agency theory's proposition that principals (owners) seek to ensure that their agents (managers) identify with principals' needs.

Agency theory assumes principals and agents have divergent interests that must be curbed by controls. It assumes that agents are highly competitive, individualistic, opportunistic, and self-serving. Davis, Schoorman, and Donaldson propose that those assumptions can be reversed to depict subordinates as collectivist, pro-organizational, and worthy of trust.[28] They argue that while agency theory provides a useful way of explaining how divergent interests can be better aligned through proper monitoring and a well-planned reward system, further theory is needed that takes a broader view than this restrictive economic perspective.

Stewardship theory states the reverse of agency theory, saying that top management, as stewards, or custodians, are motivated in the best interests of their principals.[29] Stewards place a higher value on co-operation than they do on independently seeking their own interests. They prefer co-operation to conflict and are rational, usually thinking sensibly and judiciously about what is expected of them. They are collectivist in orientation rather than individualist and therefore work towards the best interests of the group rather than selfishly seeking to satisfy their own needs in preference to those of other people. Stewardship theory warns against too much control over managers (acting as stewards) by principals because it reduces motivation and can hinder pro-organizational behaviour by the stewards. Managers' autonomy, it proposes, should be extended because they can be trusted. The two theories are very different in motivational terms: agency theory focuses on extrinsic rewards, which have a measurable market value, and stewardship theory focuses on intrinsic rewards, which are less easily quantified.

Stewardship theory, recalling Maslow and McClelland, is particularly interested in the higher-order needs of growth, achievement, affiliation, and self-actualization. In stewardship theory, people who are motivated by higher-order needs are more likely to become stewards. Stewards are motivated by intrinsic factors more than by extrinsic factors; identify highly with the organization; have high value commitments, being sincere about their ethical responsibility and work duties; will use their personal power rather than institutional power when influencing others; will try to involve employees rather than simply control them; survive better in collectivist cultures than in individualist cultures; and prefer to use lower power distance rather than high power distance (as discussed in Chapter 5) in managing others. Davis *et al.* propose that management following the principles of stewardship theory will maximize the performance of the firm and minimize costs.[30]

## Limitations

Equity theory is a theory of individual motivation that predicts individuals will make different assessments about the equity of their rewards at work. It is a theory about how groups are motivated in so far as it assumes individual motivation is fundamentally connected with judgements about the equity with which other comparable people or reference groups are treated. Equity theory predicts an employee is motivated or demotivated by judgements about the distributive justice of rewards. It is a more altruistic theory of human nature than expectancy theory. Equity theory predicts that individuals will seek to maximize equity so that a higher piece-rate worker (one who receives, for example, 50p per unit rather than 25p per unit) would feel motivated to produce less output and higher-quality work than workers on the lower rate would. In this way, the individual hopes to restore equity in the group by personally achieving a lower rate combined with high-quality work that requires a high degree of effort. Expectancy theory, on the other hand, is a hedonistic theory predicting that the individual rewarded with a higher piece rate would seek to maximize satisfaction by greater output and do so without additional attention to the quality of the work. Research on equity theory has found that employees can be subdivided into two groups, those who are relatively altruistic and behave consistently with the theory and those who are relatively less altruistic and behave more hedonistically.[31]

Agency and stewardship theories are relevant to an understanding of how individuals are motivated by interests common to the group. These theories are concerned primarily with two groups: owners and managers. Agency theory is an economic theory that implies a unitarist organization can be achieved through controlling and motivating managers to behave in the interests of owners. The theory assumes that owners' and managers' interests are in conflict but that they can be aligned more closely through appropriate controls and incentives. Stewardship theory is more collectivist than agency theory and assumes unitarism is a natural condition for a proportion of the human population. The theory predicts that through the appropriate controls and cultural context, owners will maximize managers' capability to look after owners' interests. In short, it is based on the assumption that shared interests are already managers' natural inclination.

The core content of both theories has less to say about motivation of non-managerial employees, who form the bulk of the workforce in most organizations. The two theories are therefore difficult to generalize into guidelines for HR policy and practice, although as was mentioned in the previous section, agency theory has a general affinity with hard HRM because both are based on the philosophy that human beings are rational, calculating, and self-interested beings. There is also a similarity in the assumptions of stewardship theory with soft HRM because both assume that managers will be highly committed to owners' interests whenever importance is attached to the collective interest and steps are taken to engender trust. Agency and stewardship theories are both of limited application to the broader external political environment and lack substantive historical justification. One of their most frequently quoted limiting assumptions is that motivation is determined by rational processes of decision making, even though there is considerable evidence that people often are constrained as to the options open to them in the social environment and do not habitually make decisions by a rational consideration of alternatives.[32] However, this should not become a justification for extreme and irrational methods of motivation. Unfortunately, there are occasional incidents of excessive attempts at motivating employees; for example, in July 1998 trainees in a major insurance company were encouraged to walk over hot coals with the result that seven of them needed hospital treatment.[33]

# Summary

T HREE content theories of motivation were discussed and it was noted that they all propose that people are motivated by higher-order and lower-order needs. It was found that while soft HRM aims to motivate employees by appealing to higher-order needs, hard HRM places less importance on the fulfilment of higher-order needs by concentrating specifically on motivating people only in so far as it is a means of serving the organization's strategy. Both the content theories and the four process theories that were introduced represent motivation from the perspective of individual psychology and some, such as Hackman and Oldham's theory of job design, contain prescriptions for implementing HRM. Equity theory describes how individuals are motivated by comparing themselves to other people, and the concept of what constitutes fair treatment and remuneration continues to be an important component of pay surveys and decisions on rewards policy. Agency and stakeholder theory describes ways that managers should be controlled and motivated, but is of limited application to motivating non-managerial employees. Agency theory is arguably a product of Western, individualist business thinking, stewardship theory being better suited to collectivist orientations or culture, for example, Japanese management practices. Lastly, from the industrial relations perspective, all of the motivation theories discussed tend to play down fundamental tensions and differences of interest between owners, management, and employees.

BOX 6.1
**Case Study—Motivating the Team: The HR Initiatives of a Retail Store Supervisor**

*Introduction*

Treyer is the food-store chain of Jack Macadam Holding Company Ltd. The stores tend to be smaller than those of the major players in the food retailing industry. Treyer's major competitors are Marks & Spencer and Waitrose rather than the high-volume retailers Sainsbury's and Tesco. The company has never deviated from its policy of being a provider to profitable niche markets, particularly in middle-class catchment areas. Many of the newer stores are on the edge of towns and cities, following the lead of the big players, who during the 1980s and 1990s located on the periphery of urban centres. However, the company has retained a strong base of centrally located stores and expects more competition now that major retailers are opening stores again in population centres. Distribution takes place from the central warehouse in Reading and many of the stores are located in the wealthier areas of south and central England.

Each Treyer store has a common structure and is divided into separate sections of food goods, fruit and vegetables, fish, meat and delicatessen, bakery, and general grocery products. The company's mission statement makes clear its belief that success is based on the provision of quality produce, a variety of food goods, value for money, honesty, and high standards of service.

*Appointment of new supervisor*

Imagine you are studying for an undergraduate degree at university and, in addition, have undertaken part-time employment in order to make some money and gain work experience. You have been working for a month in your local Treyer store, and before commencing employment you attended a short management training course. You were appointed weekend supervisor for the fruit and vegetable section. Currently, you are working two evenings a week and all day every Saturday.

*Poor motivation in the store*

The fruit and vegetable section suffers from poor standards of produce presentation and poor quality and inadequate levels of stock. The store has a small number of full-time staff who generally are of mature age; however, a considerable contribution to the work effort is made up by 'weekenders', who are usually teenagers from the local schools. Weekenders work at Treyer part time during weekday evenings and all day on Saturdays.

There were approximately twelve part-time staff or 'weekenders' at the time you were appointed. Immediately after your first week, the low morale of staff became obvious. General standards of discipline amongst the weekenders were inadequate, including an unsatisfactory level of personal presentation. A cursory inspection of employees' records also revealed the level of absenteeism to be quite high. At the end of your first month, you attended a management meeting at which you found out that the store had serious business problems: financial targets were not being met and levels of produce wastage were too high. You felt that some change was required, but before taking action decided to make a written assessment of the problems you would have to tackle in the fruit and vegetable section.

The heart of these problems, you were sure, lay in human resource management short-comings. There were no serious difficulties with delivery by suppliers, nor was there a problem with the quality of incoming goods on arrival at the store. You summarized the store's difficulties as requiring action in three key areas.

First, Treyer has a top-down management style and systems that are felt to be oppressive by almost all of the full-time and part-time employees. The main complaint is that there is a lack of two-way communication between the employees and their section managers and, further up the organization, between the employees and the assistant branch manager. Second, although the store's workforce is divided into teams, a general lack of team spirit is evident. This has caused people to feel demotivated and lacking direction. Third, your conversations with people have made it clear that there is a general lack of training, making it difficult for them to do their jobs properly.

You decided to divide your assessment of the HR problems into two main areas: those which, specifically in the fruit and vegetable section, could be tackled extensively by your own management initiative, and could likewise be dealt with successfully by other section managers, and then those areas that required the implementation of solutions involving higher levels of management.

You appreciated the need for everyone in the Treyer store to work as a team and implement store-wide changes; however, you also were aware how much of an influence you personally could have on improving morale. You decided to get started with training the weekenders more effectively. Treyer already had quite a strong training programme in place; the problem was that nobody in your store seemed to know about it except the few new weekend supervisors who had been trained for their jobs. The programme for week-enders took the form of a short module focused on particular topics, followed by a small number of questions to check for trainees' understanding of the material.

You introduced the training programme for the weekenders working in fruit and veget-ables and obtained permission for them to be released from their duties for half an hour each week during work time. The new training programme was supported by your own vigorous presence on the shopfloor. The pay-off in HR terms was immediate: your week-enders became more capable of doing their jobs, started to take more initiative, particu-larly with ordering of stock and presentation of goods. By the end of your third month, there were improved financial results in your section in the form of increased sales and significantly lower levels of stock wastage.

*Case Study Activity*
Analyse employee motivation in the Treyer case by applying theories of motivation.

# Study Questions

1   Define what is a content theory of motivation. Compare and contrast the three content theories discussed in the chapter: Maslow, McClelland, and Herzberg.

2   Define what is a process theory of motivation. Compare and contrast the four process theories discussed in the chapter: Latham and Locke, Porter and Lawler, Bandura, and Hackman and Oldham.

3   Evaluate hard and soft HRM using content theories of motivation and then using process theories of motivation.

4   Analyse Storey's twenty-five-item checklist on HRM and personnel management (see Chapter 1) by classifying the items according to concepts from agency and stewardship theory.

5   Select two theories of motivation and explain how they can be used to improve policy and practice in HRM.

# Further Reading

Davis, J. H., Schoorman, F. D., and Donaldson, L., 'Toward a stewardship theory of management', *Academy of Management Review* (1997), 22, 1, p. 20–47.

Vecchio, R. P., *Organizational Behavior*, 3rd edn. (Orlando, FL: The Dryden Press, 1995), chapter 5, pp. 182–213, and chapter 6, pp. 214–57.

Vroom, V. H. and Deci, E. L. (eds.), *Management and Motivation*, 2nd edn. (Harmondsworth: Penguin Books, 1992).

Wilson, F. M., *Organizational Behaviour and Gender*, (Maidenhead: McGraw-Hill, 1995), chapter 4, pp. 125–51.

# Notes

1.  Maslow, A. H., 'A Theory of Human Motivation', *Psychological Review* (1943), 50, pp. 370–96.
2.  Salancik, G. R. and Pfeffer, J., 'An Examination of Need Satisfaction Models of Job Attitudes', *Administrative Science Quarterly* (1977), 22, pp. 427–56.

3. Watson, T. J., *In Search of Management*,(London: Routledge, 1994), p. 60; Vecchio, R. P., *Organizational Behaviour*, 3rd edn., (Orlando, FL: The Dryden Press, Harcourt Brace & Company, 1995), p. 190.

4. McClelland, D. C., *The Achieving Society* (Princeton, NJ: Van Nostrand, 1961).

5. *Harvard Business Review* (Sept–Oct 1987), p. 117.

6. Vecchio defines organizational behaviour as follows: it 'is concerned with the scientific study of the behavioral processes that occur in work settings . . . The content of this field is quite broad. It encompasses such topics as employee attitudes, motivation, and performance, to name a few. And it extends to larger organizational and environmental pressures, that influence an individual's behavior and attitudes. . . .' Vecchio, R. P., *Organizational Behaviour*, 3rd edn. (Orlando, FL: The Dryden Press, Harcourt Brace & Company, 1995), p. 4.

7. Hofstede, G., *Culture's Consequences: International Differences in Work Related Values* (Beverly Hills: Sage, 1980).

8. Wilson, F. M., *Organizational Behaviour and Gender* (Maidenhead: McGraw-Hill, 1995). Webb, J., 'The open door? Women and equal opportunity at ComCo (North)', in D. Gowler, K. Legge and C. Clegg, *Case studies in Organizational Behaviour and Human Resource Management*, 2nd edn. (London: Paul Chapman Publishing, 1993).

9. Latham, G. P. and Locke, E. A., 'Goal setting: a motivational technique that works', *Organizational Dynamics* (1979), 8, 2, pp. 68–80.

10. Vroom, V. H., *Work and Motivation* (New York: Wiley, 1964).

11. Porter, L. W. and Lawler III, E. E., *Managerial Attitudes and Performance* (Homewood, IL.: Irwin-Dorsey, 1968).

12. Bandura, A., 'Self-efficacy: Toward a Unifying Theory of Behavioural Change', *Psychological Review* (1977), Vol. 84, pp. 191–215; Bandura, A., *Social Learning Theory* (Englewood Cliffs, NJ : Prentice Hall, 1977).

13. Estes, W. K., 'Reinforcement in human behavior', *American Scientist* (1972), 60, pp. 723–9.

14. Hackman and Oldman quoted in Vroom, V. H. and Deci, E. L. (eds.), *Management and Motivation*, 2nd edn. (Harmondsworth: Penguin Books, 1992) p. 260.

15. Ibid., p. 263; Hackman, J. R. and Oldham, G. R., *Work Redesign* (Reading, MA: Addison-Wesley, 1980); Hackman, J. R. and Oldham, G. R., 'Motivation through the design of work: test of a theory', *Organizational Behavior and Human Performance* (1976) 16, pp. 250–79.

16. *People Management*, 4, 24, 10 December 1998, p. 14.

17. Hofstede, G., *Culture's Consequences: International Differences in Work Related Values* (Beverly Hills: Sage, 1980).

18. Alderfer simplified Maslow's hierarchy by subdividing it into three levels of need (existence, relatedness, and growth). Alderfer, C. P., *Existence, Relatedness and Growth* (New York: Free Press, 1972).

19. Salancik, G. R. and Pfeffer, J., 'An examination of need satisfaction models of job attitudes', *Administrative Science Quarterly* (1977), 22, pp. 427–56.

20. Ibid.

21. Robbins, S. P., *Organizational Behaviour: Concepts, Controversies, Applications* (Upper Saddle River, NJ: Prentice-Hall, 1998) p. 175; Wilson, *Organizational Behaviour and Gender* (n. 8 above), p. 139.

22. Adams, J. S., 'Toward an understanding of inequity', *Journal of Abnormal and Social Psychology* (1963), 67, pp. 422–36.

23. Adams, J. S., 'Inequity in social exchange', in L. Berkowitz (ed.), *Advances in Experimental Social Psychology*, Vol. 2 (New York: Academic Press, 1965), pp. 267–99.

24. Jaques, E., *Equitable Payment* (New York: Wiley, 1961).

25. Armstrong, M., *Employee Reward* (London: Institute of Personnel and Development, 1996).

26. Torrington, D. and Chee Huat, T., *Human Resource Management for South-east Asia* (London: Prentice-Hall International (UK) Ltd, 1994).

27. Gomez-Mejia, L. R. and Balkin, D. B., *Compensation, Organisational Strategy, and Firm Performance* (Cincinnati: Southwestern Publishing, 1992).

28. Davis, J. H., Schoorman, F. D., Donaldson, L., 'Toward a stewardship theory of management', *Academy of Management Review* (1997), 22, 1, pp. 20–47.

29. Donaldson, L. and Davis, J. H., 'CEO Governance and Shareholder Returns: Agency Theory or Stewardship Theory', Paper presented at the annual meeting of the Academy of Management, Washington, DC, 1989; Donaldson, L. and Davis, J. H., 'Stewardship Theory or Agency Theory: CEO Governance and Shareholder Returns', *Australian Journal of Management* (1991), 16, pp. 49–64.

30. Davis *et al.*, 'Toward a stewardship theory of management'.

31. Vecchio, *Organizational Behaviour* (n. 6 above), p. 203.

32. Pettigrew, A., *The Politics of Organisational Decision Making* (London: Tavistock, 1973). Landy, F. J. and Becker, W. S., 'Motivation theory reconsidered', in L. L. Cummings and B. M. Staw (eds.), *Research in Organizational Behaviour*, Vol. 9 (Greenwich, CT: JAI Press, 1987).

33. *People Management*, 4, 25, 24 December 1998, p. 16.

# Chapter 7

# Financial Rewards and Performance Management

## Chapter Contents

Introduction

# Introduction

CHAPTER 4 on trade unions and industrial relations described how, in the UK, national and local systems of collective bargaining for pay determination are less common in the 1990s than they were in the 1970s. The reduction in collective bargaining arrangements has been accompanied by increased implementation of individualized rewards and performance-related pay. The new structures and systems of rewards for individual, group, and organizational performance have been accompanied by greater experimentation in formal systems of what is called 'performance management'. This chapter provides an overview of the different types of financial reward, having already explored the issues of non-financial reward extensively in the context of motivating individuals and groups in Chapter 6. It also introduces the concept of performance management, ending with an overview of Guest's proposed links between HRM and performance.

# 1 Financial Rewards

## Reward Systems

FIGURE 7.1, taken from Michael Armstrong, shows the main processes of financial rewards. As the top of the diagram depicts, reward strategy has to be consistent with human resource (or personnel) strategy, which should be in line with business strategy. The implementation of a reward strategy will feed modifications back to the human resource strategy, which in turn should lead to some modification of the business strategy. At the next level of the diagram, we see that the implementation of the reward strategy has three basic components: financial rewards, performance management, and non-financial rewards. The non-financial reward processes are designed to motivate employees through recognition, responsibility, achievement, development, and growth. According to this model, these motivators should be outcomes of the performance management processes and, following the arrows of the diagram, lead to improved individual and team performance and, from there, to improved organizational effectiveness.

The performance-management process also, as shown, feeds into the reward of variable pay, especially pay according to performance. Armstrong subdivides financial reward processes into three key areas: base pay, employee benefits, and variable pay. Base pay is determined through job evaluation studies and pay surveys that inform the

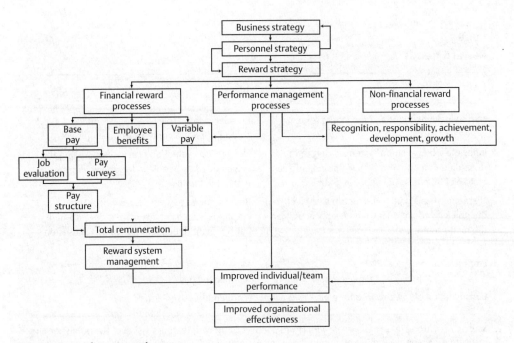

**Figure 7.1 The reward system**

*Source*: Taken from *Employee Reward* by Michael Armstrong, 1996, Figure 1, p. 7, with the permission of the publisher, the Institute of Personnel and Development, IPD House, Camp Road, London SW19 4UX.

pay structure. Employee benefits (such as company pensions and healthcare schemes) and variable pay (for example, profit sharing and bonus payments) are determined according to minimum standards set by national legislation and influenced by the requirements of the Inland Revenue and by custom and practice within the organization. All three taken together make up the total remuneration received by the individual. Where the financial reward system is motivating, improved individual and team performance should result.

Government and employers' attitudes towards rewards have been changing over the last two decades of the twentieth century. Armstrong characterizes these trends as a move away from hierarchical and rigid pay structures towards more team-based and flexible systems. His table of recent reward trends is reproduced in Table 7.1. The older systems, on the left of the table, tend to award pay according to narrowly defined jobs. The main way of obtaining more pay is through promotion; there is only some emphasis on performance-related pay, rewards tending to be consolidated around base pay. More recent trends in reward-management systems have emphasized skill and competence development; personnel development plans, according to research by the Institute of Personnel and Development (IPD), are a popular component of these systems. However, there has been less evidence of competences playing a fundamental role in organizations' pay systems, except for those engaging in organizational transformation and culture change.[1] There have also been concerted efforts to increase employees' co-operation with each other through job evaluation

TABLE 7.1
**Reward trends**

| From | To |
| --- | --- |
| Narrowly defined jobs and job standards | Broader generic roles—emphasis on competence and continuous development |
| Inflexible job evaluation systems sizing tasks, rewarding non-adaptive behaviour and empire-building and encouraging point-grabbing | Flexible job evaluation processes assessing the value added by people in their roles, often within job families |
| Hierarchical and rigid pay structures in which the only way to get on is to move up. Focus is on the next promotion | Broad-banded pay structures where the emphasis is on flexibility, career development pay and continuous improvement. Focus is on the next challenge |
| Emphasis on individual PRP | More focus on team performance through team-based pay |
| Consolidation of rewards into base pay | More emphasis on 'at risk' pay |

*Source*: Armstrong, M., *Employee Reward* (1996), Table 1, p. 19 with the permission of the publisher, the Institute of Personnel and Development, IPD House, Camp Road, London SW19 4UX.

processes that identify 'job families' (see the section on pay structures below) and overlapping categories. Broad-banded pay structures (see below) and increased focus on team-based pay are two important trends in the new reward systems. These approaches aim to involve employees in determining the structure of the reward systems and have the objective of aligning employees' attitudes more closely with the performance goals of the organization. However, it is debatable whether they form part of a new and distinct approach to HRM or are just a continuation of longer-term endeavours by management to link pay more closely to individual and organizational performance.[2] In Britain during the 1980s and 1990s, innovations in rewards systems, particularly performance-related pay, have been implemented so as to distinguish good performers from the rest, making output and productivity the focus more so than position in the organization.[3]

# Pay Structures and Systems

No matter how important job satisfaction and other intrinsic rewards are, the essential reward employees receive for their work is pay. Many pay structures and systems have been developed and any system, in practice, is something of a compromise between the different interests of employees and pressures from the external environment. This section is based on Armstrong's material on pay structures and pay systems. Pay structures are, as their name suggests, different structures for determining the pay for individuals and groups of employees. Pay systems are the processes of paying employees within a given structure. We now give a brief overview of each type of structure and system; as pay is a major element in the employment relationship, it is important to be familiar with these.

## Pay Structures

Any pay structure will have certain characteristics that it rewards in preference to others. Graded and broad-banded pay structures place more significance on such factors as length of employment with the organization (tenure) and progression through the organizational hierarchy. Structures such as individual pay range, job families, spot rates, and rate for age give more weight to, respectively, market rates combined with individual characteristics, occupation and expertise, external market rates of pay for particular jobs, and pay adjusted for age. Pay curves, pay spines, and integrated pay attempt to reconcile rewarding superior past performance with providing future opportunity for improved performance and potential for increased rewards for employees who were not top-rated but may be next time there is a pay review. All pay structures therefore possess some rationale and some bias as to what constitutes equitable treatment in rewarding employees.

**Graded** A conventional graded pay structure consists of a sequence of job grades into which jobs of equivalent value are fitted. Each grade has a pay range or band, offering the employee scope for progression within his or her grade (see Fig. 7.2).

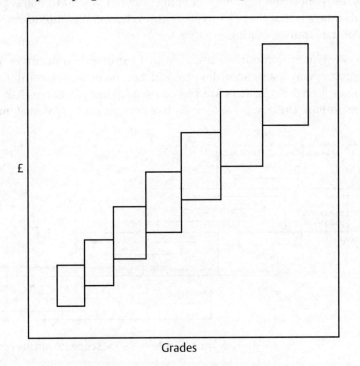

**Figure 7.2 A typical graded pay structure**

*Source:* Taken from *Employee Reward* by Michael Armstrong, 1996, Figure 13, p. 197, with the permission of the publisher, the Institute of Personnel and Development, IPD House, Camp Road, London SW19 4UX.

**Broad-banded** The recent trend has been towards reducing the number of grades and increasing the discretionary range (the range of the amount of pay or bonus an employer can award) within grades. The pay range, or band, within each grade can be made broader, and these broad-banded pay structures are used where the organization does not want to reinforce a sense of hierarchy through the pay system. Broad-banded structures allow for considerable overlap between different occupations and levels of responsibility, albeit with the maximum obtainable amount of pay usually still increasing as one progresses through the bands and being consistent with increased management responsibility. The key difference between graded and broad-banded structures is that the latter are simpler and more flexible (see Fig. 7.3).

**Individual Pay Range** Individual pay range structures specify a separate pay range for each job within categories such as senior management, middle management, and team leaders. The midpoint of the pay structure tends to be aligned with market rates, enabling the organization to compete effectively with rates of pay in comparable organizations.

**Job Families** Job family structures consist of separate pay structures for job families, which are groups of jobs evaluated as being equivalent. Each job family has its own structure that may be graded in terms of skills, competences, or responsibilities. Job family structures allow the flexibility of being able to respond to market rates; however, a disadvantage is that they can create tensions between groups of employees who do not accept the family groupings.

**Pay Curves** Pay curves, sometimes called maturity or progression curves, provide different pay progression tracks according to skill, competence, responsibility, and performance. Exceptional performers are placed on a higher pay curve than are merely effective performers. The pay curve for effective performers may stop at, for example,

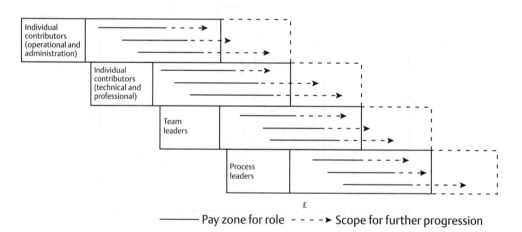

———— Pay zone for role - - - -► Scope for further progression

## Figure 7.3  A broad-banded structure

*Source:* Taken from *Employee Reward* by Michael Armstrong, 1996, Figure 14, p. 198, with the permission of the publisher, the Institute of Personnel and Development, IPD House, Camp Road, London SW19 4UX.

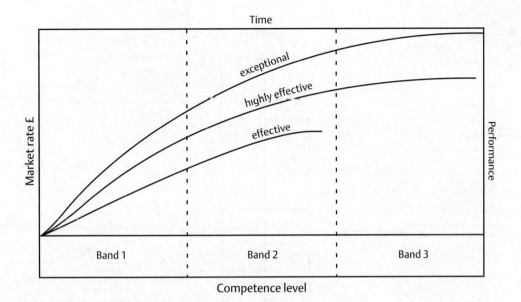

**Figure 7.4 A competence and performance-related pay curve**

*Source:* Taken from *Employee Reward* by Michael Armstrong, 1996, Figure 16, p. 201, with the permission of the publisher, the Institute of Personnel and Development, IPD House, Camp Road, London SW19 4UX.

Band 2, with only exceptional performers progressing to Band 3. Exceptional performers receive very high pay in comparison to typical market rates (see Fig. 7.4).

**Spot Rate** Spot rate or individual job rate structures use separate rates for particular jobs. These structures are used by organizations that emphasize the management's prerogative to pay whatever they wish and are useful for attracting employees with valuable skills.

**Pay Spines** Pay spines have been common in the public sector and in voluntary organizations. The various grades are organized along a single pay spine. Individuals are paid according to their grade and their point on the spine. A move to a point higher up the spine can be awarded for performance or additional responsibilities (see Fig. 7.5).

**Integrated Pay Structures** Integrated pay structures have become more popular and have been introduced to facilitate flexible working by reducing the barriers created by occupational and hierarchical pay structures. They have been commonly used during organizational change, especially in cases of de-layering the organizational hierarchy and downsizing. They also have been implemented whenever the company philosophy has moved towards single-status employment policies, whereby the organization deliberately reduces hierarchical status distinctions between employees to improve communication. These policies in the UK have often attempted to mimic either Japanese management practices or the HRM single-status policies of some US firms. For example, in 1987 the UK cable manufacturer Optical Fibres introduced a pay policy of no distinction between clerical and manufacturing workers so that all employees were to be paid a salary rather than manufacturing workers being paid

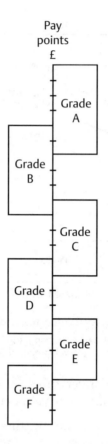

**Figure 7.5 A pay spine**

*Source:* Taken from *Employee Reward* by Michael Armstrong, 1996, Figure 17, p. 202, with the permission of the publisher, the Institute of Personnel and Development, IPD House, Camp Road, London SW19 4UX.

according to number of hours worked.[4] The introduction of new technologies in the workplace has also spurred a move towards a more integrated pay structure with the aim of encouraging greater co-operation, communication, task sharing, flexible practices, and skill development.

**Rate for Age** Rate-for-age scales link pay to the age of employees and have become relatively uncommon, although they are still used with the younger workforce, particularly young adults on formal training schemes. More recently, the UK minimum wage has included a scaling factor for young adult employees, whereby they receive a lower minimum wage than the standard.

## Payment Systems

This section reviews payment systems, commencing with the time-rate system, which is one of the most common. The other systems are divided into two categories, those that reward individual or group performance and those that reward organizational performance.

**Time Rates** Time-rate systems reward the employee for a unit of attendance at work—an hour, day, week, month, or year. Time rates are one of the most commonly used pay systems. They are relatively simple and cheap to administer and help managers forecast human resource costs. They have the advantage of being easily understood by employees, although a criticism from the perspective of HRM would be that they do not motivate performance well because there is little incentive to improve productivity or efficiency. Nevertheless, they have remained a popular payment system in the USA and UK during the 1990s.

## Rewards for Individual or Group Performance

### Individual Piecework

Individual piecework (straight piecework) schemes reward individuals directly according to their work output and have been common in agriculture for hundreds of years, although it is only in more recent centuries that individual productivity has been directly and routinely tied to monetary payment. Piecework remuneration was common in, for example, the wool and textile trade during medieval times and in manufacturing industry since the beginning of the Industrial Revolution, although it is less common now than it was at the beginning of the twentieth century. The advantages of piecework systems are that they are simple to understand and make it easy for employees to predict their earnings according to their rate of work. From the employers' perspective, piecework motivates individuals to work quickly and labour costs are directly related to the pace of work and its consequent level of productivity. A disadvantage of individual piecework systems for employers is that the quality of work often suffers from the rush to obtain high rates of output. For employees, piecework may cause undue stress and poor health after a sustained period of working.

### Work-measured Schemes

In work-measured schemes, which became popular in the 1950s and 1960s, a job or its component tasks are measured and a standard time established for performing them. These schemes reward employees for performance above the standard. They have the advantage that pay is related to productivity, the employee being expected to perform to at least the standard rate of time allowed for the job. The employee has the incentive to work harder than the standard rate, and also has the flexibility of being able to vary output according to circumstances and motivation. For a work-measured scheme to be effective, it is vital that the work be measured accurately, because employees have an incentive to exaggerate the time necessary to perform tasks in order to make incentive payments easier to obtain.

### Measured Day Work

Measured day work schemes use techniques of work measurement to determine the level of performance expected of an employee and then set an appropriate level of payment.[5] Measured day work schemes were popular in the 1960s and 1970s, when it was important for management to secure predictable levels of productivity to meet market demand. Under measured day work, the employees' pay includes an incentive payment that assumes output will be in accordance with the rate agreed. These schemes were often the subject of collective bargaining and negotiation between management and unions, and the incentive payment was given in advance, therefore obliging employees to achieve the agreed rate of productivity.

The advantages of measured day work schemes from management's point of view are that they retain freedom to deploy the workforce in the most efficient way and they encourage a high and steady rate of output. These schemes have, in the past, recognized and rewarded differentials between occupational groups of employees —for example, skilled and semi-skilled workers. This was often felt to be vitally important by unions and their members. The disadvantages of these schemes are that there is no direct individual incentive for high performance and little encouragement for innovation or improved methods of working. The individual has no control over earnings because there is no direct relationship between the individual effort made and the rewards obtained.

### Group or Team Incentives

Group incentive schemes reward the group or team with a cash payment for production output that meets an agreed target. The payment may be an equal amount to each individual or it may be made on an agreed proportional basis. Group or team incentives are a form of piecework incentive scheme that is nowadays regarded by managers as being too difficult to control.[6] These payment by results (PBR) schemes have the advantage of encouraging group discipline and teamwork, but they have the disadvantage that output can be restricted by the group because it is individual employees who determine what level of earnings they wish to achieve. This incentive scheme—in common with individual piecework, work measured, and measured day work—stresses rates and levels of productivity, while many companies now have to concentrate as much on quality as on quantity. Recent case study research on team performance— in small and medium-sized firms, pharmaceutical companies, and two call centres of large organizations—found that the more successful team initiatives paid close attention to recruitment, selection, training, and rewards. In some of the companies, unforeseen difficulties were encountered in establishing appropriate pay levels; therefore, team incentives and team-based pay should be planned before new teams are created.[7]

### Individual and Group Bonuses

Bonuses are granted in addition to base salary and paid to either individuals or groups as a reward for achievement or for completion of a project. Many reward systems incorporate individual and group bonus schemes. The advantage of individual bonus schemes is that if individuals are motivated by the bonuses to achieve targets, the schemes can be relatively easy to administer. Individual bonus systems become difficult to operate where the outputs of work are intangible, as is typical of most services, and bonus schemes can encourage individualistic and uncooperative behaviours. The advantages of group bonus schemes are that teamwork is promoted and achievement of group targets is reinforced through the rewards system. The disadvantages of these schemes are that by their very nature they can reduce individual motivation to a sole concern for achieving bonuses.

## Performance-related Pay

Performance related pay (PRP) can be defined as: 'a system in which an individual's increase in salary is solely or mainly dependent on his/her appraisal or merit rating'.[8] This rating may take into consideration not only individual output but 'other indicators of performance such as quality, flexibility, contribution to team working and ability to hit targets'.[9]

PRP systems differ from the older systems of payment by results, commission, and bonus schemes in that they assess both the outputs of work and employee behaviour. These systems enjoyed a growing popularity during the 1980s, concurrent with the move toward greater individualization of the employment relationship and away from collectivism, with many seeing PRP as a key practice of HRM.[10] An advantage of PRP is that effective, individual performance can be elicited through the rewards system: high performers are paid more than low performers are. But organizations implementing these schemes have found some common stumbling blocks: they are costly to run, employees concentrate on their objectives related to pay rather than the whole job, and they have the potential to create a sense of inequity within the organization if employees feel that managers have rewarded through favouritism rather than objective judgement of performance.[11] Researchers from the London School of Economics and Political Science found that performance-related pay in the Civil Service, hospitals, and schools has made a minority of staff work harder, but at the cost of lower morale and poorer relationships caused by greater resentment towards managers. One factor likely to increase a PRP scheme's likelihood of success, therefore, is an effective process of performance assessment sustaining a sense of equity and good working relationships.[12]

## Skill-based and Competence-based Pay

These schemes differ from the other pay systems discussed so far because they concentrate on the performance capabilities and inputs made by the employee, with the exception of some competence systems that are purely outcome-based. Sometimes these schemes will include rewards for employees' personal competences, which in effect can be similar to older versions of merit pay, whereby employees were rewarded retrospectively for personal merit (that is, behavioural traits and other inputs) rather than being directly rewarded for the outcomes of work.

For the purpose of this chapter, skill-based and competence-based systems are treated as being the same, although it is acknowledged there are differences between them. Competence-based systems are a more recent development, defining required standards of employee behaviour and performance. They are a deliberate attempt to motivate high performance,[13] or to ensure that performance meets an agreed level and occupational standard, often specified by, for example, an Industry Lead Body and approved by institutions such as the National Council for Vocational Qualifications.

Skill-based approaches are an older system and, as with the competence-based approaches, have traditionally concentrated on inputs that can be assessed by qualifications or by observing behaviour or making inferences on the basis of work outputs. Skills, therefore, can be inferred either from individual behaviour, as interpersonal skills are, or from the results of the employee's applying technical/occupational skills to work tasks. In practice, the terms 'skill' and 'competence' have often been confused.[14] In the context of job analysis, Armstrong proposes treating skills separately as 'inputs' and competences as 'behaviours' and 'achievement'. He distinguishes between 'knowledge and skills', which are inputs (what the employee has to be able to know and do); behaviour, which consists of 'process competences' (how the employee is expected to behave); and achievement, which consists of 'output competences' (what the employee is expected to achieve).[15]

In the 1980s and 1990s, these systems of pay have been used by organizations to encourage employees to develop their skills and competences. An employment trends survey, conducted by the Confederation of British Industry (CBI) and the William Mercer consultancy, involving over 670 employers and 2.4 million employees, found that two-thirds of firms are using competences as part of the means of determining pay.[16] Organizational downsizing and de-layering frequently have had the short-term result of intensifying employees' work and broadening their responsibilities. Some companies switched away from performance-based systems of pay to emphasize more greatly the acquisition of new skills and competences with the aim of stimulating employees to behave and develop in ways consistent with the planned direction of organizational change. The skills and competences that get rewarded can be very broad, ranging from soft skills/competences, such as teamwork and communicating with customers, to technical skills, such as operating new technology and systems. In the computer and information industries, Unisys and IBM are two examples of companies that during the early 1990s implemented skill-based and competence-based pay systems. Recent competence-based systems have covered a wider range of behaviours and attributes than skill-based systems do,[17] rewarding inputs such as teamwork, customer orientation, innovation practices, accountability, and motivation.

IBM, during the turbulent world-wide business conditions of the early 1990s, adopted a broad-band pay system sensitive to market pay rates and then combined it with a pay element emphasizing development and employability. A central purpose of many skill-based and competence-based systems has been to stress that employees must continuously improve their work practices and develop themselves, therefore maximizing both the competitiveness of the organization and their own employability. These demanding systems are in stark contrast to the older pay systems, which traditionally emphasized internal promotion and encouraged employees to assume there was a job for life in the organization.

## Cafeteria or Flexible Benefit Systems

These benefit systems have become popular in the USA and UK because they give employees more choice in determining their remuneration packages. They focus on variable pay rather than basic pay, by concentrating on benefit packages. Bhs (British Home Stores) was one of the first companies in the UK to introduce a cafeteria pay system that provided managers with the opportunity to choose from different levels of life insurance cover, private medical care, annual holiday entitlement, disability insurance, and other benefits. Advantages of cafeteria systems, from the employer's perspective, are that they are flexible and, when well-managed, can be tax-effective and reduce employer risks and liabilities during insurance claims because the employer has offered the employee clear choices over pay and benefits. This has become more of a significant issue in the USA and, to a lesser but growing extent, in the UK, where individual employees are becoming increasingly litigious in disputes with their organizations, sometimes winning substantial court settlements that are very costly to the employer.

# Rewards for Organizational Performance

### Gainsharing

Gainsharing is a bonus plan which gives employees a share of the financial gain made by the organization's improved performance. It is an alternative to the individualized rewards of performance-related pay, relating rewards to organizational performance. The potential advantages of gainsharing are that it allows employees to have control over their work and encourages teamwork and co-operation. If productivity rises and the organization gains, then everyone gains. These schemes intend to focus employees' attention on the key issues influencing organizational performance. A gainsharing scheme operates on a formula agreed between management and employees whereby everyone shares in the gains resulting from effective work performance. Modern versions are most often based on measures of value-added performance, calculated by deducting expenditure on materials and purchased services from sales.

### Profit sharing

With profit sharing, employees are paid a proportion of the organization's pre-tax profits. Profit-sharing schemes have become more attractive to companies following recent changes in taxation. The Conservative governments of the 1980s were keen to encourage companies to use profit sharing as a means of educating people to become more conscious of the profitability of their employing organization. The tax relief on these schemes meant that employers could provide extra benefits to employees without increasing company contributions. Traditionally, profit-related pay schemes were non-Inland Revenue approved profit-sharing schemes, whereby eligible employees were awarded cash from a pool according to a formula that was at the discretion of the company and did not have to be published. However, in the 1980s, with the tax incentive from the Inland Revenue, it became possible to award employees approximately 3–6% profit-related pay on top of their salaries without having to pay any tax on that element of pay. The maximum amount allowed in any one year has been £3,000 or 10% of total pay, whichever is greater.

Inland Revenue approved profit-sharing schemes allocate profits to a trust fund that obtains shares in the organization for employees. The 1978 Finance Act made provisions for companies to distribute shares to employees free of charge. The period between shares being obtained by the employees and the actual release of payments to them can be prolonged. Further, stock market fluctuations make the eventual worth of the shares uncertain. These difficulties reduce the extent of employees' belief that there is a direct relationship between their own efforts and the eventual profitability of the organization.

### Save-as-you-earn

Inland Revenue approved save-as-you-earn (SAYE) employee share-option schemes have made it easier and more tax-efficient for organizations to buy shares for full-time employees, who have the opportunity to cash in their shares after an agreed period of time. The 1980 Finance Act enabled employees to have options to buy, hold, and sell shares. Schemes required employees to save for five or seven years, but more recently it has become possible for employees to sell their shares after only three years. Employees don't pay any tax on the income from selling their shares unless the income is high enough to be subject to capital gains tax. The management of these schemes, particularly in large organizations, has become quite complex, and the administration costs alone amount to many thousands of pounds. Recently companies have become increasingly concerned that as the tax relief is withdrawn from these schemes, the total rewards bill will increase substantially.

A key purpose of schemes that reward organizational performance is to make employees and managers more profit-conscious and to align their interests with those of the company. A disadvantage of profit-sharing and employee share-option schemes is their complexity, which renders them difficult for employees to understand. Employers who have been engaged in profit-sharing and employee share-option schemes for some years—for example, BT, Barclays, Sainsbury's, and Tesco—have had to set up administration and information services to make sure that employees are well informed and involved. Research studies of these schemes have found that they do not strongly motivate employees to perform better at work,[18] although they are motivating to some extent, for example, through increasing job satisfaction.[19] The extent to which employees feel personally rewarded by the schemes is strongly moderated by other factors, such as individual preferences for participation[20] and position in the organizational hierarchy.[21] Some research suggests that motivation is moderated by the extent to which the individual is intrinsically or extrinsically motivated.[22] Employees who are extrinsically motivated are thought to be satisfied only when the actual reward is calculated to be a fair return on effort. Intrinsically motivated employees tend to be more satisfied with the fact that the schemes facilitate wide employee ownership and, in general, they will make less precise assessments of the actual financial benefit they derive from the schemes.

### Final Remark on Pay Structures and Payment Systems

As was mentioned at the beginning of the section on payment systems, time rate systems have remained popular partly because they are a comparatively simple means of rewarding employees and are less likely to lead to disagreement over the amount awarded. John Storey contrasts personnel management with HRM on the issue of pay (see Storey's twenty-five-item checklist in Chapter 1) saying that a personnel

**TABLE 7.2**

**Purcell's types of performance pay system**

| Type of performance | Unit of performance | |
| --- | --- | --- |
| | Individual | Collective |
| Output | Piecework | Measured daywork |
| | Commission | Team bonus |
| | Individual bonus | Profit sharing |
| | Individual performance-related pay | Gain sharing |
| Input | Skill-based pay | Employee share- |
| | Merit pay | ownership schemes |

*Source*: Purcell (1993), unpublished, cited by Kessler, I., 'Reward Systems', in J. Storey (ed.), *Human Resource Management: A Critical Text* (London: Routledge, 1995), p. 256

management approach rewards employees according to fixed grades but HRM uses performance-related pay. John Purcell[23] has summarized performance-based pay systems in two dimensions: the type of performance and the unit of performance rewarded. The type of performance he categorizes as either output or input, the majority of performance-based pay systems rewarding output performance. The unit of performance he subdivides into individual and collective systems. Individual systems include piecework, commission, individual bonus, individual performance-related pay, skill-based pay, and merit pay. Collective systems include: measured daywork, team bonus, profit sharing, gainsharing, and employee share-ownership schemes. Purcell's summary of types of performance-based pay system is shown Table 7.2.

Occasionally, organizations have completely changed their pay structures and systems in an attempt to signal change and motivate new employee behaviours and attitudes. McDonalds and Burger King, for example, launched new initiatives on pay and career prospects in a massive recruitment drive and battle for market share. Both companies had been paying well below the Low Pay Commission's minimum level and were said to be anxious not to be caught in negative publicity that would reinforce the 'McJob' image.[24] However, the majority of organizations' structures and systems have evolved over time, with pay structures being modified and systems progressively becoming more complex as management seek to motivate and reward employees for improved organization performance.

# Top Management Pay

Traditionally, managers have been paid more than most of their subordinates. The structures and systems for rewarding managers are similar to those for rewarding employees, although for management in many companies there is a wider range of schemes available, related to profit sharing, performance bonuses, share options, pensions, and other benefits. Executive share schemes specifically give executives options to acquire shares at fixed prices. These schemes aim to give executives a stronger sense of ownership of their organizations and more closely align their interests with those of the shareholders (see the section on agency theory in Chapter 6). Some of these schemes have been very generous, providing managers with as much as, or more than, the value of their annual pay packages. The gap between employees' pay and top managers' pay has widened, particularly during the 1980s, when directors' pay rose, in real terms, higher than employees' pay did: according to the National Institute for Economic and Social Research, during the period 1985–90 directors' pay increased by 77%, while employees' pay increased by only 17%.[25]

Management of executives' rewards has become a frequently debated issue during the 1990s and has led to the publication of three influential reports: The Cadbury Report (1993); The House of Commons Employment Select Committee's Report (1995); and the Greenbury Report (1995). These reports have advised greater control over executives' rewards by increasing the transparency of the reward systems through measures including tighter service contracts, use of remuneration committees involving non-executive directors, and wider publication of the remuneration policy for directors and publication of the figures of their actual individual remuneration.

# 2 Performance Management

PERFORMANCE management is an approach used by organizations to try to achieve strategic goals consistently through better formal and informal motivation, monitoring, evaluating, and rewarding of performance. Performance management systems grew in popularity during the 1980s because they were thought to facilitate rigorous specification of performance standards and measures and increase the likelihood of achieving organizational goals at a time when organizations needed to respond to increasingly competitive business conditions. They also were a move away from collectivism towards greater individualization of the employment relationship.[26]

During the 1990s there has been increased interest among HRM practitioners and researchers in high-performance or high-commitment practices, and there is evidence for a link between adoption of high-performance HR practices and superior organizational performance. US researchers Pfeffer and Huselid claim that adoption of their best practices, when combined with long-term commitment and consistent performance measurement according to high standards, will result in superior performance.[27] David Guest sees Huselid's work as a potential breakthrough for HRM theory and practice:

Using company market value as the key indicator, he [Huselid] found that firms with significantly above-average scores on the index of high-performance work practices (in technical terms, this meant one standard deviation above the mean) provided an extra market value per employee of between £10,000 and £40,000. On this basis, an investment in HR pays off handsomely.

Given these seemingly huge financial benefits, what are the specific practices that provide such an advantage? One thing is clear from all of the research: there is no value in investing heavily in specific practices. Performance-related pay, psychometric tests in selection or extensive training will not in themselves bring bottom-line results. The key lies in having the right 'bundle' of practices—and the challenge for personnel managers is to find it.[28]

However, Stephen Wood from the London School of Economics and Political Science observes that UK companies are failing to derive benefit from high-commitment management because they do not implement the practices consistently and over the longer term.[29] These companies are underachieving by taking the classic British short-term and piecemeal approach to strategy.

## The Four Components

In 1996, Marchington and Wilkinson proposed four principal components of performance management (see Fig. 7.6). Performance management is a continuous process whereby employees know the performance expectations for their work and are supported by managers and their peers to achieve these expectations. This informal and formal support should occur consistently throughout the year. All individual performance is formally reviewed and appraised once or twice a year. Following the formal

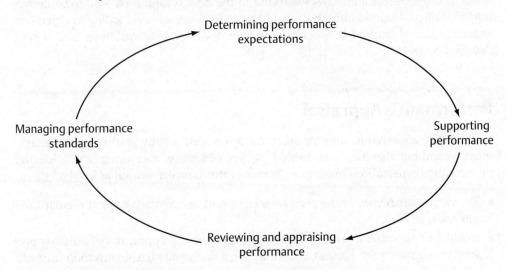

**Figure 7.6  Four components of performance management**

*Source:* Taken from *Core Personnel and Development* by M. Marchington and A. Wilkinson, 1996, Figure 5, p. 135, with the permission of the publisher, the Institute of Personnel and Development, IPD House, Camp Road, London SW19 4UX.

appraisal interview, actions are decided by employee and manager that aim to achieve new levels of performance, to implement training programmes and other development initiatives, and to find ways of resolving performance difficulties or failures. In large organizations—for example, public-sector local authorities—follow-up actions include the management of absenteeism.

Connock stresses that performance management places great emphasis on the future and on achievement using 'SMART' objectives and targets (specific, measurable, achievable, realistic, time-constrained).[30] The process places importance on setting key accountabilities, agreeing future objectives for them, agreeing measures and standards to be obtained, and assigning time-scales and priorities. Formal, sophisticated monitoring techniques also play an important role in performance management, as shown by the Fourth Workplace Employee Relations Survey (1998). The survey found that there is a group of HR practices associated with performance management: psychometric testing, use of employee attitude surveys, and performance appraisal. Performance management systems use formal employee appraisal as a central component, but they should not be seen as appraisal under a new name. These systems include a number of human resource activities, and typical features are: well-communicated mission statements, regular communication on progress according to business plans, integration with quality management policies, a clear focus on senior managers' performance, use of performance-related rewards, and a strong emphasis on training and development tailored to achieve performance expectations.

The demerger of ICI into ICI and Zeneca led to new systems of performance management in the two demerged companies. ICI introduced what was known as the 'Triple A' project (accountability, achievement, autonomy), which was designed to manage individual performance, making it more closely aligned with the strategic needs of the business. Employees working in the new system were said to be better-informed about their accountabilities and their achievements according to objectives and targets, and learned to work with newly devolved responsibilities and within devolved budgets.[31]

## Performance Appraisal

Performance appraisal is not only a central component of any performance management system but also the main, formal method of setting, measuring, and achieving performance expectations. Anderson defines performance appraisal as involving:

- The systematic review of the performance of staff on a written basis at regular time intervals; and
- Holding of appraisal interviews at which staff have the opportunity to discuss performance issues, past, present and future, on a one-to-one basis, with their immediate line manager.[32]

Harrison suggests that performance appraisal used within performance management systems requires four activities, as shown in Fig. 7.7, which are part of the role of

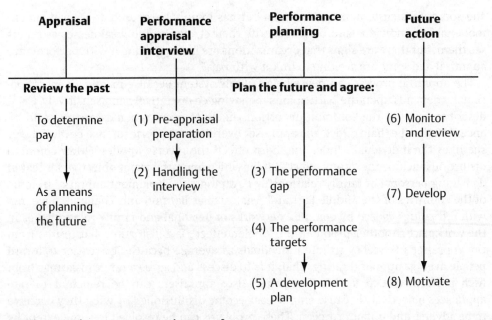

**Figure 7.7  The manager's role in performance management**

*Source*: Harrison, *Human Resource Management: Issues and Strategies* (1993), Figure 10.3, p. 262. Reprinted by permission of Pearson Education Limited.

all line managers.[33] The manager must appraise and review the past; conduct the performance appraisal interview; plan the future and agree performance targets and development plans; and follow up the interview with future action.

The immediate line manager is not always the person who acts as the appraiser. In parts of the UK armed forces and civil service, the manager's manager has taken on the appraiser's role, it being assumed that he or she holds a more impartial view of the employee's performance.[34] A common problem with this method is that the higher-level manager is not always very well acquainted with the employee's day-to-day work, aspirations, or performance. Most appraisals that aim to involve employees and to be 'transparent systems' (in which personal records and judgements are open to inspection by the appraised individual) incorporate self-appraisal as a necessary component of the review process.

Other less commonly used appraisal methods are 'upward appraisal', whereby employees appraise their managers. This approach has been used successfully in large organizations such as the retail companies Tesco and Asda. Peer appraisal has found more popularity in the professions, such as in universities and, to a lesser extent, in general medical practice.[35] Research suggests that 'multi-appraisal' methods, which are the most comprehensive because data are collected from all around an employee (a '360-degree appraisal'), sometimes from inside and outside the organization, provide a fuller picture and limit the danger of distortion from using one perspective.[36] Since the early 1990s, 360-degree feedback has been adopted in Britain across a range of public- and private-sector organizations involving subordinates, peers, superiors, and sometimes customers and suppliers. It has mainly been used as a development tool enabling individuals to better identify their strengths and weaknesses as others see them, but there are signs that organizations are incorporating it with performance appraisal and some are seeking to link it with pay.[37]

The appraisal process can never be a fail-safe system because its effectiveness continually depends upon the participants' behaving co-operatively and sensitively. Grint describes some of the common distortions likely to occur when assessing performance.[38] Under the 'halo effect' the appraiser overestimates performance because he or she likes the individual. Under the 'horn effect' the reverse applies. Other common distortions include the 'crony effect', under which appraisal is not objective for fear of damaging personal or family relationships. Attempts to implement appraisal in some of the countries of the Middle East and Asia, such as Bahrain and Thailand, have met with difficulties caused by complex networks of personal and family relationships in the workplace. Another problem, the 'Veblen effect', is a distortion that results from the appraiser's tendency to rate individuals as average because it is easier to award people average appraisal ratings than it is to discuss and agree a range of ratings from high performance to low performance. Also, appraisers can be reluctant to rate appraisees objectively because employees become disillusioned by what they perceive to be adverse and unfair criticism. These problems can be resolved to some extent by proper training of managers and employees in the appraisal process, particularly by developing their skills in getting the best out of the written reviews and the face-to-face interview. Appraisal systems have to be sensitive to norms of national culture and may have to be implemented in different ways. A research investigation on performance appraisal comparing practice in Hong Kong and Great Britain found that British appraisals were more participative and less directive than Hong Kong appraisals.[39]

Fletcher and Williams say that appraisal is often difficult to implement effectively because it requires managers to perform adequately in two potentially contradictory roles, those of 'judge' and 'helper'.[40] These assessment and development roles in appraisal systems have been known for many years. McGregor described appraisal as having three objectives. First, there is an administrative objective, which is judgemental about the employee's career, such as determining who gets promoted and rewarded (the 'judge' role). Second, appraisals have the objective of being informative—making judgements about an employee's performance, strengths, and weaknesses. Third, as well as performing this judgemental function of categorizing individuals, appraisals must be motivational, creating learning experiences that motivate employees to develop themselves and improve their performance (the 'helper' role).[41]

To summarize, four essential elements of performance management are:

(1) setting individual objectives which support achieving the business strategy;
(2) performance appraisal;
(3) review of pay and rewards including performance-related pay; and
(4) organizational capability review—the performance management system must influence the business strategy.[42]

# Kaplan and Norton's Balanced Scorecard

One recent innovation in performance management that has attracted the attention of senior management in companies[43] and that satisfies the features listed above is Kaplan and Norton's version of the 'balanced scorecard',[44] a management system designed to encourage what the authors call 'breakthrough performance' in product, process, customer, and market development. The scorecard presents four different perspectives on performance measurement: financial, customer, internal business, and innovation and learning. Kaplan and Norton say that, in the past, managers failed to utilize this range of perspectives and have stuck too closely to short-term financial measures such as return on investment (ROI), sales growth, and operating income. These financial measures are important, but in terms of the 'balanced scorecard' they represent just one-quarter of the picture. The scorecard or the financial measures should be used, they say, as a means of bench-marking performance on projects and in new growth businesses.

Figure 7.8 shows that the balanced scorecard is a management process involving four main steps. First is deciding the vision of the future. Second is determining how this vision can become a competitive advantage for the organization as seen from four perspectives: shareholders, customers, internal management processes, and ability to innovate and grow. The third step is determining from these four perspectives the critical success factors, and the final step is identifying the critical measurements for ascertaining how far along the organization is on the path to success.

Kaplan and Norton give several examples of the balanced scorecard in practice. One case study involves a company called Rockwater, a subsidiary of a global engineering and construction company, Brown & Root/Halliburton. The measures used by organizations depend on the critical success factors identified in the balanced scorecard. For Rockwater, from the financial perspective, critical measurements included return on capital employed (ROCE), cash flow, and sales backlog. From the customer perspective, measures included customer ranking surveys, the customer satisfaction index, market share, and the pricing index. From the internal business perspective, critical measurements included hours spent with customers on new work, success rates of tenders, amount of rework required, and success in project performance, particularly meeting new customer needs. From the innovation and learning perspective, measures included staff attitude survey results, percentage of revenue from new services, revenue per employee, and employee suggestions. Kaplan and Norton's approach has been said to be influential, with 60% of the top 100 UK companies confirming that they use the balanced scorecard.[45]

# HRM Practices and Outcomes

David Guest, whose soft HRM model was introduced in Chapter 1, says that people will take HRM more seriously when research delivers better evidence for the linkage

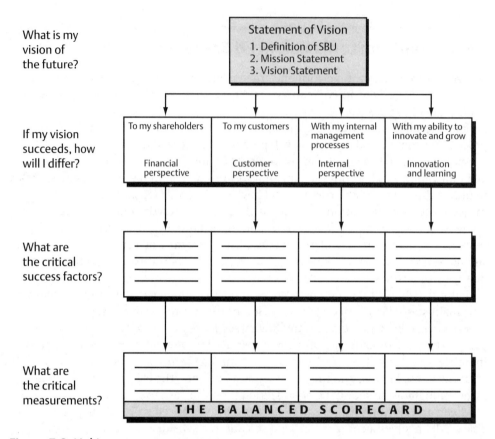

**Figure 7.8 Linking measurements to strategy**

*Source:* Reprinted by permission of *Harvard Business Review*. From 'Begin by Linking Measurements to Strategy' by R. S. Kaplan and D. P. Norton, September–October 1993, p. 139. Copyright © 1993 by the President and Fellows of Harvard.

between HRM and organizational performance.[46] Guest criticizes previous research for not paying enough attention to the nature of organizational performance and for not providing a strong rationale for specific HR practices. He recommends that better theories of performance be created, citing the balanced scorecard (introduced in the preceding section) and the expectancy theory of motivation (discussed in Chapter 6). Recent research on HRM in the world automotive industry found that high individual performance depends on three factors: skill, effort, and appropriate role perception; all three were originally proposed in expectancy theory.[47]

Reminiscent of his own earlier prescriptive model, Guest proposes three HRM outcomes linked to practices: quality, commitment, and flexibility. Quality outcomes are linked to practices concerned with selection, development, and quality. Commitment is linked to employee relations, promotion, and rewards. Flexibility links with structural characteristics and with formal and informal communication and teamwork. The detail of the HRM practices linked to outcomes is laid out in Fig. 7.9.

Selection
Socialization
Training and development          ⟶          Skills and Ability
Quality Improvement programmes                (Quality)

Single status
Job security
International promotion           ⟶          Effort/Motivation
Individualized reward systems                 (Commitment)

Communication
Employee involvement
Team working                      ⟶          Role Structure and Perception
Job design                                    (Flexibility)
Flexible job descriptions

### Figure 7.9  HRM and performance

*Source*: Guest, 'Human Resource Management and Performance: a review and research agenda', *The International Journal of Human Resource Management* (1997), p. 269

Reviewing empirical research on the link between HRM and performance, Guest comes to the conclusion that, first, higher performance outcomes are more likely where HR practices link to business strategy and the external environment.[48] Second, most strongly supported of all in a growing number of research studies is the link between high performance HRM practices and better organizational performance as indicated by productivity, labour turnover, or financial indicators. Third, there is some evidence for superior performance where coherent groups of practices are deliberately applied. This is known as the HRM 'bundles' approach, which aims to achieve high performance by utilizing mutually reinforcing clusters or 'bundles' of HRM practice.

# Summary

THIS chapter has reviewed ways of financially rewarding employees and has identified some of their strengths and weaknesses. Payment structures and systems reward different aspects of employees' work. Some structures are comparatively simple, such as graded pay structures, and have tended to measure performance only periodically and prior to salary progression. Others, such as pay curves, are more complex and depend on more frequent measures of performance in calculating the amount of reward due.

Similarly, some systems of pay are comparatively simple—for example, time rates have worked with very rudimentary records of attendance—while others are more complex, such as work-measured and performance-related pay systems. Most systems focus on rewarding either individual or group or organizational performance. Performance-related pay requires making individual distinctions between employees based on their performance for the purpose of allocating different proportions of pay. Group bonus schemes reward groups of employees for having achieved targets. Gainsharing and SAYE schemes establish a fixed proportion for employees who are then rewarded an equal or proportional share of the returns from the performance of their organization. The way that employees are paid reveals assumptions about what is to be valued and who is to be rewarded. The structures and systems make important statements about how pay should and can motivate performance in the workplace.

BOX 7.1
## Case Study—Performance Appraisal in a Midlands Car Manufacturing Plant

*Introduction*
Imagine you have been working for one year in an international car company plant located in the Midlands. You are a team leader working on the production line and your appraisal interview is due in three weeks' time. You will be appraised by your line manager. The system is an open one in so far as all of the written documentation is available to you, your line manager, and the line personnel manager. You are reflecting on what you have done before you commit your ideas to paper.

*Appraisee's Brief*
Your team, along with others in the company, has been asked to come up with ways of introducing quality improvements and cost savings. One project you worked on for your part of the production line was very successful. Your team estimated that it was costing the company £1,500 per year to revamp the car floor mat. The mats were getting scratched during assembly and the minimum repair cost was £75 per vehicle. Your team has cut that area of waste down to zero, simply by introducing a rubber mat that could be laid on top of the floor mat, thus preventing any scratching and waste. Your team's cost projection is that, if this innovation is introduced for other teams, it could lead to savings in the region of £50,000 a year.

You have enjoyed your first year as team leader and the job is a challenging one with twelve people to manage on a daily basis.

Your team has responsibility for talking directly to suppliers wherever there are improvements that can be made. The relationship between shop floor employees and management is generally felt to be good, and the organization is flatter and less hierarchical than it used to be. There no longer seems to be the 'us and them' mentality that characterized the plant ten years ago. Your team is highly committed to productivity and quality targets, and everyone feels they all are in the same boat. Your team is aware of the increasingly competitive global markets, and the management style emphasizes that employees must work smarter and not just harder. The team is informed by line management communications, personnel and employee involvement, fellow workers, and you yourself about new business challenges and how to meet them through achieving weekly and monthly targets.

You have had some opportunity for self-development; for example, you gave a presentation on team briefing to another manufacturing company at their annual conference. Also, you have met the managing director, who periodically visits the track to talk directly with shop floor employees and listen to issues they want to discuss.

Formal team briefings are held weekly. All of the team leaders meet beforehand for a management meeting and briefing from a representative of senior management. The team leaders then go back to brief their own teams at the start of the shift. These meetings take approximately twenty minutes and team leaders present an update on the situation, then set and review targets for the coming week and ensuing months. The briefing is a two-way communication process because members are expected to participate and raise any issues they want to air with the group.

Your team's composition has changed recently, through the re-introduction of a Saturday morning shift, which had been abandoned during the recession when production was down. The changes have caused some difficulties because the three members who had to leave in order to join another shift were well-liked and part of a very positive working relationship. Your team is now having to learn how to work with three new people and morale is not as high as it was over the last year. Time has been spent properly inducting the new team members, and although the group is not yet as cohesive as it should be, you are confident that over the next few weeks, with on-the-job development and effective management on your part, the team will mould once again into a high-performing work group.

For one month, your team had a graduate engineer who was working for you as part of a government-supported training scheme. He pointed out from an outsider's perspective some basic improvements to the work processes, which your team enthusiastically listened to and quickly adopted. One straightforward innovation that has saved time and money is that the team now take car seat parts in batches of two or three rather than one at a time. Another innovation suggested by the graduate engineer was to get maintenance to paint more red lines on the floor to guide stacker trucks. The new lines prevent trucks from parking up too close to your team. Although no accident had yet happened, this proactive approach to health and safety is strongly encouraged by the company.

Your line manager has been very helpful and you have enjoyed working with her on planning tasks, reviewing production schedules, and identifying training and development needs for the team. You are ambitious and want to enrol for a part-time diploma in management at your local university. However, this will mean taking some time off work and having a member of the team act as team leader. There was another person trained and experienced as a team leader, but he was one of the three who recently left. So, there is no one in the team trained in that position, although two individuals have come forward, and you have not yet had time to discuss with your line manager the on-the-job development and training these two members require.

The management style in your company, according to the long-serving members of the team, used to be somewhat autocratic. The culture has changed and now is participative and open. People on the shop-floor say that they feel more confident and able to talk both to managers and to employees from other parts of the plant. They are ready to voice their own opinions, listen to others' criticism, and act positively and decisively. High standards of communication and performance are expected of everyone, and teams likewise expect proper support from their team leaders and adequate resources to undertake the goals set for them.

One team member has noticed that there are no telephone directory entries for many people employed by component supplier firms. The company has already been dealing with this issue centrally through the purchasing and supply department. However, there is one individual in your team who is convinced it would be better for the team to compose its own list. You appreciate how time-consuming it will be to set about compiling and updating a list of relevant external phone numbers and phone extensions. Given the current workload your team is facing, it does not make sense for the task to be done locally. You are aware that this team member is a highly enthusiastic individual who sometimes reacts over-sensitively to setback and failure. His personality is such that he can become easily disappointed. You have managed to delay him from starting on his phone project, but have not yet been able to tell him directly that it is not feasible. When you last broached the topic with him, he used it as an opportunity to sell you the idea rather than listen to your explanation of the impracticality of his proposal. Furthermore, there is a new empowerment programme under way in the company and you do not want to risk being seen as acting negatively towards this new HR initiative. You discussed the telephone directory project with your line manager before talking to the team member, but although you followed her advice it did not lead to the result she had predicted.

The team members have reviewed their working relationship and the overall atmosphere within the team. After a full and frank exchange, they concluded that members were able to express their feelings and that their ideas were being taken up by the company, particularly through the suggestion scheme. They were positive about incorporating the three new members and everybody endorsed the quality management targets, saying they made the team's priorities clearer.

New targets for reducing waste have been introduced by the company and the team is pleased with its results. Very few items that are the team's direct responsibility have had to be scrapped; however, some scrap items have been coming from further up the line. The team has been effective in identifying these scrap items and sending them back to their originators, although this has sometimes negatively affected your team's output. You know that some influential members of the team feel that you have not done enough to ensure the scrap items aren't dumped on the team again in the future. You have talked about the scrap problem with the other team leaders responsible and also separately with your own line manager. It is likely that the scrap problem will continue until new software is installed for controlling the carousel, thus enabling changes to the work process. At present, some of the other teams are having to work weekend overtime to make up for lost time caused by faults identified in the computer software.

Overall, you have enjoyed your first year as team leader and are keen to get ahead. You appreciate that you have at least another year of hard work as team leader before promotion is likely. You are looking forward to your appraisal interview and hope that your line manager will make it clear what your next step will be in your career with the organization.

*Case Study Activity*
On the basis of the information above, complete the appraisal forms and, with a colleague acting as your line manager, role-play the appraisal interview. Your lecturer will need to provide the 'line manager' with a short brief giving additional information for the role play (this brief is not provided in this textbook).

# PEUGEOT

# PERFORMANCE APPRAISAL

## GUIDELINES AND PREPARATION DOCUMENT FOR EMPLOYEES

### INTRODUCTION

These guidelines have been developed to help you prepare for the Performance Appraisal process and should be used in conjunction with the Appraisal and Training/Development Planning Record Sheet.

In this document the appraisal process is explained under three main headings:

1. PREPARATION AND TIMING
2. COMPLETION OF RECORD SHEET
3. POST APPRAISAL ACTION

These issues are discussed more fully below.

### 1. PREPARATION AND TIMING

Successful performance appraisal preparation is best achieved by:

- reading the guidelines and completing the forms well in advance of the appraisal meeting – the appraisal documentation should be issued to you 7–10 days prior to your meeting
- agreeing a date/time with your Manager/Supervisor for the appraisal interview
- contributing to the meeting which should be viewed as a two way exchange of information and ideas.

### 2. COMPLETION OF THE APPRAISAL/DEVELOPMENT PLANNING RECORD SHEET

The format of this preparation document is similar to that of the Record Sheet which covers five main sections:

- Achievement of objectives/targets for the previous year
- Methods of working
- Dealing with people
- Objectives/targets for next year
- Training and development

Each of these is explained in more detail overleaf.

Figure 7.10  Peugeot Appraisal Guidelines

*Source*: Peugeot appraisal form and guidelines reproduced here by kind permission of Peugeot's Training and Development Function.

## 2.1 ACHIEVEMENT OF PAST OBJECTIVES/TARGETS

Consider how successful you were in achieving the objectives set for the previous year. It may be necessary to take into account any revisions or changed circumstances. You may also wish to refer to notes made during interim review meetings or make reference to the completion of projects or major pieces of work which contributed to the achievement of the objectives/ targets.

## 2.2 METHODS OF WORKING

When reviewing this area you may wish to consider how effectively you:

- planned and scheduled your work
- identified and solved existing or potential problems
- made decisions and communicated your plans
- controlled and managed key resources at your disposal
- suggested/initiated quality improvements to the product or service for which you have responsibility

## 2.3 DEALING WITH PEOPLE

To prepare this area you should consider your approach to the development of customer and supplier relationships and the management and supervision of others if appropriate. Factors which could be included in your review are detailed below.

## (a) Customer and Supplier Relationships

Whilst working towards the achievement of your objectives consider how successfully you:

- identified your customers and suppliers
- established their needs
- developed effective communication
- evaluated any action you took to improve the product or service offered
- adopted an appropriate personal style when dealing with customers and suppliers.

## (b) Managing/Supervising Others (where appropriate)

Consider how effectively you managed or supervised others. How well did you:

- communicate with and direct your team
- involve individuals and enhance the commitment of the team
- motivate individuals and develop a positive team spirit
- identify training/development needs and implement appropriate action.

(N.B. 'Managing/Supervising Others' could include indirect supervision e.g. project group leader.)

## 2.4 OBJECTIVES TARGETS FOR NEXT YEAR

Prior to the appraisal meeting your Manager/Supervisor will be developing what he/she considers to be your objectives/targets for the next year. Please consider and state during the meeting what you believe they are or should be.

> During the appraisal process it is extremely important that you put forward your point of view and ideas. Where appropriate these will be combined with those of your immediate Manager/Supervisor and recorded in the relevant sections of the Record Sheet. In addition, you may wish to make further comments once the appraisal form has been completed. Space has been provided on the Record Sheet for this purpose.

## 2.5 TRAINING/DEVELOPMENT NEEDS

The appraisal discussion provides the opportunity to discuss several aspects of your training and development.

### (a) Training needs within the current job

Your Manager/Supervisor has been asked to consider whether you have any training needs. In considering this question he/she will review not only how you achieved your previous objectives/targets, but also what assistance you might require to meet any new objectives. We believe it is important that you contribute to this process and therefore suggest you consider:

- how effectively did you achieve previous objectives?
- what further skills/knowledge/awareness might have helped improve your effectiveness?

In addition, during the appraisal meeting, you should discuss what skills/knowledge/awareness would help you achieve your new objectives/targets.

### (b) Longer term development

The appraisal meeting gives you and your immediate supervisor/manager the opportunity to discuss your career aspirations should it be appropriate to do so. You may wish to discuss:

- your general career aspirations
- the type of jobs that you might want to be considered for in the future (including whether you would want to work in other departments and locations)
- what training/development action you could take to improve your chances of achieving your career aims.

In most cases the discussion of 'longer term development' should focus on development over approximately the next five years.

**PEUGEOT**

# APPRAISAL AND TRAINING/DEVELOPMENT PLANNING

## RECORD SHEET

NAME
........................................................................................................

IDENTITY NUMBER
........................................................................................................

POSITION
........................................................................................................

DEPARTMENT
........................................................................................................

NAME OF APPRAISER
........................................................................................................

DATE COMPLETED
........................................................................................................

*This document should be completed during or preferably immediately following the appraisal meeting.*

*The individual concerned, the Appraiser, the Appraiser's Manager and the line Personnel Manager, should each receive a copy of the completed document.*

**Figure 7.11  Peugeot Appraisal Record Sheet**
*Source*: Peugeot Training and Development Function.

## ACHIEVEMENT OF PAST OBJECTIVES/TARGETS

...........................................................................................................................
...........................................................................................................................
...........................................................................................................................
...........................................................................................................................
...........................................................................................................................
...........................................................................................................................
...........................................................................................................................
...........................................................................................................................
...........................................................................................................................
...........................................................................................................................
...........................................................................................................................
...........................................................................................................................

## METHODS OF WORKING

...........................................................................................................................
...........................................................................................................................
...........................................................................................................................
...........................................................................................................................
...........................................................................................................................
...........................................................................................................................
...........................................................................................................................
...........................................................................................................................
...........................................................................................................................
...........................................................................................................................
...........................................................................................................................
...........................................................................................................................

## DEALING WITH PEOPLE

...........................................................................................................................
...........................................................................................................................
...........................................................................................................................
...........................................................................................................................
...........................................................................................................................
...........................................................................................................................
...........................................................................................................................
...........................................................................................................................
...........................................................................................................................
...........................................................................................................................

## OBJECTIVES/TARGETS FOR NEXT YEAR

...........................................................................................................................
...........................................................................................................................
...........................................................................................................................
...........................................................................................................................
...........................................................................................................................
...........................................................................................................................
...........................................................................................................................
...........................................................................................................................
...........................................................................................................................

## TRAINING/DEVELOPMENT NEEDS

### Methods of working

......................................................................................................................................
......................................................................................................................................
......................................................................................................................................
......................................................................................................................................
......................................................................................................................................
......................................................................................................................................
......................................................................................................................................
......................................................................................................................................

### Dealing with people

......................................................................................................................................
......................................................................................................................................
......................................................................................................................................
......................................................................................................................................
......................................................................................................................................
......................................................................................................................................
......................................................................................................................................
......................................................................................................................................

### Other needs

......................................................................................................................................
......................................................................................................................................
......................................................................................................................................
......................................................................................................................................
......................................................................................................................................
......................................................................................................................................
......................................................................................................................................
......................................................................................................................................

### Longer term development

......................................................................................................................................
......................................................................................................................................
......................................................................................................................................
......................................................................................................................................
......................................................................................................................................
......................................................................................................................................
......................................................................................................................................

### INDIVIDUAL'S COMMENTS

......................................................................................................................................
......................................................................................................................................
......................................................................................................................................
......................................................................................................................................
......................................................................................................................................
......................................................................................................................................
......................................................................................................................................

Appraiser's Signature ......................................Individual's Signature ......................................

## TRAINING AND DEVELOPMENT NOTES

..................................................................................................................
..................................................................................................................
..................................................................................................................
..................................................................................................................
..................................................................................................................
..................................................................................................................
..................................................................................................................
..................................................................................................................
..................................................................................................................
..................................................................................................................
..................................................................................................................
..................................................................................................................
..................................................................................................................
..................................................................................................................
..................................................................................................................

### 3. POST APPRAISAL ACTION

Once the Record Sheet has been completed and signed you will receive a copy. Your Appraiser's Manager and the line Personnel Manager will also receive copies.

If you do not wish to sign the document you should give some sort of explanation in the section headed 'Individual's Comments'. In addition should you strongly disagree with the appraisal you can refer the issue to the next level of management.

The Personnel and Training function will provide your manager with follow-up advice and assistance on how the identified training and development needs can be met. They will also assist with the development of your training plan which will be communicated to you via your Manager/Supervisor.

# Study Questions

1   Define and explain three payment structures of your choice. Discuss the difficulties likely to be encountered from moving from one pay structure to another.
2   Define two payment systems of your choice, one based on rewarding individual performance and the other on rewarding organizational performance. Explain the likely benefits and drawbacks of their joint implementation.
3   Discuss how alternative payment structures and systems might suit different organizations operating within different markets.
4   Define performance management and discuss how far it is consistent with models and frameworks of HRM introduced in Chapter 1.
5   Write a short report recommending, for a selected case organization, how Kaplan and Norton's balanced scorecard should be integrated with HR policy and practice.

# Further Reading

Armstrong, M., *Employee Reward* (London: Institute of Personnel and Development, 1996).

Kessler, I., 'Reward Systems', in J. Storey, *Human Resource Management: A Critical Text* (London: Routledge, 1995), pp. 254–79.

Marchington, M. and Wilkinson, A., *Core Personnel and Development* (London: Institute of Personnel and Development, 1996), Section 6: Employee Reward, pp. 293–357.

Stiles, P., Gratton, L., Truss, C., Hope-Hailey, V., and McGovern, P., 'Performance Management and the Psychological Contract', *Human Resource Management Journal* (1997), 7, 1, pp. 57–66.

# Notes

1.  Kessler, I., 'Reward Systems', in J. Storey (ed.), *Human Resource Management: A Critical Text* (London: Routledge, 1995), pp. 254–79 at p. 256; Baron, A. and Armstrong, M., 'Out of the tick box', *People Management* (1998), 4, 15, 23 July, p. 38.
2.  Kessler, 'Reward Systems', p. 256.
3.  Poole, M. and Jenkins, G., 'Developments in human resource management in manufacturing in modern Britain,' *International Journal of Human Resource Management* (1997), 8, 6, December, pp. 841–56 (see p. 852).
4.  Bratton, J. and Gold, J., *Human Resource Management: Theory and Practice*, 2nd edn. (Basingstoke: Macmillan Business, 1999).

5. Cowling, A. and James, P., *The Essence of Personnel Management and Industrial Relations* (London: Prentice Hall, 1994); Armstrong, M. and Murlis, H., *Reward Management*, 3rd edn. (London: Kogan Page, 1994).

6. Armstrong, M., *Employee Reward* (London: Institute of Personnel and Development, 1996), pp. 271–9.

7. Kinnie, N. and Purcell, J., 'Teamworking', *People Management* (1998), 4, 9, 30 April, p. 35.

8. Swabe, A. I. R., 'Performance-related pay: a case study', *Employee Relations* (1989) Vol. 11, No. 2, pp. 17–23 (see p. 17).

9. Kinnie, N. and Lowe, D., 'Performance related pay on the shopfloor', *Personnel Management* (1990), November, pp. 45–9 (see p. 45), cited in I. Beardwell and L. Holden, *Human Resource Management: a contemporary perspective* (London: Pitman, 1997), p. 575.

10. Storey, J., *Developments in the Management of Human Resources*. Oxford: Blackwell, (1992).

11. Marsden, D. and Richardson, R., 'Performing for pay? The effects of "merit pay" on motivation in a public service', *British Journal of Industrial Relations* (1994), 32, 2, June, pp. 243–62, at p. 251; *People Management* (1998), 4, 15, 23 July, p. 11.

12. Marchington, M. and Wilkinson, A., *Core Personnel and Development* (London: Institute of Personnel and Development, 1996); Kessler, I., 'Performance pay', in K. Sisson (ed.), *Personnel Management: A Comprehensive Guide to Theory and Practice in Britain*, 2nd edn. (Oxford: Blackwell, 1994).

13. Cockerill, A., 'The kind of competence for rapid change', *Personnel Management* (1989), 21, 9, September, pp. 532–56; Cockerill, A., 'Managerial competence as a determinant of organizational performance', unpublished PhD thesis (University of London, London Business School, 1990); Schroder, H. M., *Managerial Competence: The Key to Excellence* (Iowa: Kendall-Hunt, 1989); Boyatzis, R., *The Competent Manager: a Model for Effective Managers* (New York: Wiley, 1982).

14. Woodruffe, C., 'What is meant by a competency', in R. Boam and P. Sparrow, *Designing and Achieving Competency: A Competency-Based approach to Developing People and Organizations* (Maidenhead: McGraw-Hill, 1992), pp. 16–30 at p. 29: '. . . competencies are dimensions of behaviour which are related to superior job performance.'

15. Armstrong, *Employee Reward* (n. 6 above), pp. 177–82.

16. *People Management* (1998), 4, 16, 13 August, p. 15.

17. Marchington, M. and Wilkinson, A., *Core Personnel and Development* (London: Institute of Personnel and Development 1996), p. 334.

18. Long, R., 'The effects of employee ownership on organizational identification, employee job attitudes, and organizational performance: a tentative framework and empirical findings', *Human Relations* (1978), 31, 1, pp. 29–48; Baddon, L., Hunter, L., Hyman, J., Leopold, J., and Ramsay, H., *A Critical Analysis of Profit-sharing and Employee Share Ownership* (London: Routledge, 1989); Dunn, S., Richardson, R., and Dewe, P., 'The impact of employee share ownership on worker attitudes: a longitudinal case study', *Human Resource Management Journal* (1991), 1, 3, Spring, pp. 1–17.

19. Poole, M. and Jenkins, G., 'How employees respond to profit sharing', *Personnel Management* (1988), July, p. 33; Bakan, I., 'The effect of profit sharing and share option schemes on employee job attitudes', unpublished PhD thesis, Coventry University, June 1999.

20. Oliver, N., 'Work rewards, work values and organizational commitment in an employee owned firm: evidence from the UK', *Human Relations* (1990), 43, 6, pp. 513–26.

21. French, J. L., 'Employee perspectives on stock ownership: financial investment or mechanism of control?', *Academy of Management Review* (1987), 12, pp. 427–35.

22. Klein, K. J., 'Employee stock ownership and employee attitudes: a test of three models', *Journal of Applied Psychology Monograph* (1987), 72, 2, pp. 319–32.

23. Purcell (1993), unpublished, cited by Kessler, I., 'Reward Systems', in J. Storey (ed.), *Human Resource Management: A Critical Text* (London: Routledge, 1995), pp. 254–79 at p. 256; Crystal, G. S., *In Search of Excess: the Overcompensation of American Executives* (New York: W. W. Norton, 1991).

24. *People Management* (1998), 4, 2, 22 January, p. 16.

25. National Institute for Economic and Social Research (London: NIESR, 1994).

26. Jenkins, A., 'The French Experience of Flexibility: Lessons for British HRM', in P. Sparrow and M. Marchington (eds.), *Human Resource Management: The New Agenda* (London, Pitman Publishing, Financial Times, 1998), pp. 259–71 at pp. 269–70.

27. Pfeffer, J., *Competitive Advantage through People* (Boston, MA: Harvard Business School Press, 1994); Huselid, M. A., 'The Impact of Human Resource Management Practices on Turnover, Productivity and Corporate Financial Performance', *Academy of Management Journal* (1995), 38, 3, pp. 635–72.

28. Guest, D., *Personnel Management* (1998), 4, 21, 29 October, pp. 64–5.

29. Wood, S. and Albanese, M., 'Can We Speak of a High Commitment Management on the Shop Floor?', *Journal of Management Studies* (1995), 32, 2, pp. 1–33.

30. Connock, S., *HR Vision: Managing a Quality Workforce* (London: Institute of Personnel Management, 1991).

31. Cully, *People Management* (1998), 4, 21, 29 October, p. 71; Marchington and Wilkinson, *Core Personnel and Development* (n. 12 above), pp. 136–7.

32. Anderson, G., 'Performance appraisal' in B. Towers (ed.), *The Handbook of Human Resource Management*, 2nd edn. (Oxford: Blackwell, 1992), pp. 196–222 at p. 198.

33. Harrison, R., *Human Resource Management: Issues and Strategies* (Wokingham: Addison-Wesley, 1993), p. 262.

34. Unpublished internal review (1995) of the performance appraisal system of one part of the MoD conducted by a member of the British Forces.

35. Peer appraisal tends to be popular amongst senior groups of professionals who resist appraisal by other non-professionals. The evidence from research on professional partnerships is that below partner level the main method of appraisal is superior-subordinate. Further reading on appraisal in professional firms: Morris, T. J. and Pinnington, A. H., 'Evaluating strategic fit in professional service firms', *Human Resource Management Journal* (1998), Vol. 8, No. 4, pp. 1–12.

36. Grint, K., 'What's wrong with performance appraisals? A critique and a suggestion', *Human Resource Management Journal* (1993), 3, 3, pp. 61–77.

37. Fletcher, *People Management* (1988), 4, 19, 1 October p. 46.

38. Grint, 'What's wrong with performance appraisals?'

39. Snape, E., Thompson, D., Yan, F. K., and Redman, T., 'Performance appraisal and culture: practice and attitudes in Hong Kong and Great Britain', *International Journal of Human Resource Management* (1998), 9, 5, October, pp. 841–61 (see p. 841).

40. Fletcher, C., and Williams, R., 'The route to performance management', *Personnel Management* (1992), October, pp. 42–7.

41. McGregor, D., *The Human Side of Enterprise* (New York: Harper Row, 1960).

42. Williams, S., 'Strategy and objectives', in F. Neale (ed.), *The Handbook of Performance Management* (London: Institute of Personnel Management, 1992), pp. 7–24.

43. Sparrow, P. and Marchington, M., 'Re-engaging the HRM Function', in P. Sparrow and M. Marchington (eds.), *Human Resource Management: The New Agenda* (London: Pitman Publishing, The Financial Times, 1998), 296–313 at p. 309.

44. Kaplan, R. S., and Norton, D. P., 'Begin by linking measurements to strategy', *Harvard Business Review* (1993), September–October, pp. 134–42.

45. Sparrow and Marchington, 'Re-engaging the HRM Function' (n. 43 above), p. 309.

46. Guest, D. E., 'Human Resource Management and Performance: a Review and Research Agenda', *International Journal of Human Resource Management* (1997), 8, 3, June, pp. 263–76.

47. MacDuffie, J. P., 'Human Resource Bundles and Manufacturing Performance: Flexible Production Systems in the World Auto Industry', *Industrial Relations and Labor Review* (1995), 48, pp. 197–221.

48. Schuler, R. S. and Jackson, S. E., 'Linking Competitive Strategies with Human Resource Management Practices', *Academy of Management Executive* (1987), 1, 3, pp. 207–19; Lawler, E. E. III., 'The strategic design of reward systems', in C. Fombrun, N. M. Tichy and M. A. Devanna, *Strategic Human Resource Management* (New York: John Wiley & Sons).

# Chapter 8
# Learning and Development

## Chapter Contents

# Introduction

T HIS chapter focuses on innovative ideas and practices in employee learning and development. First, it identifies the importance accorded to learning and development within human resource management, then investigates ways of creating a 'learning organization' and, finally, examines current policy and practice in employee development.

Chapters 2, 3, and 4 on the context of HRM have described how difficult it is for managers to maintain a long-term perspective on employee development and have shown it to be strongly influenced by national policy and by funding of education and training provision through state-subsidized institutions. Obstacles to implementing the learning organization exist and Chapter 2 on the environment of HRM has clarified the particular problems of the UK context for employee training and development. In summary, there is less of an institutional framework for training in the UK market system than in other developed countries, such as France and Germany, where there is greater legislative support and more frequent partnerships between education providers and employers. Training in the UK became more *ad hoc* following the abolition of the Industrial Training Boards (ITBs). Furthermore, it is difficult to plan and invest in training employees because there are strong pressures on management to reduce costs wherever possible and to deliver short-term financial returns. Compounding the demanding financial performance requirements faced by companies is the fact that UK financial institutions prefer to lend money on a short-term basis, making it still more difficult to invest in human assets, particularly whenever the return on the investment is either long-term or difficult to quantify. Employers in the UK traditionally have not sought to compete by long-term investment in employee development, preferring when possible to use lower skilled and lower cost labour or to recruit trained people directly from the external labour market.[1] There are, in addition, particular gaps in intermediate-skills training provision which are much more prevalent in the UK than in other European countries where more craft and technical apprentice training schemes remain. To sum up, a coherent and strategic approach to training and development is difficult enough to achieve in any company, but even more so in the UK environment.[2]

Many of the criticisms showing the UK environment to be inimical to developing human resources also apply to the USA. From an industrial relations perspective, Kochan and Osterman argue that Japanese and German corporations have been better than US firms at institutionalizing human resource practices that lead to competitive advantage.[3] They are sharply critical of the North American institutional context, observing there are particular obstacles for small and medium-sized employers (SMEs) who wish to compete by fostering a highly skilled, highly paid workforce. The labour market environment offers SMEs few incentives to train all of their employees to the highest level, for fear of loss of the HR investment from poaching by competitors. In contrast to overseas competitors, US employers are often isolated from each other and relationships with key trading partners and international competitors are adversarial, low-trust, and hostile. The net result of these circumstances is that they promote short-term thinking and a limited investment in human resources.

Adoption of human resource practices, and their sustainability, is heavily influenced by macro-factors, particularly capital markets, corporate governance structures, institutional infrastructure, and government policies. Kochan and Osterman argue that US management has not in the past paid sufficient attention to the macro-factors of the American environment, tending to concentrate on issues concerning product markets, labour markets, technology, competition strategy, managerial values, and the distribution of power within the organization. They propose that there is a link between HR and performance. The process begins with high investment in human capital and superior organizational practices, leading ultimately to a competitive society with high living standards. They say the following about their model, shown in Fig. 8.1:

The key argument is that achieving competitiveness at high standards of living requires a high rate of growth in productivity, product innovation, and adaptability to changing markets. This in turn requires corporate strategies that give high priority to developing and fully utilizing the skills of the work force. Finally, the gains of improved productivity must be distributed in an equitable fashion to the multiple stakeholders who helped create them and reinvested in ways that ensure future generations improved standards of living.[4]

Kochan and Osterman's model assumes that for wealth to be created, productivity must be improved; this includes increasing the efficiency of firms and the economy in

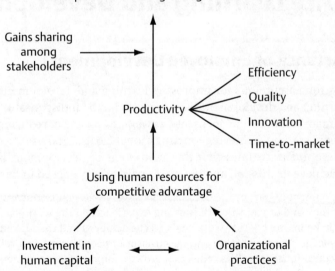

**Figure 8.1 Human resources and national competitiveness**

*Source*: Reprinted by permission of Harvard Business School Press. From *The Mutual Gains Enterprise* by T. A. Kochan and P. Osterman, Boston, MA 1994, p. 6. Copyright © 1994 by the President and Fellows of Harvard College; all rights reserved.

utilizing scarce resources. If enterprises are to be competitive in the global market-place, products must be continuously improved according to the quality standards that are important to customers, and time-to-market must be rapid and responsive. Their concept of productivity is broader than just efficiency, also implying enlarging the capability of firms and the economy as a whole to innovate and utilize new technologies. Ways of developing a more highly skilled workforce through the practices of the learning organization and training and developing employees to become more innovative are discussed in this chapter.

Fundamental change towards 'learning organizations' seems unlikely at the time of writing. One of the preconditions for it is for greater influence to be applied at the level of the state and on financial institutions to facilitate and respect employees' long-term learning and development. Creating a high-skills economy involves more than just ensuring skill supply for the nation's skill needs; it means addressing major structural issues such as the role of business networks, research and development, investment, and product innovation.[5] This chapter acknowledges the difficulties employees face in seeking better opportunities for learning and development, and does not pretend that learning and development will often be at the top of a line manager's agenda when he or she is facing short-term business pressures. The chapter also informs the reader about innovations in learning and development over the last thirty years and, most important, offers insight into what might be achieved.

# 1 What Are Learning and Development?

## The Importance of Employee Development

THERE are strong arguments for improving learning and development in organizations. Learning and development have been said to be indispensable components of strategic human resource management,[6] as well as a means of reducing uncertainty in the market-place and achieving organizational goals.[7] Harrison's definition of employee development assumes that the main point of development is to help the organization achieve its mission and business goals, as is proposed in hard HRM.

Employee development as part of the organization's overall human resource strategy means the skilful provision and organization of learning experiences in the workplace in order that performance can be improved, that work goals can be achieved and that, through enhancing the skills, knowledge, learning ability and enthusiasm of people at every level, there can be continuous organizational as well as individual growth. Employee development must, therefore, be part of a wider strategy for the business aligned with the organization's corporate mission and goals.[8]

Research suggests that this argument is consistent with the views of many UK business managers.[9]

Even in companies, such as Rover Group, that promote some individual learning and education separable from the direct needs of the business, top management would tend to agree with Harrison's perspective. Rover Group's 'Learning Business' initiative has given funding to employees to take courses in topics as wide-ranging as sheep husbandry and in-shore navigation. Its purpose was to increase employees' willingness and ability to learn in order that they could work more productively and innovatively. But the Rover Group New Deal, a contract made in 1992 between Rover Group and its employees, makes abundantly clear the basic commitment that employees must have to the business and the organization and is consistent with Harrison's assertion quoted above that employee development is part of the wider strategy of the business. Rover Group's New Deal refers to, amongst other issues of the employment relationship, employee involvement, employee development initiatives, and the importance of employees' focusing on quality and the needs of the business.[10]

## Definitions

To understand what we mean by 'learning' and 'development' in the organizational context, we need to define the commonly used terms 'learning', 'training', and 'education'. There are a variety of processes of learning and it takes place in many different contexts. The glossary of training terms published by the Department of Employment (DOE), which is now part of the Department for Education and Employment (DfEE), defined learning as:

The process whereby individuals acquire knowledge, skills and attitudes through experience, reflection, study or instruction.[11]

Training tends to be defined more narrowly than is learning or education. The DOE's glossary defined training as:

A planned and systematic effort to modify or develop knowledge/skill/attitude through 'learning' experience, to achieve effective performance in an activity or range of activities.[12]

Education was more broadly defined by the DOE as:

A process and a series of activities which aim at enabling an individual to assimilate and develop knowledge, skills, values and understanding that are not simply related to a narrow field of activity but allow a broad range of problems to be defined, analysed and solved.[13]

So, according to a broad interpretation of education, its purpose is to provide individuals with an understanding of the traditions, ideas, and values important to the society in which they live and to help them acquire and develop skills in learning, creativity, and communication. A difficulty that all three of the above definitions are said to have in common is that they are rooted in an individualist conceptualization of the world. That is to say, they concentrate on the individual to the exclusion of more collectivist concepts of learning, such as learning in teams, organizations, and the community.

# HRM v. Personnel Management Perspectives

HRM and personnel management perspectives on employee development are different: personnel management concentrates on controlled access to courses and formal training interventions that occur off the job, while HRM is more concerned with creating learning companies. Storey includes 'training and development' as one of his twenty-five points of difference and one of the key 'levers' in managing the human resource (see Chapter 1). Overall, Storey's levers for HRM emphasize managing individuals and the culture of the organization. Teamwork, managing climate and culture, having fewer pay grades, and wide-ranging cultural, structural, and personnel strategies are all part of the new HRM approach. In any one company, it should be remembered, most of these levers were management aspirations or plans under implementation rather than organizational reality.[14] Storey and Sisson have since voiced concern over what they argue is a gap between the rhetoric—'people are our greatest asset'—and the reality, namely that the UK is not a 'development-oriented, flexible, well-motivated, efficiently operating, highly skilled and well-paid economy'.[15] A recent survey on British manufacturing companies provides evidence that numerical and financial flexibility initiatives in the form of part-time work and fixed-term contracts strongly outweigh the development of multiple skills.[16] Sectors of the economy that are union-free have in general failed to introduce new HR initiatives and contracting-out of services has not led to improved HRM. Storey and Sisson recommend the UK find a better balance between individualism and collectivism in managing its human resources and industrial relations. Development of employees' skills and careers has become a focal point for recent industrial unrest and this may lead to more development opportunities within some companies where unions are influential or where individual grievances lead to significant employee-relations problems. These problems could be resolved in the future by a more proactive policy on employee development. An example of individual grievances erupting into collective action in a non-unionized company is the strike by cast members of the Disneyland Paris parade (including those portraying the big-name Disney characters Snow White and the Seven Dwarfs, Mickey and Minnie Mouse, and Goofy), which made newspaper headlines in the summer of 1998. The action lasted for one month but did not spread further throughout the non-unionized workforce. The major complaint was that the company was not providing the performers with development opportunities in ballet skills to enhance their careers and increase their employability.[17]

Storey and Sisson conclude that employee trust, commitment, and capability must be continuously improved to attain a high-quality workforce. Storey is unconvinced that HRM can ever be 'owned' by line management working in devolved business units with no strategic HRM and a climate dominated by short-term targets.[18] He optimistically proposes that the recent trends towards business process re-engineering, zero-based budgeting, outsourcing, and focusing on core processes will lead to less bureaucracy in organizations—and unavoidably challenge managers to rediscover the basic tenets of HRM. Future organizational success depends on a consistent and coherent approach to HRM, particularly the basics such as the human resource cycle of recruitment and selection, appraisal, development, and rewards. Management therefore must adopt a long-term perspective and responsibilities for provision of HR/IR must be clearer and more effectively co-ordinated at the various levels of the organization than they have been in the past. Storey and Sisson have argued, however, that this is extremely difficult in the UK and therefore managers interested in working towards the learning organization should be realistic about what can be achieved in the short term.

# 2  Creating the Learning Organization

CREATING the learning organization is a strategy for sustainable development in which more organizations may take a greater interest in the future, but as yet it is still mainly a vision of what might be. It is claimed to be not simply a new way of training individuals, but an approach to wider processes of learning that enable continuous transformation of the organization.[19] Pedler *et al.* have been influential in disseminating the learning organization concept in the UK and they define learning at the 'whole organization level' as follows: 'A learning company is an organization that facilitates the learning of all its members and continuously transforms itself.'[20] By 'members' of the organization they mean the full range of key stakeholders: 'employees, owners, customers, suppliers, neighbours, the environment and even competitors'.[21]

## Innovations in Training and Development

The following section traces the antecedents of the learning company concept, based on work by Pedler *et al.* In the UK during the 1950s, when labour was in short supply, training was either given only where needed in response to a specific problem or centred around the pursuit of qualifications and skills for promotion purposes.[22] By the mid-1960s, systematic approaches to training were becoming more common, particularly in large organizations, which were further encouraged to formalize training provision following the establishment of the Industry Training Boards (ITBs). As was mentioned in Chapter 2 on the environment of HRM, The Industrial Training Act of 1964 created the system whereby industry boards had power to raise a levy from companies to fund training. Companies were expected to produce training plans and reports. The ITBs played an important role in promoting better formal organization and improved design of training programmes, and, at their height, there were twenty-seven boards covering training arrangements for fifteen million employees. Unfortunately, companies were said to find them too bureaucratic and inflexible and, in 1973, a new national, central body—the Manpower Services Commission—was established to co-ordinate response to national training needs.

The systematic approach to training continued into the 1970s but often failed to produce desired outcomes because, so Pedler and his co-authors claim, it was unworkable.[23] As a consequence of its impracticality, employees became demotivated and felt undervalued. The systematic approach uses rational methods of planning, preparing, delivering, assessing, and evaluating training. It draws on models of learning and instruction[24] and operates on the assumption that outcomes should be specified, measured, and assessed. Where the training intervention fails, corrective action must be applied. Action might be, for example, improved planning, redesign of the content, or use of different systems and techniques of delivery.

Another development movement is organization development (OD), which has been more prevalent in the USA than in the UK and focuses on transforming individuals to help them become more open to personal learning and change, more emotionally sensitive, and more effective in dealing with people.[25] OD is a long-term approach to improving the organization's change processes, problem solving, and renewal. It is carried out with the help of internal or external consultants who assist management and employees in problem solving. The OD interventions pay attention to the interpersonal behaviour of individuals and groups, particularly their emotions and feelings, and expect people to become more open-minded, tolerant of each other, and better communicators. The OD programme is based on the integrity of the individual, and the consultants often have backgrounds and training in such fields as counselling and psychotherapy.[26]

A few large UK organizations have experimented with the OD movement, but Pettigrew reports that OD has been only marginally successful because it is too different from the attitudes and behaviour of dominant management cultures.[27] The chemicals and plastics multinational company ICI, for example, tried to implement OD methods. While its culture differed from site to site of the company, it tended to be either bureaucratic or technocratic, and neither of these cultures is amenable to OD interventions. Bureaucracies are generally too inflexible and hierarchical to allow the learning organization to flourish. Technocracies are also unreceptive because they value too much the technical expertise and rational decision making of elite groups, thus failing to encourage the commitment, communication, and involvement of employees. Interestingly, in June 1993 ICI demerged its pharmaceutical business into a separately owned company, Zeneca, in recognition that the industries ICI as a whole competed in were such different businesses that the pharmaceutical area was considered better off separately owned and managed.

Pedler *et al.* argued that by the 1980s, three different approaches to learning and development were evident. First, the OD approach was still being used in some companies but failing to deliver long-term significant benefits. Second, self-development and action learning were generally being used as an excuse for lack of real support for training and development. Self-development, when applied with clear commitment from top management, aims to solve poor transfer of training by developing more motivated and self-directed employees. The approach was based on learner-centredness and the learner having control over the processes of learning. The aim is to gain improved transfer of learning to the workplace; formal training and development interventions, although important, are not the facilitators' and trainers' main objective. They instead aim to empower people to learn from their actions and to act on their learning.[28] Typical roles of the manager or trainer in facilitating individual employees' self-development are those of instructor, coach, or mentor. Which role is selected depends on its appropriateness for learning. Instructing helps individuals best when they need directing, coaching is best when some guidance is required, and mentoring is called for when development takes place over a long period of time. Mentors offer support and experience and often, but not always, are of higher positional authority in the organization than the individual being mentored. Action learning is a technique pioneered by Reg Revans, involving tailor-made management development based on real-life problems.[29] A common approach is to form a small group into an 'action learning set' and provide an opportunity for reflecting on a major project or projects occurring over several weeks or months. The projects are based on real workplace problems and have objectives derived from needs of the business that have been identified by senior management. The third approach to learning and development in the 1980s came about when there was a lot of excitement and enthusiasm generated by the American management gurus making pleas to top executives to change their organizations' cultures and to create excellent companies.[30] Unfortunately, it did not significantly alter employees' exposure to training and development,[31] and the claims that financial performance could be improved by adopting 'excellent company' practices have been in doubt since the research was first published.[32]

According to Pedler *et al.*, the problem with all of these approaches—OD, self-development and action learning, and excellent company cultures—was that it was felt companies were making too many changes with too little effect.[33] Interest grew during the 1980s in quality management and Japanese management practices, partly because they were seen to be integral to Japanese companies' business success. Inspection of these practices showed formal on-the-job training to be very important. However, many other important management considerations were also raised that were not so much about training or development interventions as about making a concerted and collective approach to continuous improvement of the organization. Japanese management practices seemed to be able to develop employees who will work with high organizational commitment, high involvement, and low conflict with management. Pedler *et al.* represented graphically the historical occurrence of innovation in training and development as a timeline, shown in Fig. 8.2.

The reader should note that the Pedler representation of the move from systematic training methods to the learning company concentrates on the history of innovation in training and development and has been discussed for that reason. Their timeline identifies the development of new ideas over time, but should not be taken out of this context, which would be to accord a more significant role to these innovative approaches than they actually have had on employee development within most UK work places.

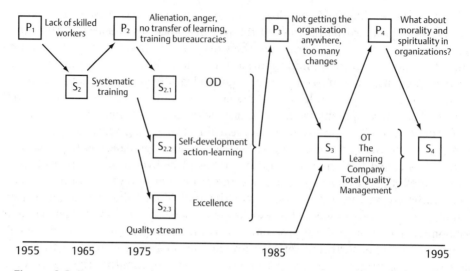

**Figure 8.2 From systematic training to the learning company**

*Source*: Pedler, M., Burgoyne, J. and Boydell, T. (1991) *The Learning Company: A Strategy for Sustainable Development*, Maidenhead: McGraw-Hill, Figure 2.9, p. 17. Reproduced with the kind permission of McGraw-Hill Publishing Company.

## The Learning Company

The learning company is a set of aspirations more than a reality and represents a synthesis of ideas for development, including self-development, action learning, OD, quality management, and organizational transformation (OT). Various writers have proposed ground rules for becoming more like a learning company; Pedler *et al.* propose eleven, organized under five general categories, shown in Box 8.1.

> BOX 8.1
> ### How Companies Become Learning Companies
>
> Strategy
>
> *1. The Learning Approach to Strategy*
> Strategy and direction are regularly updated. Policy and strategy are structured as learning processes. Experimentation, frequent modification, and feedback.
>
> *2. Participative Policy Making*
> All members participate so that policy making is significantly influenced by stakeholders. Use of appraisal and career planning discussions for policy development within an organizational climate that encourages employees to express conflicting views and differences.
>
> Looking In
>
> *3. Informating*
> Information, databases, and communication systems are used in the company for a variety

of learning purposes. Readily available information on departments/sections is made available through use of computers. Information technology used to facilitate understanding and decision making.

### 4. Formative Accounting and Control

Systems of accounting and reporting are structured to assist learning. Everyone feels responsible and accountable for work group/unit. Accounting and finance are advisory and the system encourages individuals to undertake risks involving venture capital.

### 5. Internal Exchange

Co-operation between groups (e.g. departments) within the organization; treating each other as internal customers and ensuring that goods and services are delivered according to agreement, on time and at the right cost.

### 6. Reward Flexibility

Discussion of and experimentation with reward systems. All participate in determining the reward system and the basic values underpinning it, and there is shared use of flexible working, enabling individuals to make different contributions and be rewarded accordingly.

## Structures

### 7. Enabling Structures

Experimentation with new forms of organizational structure. Structure and rules are regularly discussed, reviewed, and changed. Appraisal is focused on developmental aspects with careers flexibly structured to allow for experimentation, growth, and adaptation.

## Looking Out

### 8. Boundary Workers as Environmental Scanners

All employees monitor and report on activities and events outside of the company. Company regularly receives intelligence reports on the economy, markets, technological developments, and world trends. Internal meetings regularly review the business environment and external meetings are frequently held with stakeholders (e.g., customers, suppliers, and community members). Learning events and meetings with business partners.

### 9. Inter-company Learning

Employees go on job attachments to work for a specified period of time for business partners. Participation in joint ventures with partners to develop new products and markets. Use of benchmarking to learn best practice from other industries.

## Learning Opportunities

### 10. Learning Climate

A positive attitude to the principles of continuous improvement. Employees are always trying to learn and do better, including learning from what went wrong. People take time to question their own practices and will get others to help them when needed. Differences of all sorts are recognized and positively valued as essential to learning and creativity.

*11. Self-development Opportunities for All*
Open-access, resource-based learning available for employees and external stakeholders. People are encouraged to be active self-developers. Appraisal and career planning concentrate on identifying and exploring individual learning needs. Self-development budgets are used.

*Source*: Pedler, M., Burgoyne, J. and Boydell, T., *The Learning Company: A Strategy for Sustainable Development* (1991), Figure 3.1, pp. 26–7. Reproduced with the kind permission of McGraw-Hill Publishing Company.

In the US, Peter Senge and his colleagues from the Massachusetts Institute of Technology have worked with many executives in helping their companies to become learning organizations. Senge recommends that organizations encourage more adaptive and generative learning.[34] Adaptive learning is important for adapting to changes in the environment and has become particularly important for bureaucratic organizations, which have generally been slow to react to external change. Generative learning is particularly important for creating new ideas, products, and processes, for example, in new product development, innovation, and quality management. Senge cites the Japanese corporations of the 1980s as being effective in both adaptive and generative learning. He recommends three critical processes for building learning organizations: building shared visions, surfacing and challenging mental models, and engaging in systems thinking.

Building shared visions is a continuous process involving the distribution of leadership skills amongst a number of employees and the creation of shared visions by communicating, analysing, and blending individual visions. Uncovering and testing mental models is a discipline that aims to challenge assumptions within organizations with the aim of encouraging learning. False assumptions need to be questioned and managers have to become more skilled in understanding and exploring other points of view. Senge says that managers learn to be good at advocating their preferred viewpoint but must be able to balance their presentation and persuasion skills with the ability to inquire meaningfully into others' views and opinions. This means being able to distinguish what Argyris and Schon call 'espoused theory' from 'theory in use'.[35] The espoused theory is what people in organizations claim to be the theory that the organization operates under, while the theory in use is the ideas they actually use. For most individuals part of the solution in more successfully surfacing and testing mental models is to recognize and defuse defensive routines. These are routines which we all use to avoid plain speaking or uncomfortable issues; often, these defensive routines destroy full and frank discussion. By 'engaging in systems thinking', Senge means focusing systematically on underlying trends and forces of change. This is the ability to see interrelationships and dynamic complexity and ultimately to identify solutions. Senge says that good leaders often are systems thinkers capable of focusing on high-leverage changes, that is, changes that require minimum effort but lead to significant improvement.

# The Learning Cycle

The learning organization is about individual and organizational change (organizational change will be covered in detail in Chapter 9) and about creating the conditions for better learning. It is more collectivist than are traditional learning theory and instructional design, which have roots in disciplines such as information science and cognitive and developmental psychology. Dixon proposes that there is an 'organizational learning cycle', a way that we can learn collectively.[36] Dixon's cycle borrows heavily from work by Kolb, who is best known for his theory of individual, experiential learning.[37] Dixon's and Kolb's learning cycles are both four-stage processes of continuously revising and creating knowledge.

Kolb's experiential learning cycle proposes that an individual's learning progresses through four stages: concrete experience, reflective observation, abstract conceptualization, and active experimentation (see Fig. 8.3).[38] The first stage requires generating ideas through experience. During the second stage the individual integrates and reflects on the experience. The third stage involves drawing conclusions and abstracting lessons or concepts from the material experienced and reflected upon. The fourth stage involves testing out theories or ideas, which then returns the individual to seeking more concrete experience, and so on. In a perfect world, Kolb says, the individual would have a balance of abilities consistent with his or her four stages of the learning cycle.[39]

In reality, most people develop learning styles that emphasize some abilities over others.[40] For example, a finance manager with strong mathematical skills may prefer

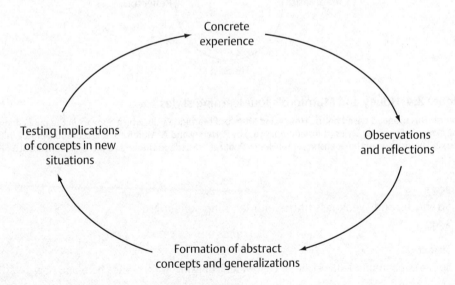

**Figure 8.3  Kolb's experiential learning cycle**

*Source*: Kolb, D. A. (1996) 'Management and the Learning Process' in pp. 270–87, K. Starkey, *How Organizations Learn*, London: Thomson Publications, p. 271.

abstract conceptualization and active experimentation, while a sales manager may have greater interest in learning from concrete experience and reflective observation. This is not to say that one should be too quick to stereotype people or occupations; within any group there will be a range of abilities and preferences. One of the main roles of the learning styles in employee development has been to improve individuals' learning and their interpersonal communication by making them more aware of their own and others' learning styles.

# Individual Learning Styles

Honey and Mumford propose a model similar to Kolb's in which individuals have a mixture of four learning styles, normally with a preference for one or two of the styles.[41] Honey and Mumford's learning styles questionnaire (LSQ) and Kolb's learning styles inventory (LSI) are both diagnostic tests to help individuals identify their strengths, weaknesses, and development needs. The four learning styles, based on Kolb's theory of stages in the learning cycle, are: activitist, reflector, theorist, and pragmatist. Box 8.2 provides a short definition of each style along with its potential strengths and weaknesses.

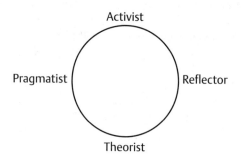

### Figure 8.4 Honey and Mumford's four learning styles

*Source*: This model is based on the Honey and Mumford Learning Cycle, which appears in the publication *The Manual of Learning Styles* (third edition, 1992) by P. Honey and A. Mumford. It is reproduced here with the kind permission of the publisher, Peter Honey Publications Ltd., 10 Linden Avenue, Maidenhead, SL6 6HB.

---

BOX 8.2
## Strengths and Weakness of the four learning styles
Activist

*Strengths*
Sociable, open-minded, welcomes challenge, highly involved, prefers here-and-now

*Weaknesses*
Bored by implementation details and the longer term, always seeks the limelight

Reflector

*Strengths*
Good listener, tolerant, sees different perspectives, postpones judgement, cautious

*Weaknesses*
Takes a back seat in meetings, low profile, distant

Theorist

*Strengths*
Integrates observations with theory, rational, objective, analytical

*Weaknesses*
Perfectionist, detached, impatient with subjective and intuitive thinking

Pragmatist

*Strengths*
Experimenter, quick to adopt and try out new ideas, practical, down-to-earth

*Weaknesses*
Impatient with theory, impatient with open-ended discussion

No learning style has a monopoly of the virtues, and the strengths of each of the learning styles are not appropriate for all situations. What is a strength in one situation may become a weakness in another. This is one reason why, when a group works as a team, it is often able to perform better than solitary experts. A good example of this is what happened during a week of team-building exercises in a major car company when engineers pitted their wits against those of groups of non-specialists from a variety of disciplines (operations, finance, IT, purchasing, etc.) in performing specific tasks. The engineers were shocked to find they didn't perform tasks involving a significant engineering element as well as the non-specialists did. The hard lesson for them was that better teamwork, using a range of learning styles to implement the full learning cycle, is a real strength and the possession of professional occupational expertise is not sufficient on its own.[42]

# Organizational Learning

As was mentioned in the last section, Dixon's organizational learning cycle is geared to the collective organization and not individuals.[43] Kolb's learning cycle was developed to represent individuals' learning, but was modified by Dixon to represent organizational learning. Dixon's cycle, which contains four stages similar to Kolb's, is shown in Fig. 8.5.

In Dixon's organizational learning cycle, information is widely generated by utilizing the external and internal environments. It is collected continually and from

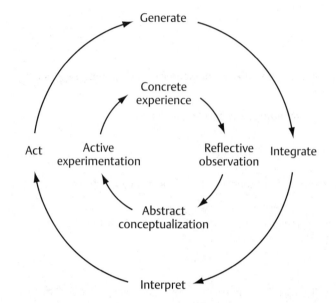

**Figure 8.5  Dixon's and Kolb's learning cycles**

*Source*: Dixon, *The Organizational Learning Cycle* (1994), p. 46, McGraw-Hill, Figure 4.2, p. 46.

multiple sources. Internally, it is generated by experimentation, analysis of mistakes and successes, and the use of data for self-correction. Further, research and development is not the exclusive preserve of an isolated R&D department, but is conducted by line management. Information is integrated into the organizational context by disseminating it accurately and in a timely manner. The flow of information is unimpeded and employees are rewarded for accurate reporting on what they have found rather than for just saying what they think they are expected to say. Information sharing is encouraged through job design that focuses on multi-skilling and multi-functioning. Where possible, staff positions such as personnel and marketing are integrated with line management. Information is collectively interpreted by encouraging all employees to discuss their different interpretations with each other. Rather than funnelling information to a conclusion, individuals are expected to be more open-minded, flexible, and questioning of their own points of view. Frequent interactions, keeping the organization limited in size, and treating everyone equally are other methods of collective interpretation. In summary, everything is held to be open to question. Action is taken giving authority and control to the local level of the organization. This is done according to centrally agreed, critical specifications. There are no penalties for failure, when taking reasonable risks, and the reward system uses profit sharing and stimulates committed and innovative action.

The organizational learning cycle depends on a supportive organization structure and culture; further, it assumes individuals will be motivated to learn. Western companies have been criticized in the past for encouraging functionally divided careers that have motivated ambitious managers and employees to work for the good of their own work group and function rather than to the strategic benefit of the company. Ford of Europe, a US-owned company operating in Europe, had an organizational structure described as 'functional chimneys'. The functional structure encouraged vertical communication and a high degree of specialization in areas such as finance, accounting, and product planning, but had the negative effect of making Ford employees internally competitive rather than focused as one group serving its automobile markets. Competition from overseas manufacturers, particularly Asian car manufacturers, became more intense in the late 1970s and 1980s, forcing Ford executives to reconsider the effectiveness of both their business strategies and the internal organization. As is often the case for many companies across the world, it takes a big shock caused by a development in the external environment to persuade managers of the need to act quickly and make fundamental changes.[44]

Starkey and McKinlay have researched Ford of Europe's improvement of the product development process.[45] In short, Ford's costs were too high and the time-scale too long. Japanese companies such as Mazda, Toyota, and Honda were identified as leaders in product development and their approach was very different from Ford's. These Japanese companies were more integrated and cross-functional organizations using distinct management practices (as was discussed in Section 3 of Chapter 1). Ford learnt a lot from Mazda by having a 25% equity stake in the company. It learnt from Mazda's successful practice of simultaneous engineering, judged to be a new approach and a step beyond matrix management (a popular form of organization for innovation and project management in the engineering industry), because it operated with a tighter co-ordination of product development and manufacturing. In 1989, Ford was facing the need to reduce its new product cycle time by eighteen months just to become competitive. Ford had had problems in the past with either manufacturing dominating and compromising product design or, vice versa, product design remaining aloof from manufacturing, leading to inefficiencies and operational problems. Both problems were caused by compartmentalized thinking and a failure of functional integration.

Mazda stresses four factors for successful simultaneous engineering: communication between product development and manufacturing; formal co-operation including cross-functional careers; team culture and shared responsibility; and customer-driven processes. Employee development in Ford will be of strategic benefit only where it can stimulate improved innovation and new ways of working. Following Mazda's example, an important part of the development process is to facilitate increased lateral communication and decreased functional separation. Separate and isolated employee development programmes will not take the company far enough in the highly competitive world automobile market. Employee development must occur in improved cross-functional work environments and reinforce new structures of organizational learning. Managers and employees must learn to co-operate and integrate their activities more effectively rather than coexist under conditions of internal competition, isolation, and status divisions. The evidence then is that the structure and culture of Japanese corporations have been more successful than those of Western companies in facilitating some aspects typical of the learning organization, such as information sharing throughout the company, on-the-job learning, teamwork, and routine development of subordinates by managers.

# 3  Employee Development

## Thinking More Broadly about Development

HRM claims to have a more proactive approach to employee development than personnel management does. HRM is said to view promoting and facilitating continuous learning as everybody's responsibility. In the past, the separate training function of the organization was considered responsible for learning and development, it being almost exclusively the duty of a small department staffed by a training manager and trainers. In some companies, training has been seen as part of the personnel function, and line managers have tended to avoid responsibility for identifying development needs and supporting training and development. In the learning organization, employee development does not centre exclusively upon the training or personnel department; rather, as in HRM, it is considered the responsibility of everyone in the organization, and particularly line management.

An important part of the management of employee development is to decide what tasks are the responsibilities of which party—employees, their line managers, or, where it exists, the training department. The training or HR department will provide for some needs; others will be best met by contracting external providers. For example, it may be found to be more cost-effective and time-saving to pay a specialist training consultancy to run a two-day training course on assertiveness skills rather than to 'upskill' the in-house trainers to be able to deliver it themselves. In HRM, training and development have a big role to play in innovation.[46] Much of the employees' development will be informal and occur through on-the-job learning; however, there is often additional need for structured, off-the-job learning programmes. Trainers and HR facilitators are now most frequently encouraged to develop their role as change agents in managing change (see Chapter 9). The trainers must therefore be highly flexible and supportive of innovation, and some of them will play major parts in organization-wide change through partnership with managers, idea generation, and sponsoring and 'orchestrating' innovation. Here, facilitation and co-ordination skills are more important than imparting instruction or assessing individuals' skills.

Research on innovation in organizations has found that major technological changes frequently come from outside the industry; mature product markets and their leading companies generally don't spawn the new breakthrough product that undercuts them.[47] The transistor, for example, was not a product of companies that were manufacturing vacuum tubes. There are some companies—although they are unusual—that seek to innovate continuously, such as 3M, which has a business mission committed to developing new products that are first to market. These are high-investment products that often have high profit margin sales for a comparatively short and fixed period of time. 3M knows that profitable innovation most often comes from listening to customers and having an internal organization that can learn, acquire promising small entrepreneurial technology companies, and enter into joint ventures with business partners. For years, 3M has encouraged lateral and informal communication as well as using the formal organization structure for funding ideas and promoting product champions.[48] Galbraith recommends that, if organizations wish to innovate, they must attend to four design components: structure, processes, reward systems, and people. The structure must encourage idea generators, sponsors, and orchestrators. It must be differentiated enough to allow variability of ideas and activities and possess small pools or 'reservations' of resources. The processes must involve planning ahead for innovation, idea generating, blending ideas, and managing innovative products. The reward system should provide opportunities, autonomy, promotion, and recognition for individuals and groups who are successful innovators. Finally, Galbraith says, people must be selected and encouraged to self-select and then the necessary training and development must be provided.

The next three parts of this section review current innovations in the policy and practice of employee development: outdoor development to promote teamwork and organizational commitment, open learning methods and training technology tools to improve employees' access to learning and development, and the use of competences in employee development.

# Outdoor Development

Outdoor development courses have been used in some companies (for example, Fujitsu) for inculcating teams with company values or as part of induction for new recruits. The learning activities on these courses aim to motivate employees and develop their skills in leadership, teamwork, problem solving, decision making, and creativity. There are a number of specialist providers of this type of training; however, to be successful, pro-grammes must be carefully planned and properly supported in the workplace, includ-ing making sure that a critical mass of delegates obtain places. Experienced companies aim to maximize the benefits of these programmes by ensuring that the facilitators and trainers running them are well-informed about the company's strategy, culture, and employee attitudes. Managers of the employees attending these courses give pre-course briefings and post-course feedback and organize follow-up activities to ensure the maximum transfer of learning back into the workplace. If these activities are not performed, the outdoor development will not be appropriately contextualized and delegates will complain that the outdoor events were not relevant or, more disappoint-ing still, that expectations were raised and then not met back at work. Marchington and Wilkinson report problems with outdoor development where programmes have been poorly managed and inadequately supported by employing organizations.[49] They also quote some of the ground rules for increasing the chances of success:

- integration with other training activity and with organizational goals;
- clear and achievable objectives which are monitored and relate back to the work-place; these need to be established in conjunction with the outdoor trainers;

- rigorous checks on safety offered by providers;
- tutors and trainers who are skilled at undertaking ongoing reviews of the courses, both of a structured and unstructured nature;
- programmes tailored to individual and company needs;
- a sense of ownership on the part of the delegates.[50]

Jones has examined a number of the claims for outdoor management development and argues that one of its most potent strengths is in improving individuals' ability to learn.[51] Jones cautions against counter-productive outdoor development, for example, sessions that unnecessarily reinforce status relationships at work, often resulting in an over-assertion of power and authority of the organizational hierarchy.

## Technology-based Learning and Open Learning

Large corporations and financial institutions began to experiment on a larger scale with open, flexible, and distance learning methods in the 1980s. Organizations such as BT have used computers for instructing field engineers and for simulation training (in, for example, circuit fault diagnosis) for over twenty-five years. The technology platforms have become increasingly more capable of delivering high-quality multimedia presentations that respond flexibly to individual queries, answers, and decisions. Training technologies using computers and audiovisual machines have a history of usage and experimentation in education and training going back over the last four decades. The 1960s saw the development of the instructional design movement and audiovisual learning programmes. It was the period when 'teaching machines' were introduced, the more sophisticated ones being controlled by computer. There was a great deal of interest in the use of educational television, film, overhead projectors, and 35mm slide displays. The 1970s brought video cassettes and, when the price of Xerox machines went down, greater use of photocopied handouts. The 1980s saw more sophisticated software programming and the use of more powerful microcomputers. It was a decade when interactive video (computer-controlled videodiscs) had a brief heyday in large company training by providing an advanced form of computer-based training and utilizing a range of video, graphics, and audio material. The 1980s were a decade of experimentation and a period of government-funded projects in new software technologies, especially artificial intelligence.

The 1990s have seen a continued improvement in the use of the technologies of the 1980s in both work and home environments. Personal computers (PCs) are much more prevalent in offices, educational institutions, and training organizations. Multimedia capabilities have become more available through improved technologies in Windows and hypermedia software, computer graphics interfaces, and in-built CD peripheral devices. Children are developing IT literacy skills as a normal part of their upbringing with home computer games and widespread availability of PCs in schools. The 1990s have been a decade of steadily increasing usage of advanced multimedia technologies in large companies and in the home. Training technologies can be flexible to a range of learning aims in basic technical skills and 'soft' or 'people' skills (for example, interpersonal communication). Computer-based training offers a learning experience in which the path the learner takes through the material can be highly individualized yet restricted so that all users ultimately achieve the final objectives. On the one hand, training technologies can help in 'closed' tasks; for example, a bank employee can learn how to process a customer payment involving ten to twenty steps that have to be learnt and practised until the employee is competent. On the other hand, the learning might be more open-ended: individuals or groups browsing through a large database of stills, video clips, and computer simulations to acquaint themselves with an area of a country or a complex plant or piece of CMC machinery, for example.

Open learning centres were established as new facilities in many large companies and education institutions during the 1980s and 1990s. Depending on how they are defined, their origins can be traced back to open-access education and training technologies of the 1960s or further back to correspondence courses, institutes, specialist libraries, and societies of the 1800s. Derek Rowntree proposes that open learning can be considered in two different contexts: philosophy and method.

- A philosophy: a set of beliefs about teaching and learning that involve reducing barriers to access and giving learners control over learning.
- A method: a set of techniques for teaching and learning. Open learning using self-study materials and a range of media such as print, audio cassettes, television, computers, and so on.[52]

National provision of open learning in the UK was begun by some noteworthy institutions that have given people an opportunity to learn who otherwise would not have been able to study on traditional, formal programmes. A number of other countries have a wealth of experience and expertise in open and distance learning, particularly the USA, Canada, and Australia, where large distances have rendered it impractical for some rural populations to pursue traditional face-to-face methods of education. The National Extension College (NEC) was established in 1963 to give adults a second chance in academic and vocational studies, learning mainly from specially written courses, sometimes using TV programmes. This was followed by the Open University (OU), established in 1971 to provide distance learning, supplemented by occasional workshops and summer schools. Nearly two million people have studied with the OU. It has a world-wide reputation for its high-quality course materials developed by teams of specialists and its flexible system of credit-based undergraduate degrees, diplomas, and certificates. In 1987, the Open College was established by the government to transform vocational education and training in the same way that the OU had managed to influence attitudes in higher education. The Open College failed to achieve its targets, and there is still a lot of work to do through the Training Enterprise Councils (TECs) and other education and training bodies to encourage open learning, particularly in the small and medium-sized enterprise. Technology comes into play again here, linking students in open and distance learning programmes with teachers located at a central institution. Some companies such as BT, Prudential Corporation, and Price Waterhouse began to experiment more with training technologies in open and distance learning during the 1980s.[53] The increasing geographical spread of many large organizations' operations, combined with improvements in hardware and software, have encouraged managers' interest in technology-based training.

The media technologies used for open learning in the last decade of the twentieth century are more sophisticated and versatile than the products available in the 1960s. Reynolds and Iwinski recommend using the term 'technology-based learning' ('TBL'), in preference to 'technology-based training', to cover the full variety of information and communication technologies.[54] Many of the uses for TBL involve informal and unplanned learning through media such as interactive media, video and computer teleconferencing, simulators, and virtual reality devices. The use of Internet and Intranet (Internet services exclusive to one organization and its chosen partners) has grown rapidly throughout the 1990s. Corporate companies such as BP have made creative and intensive use of computer databases, computer conferencing, and Intranet services to promote 'breakthrough advances' in learning by employees. In the words of BP chief executive John Browne, 'Leadership is all about catalyzing learning as well as better performance.'[55] Large organizations have had a leading role in the development and distribution of TBL in the UK. It has been used for over ten years in diverse industries, including telecommunications (for example, BT), banking (Lloyds-TSB, Barclays), financial and insurance services (Abbey National), oil (BP, Shell), and automotive (Rover, Ford, Jaguar). The government has played a critical role in financing and promoting new technologies in training through institutions such as the DTI (Department of Trade and Industry), DfEE (Department for Education and Employment) and the NCET (National Council for Educational Technology).

Banks and financial services have been one of the most proactive industry sectors in using computers and new technologies for training and employee development. Lloyds Bank and TSB are one example of this. Both were regular users of technology-based training prior to the 1996 merger forming Lloyds-TSB. Lloyds and TSB have both used computer-based training and audiotape since the mid-1980s for open learning. In 1985, Lloyds invested in interactive video (IV) and were thus comparatively early adopters of IV technology, and they quickly moved on to developing compact disc (CD) training materials. From 1990 onwards, Lloyds was able to deliver CD training via the Branch Automated System (BAS) and Wide Area Network (WAN). These TBL programmes take approximately fifteen minutes for the trainee to complete, are multimedia-based, and involve practical training in skills such as 'product training', 'daily risk management', 'a quality welcome', 'sales management' and 'coaching for results'. Before the merger, Lloyds had over one hundred open learning centres and TSB had over one hundred learning resource centres. Post-merger, Lloyds-TSB planned to further increase its provision of open learning to nearly 300 centres. The two main groups of employees being trained through open learning are clerical and junior management. Open learning and training technologies are only part of Lloyds-TSB's total training provision. Traditional forms of in-house training and external courses through education and training providers are also used. The Lloyds-TSB merger joined two organizations that both had a tradition of in-house and external management development, clerical training, and open learning centres.

# Management Development

HRM places more importance on management development than did traditional personnel management; hence this last part of Section 3 reviews recent initiatives in management development and particularly the competence movement. Storey's twenty-five-item checklist (see Chapter 1) advises, from the viewpoint of HRM, that line management use transformational leadership and that general, business, and line managers be the key HR decision makers.[56] Under HRM, managers' core skills are those of facilitation rather than negotiation. In later work Storey says increased activity in the field of management development has raised as many questions as it has answered.[57] How, he asks, should management development be conceptualized? What are the main methods and techniques? What are management competences and how effective has the Management Charter Initiative (see p. 205) been since it was launched in 1988? What factors influence the provision and effectiveness of management development?

Under conditions of greater instability and increased global competition, Storey argues, managers capable of reliable and efficient performance, high conformity, cost reduction, and what are called 'satisficing' behaviours ('social pleasers') do not have enough capabilities to ensure a well-managed organization. Other competences of a more entrepreneurial and flexible nature are now sought after, particularly at the higher levels of the organization. An idea of what these new competences might be can be gained from Gareth Morgan's research study, reported in his book *Riding the Waves of Change*.[58] His study of emerging managerial competences was funded by Shell Canada and involved senior executives, twenty of whom participated in a round-table forum. The competences they identified were: reading the environment, proactive management, leadership and vision, HRM, promoting creativity, learning and innovation, skills of remote management (particularly facilitation and empowerment), using information technology as a transformative force, managing complexity, and developing contextual competences (particularly building alliances and social responsibility). The interested reader is advised to consult the book for more detail of the scope and content of these proposed competences. Reading the environment requires competence in scanning and gathering intelligence, forecasting, scenario planning, and identifying key points of change. Human resource management, they propose, involves valuing people as key resources, developing abilities during organizational change, getting the best out of specialist and generalist qualities, and managing in an environment where all managers and employees are, ultimately, equals.

Management development during the 1980s became more connected than it previously had been with managing organizational change (see Chapter 9), the reduction of middle management and their replacement by work teams that are tightly performance-managed.[59] These management development programmes have had common aims, such as making managers more innovative, risk-taking, and 'business-like'.[60] Facilitators of change have sought to make managers aware of the change in company values and the need to concentrate on providing quality customer services at competitive prices. The methods of delivery have normally combined both formal and informal methods of development. Managers have had to attend change conferences and formal skills training in new values, work methods, and systems. Informally, it is known that those who are most likely to survive in the organization are those able to enact the new values with commitment and responsibility.

While there are some opportunities for promotion in organizations, there has been a general de-layering of the management hierarchy and downsizing, meaning that development is a required part of the job and not something done only to managers who either lack necessary skills or who are being developed for promotion. Many of the methods and techniques used in management development apply equally to other employees. Indeed, if organizations develop their managers, they must similarly advance the attitudes and skills of subordinate employees; otherwise problems of communication and skill shortages will result further down the line. As was mentioned in section one of this chapter, some companies, such as Rover Group, have implemented ambitious employee development and assistance programmes to ensure the whole organization is receptive to learning new skills and ideas and improving themselves.[61]

Other countries have different traditions of management development. The American approach involves provision of formal business education in colleges and universities with a very high output of MBA graduates.[62] The French have favoured recruiting top management material from élite schools, known as Grandes Écoles, and the Germans have pursued in-depth technical and university education with relatively little emphasis on formal business qualifications, until more recently. The MBA degree was not available in German universities in the 1980s and early 1990s and the few who studied for it did so through collaboration with foreign providers such as Henley Management College, Cranfield University and the OU. The Japanese approach favours recruiting raw material from top universities and then training managers in-company over the years through a process of continuous development, with developing one's subordinates being a key role of the Japanese manager.[63] The Japanese and German approaches have both favoured strong internal labour markets for management development, which leads to high likelihood of promotion from within the organization and routine, planned employee development of the core workforce.

The importance attached to competence development for management is usually traced back to a number of reports of the mid-1980s, saying what many people in business had for some time been acutely aware of—that managers were receiving inadequate formal and informal development.[64] It is hard to quantify informal development, but easier to measure formal development (for instance, in number of training days per year). During the time of those reports, managers were receiving approximately one day of training a year on average, although provision was highly skewed, with the majority receiving none. The amount of training for managers in the UK has steadily grown and continued to grow throughout the national recession of the early 1990s, but according to most researchers the UK still lags behind its major competitors.[65] An employee in a professional occupation is five times more likely to receive training than an unskilled employee, but only a few UK companies have been consistent over recent years in resourcing management training.[66] The amount of formal training input is only one measure of management development, which says nothing directly about the quality and effectiveness of the provision, but it is at least one indicator that, overall, if not very rapidly in the UK, provision is gradually improving.

---

BOX 8.3
### The Management Charter Initiative

The Management Charter Initiative (MCI) was launched in 1988 by the Confederation of Business and Industry (CBI), the British Institute of Management (BIM) and the Foundation for Management Education. An employer-led body named the National Forum for Management Education and Development was formed. The MCI is specifically responsible for improving and assessing management functional competences and has developed National Occupational Standards for managers. These standards are a nationally recognized and accredited system for developing more effective managers in the workplace. The MCI standards are linked at different levels of management to National Vocational Qualifications (NVQs), which, as was mentioned in Section 3 of Chapter 2, are divided into levels 1–5, reflecting increasing levels of difficulty.

There are seven key roles in the MCI Occupational Standards for Managers and each is divided into units. The units subdivide into elements, which themselves consist of performance criteria together with underpinning knowledge and understanding. Assessment of the standards is primarily work-based and involves testing the knowledge and understanding required for consistent performance. The assessor essentially wants to know what a manager can do and that he or she can perform competently.

In summary, the standards consist of:

Key Roles
Units
Elements
Performance criteria
(underpinning knowledge and understanding)

The seven key roles are:

A:  Manage activities
B:  Manage resources
C:  Manage people
D:  Manage information
E:  Manage energy
F:  Manage quality
G:  Manage projects

There is space here to give details on only one example.

### Key Role C: Manage people

This role describes the work of managers in getting the most from their teams. It covers recruiting, training, building the team, allocating and evaluating work, and dealing with people problems. It also includes managing oneself and managing relations with others at work.

*Units*

C1  Manage yourself

C2  Develop your own resources

C3  Enhance your own performance

C4  Create effective working relationships

C5  Develop productive working relationships

C6  Enhance productive working relationships

C7  Contribute to the selection of personnel for activities

C8  Select personnel for activities

C9  Contribute to the development of teams and individuals

C10  Develop teams and individuals to enhance performance

C11  Develop management teams

C12  Lead the work of teams and individuals to achieve their objectives

C13  Manage the performance of teams and individuals

C14  Delegate work to others

C15  Respond to poor performance of teams and individuals

C16  Deal with poor performance in your team

C17  Redeploy personnel and make redundancies.

*Source: What are Management Standards?—An Introduction* (Management standards information pack, Management Charter Initiative (1997), MCI, Russell Square House, 10–12 Russell Square, London WC1B 5BZ.

The standards can be assessed at different NVQ levels of qualification. Level 3 is for practising managers or supervisors, and levels 4 and 5 for higher-level managers. At different levels some units are mandatory and some are optional, thus providing some choice for individuals with different job responsibilities and career goals.

The assessment criteria are straightforward and assessors often assess the manager at the level of an element because it contains a group of related performances. The manager is assessed according to one of three judgements: competent, insufficient evidence, and not yet competent. If the candidate is competent in an element, then he or she will move on to other elements or units of the standards. If there is insufficient evidence, then more evidence has to be gathered before the assessor can make a judgement. If the result is 'not yet competent', then more learning and development has to take place before new dates for assessment are agreed. The assessment methodology is criterion-based, meaning that, to pass, a candidate must meet an objective standard of competence that is nationally specified and understood. It is not a norm-based system by which an arbitrary number below average attainment fail whatever the objective standard of the whole group.

The competence movement in education and training has been a national UK government policy priority since the establishment in 1985 of the National Council for Vocational Qualifications. Competences are a way of specifying capabilities that can be assessed and developed according to nationally agreed criteria. They are a method of rationally planning and detailing the attainments of individuals and, ultimately, the whole workforce. Their purpose is to ensure a more competent workforce capable of performing competitively in global and domestic markets. Functional management competences have been criticized for being too generic and non-specific, and for being too bureaucratic and over-rational, particularly the high workload created in assessment activity. However, the movement is little more than ten years old and its immediate intellectual forebears stretch back over just twenty years.[67] There has been some interest in the UK competence-based approach from other countries, including France, Germany, and Japan. Recent research evidence has found that social competences (for example, punctuality, loyalty, creativity, customer orientation, responsibility, and co-operation) are an area that employers are paying greater attention to by selecting and developing employees using a 'fit to team' attitudinal model rather than a 'fit to job' functional model.[68] Case study research of organizational learning in Fiat, Motorola, Mutual Investment Corporation, and Electricité de France found it was stimulated by influential managers' recognition of the difference between what was significant and what had been achieved in the past and their identification of which resources needed to be further developed. The authors recommend that learning should link intangible human resources (e.g. knowledge, skills, and expertise) to core competences.[69]

# Summary

T HE learning organization is a set of aspirations more than it is a reality. US and UK variants of the learning organization make recommendations on improving employee development to benefit individuals and their employing organizations. Innovations in training and development have been discussed in this chapter. Three such innovations—systematic training, OD, and action learning—notwithstanding their longevity have not been especially influential for the majority of organizations and have all come under criticism from employers for being ineffectual and expensive. Specific tools for employee development—the learning cycle and learning styles —have been described. They have continued to be applied during the late 1990s by some companies, albeit in a somewhat *ad hoc* manner, in certain aspects of training and development. More recently, Kolb's learning cycle has been extended by Dixon into a practitioner framework for organizational learning, but has had considerably less impact on managers interested in the learning organization[70] than did earlier work by Senge and Pedler *et al.*

The use of open learning and training technologies has had slow but continuous development in UK training and education since the late 1970s, but one of the major reasons for their longevity is the attractiveness to employers of their claims to reduce education and training costs, especially the number of human resources employed in delivery. The competences approach used in employee resourcing (especially for selection and recruitment), as discussed in Section 2 of Chapter 5, has also been a recent innovation in employee development. We concentrated on one example of the use of functional competences for management development, but the MCI standards have not been especially influential during the first ten years of this government and multi-employer initiative. Employers have tended to concentrate more on attitudinal competences rather than functional standards, partly because attitudinal competences are more often specific to the internal labour market of the employing organization while NVQ standards are said to be less relevant and furthermore are generic, portable qualifications in the external labour market.[71]

Overall, this chapter has acknowledged the difficulty of creating learning companies in practice and characterized past innovations in training and development as tending to be short-lived and of limited influence. Nevertheless, the learning organization offers a challenging vision of the future—a new organizational culture, a philosophy of lifelong learning, and long-term investment in people.

---

BOX 8.4

### Case Study — New Pressures for Learning and Development in the Fork-lift Truck Factory of Smarna Gora Holdings

The following case study is a good example of much broader employee development needs that arose when a company found itself changing its business from trading within a socialist economy to operating in a transitional capitalist economy and being exposed to global market competition. The case compares the company's situation at the end of the socialist era in 1990 and its situation in 1997.

*1990*

The company has a total of 2,000 employees and is divided up into five different factories: turbine (water, electricity production), pump (water), industrial equipment (presses, hydraulic equipment), fork-lift truck, and work factory (cranes, cement, mechanical parts). The fork-lift truck factory has 250 employees and is organized into four departments: construction, commercial, finance, and technical. The commercial department is divided into buying and selling. The technical department is divided into planning, production, storage, and maintenance.

In 1990, the company was functioning within the Socialist system, which focused on production. It is based in Slovenia, which at the time was a state of Yugoslavia. Igor Pavlin, the manager for the factory's operations, said:

There was no planning done at the organizational level and no emphasis on markets nor much on management. There was no client orientation and no need to compete with European countries. The market was almost exclusively Yugoslavia.

Consumption was greater than production and there was no strong need to invest in new product development. The majority of investment went into the construction department. Organizational commitment was low, with lower-level employees not feeling much responsibility for their work or the organization. Management did not help the situation by placing low importance on efficient methods of working. As for industrial relations, the syndicate structure (trade union) was very strong in influencing how the organization was run and the system of management was strongly paternalistic, making additional assets available for the factory's use so that employees could rent company houses and travel to company holiday sites.

*1997*

There has been considerable downsizing and rationalization of Smarna Gora Holdings and the number of factories has been reduced since 1990. The turbine and pump factories have been combined and so have industrial equipment and the work factory.

In the fork-lift truck factory the commercial department has combined buying and selling to reduce head count and to simplify horizontal communication across the organization. Storage has been moved from the technical department to the commercial department. The number of employees has been reduced to 130 and the work is now more dominated by the commercial department rather than the emphasis being on production. Management have agreed with employees the mission and vision of the factory. It is documented and available to everybody.

Smarna Gora Holdings has a good reputation in other Eastern European countries and there are initiatives being taken with the turbine section of the recently formed turbine and pump factory to raise the profile of the company in Western markets to gain a market share. The company is developing a global orientation and making strong use of previous trading relationships with countries such as Iran and India.

Igor Pavlin said the company is about to create a new managerial post for human resource management that will have ambitious targets for employee development over the next three years. Igor explained the challenges facing the new manager:

Changing the culture involves changing the mindset of the employees. For example, in construction there are now six new types of fork-lift truck which require additional skills and experience within the company. The workforce needs training and education to meet the changing technology requirements. Skill shortages have become apparent in some of the semi-skilled and skilled jobs, like turning and welding. The whole operation has to meet higher quality standards—ISO 9001—and work with more complex technologies. The departments have to attend to improving teamwork and are addressing difficulties in recruitment and training needs of the existing workforce, particularly additional knowledge, both technical and managerial. Job responsibilities and tasks have been enlarged as a result of the reduced number of people employed in the business. New computer systems are being introduced and modifications being made to be compatible with ISO 9001.

The financial situation is precarious across the new countries of the old Yugoslavia, due to the war and internal political difficulties associated with the dismantling of the old socialist state. The national market was closed during the war and is predicted to be weak over the next five years. There have been cash-flow problems relating to difficulties in raising finance through the banks, with risk countries not making payments according to schedule (for instance, two-month repayment periods have increased to a staggering two years), and a general reduction in productivity.

There have been problems leading to strikes by the workers, said to be prompted by the unions. One national syndicate organized a work stoppage for two hours in order to obtain and negotiate the divulgence of more information by employers. Igor explained the worsening conditions of the workforce, which he saw as likely to continue unless the factory's products become more competitive on the export market and employees change their job attitudes, especially their work commitment and skill development. Igor was positive about the capability of the factory to succeed, although he did not mince his words about the very great human resource difficulties and challenges that lay ahead:

The workers have lower wages than before, about equivalent to 500 Deutschmarks a month. There are fewer fringe benefits, harder and longer work, and their overtime payments are late. Some of our employees live ten to fifty kilometres outside of Ljubljana [the city where the factory is based] and don't identify strongly with the strategic needs of the organization. We need greater organizational commitment and better skills for the competitive marketplace.

*Case Study Activity*
1. Identify the positive and negative pressures on learning and development in the fork-lift truck factory of Smarna Gora Holdings. Ensure your answer covers both external and internal pressures.
2. Write a ten-point plan for both management and employee development in Smarna Gora Holdings over the next five years. Ensure that you order your points for priority of action.

# Study Questions

1   List some of the innovations that have occurred in training and development and outline their strengths and weaknesses.

2   Analyse the relationship between Kolb's, Honey and Mumford's, and Dixon's theories of learning.

3   Select an organization in which you or a colleague has worked. Using the Pedler, Burgoyne, and Boydell framework, assess how far it approximates to a learning organization.

4   Write a detailed training and development rationale for technology-based learning and open learning in an organization that you have studied. Include the following issues: cost benefits, speed of response, flexibility of delivery, ease of use, individualization of learning, and creating the learning organization.

5   Find out more information from the MCI about the management standards. Devise a career development plan for yourself and the group assuming you are in the employment of your choice over the coming five to ten years.

# Further Reading

Dixon, N. M., *The Organizational Learning Cycle: How We Can Learn Collectively* (London: McGraw-Hill Book Company, 1994).

Guest, D. E., 'Human Resource Management and Performance: a Review and Research Agenda', *International Journal of Human Resource Management* (1997), 8, 3, June, pp. 263–76.

Pedler, M., Burgoyne, J., and Boydell, T., *The Learning Company: A Strategy for Sustainable Development* (Maidenhead: McGraw-Hill, 1991).

Starkey, K. and McKinlay, A., 'Product Development in Ford of Europe: Undoing the Past/Learning the Future', in K. Starkey (ed.), *How Organizations Learn* (London: International Thomson Business Press, 1996), pp. 214–29.

# Notes

1. Finegold, D., 'The implications of training in Britain for the analysis of Britain's skill problem: how much do employers spend on training?' *Human Resource Management Journal* (1991), 2, 1, Autumn, pp. 110–15.

2. Finegold, D. and Soskice, D., 'The failure of training in Britain: analysis and prescription', *Oxford Review of Economic Policy* (1988), 4, 5, Autumn, pp. 41–53.

3. Kochan, T.A. and Osterman, P., *The Mutual Gains Enterprise: Forging a Winning Partnership Among Labor, Management, and Government* (Boston, MA: Harvard Business School Press, 1994).

4. Kochan and Osterman, *The Mutual Gains Enterprise*, pp. 5–6; Boydell, T. H., *A Guide to the Identification of Training Needs* (London: British Association for Commercial and Industrial Education, fourth impression, 1990); Boydell, T. H. and Leary, M., *Identifying Training Needs* (London: IPD, 1996).

5. Keep, E., 'Missing links', *People Management* (1999), 5, 2, 28 January, p. 35.

6. Hall, D. T., 'Human resource development and organizational effectiveness', in C. J. Fombrun, N. M. Tichy, and M. A. Devanna, *Strategic Human Resource Management* (New York: John Wiley & Sons, 1984), pp. 159–81.

7. Starkey, K., *How Organizations Learn* (London: Thomson International Business Press, 1996), p. 1.

8. Harrison, R., *Employee Development* (London: Institute of Personnel and Development, 1992), p. 4.

9. Stiles, P., Gratton, L., Truss, C., Hope-Hailey, V., and McGovern, P., 'Performance management and the psychological contract', *Human Resource Management Journal* (1997), 7, 1, pp. 57–66 (see Table 1, p. 59).

10. Rover Group, 'Rover Tomorrow—Now—The New Deal—The Way Forward' (1992), p. 20.

11. Department of Employment, *Glossary of Training Terms*, 2nd edn. (London: HMSO, 1978).

12. Ibid.

13. Ibid.

14. Storey, J., *Human Resource Management: a Critical Text* (London: Routledge, 1995), p. 26.

15. Storey, J. and Sisson, K., *Managing Human Resources and Industrial Relations* (Milton Keynes: Open University Press, 1993), p. 223.

16. Poole, M. and Jenkins, G., 'Developments in Human Resource Management in Manufacturing in Modern Britain', *International Journal of Human Resource Management* (1997), 8, 6, December, pp. 841–56 (see pp. 854–5).

17. *People Management* (1998), 4, 16, 13 August, p. 11.

18. Storey, *Human Resource Management: a Critical Text*, p. 384.

19. Pedler, M., Burgoyne, J., and Boydell, T., *The Learning Company: a Strategy for Sustainable Development* (Maidenhead: McGraw-Hill, 1991), p. 1.

20. Ibid.

21. Ibid., p. 19.

22. Ibid., p. 13.

23. Ibid., pp. 13–14.

24. The models the systematic approach draws on come from the following: Bloom, B. S. (ed.), *Taxonomy of Educational Objectives, the Classification of Educational Goals*, by a committee of college and university examiners (New York: David McKay Co., 1956);

Gagné, R. M., *Essentials of Learning for Instruction* (Illinois: Holt, Rinehart and Winston, 1975); Romiszowski, A. J., *Producing Instructional Systems* (London: Kogan Page, 1986).

25. Argyris, C., 'Skilled incompetence', in K. Starkey (ed.), *How Organizations Learn* (London: Thomson Business Press, 1996), pp. 82–91; Argyris, C. and Schon, D. A., *Organizational Learning: a Theory of Action Perspective* (Reading, MA: Addison Wesley, 1978); Schein, E., *Organizational Psychology* (New Jersey: Prentice-Hall, 1988).

26. Counselling: Summerfield, J. and van Oudtshoorn, L., *Counselling in the Workplace* (London: Institute of Personnel and Development, 1995); Human Relations: Mayo, E., *The Human Problems of an Industrial Civilization* (New York: Macmillan, 1933); Gestalt Psychology: Lewin, K., *Field Theory in Social Science* (New York: Harper, 1951); Psychotherapy: Perls, F. S., Hefferline, R., and Goodman, P., *Gestalt Therapy: Excitement and Growth in the Human Personality* (Harmondsworth: Penguin (reprinted), 1977); Transactional Analysis: Berne, E., *Transactional Analysis in Psychotherapy* (New York: Grove Press, 1961); Berne, E., *Games People Play: the Psychology of Human Relationships* (New York: Grove Press, 1964); Rogers, C., *On Becoming a Person: a Therapist's View of Psychotherapy* (London: Constable, 1961); Socio-technical Systems Theory: Trist, E. L. and Bamforth, K. W., 'Some social and psychological consequences of the longwall method of coal-getting', *Human Relations*, (1951), 4, 3–38; Trist, E. L., Higgin, C. W., Murray, H., and Pollock, A. M., *Organizational Choice* (London: Tavistock Institute, 1963).

27. Pettigrew, A. M., *The Awakening Giant* (Oxford: Blackwell, 1985).

28. Megginson, D. and Pedler, M., *Self-development: a Facilitator's Guide* (Maidenhead: McGraw-Hill, 1992).

29. Revans, R., *Action Learning* (London: Blond & Briggs, 1980); Revans, R., *The ABC of Action Learning* (London: Chartwell-Bratt, 1983).

30. Peters, T. J. and Waterman, Jr, R. H., *In Search of Excellence: Lessons from America's Best Run Companies* (New York: Harper and Row, 1982); Deal, T. E. and Kennedy, A., *Corporate Cultures* (Reading, MA: Addison-Wesley, 1982); Kanter, R. M., *The Change Masters: Corporate Entrepreneurs at Work* (London: Allen & Unwin, 1984).

31. Pedler *et al.*, *The Learning Company* (n. 19 above), p. 15.

32. Legge, K., *Human Resource Management: Rhetorics and Realities* (Basingstoke: Macmillan, 1995), p. 80.

33. Pedler *et al.*, *The Learning Company* (n. 19 above), pp. 15–17.

34. Senge, P., *The Fifth Discipline: The Art and Practice of the Learning Organization* (New York: Doubleday/Currency, 1990); Senge, P., 'The Leader's New Work: Building Learning Organizations', in K. Starkey (ed.), *How Organizations Learn* (London: Thomson International Business Press, 1996), pp. 288–315.

35. Argyris and Schon, *Organizational Learning* (1978) (n. 25 above).

36. Dixon, N. M., *The Organizational Learning Cycle: How We can Learn Collectively* (Maidenhead: McGraw-Hill, 1994).

37. Kolb, D. A., *Individual Learning Styles and the Learning Process* (Massachusetts Institute of Technology Sloan School Working Paper No. 535-71, 1971); Kolb, D. A., Rubin, I. M., and McIntyre, J. M., *Organizational Psychology: An Experiential Approach* (Englewood Cliffs, NJ: Prentice-Hall, 1974).

38. Kolb, D. A., *Experiential Learning* (Englewood Cliffs, NJ: Prentice-Hall, 1984).

39. Kolb, D. A., 'Management and the learning process', in K. Starkey, *How Organizations Learn* (London: Thomson International Business Press, 1996), pp. 270–87.

40. Ibid.; Mumford, A., 'Individual and Organizational Learning: the Pursuit of Change', in *Managing Learning* (London, The Open University: Routledge, 1994).

41. Honey, P. and Mumford, A., *A Manual of Learning Styles*, 1st edn. (Maidenhead: Peter Honey, 1981), pp. 25–9; Honey, P. and Mumford, A., *A Manual of Learning Styles*, 3rd edn. (Maidenhead: Peter Honey, 1992); Mumford, A., Honey, P., and Robinson, G. *Directors'*

*Development Guidebook* (London: Institute of Directors and Employment Department 1991).

42. Verbal communication (1996) by UK-based manager in a major automotive company.

43. Dixon, N. M., *The Organizational Learning Cycle: How We can Learn Collectively* (Maidenhead: McGraw-Hill, 1994).

44. Pettigrew, *Awakening Giant* (1995) (n. 27 above).

45. Starkey, K. and McKinlay, A., *Strategy and the Human Resource* (Oxford: Blackwell, 1993); Starkey, K. and McKinlay, A., 'Product development in Ford of Europe: undoing the past/ learning the future', in K. Starkey (ed.), *How Organizations Learn* (London: Thomson International Business Press, 1996), pp. 214–29.

46. Guest, D. E., 'Human Resource Management and Performance: a Review and Research Agenda', *International Journal of Human Resource Management* (1997), 8, 3, June, 263–76.

47. Galbraith, J. R., *Organization Design* (Reading, MA: Addison-Wesley, 1978); Galbraith, J. R., 'Designing the Innovating Organization', in K. Starkey (ed.), *How Organizations Learn* (London: Thomson International Business Press, 1996), pp. 151–81.

48. Peters and Waterman, *In Search of Excellence* (1982) (n. 30 above), pp. 224–34.

49. Marchington, M. and Wilkinson, A., *Core Personnel and Development* (London: Institute of Personnel and Development, 1996).

50. *Employee Development Bulletin* (1991) 14, p. 9, quoted in Marchington and Wilkinson, *Core Personnel and Development*.

51. Jones, P. J., 'Outdoor management development: a journey to the centre of the metaphor', in C. Oswick and D. Grant (eds.), *Organization Development: Metaphorical Explorations* (London: Pitman Publishing, 1996), pp. 209–25.

52. Rowntree, D., *Exploring Open and Distance Learning* (London: Kogan Page, 1992).

53. Pinnington, A. H., 'The formative evaluation of interactive video', unpublished PhD thesis (Henley Management College and Brunel University, Uxbridge, 1990).

54. Reynolds, A. and Iwinski, T., *Multimedia Training: Developing Technology-based Systems* (New York: McGraw-Hill, 1996); Browne, J., 'Unleashing the power of learning: an interview with British Petroleum's John Browne', *Harvard Business Review* (1997), September–October, pp. 147–68, reprint number 97507.

55. 'Unleashing the Power of Learning: An Interview with BP's Chief Executive John Browne', *Harvard Business Review* (1997), Sept.–Oct., p. 168.

56. Storey, J., *Developments in the Management of Human Resources* (Oxford: Blackwell, 1992).

57. Storey, *Human Resource Management* (1995) (n. 14 above).

58. Morgan, G., *Riding the Waves of Change: Developing Managerial Competencies for a Turbulent World* (San Francisco, CA: Jossey-Bass Inc, 1988).

59. Sparrow, P. and Marchington, M., *Human Resource Management: The New Agenda* (London: Financial Times, Pitman Publishing, 1998), p. 6.

60. Storey and Sisson, *Managing Human Resources and Industrial Relations* (1993) (n. 15 above), p. 163.

61. Some of these programmes have awarded employees fixed sums of money to spend on internal training and education (for example, £180 each year). Some of the courses have not been directly related to their work tasks (for example, sheep husbandry), and some are similar to what has previously been offered solely through the WEA (Workers' Educational Association) and part-time adult further education (for example, foreign language skills for tourists).

62. Wharton Business School was established to provide business education in the 1880s, while comparable UK institutions such as Henley Management College and London Business School were both formed in the period after the Second World War and have been producing MBA graduates only since the late 1960s to early 1970s.

63. Storey and Sisson, *Managing Human Resources and Industrial Relations* (1993), p. 171.

64. Constable, J. and McCormick, R., *The Making of British Managers* (London: British Institute

of Management, 1987); Handy, C. B., *The Making of Managers* (London: Manpower Services Commission/National Economic Development Office/British Institute of Management, 1987); National Economic Development Office/Manpower Services Commission, *People: The Key to Success*, (London: NEDO, 1987); Mangham, I. and Silver, M. S., *Management Training: Context and Practice* (London: Economic and Social Research Council, 1986).

65. Storey and Sisson, *Managing Human Resources and Industrial Relations* (1993); Keep, E., 'Vocational education and training for the young', in K. Sisson (ed.), *Personnel Management: a Comprehensive Guide to Theory and Practice in Britain* (Oxford: Blackwell, 1994), pp. 299–333; Marchington and Wilkinson, *Core Personnel and Development*, (1996) (n. 49 above).

66. Ashton, D and Felstead, A., 'Training and development', in J. Storey, *Human Resource Management: A Critical Text* (London: Routledge, 1995), pp. 248–50.

67. Boyatzis, R., *The Competent Manager* (Chichester: John Wiley, 1982); Schroder, H. M., *Managerial Competence: the Key to Excellence* (Iowa: Kendall-Hunt, 1989).

68. Sparrow and Marchington, *Human Resource Management* (1998) (n. 59 above), p. 127.

69. Dibella, A. J., Nevis, E. C., and Gould, J. M., 'Understanding organizational learning capability', *Journal of Management Studies* (1996), 33, 3, May, pp. 361–79 (see pp. 377–8); Sparrow, P. and Hiltrop, J.-M., *European Human Resource Management in Transition* (Hemel Hempstead: Prentice-Hall, 1994).

70. Dixon, *The Organizational Learning Cycle* (1994) (n. 43 above).

71. Sparrow, P., 'New organisational forms, processes, jobs and psychological contracts: resolving the HRM issues', in P. Sparrow and M. Marchington (eds.), *Human Resource Management: The New Agenda* (London, Financial Times: Pitman Publishing, 1998), pp. 117–41, at p. 127.

# Chapter 9
# Managing Change

## Chapter Contents

Introduction

# Introduction

H UMAN resource specialists nowadays are said to be giving more time to diagnosing, planning, facilitating, and reinforcing organizational change than they have in the past. Organizational change can be minor and smooth or major and transformational. Chapter 2 explained how, in the 1980s and 1990s, many public-sector organizations in the UK were privatized and large companies underwent major restructuring often accompanied by reduction of the workforce. Increased uncertainty in domestic and world markets and increased threats of loss of business due to fiercer competition have put pressure on management to be effective in managing internal organizational change. Managing change has been a central concern in the UK for government and the public sector, implementing rolling programmes of financial change, new systems of public-sector management, and substantial downsizing of the number of civil servants employed in the country.[1] Managing change has also become a critical issue in many countries across the world as a consequence of increased activity by national governments in restructuring, contracting out, and privatization of public sector services. Likewise, companies in these countries have found themselves under greater pressure since the 1980s to initiate major programmes of organizational change, raising questions about how the process should be managed.

In Chapter 4 we examined the nature of industrial relations in the UK, identifying the move away from joint regulation to unilateral regulation. Since 1979, greater importance has been attached to unilateral regulation and private- and public-sector managers are often assigned roles as leaders of organizational change, which raises questions on how change is being achieved. In this chapter, we review some of the influential literature on managing change. Many of the frameworks of change outlined below are compatible with the philosophy of HRM and unilateral regulation. For example, in Storey's twenty-five-point framework (see Chapter 1) under 'HRM' two of the points are that managers should show transformational leadership and manage the climate and culture of the organization. The majority of the guidelines for managing change discussed in this chapter adopt a managerialist and unitarist perspective, but are reviewed with the expectation that the reader will discuss these critically and understand them in conjunction with ideas and perspectives on HRM presented in previous chapters.

Chapter 9 subdivides into five sections. In the first two sections, we review the developing debate in the management literature over the last two decades of the twentieth century and its change of emphasis away from a preoccupation with optimal organizational structure towards more interest in changing the organizational culture. Next, three frameworks of change are introduced; then we explore some of the widely known work on the scale and implementation of change. Finally, the role of the HR function in the management of organizational change is briefly evaluated.

# 1 From Organizational Structure to Organizational Culture

I N the 1970s, it was commonplace for practitioners and academics in the management field to stress the importance of organizational structure. In 1962 in the USA, Chandler researched companies' historical growth and diversification into multidivisional firms and concluded that 'structure follows strategy'.[2] By this he meant that how the company is organized to achieve its goals (structure) must be consistent with the business strategy. In the UK, the well-known Aston school undertook studies of specific dimensions of organization structure, such as specialization, standardization, formalization, centralization, and configuration.[3] Research of this nature was full of discussion about what constituted optimal and suboptimal structure of an organization's systems, procedures, plans, and controls.

By the beginning of the 1980s, Japanese manufacturing companies had made significant inroads into traditional US and European domestic markets, particularly in the automotive and consumer electronics industries. These Japanese businesses were achieving success through higher productivity, better quality, lower cost, and a quicker responsiveness to customers. Although much of the Japanese quality philosophy had originated in the USA with 'quality gurus' such as W. Edwards Deming and Joseph M. Juran,[4] the operations and quality systems of these companies were different to those in the West, and, overall, the Japanese industry structure and the national and organizational cultures were distinctive in many ways. Some Western business leaders who visited Japanese companies in the late 1970s and early 1980s were strongly influenced by what they saw and were convinced their companies would have to change if they were to survive in the increasingly competitive world market-place.[5]

In the 1980s, partly in response to the rising power of the economies of the Pacific Rim, the focus of interest in management consultancy and writing moved from issues of organizational structure[6] to organizational culture. Ed Schein from the Massachusetts Institute of Technology defines the culture of an organization or group as:

A pattern of shared basic assumptions that the group learned as it solved its problems of external adaptation and internal integration, that has worked well enough to be considered valid and, therefore, to be taught to new members as the correct way to perceive, think, and feel in relation to those problems.[7]

Schein goes on to say that his concept of culture involves understanding how groups socialize new members into the group, identifying the behaviours that groups nurture and reward, and appreciating that large organizations will have a corporate culture and subcultures. Schein believes that leaders can create group culture, as did Deal and Kennedy, whose advice on changing organizational culture met a clear need amongst senior executives in the 1980s when many companies in the USA and Western Europe were suffering a crisis of business confidence in their traditional home markets.[8] Deal and Kennedy's perspective on culture change concentrates on the more symbolic aspects of management, highlighting differences in national and organizational cultures and extolling the virtues of charismatic leadership, entrepreneurialism, vision and values, rites and rituals of corporate life, and 'the way we do things around here'.

Deal and Kennedy proposed a new challenge to management and employees, asking them to think about their organizations as 'strong' and 'weak' cultures. America's great companies were not merely organizations, they said, but successful, human institutions. The high performers were 'strong culture' companies, for example, Caterpillar Tractor, General Electric, DuPont, Price Waterhouse, 3M, IBM, Procter & Gamble, Hewlett-Packard, and Johnson & Johnson. Deal and Kennedy said that high-performing companies owe their success to the development of a strong culture and listed five situations when change is necessary and the culture needs reshaping; the first two in particular, relating to the environment, were perceived to be significant in the 1980s:

- when the environment is undergoing fundamental change, and the company has always been highly value-driven;
- when the industry is highly competitive and the environment changes quickly;
- when the company is mediocre, or worse;
- when the company is truly at the threshold of becoming a large corporation—a *Fortune* 1000-scale corporate giant;
- when the company is growing very rapidly.[9]

It has often been said that only when a dramatic change occurs in the external environment do companies become motivated to undertake large-scale organizational change. Pettigrew's study of the ICI corporation is a good example of the vital importance of the external environment in persuading people to recognize the need for change.[10] Pettigrew found that it was not until the organization was facing a substantial crisis threatening its long-term existence that fundamental change started to occur, on that occasion under the leadership of John Harvey-Jones.

In some respects, ICI had a strong culture already, but it had become inappropriate when the environment changed fundamentally. Its culture was felt by managers such as Harvey-Jones to be too elitist, bureaucratic, and inward-looking to remain a major player in the world chemicals industry. The need to adapt had been recognized within parts of the company for years, but (as mentioned in section 2 of Chapter 8) ICI's organizational development programmes and other change initiatives had received half-hearted support from top management and were insufficient to stimulate substantial change. The external environment became the determining factor when the growing threat to the company's business interests was ultimately recognized in the form of reduced profitability and the worst losses ICI had ever experienced.

During the 1980s, consistent with the move towards unilateral regulation of the employment relationship, top management paid more attention to ensuring managers were visible to the rest of the workforce in implementing change. The greater significance accorded to managers in leading change reinforced the message that joint regulation was no longer practical because it was an obstacle to visionary leadership and the exercise of management prerogative.

## 2 Strong Cultures and Excellent Cultures

ONE line of thinking on managing change, which emerged in the USA during the 1980s, is that its essence lies in managing the organizational culture. A variety of high-performing US corporations were considered by some researchers from Harvard Business School and the consulting company McKinsey to be successful because they had the right culture. Peters and Waterman popularized the approach of managing culture in their book, *In Search of Excellence*.[11] The 'excellent company' and 'strong culture' approaches come from the same group of people.[12] As well as having the same origins, both approaches are committed to the concept of 'transformational' leadership and effective cultural management.

Advocates of the 'excellent-company' approach became increasingly convinced by the argument that strong culture is a major key to business success, although events over the ensuing years have called this into question as some of their 'excellent' companies have experienced difficulties. For example, 'Walt Disney was to produce a string of films that were failures, Caterpillar experienced declining demand for its heavy plant machinery, and Atari, the name once synonymous with computer games, almost disappeared entirely'.[13] The excellent-company study has been criticized for not being very thorough in terms of research design;[14] nevertheless, the eight attributes that Peters and Waterman said make an excellent company have remained influential. One measure of the considerable interest at the time in the excellent-company approach was that, at the height of its popularity, the book was selling more copies than the Bible. A possible explanation for its appeal lies in the eight attributes' cultural acceptability to US organizations. The attributes emphasize qualities of individualism, autonomy, medium to low power distance (as explained in section 1 of Chapter 5), and tolerance of ambiguity. The 'excellent company' attributes are as follows:

(1) a bias for action—getting on with it;
(2) close to the customer—understanding and responding to what the customer wants;
(3) autonomy and entrepreneurship—fostering leaders and innovators;
(4) productivity through people—treating employees as the root source of quality and productivity gain;
(5) hands-on, value driven—being close to the job, no matter what one's job status;
(6) 'stick to the knitting'—doing things you know how to do well;

(7) a simple form, lean staff—keeping the organizational structure simple, with few corporate staff;

(8) simultaneous loose–tight properties—pushing autonomy right down to the shop floor while a few core values (e.g., reliability) are rigidly adhered to.[15]

The eight attributes are general enough to be open to a variety of interpretations on what constitutes excellence, thus facilitating alternative ways that top managers could see the excellent company concept as being relevant, at least in part, to their own organization. Peters and Waterman's case descriptions are situated in diverse industries with exemplary companies ranging from, for example, 3M, a manufacturing company with a long-standing reputation for first-to-market product innovation, to McDonald's, a company famous for its successful global operations in fast food. Peters and Waterman believed American organizations had become too bureaucratic and over-centralized. Top management concentrated too exclusively on rational, top-down decision making and achieving short-term results; consequently, so they argued, companies were failing to win real commitment from their employees. The message from Peters and Waterman was that employees' commitment has to be won through treating them as valued assets.[16] In short, they believed employees will respond positively to the soft HRM approach, or, in Tom Peters' words, 'It all comes down to people.'[17]

---

**BOX 9.1**

## A Recipe for Successful Change

Based on their experience of private- and public-sector organizations, Terrence Deal and Allan Kennedy formulated this 'how-to' of successful organizational change:

Position a hero in charge of the process. A strong leader must be put in place to lead the change. The selected person must have the necessary vision and tenacity to take the process through to completion and be someone who employees will come to see as a hero.

Recognize a threat from outside. Strong-minded individuals won't be enough unless they can point to circumstances that show the need for change. As was discussed above, the external business environment can have a strong influence on how far employees are prepared to accept change. The threat of competition and factors in the external environment must be communicated to motivate cultural change and persuade people to leave old customs and practices behind.

Make transition rituals the pivotal elements of change. Often, the culture change is a radical departure from old ways of doing things and people need time to 'mourn' the loss of the old and learn to appreciate the new. This period of transition is necessary and should not be ignored. Transitions should be facilitated by the organization.

Provide transition training in new values and behaviour. The company must provide opportunities for training and acculturation to the new set of values normally involving changes in attitudes and behaviours. Often, to mark the inception of the new culture, different language and symbols used for communication within the organization are encouraged.

It is vital that organizational change is led by members of the organization; otherwise employees will question the extent of management commitment. However, it is common for consulting firms to assist with diagnosing, planning, and facilitating change. Deal and Kennedy recommend the use of outsiders, using the colourful phrase 'Bring in outside shamans'. They can add valuable experience gained from working on analogous programmes with other companies; in addition, they bring an outside perspective and help to give more objectivity to what are often emotionally charged events.

Major programmes usually involve changes in organizational structure. Change to the structure leads to new formal systems and changed procedures, redistributes power within the organization, and reinforces new ways of working. Using the language of culture change, Deal and Kennedy recommend that organizations 'build tangible symbols of the new directions'. Naturally, when such changes involve job loss, employees worry about their security. Too much angst and anxiety and a lack of trust can lower morale and productivity in the company.[18] Therefore, they argue, the 'people side' of the change process must be paid adequate attention if it is to be successful over the long term. Insist, Deal and Kennedy say, on the importance of security in transition. This requires making what are perceived to be reasonable or even generous redundancy settlements. It involves re-establishing a sense of security through clearly communicated plans and redundancy programmes, primarily through top management's remaining true to their word so that employees know where they stand and can then plan accordingly. The organization needs to make sure that it pays good attention to those whom it wants to retain; otherwise they will feel like 'survivors of the wreckage rather than winners of the game'.

Deal and Kennedy's book is primarily targeted at management and advises managers to exercise the management prerogative through exemplary leadership and by managing the culture of the organization. As the authors summarize it:

Sometimes, change is necessary and not all bad, although it is almost always risky, expensive, and time-consuming. Indeed, the difficult part of change is changing the culture. But cultures can be changed if the managers who would change them are sensitive enough to the key cultural attributes—heroes, values, rituals—that must be affected if the change is to succeed.

*Source*: Deal and Kennedy, *Corporate Cultures: The Rites and Rituals of Corporate Life* (1982), p. 176.

# 3    Frameworks of Change

FRAMEWORKS of the process of change are of importance to general managers and HRM practitioners because they want to achieve results as smoothly and quickly as possible. Frameworks are equally important to academics, as they help them to understand the causes, reasons, and processes of change. This section reviews three frameworks utilized by consultants, general managers, and HR practitioners for managing change. The first, by Kurt Lewin, is fifty years old and continues to be used by some of the UK's major companies during change conferences and training events.[19]

## Lewin's Force Field Analysis

Kurt Lewin's force field analysis[20] is one of the early frameworks of change used in the management field and is still a popular tool, but it has been criticized for over-simplifying the change process, which it undoubtedly does. More complex frameworks of change are available, for example, processual analysis.[21] These other academic approaches to organizational change are well worth becoming acquainted with but are beyond the scope of this chapter, which focuses on unitarist approaches to managing change (interested readers should consult the list of further reading at the end of the chapter).

Kurt Lewin had an interest in models of change that used dynamic and topographical concepts derived from physics and mathematics (topographical concepts involve detailed description and map-like representation). He is one of the most frequently quoted people on the subject of change and his Three Steps framework of force field analysis is a normative description of people's tendency to resist change (see Fig. 9.1).[22] His approach assumes people naturally resist change but can be persuaded to change when the causes of their resistance are dealt with appropriately. This section concentrates primarily on the individual factors leading to resistance to change; however, the broader structural and political factors are just as important and should be identified in addition to analysing organizational change using the force field approach.

Lewin's framework portrays change as a dynamic process in which individuals have to progress through three stages: unfreezing, which means recognizing the need for change; changing, which means overcoming and reducing the 'forces of resistance' and utilizing and strengthening 'driving forces'; and refreezing, which means habituating the change (see Fig. 9.2).

The application of Lewin's force field theory to management practice is simpler than his original academic psychological research[23] and incorporates more recent concepts from psychology on individual change. These and other ideas from the management literature are now discussed in the remainder of this section. The Three Steps approach argues that the change process naturally involves dealing with people's resistance. We all develop habits in our daily tasks and sometimes these behaviour patterns interfere with our recognizing the need for change. Once the individual shows a readiness to alter his or her behaviour or at least has acknowledged the need for change, the change agent (i.e., the person or group that is pushing for the change) can progress the process of change in two main ways: first, by overcoming and reducing the forces of resistance and, second, by strengthening the driving forces. The change will be all the easier to implement where it involves a definition of the employees' role that is consistent with social, cultural, and legal expectations commonly held by the work group.[24] Generally, change programmes progress more effectively when they are able to appeal to cultural values already held by the group as a means of motivating them to do things differently.

In organizations, employees will often psychologically resist change when it involves altering their work values and self-concept; for example, some professionals

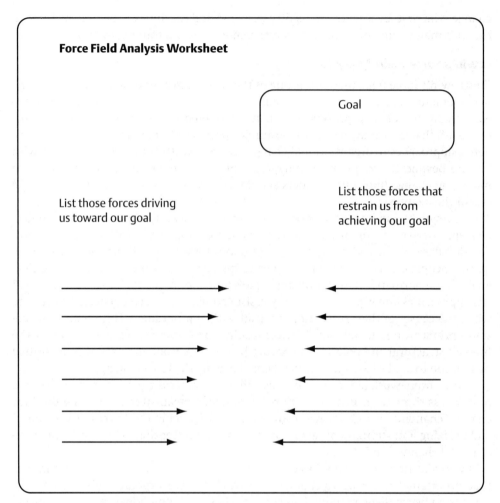

**Figure 9.1  Force field analysis**

*Source*: based on Lewin, K. (1947) 'Frontiers in Group Dynamics', *Human Relations* 1:5–42, and (1951), *Field Theory in Social Science*, New York: Harper.

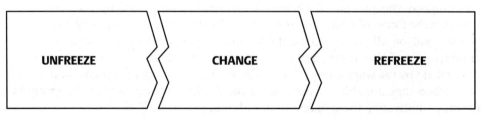

**Figure 9.2  The change process**

*Source*: based on Lewin, K., (1947, 1951) as above.

find marketing and administration duties unsatisfying when they take up time that could have been spent executing professional work. Many professionals in the public and private sector are facing increased responsibility for marketing and administration and some of them are ambivalent about how much of their newly defined role they should accept.[25] Their reluctance to change is partly a consequence of their occupational commitment to professional work; their unwillingness to take on more duties is rarely just a case of irrational resistance.[26]

Change can increase the amount of ambiguity felt by employees and becomes problematic whenever they are unclear about what is wanted from them. Resistance to change occurs when it creates too much role incompatibility for employees.[27] For example, expecting shopfloor workers to communicate with a larger number of teams and managers in the plant will mean they have to adopt a broader role set; that is, they will have to co-operate with various groups and learn to behave and respond to different expectations. Some employees will find developing a broader set of relationships at work to be a stimulating new challenge and personally fulfilling; however, others may find these new relationships to be incompatible with their more restricted concept of self and experience increased role strain and stress.

People adopt various strategies for resolving role problems that they feel to be stressful, and some psychological coping mechanisms act as blocks to personal change. Three of the more common coping mechanisms are repression, withdrawal, and rationalization.[28] Repression occurs when individuals force the unpleasant issue away from consciousness into the subconscious; withdrawal occurs when individuals physically or psychologically distance themselves from unpleasant circumstances (for example, absenteeism, poor participation in meetings); and rationalization happens when individuals fabricate stories to justify actions that require explanation, substantially avoiding or altering the truth.

If the change programme creates unclear role expectations, this too leads to uncertainty and resistance. Therefore, effective change agents will identify in advance any areas of potential uncertainty and make clear how people's work is to be evaluated, what the scope is for advancement and responsibility, and exactly what the new expectations are of individual employees' performance.[29] Effective change programmes should take account of the fact that some people have a higher tolerance of stress than others do. The management of individual stress has become recognized as a higher priority for managers, who have seen it as a more significant employee-relations problem in the 1990s than working days lost through industrial disputes.

> By 1994 the CBI and Percom survey reported that 171 million working days were lost in the UK through sickness, compared with half a million lost through industrial disputes. We estimate that between 30 and 40 per cent of all sickness absence is stress-related.[30]

Resistance to change also has to be seen in this light because people who are 'resistant' are not necessarily being stubborn but may be slower in having 'insight' into the situation. Resistance is sometimes portrayed by consultants and managers as the result of employee weakness and individuals may be stereotyped and called saboteurs, shirkers, dinosaurs, ostriches, loony lefties, and so on. Such stereotyping of resistant groups of people occurs more openly in spoken dialogue and the news media than it does in textbooks, and is a means of representing resistance as both irrational and destructive to the collective good. Stereotyping can prevent the voicing of fundamental issues and ignore valid alternatives and directions for change. For example, the stereotyped groups may believe, rightly or wrongly, that they are not participating sufficiently in processes of organizational decision making that affect their lives or they may have interests and cherished values that are threatened by the change, but could be better accommodated.

### Reger *et al.* on Reframing the Organization

Recent attempts to establish Total Quality Management in US and UK companies have drawn attention to obstacles to institutionalizing change (the last of Lewin's Three Steps) created by the difficulty of habituating employees to new ways of working. Reger, Gustafson, Demarie, and Mullane have written about why implementing total quality is easier said than done.[31] Reger *et al.* argue that fundamental change is most likely to be successful where the proposed change is aligned with people's positive beliefs about the organization's ideal identity. If the change fits with people's idea of where they would like the organization to be, then they are more likely to support it wholeheartedly. On the other hand, if the radical improvements threaten people's core values and they see the change as attacking what they cherish in the organization, then they will resist it.

Management have two options in this situation, say Reger *et al.*: either to change people's sense of what is ideal or to change their sense of what the current situation is. Their framework of change calls for balance. On the one hand, change must be of sufficient magnitude to overcome what is called cognitive inertia; in other words, people must consider it worth doing and not perceive it to be pointless. However, on the other hand, change must not seem so great that it offers a future that people think is overly idealistic or impossible to achieve. The art, they say, lies in getting the change to fall in between the two extremes and within what the authors call the 'change acceptance zone' (see Fig. 9.3).

One strength of considering the 'probability of change acceptance' is that it encourages management to plan the implementation of TQM by taking into account the likely extent of employee acceptance and resistance. A limitation is that it presents employees' acceptance of change within a framework that has an implicit preference for unilateral regulation and does not take sufficient account of the extent that TQM may, for example, be felt by employees to be benefiting large shareholders more than themselves. This occurs when TQM comes to be perceived as work intensification for no concrete reward, rather than viewed as a work philosophy for improving product and service quality in order to increase the competitiveness of the organization.[32]

### Burns on Personal Change

With the aim of promoting psychological well-being in the workplace, Robert Burns advises that employees, and managers especially, should learn to cope more effectively with change.[33] Burns offers a concept of change seen in terms of personal adaptation, recommending that we get to know ourselves better and develop more effective personal strategies for coping with stress. Humans, he says, generally prefer stability but

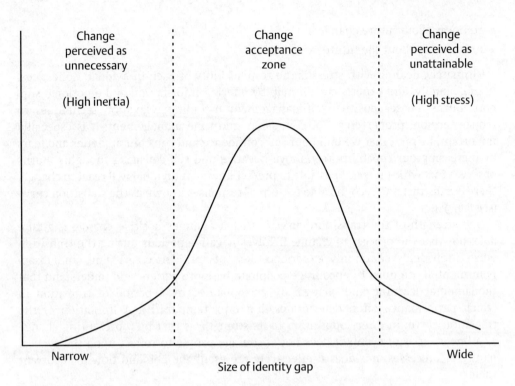

**Figure 9.3  Reger et al., on reframing the organization**

*Source*: Republished with permission of Academy of Management, PO Box 3020, Briar Cliff Manor, NY 10510-8020, from *Reframing the Organisation: Why Implementing Total Quality is Easier Said Than Done*, Fig. 3, p. 576), R. K. Reger, L. T. Gustafson, D. M. Demaric and J. V. Mullane, *Academy of Management Review* 1994, vol. 19, No. 3. Reproduced by permission of the publisher via Copyright Clearance Center, Inc.

nowadays everyone must become more skilled in living under rapidly changing conditions of work. Common stress factors on the job should be identified and, where possible, sources of stress reduced and proactively managed by the organization. Burns lists the following as having the potential to cause stress:

- thwarted career development
- lack of job security
- too much or too little work/responsibility
- inability to adapt to new work practices
- boring/meaningless work
- little support from management
- lack of required skills
- inability to use existing skills
- inadequate training/reskilling
- lack of involvement in decision making
- lack of socio-emotional support/counselling

- rumours about future change
- uncertainty about the future.[34]

Ultimately, dealing with stress is the responsibility of each individual. Colleagues, friends, family, and experts can all help by offering information and emotional support. Burns advises positive self-management including relaxation techniques to reduce tension, proper diet, exercise, sleep, and time management. It is especially important, he says, that we build our self-confidence and confront anxieties and fears by increasing our capability to remove negative and self-defeating thoughts. Burns observes that whilst it is not possible to predict how an individual will react to change, there is a distinct and recognizable pattern of responses known as the transition curve (see Fig. 9.4).

One strength of the transition curve is that it assumes positive change is attainable, but that the process of change involves negative periods during the transition when individuals commonly experience loss of confidence, grieving, and disappointment. It attempts to encourage people to be more patient and understand that fundamental learning and change are accompanied by a period of transition in which performance often deteriorates, but only temporarily. A limitation of the transition curve, in direct opposition to its strength, is that by representing change as a linear series of events it does not encourage people to reflect upon the cyclical nature of processes, nor does it effectively represent the ebb and flow of recurrent themes.

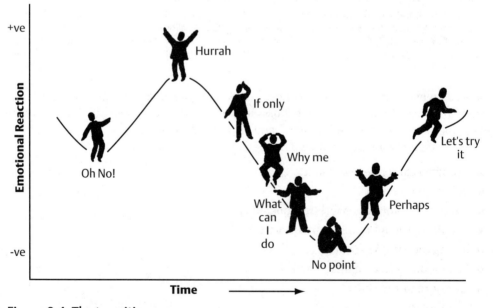

**Figure 9.4 The transition curve**

*Source:* Burns, R. (1993), *Managing People in Changing Times—Coping with change in the workplace—A Practical Guide*, London: Allen and Unwin, Fig. 1, p. 21.

# 4    Implementing Change

W E have identified the growing interest in managing change amongst managers and within the HR function, and have reviewed three frameworks of change. This section now turns to guidelines for implementing change.

### Nadler and Tushman

Over the last two decades of the twentieth century in the USA and UK, many large organizations have restructured, de-layered, and implemented planned change.[35] In an *Academy of Management* article on large-scale organizational change, Nadler and Tushman propose four types of organizational change: tuning, adaptation, reorientation, and re-creation (see Fig. 9.5). These types vary according to the scope of change (either incremental or strategic) and the relationship of the change to external events (either an anticipatory or a reactive relationship).

Incremental change is a change to only one element of the organization and is consistent with existing plans and practices—for example, changing the company pay and rewards system to adapt to new developments in the external labour market. Strategic change constitutes change that affects the whole organization and marks a reshaping or even a breaking away from previous approaches. An example of this would be breaking out of the conceptualization of the product-market environment the company has historically operated within. Anticipatory change is, as the phrase suggests, change made by the organization in anticipation of events occurring in the external environment, such as government rules being simplified and repealed to deregulate trade in an industry sector. The deregulation of the air freight business and consequent growth of operations for companies such as Federal Express is one example of this. Reactive change is simply where the

|  | *Incremental* | *Strategic* |
|---|---|---|
| *Anticipatory* | Tuning | Reorientation |
| *Reactive* | Adaptation | Re-creation |

**Figure 9.5 Nadler and Tushman's four types of organizational change**

*Source*: Republished with permission of Academy of Management, PO Box 3020, Briar Cliff Manor, NY 10510–8020, from Organisational Frame Bending: Principles for Managing Reorientation (Exhibit 2), D. A. Nadler and M. L. Tushman, Academy of Management Executive, 1989, vol. 3, No. 3, pp. 194–204. Reproduced by permission of the publisher via Copyright Clearance Center, Inc.

organization reacts to events in the environment—for example, a response by a major retail company to the unanticipated signalling of a price war by a key competitor.

The four types of organizational change shown in the four boxes comprise either an incremental or a strategic scope and either an anticipatory or a reactive relationship to external events. Tuning is anticipatory and incremental and as such involves the lowest intensity of 'shock' and discontinuity. According to Nadler and Tushman, it is a way of increasing efficiency and is not a response to an immediate problem. Adaptation is reactive and incremental and has the second-lowest intensity of shock. It is a response to external events but does not involve fundamental change throughout the organization. The two strategic scopes of change have higher relative intensity, re-creation often bringing the biggest shock—because it is unanticipated and unplanned—and reorientation the second-biggest shock. Reorientation is a change made with the luxury of time afforded by having anticipated future events and is described as 'frame-bending' change, whilst re-creation marks a radical departure from the past and is 'frame-breaking'.

## Todd Jick

Professor Todd Jick, in a Harvard Business School teaching case study on implementing change, proposes three roles for those involved in the change: change strategists, change implementers, and change recipients.[36] The change strategists are responsible for the early work: they identify the need for change, create a vision of the desired outcome, decide what change is feasible, and choose who should sponsor and defend it. The change implementers make it happen and shape, enable, orchestrate, and facilitate successful progress. The change recipients are the institutionalizers of the change who have to adopt and adapt.

Jick offers ten 'commandments' for implementing change:

(1) analyse the organization and its need for change;
(2) create a shared vision and common direction;
(3) separate from the past;
(4) create a sense of urgency;
(5) support a strong leader role;
(6) line up political sponsorship;
(7) craft an implementation plan;
(8) develop enabling structures;
(9) communicate, involve people, and be honest;
(10) reinforce and institutionalize change.[37]

When following the first commandment, 'analyse the organization and its need for change', the change strategists, Jick recommends, should examine the forces for and against change (as in Lewin's force field analysis). He gives further advice:

■ explain change plans fully;
■ skilfully present plans;
■ make information readily available;
■ make sure plans include benefits for end users and for the corporation;

- spend extra time talking;
- ask for additional feedback from the workforce;
- start small and simple;
- arrange for a quick, positive, visible payoff;
- publicize successes.[38]

Given that this is a textbook on HRM, it is also worth drawing attention to Jick's advice for the ninth commandment, 'communicate, involve people, and be honest'. Jick recommends that employees be prepared for both positive and negative effects of change.[39] This should be done by encouraging dialogue between management and employees. The employee preparation should:

- be brief and concise;
- describe where the organization is now, where it needs to go, and how it will get to the desired state;
- identify who will implement and who will be affected by the change;
- address timing and pacing issues regarding implementation;
- explain the change's success criteria, the intended evaluation procedures, and the related rewards;
- identify key things that will not be changing;
- predict some of the negative aspects that targets should anticipate;
- convey the sponsors' commitment to the change;
- explain how people will be kept informed throughout the change process;
- be presented in such a manner that it capitalizes on the diversity of the communication styles of the audience.

The aspiration of the above list is illustrated by the following quotation from a well-known practitioner of change, Jack Welch, CEO of General Electric:

The best companies now know, without a doubt, where productivity—real and limitless productivity—comes from. It comes from challenged, empowered, excited, rewarded teams of people. It comes from engaging every single mind in the organization, making everyone part of the action, and allowing everyone to have a voice—a role—in the success of the enterprise. Doing so raises productivity not incrementally, but by multiples.[40]

Change, then, needs to be managed if organizations are to survive and prosper over time.[41] Arguably, it is only by winning and nurturing the commitment of employees that change will be sustained in organizations. Managers and employees act within an organizational structure and culture that they inherit, work with, and re-create. Some will re-create their organization anew, others will replicate it as before.

# 5 The Role of the HR Function

B oth hard and soft versions of HRM theoretically portray human resources as potentially valuable strategic assets, and since the first HRM texts of the 1980s, new theories have been proposed on how to develop human potential and obtain competitive advantage through human resources.[42] In practice, as this book repeatedly emphasizes, US and UK companies have been more influenced by short-term considerations than have Japanese companies, traditionally known for their long-term vision. Paradoxically, though, in the latter half of the 1990s, it is the Japanese multinational companies that are being eclipsed by US companies as 'trend-setters' in progressive HRM and in the contingent response to the environment that leads to superior performance.[43] In-depth studies of working conditions in Japanese-owned companies operating in Great Britain have found positive responses to Japanese management practices from some employees, but the balance of the recent evidence has been that workers are concerned about the consequence of these practices in relation to health and safety, intensity of work, understaffing, and rigidly standardized jobs.[44] However, this is not to say that US companies, in contrast, are able to transfer their HRM practices across cultures completely. For example, a study of Dundee NCR found that recruitment, training, pay, benefits, and pensions followed US parent company policy but other areas of HR policy and practice were adapted to suit the local environment.[45]

Marchington and Wilkinson observe that responsibility for HRM[46] has over recent years been split up and handed to a wider range of people outside of the traditional personnel department. In the 1990s there are more consultants than were available to senior and line managers twenty years earlier. There are more large, multi-disciplinary firms, notably management consultancies and the consultancy arms of the major accountancy practices, specialist HR consultancies, independent consultants, academics, and professional groups and associations such as the Institute of Personnel and Development (IPD), Management Charter Initiative (MCI), and the Industrial Society—all with interests in advising on HRM. Companies are now more willing to buy consultancy services, and one important consequence of the greater availability of expertise is the need for employed practitioners of personnel management and HR to be able to compete against external providers. If the trend continues, they will have to become more capable of winning competitive tenders and develop their skills in quantifying the business benefits of their activities.[47] They need to be more effective in persuading top management of their understanding of the business and, in general, improve their credibility with line management.

The problem of personnel or HR function credibility is not new,[48] but some academics who have researched HRM for over ten years are cautiously optimistic. Tyson and Fell say that the HR function has become more split up amongst several groups.[49] The new HRM in organizations is more likely to consist of high-level (strategic) change agents, internal and external consultants working in partnership with line management, and basic administrators serving line management demand. They warn against making extreme predictions, whether euphoric or pessimistic, and recommend we look for new forms of capitalist organizations, featuring, for example, a changed stakeholder role for shareholders with a broader, ethical, and environmental responsibility.

# Summary

THIS chapter has reviewed the growth of interest in organizational culture and discussed three frameworks for managing change and two for implementing change. Senior and middle management have a vital role to play in establishing the organizational culture and managing the process of change, but ultimately success relies just as much on all employees as it does on the actions of individual managers. These frameworks all have in common the assignment of more responsible and proactive behaviour, especially for management, which is in accordance with the spirit of HRM conveyed in Storey's twenty-five-point contrasting of personnel management with HRM (see Chapter 1). The disadvantage of the frameworks and guidelines on managing change is that by concentrating on leadership by managers and portraying employees as passive recipients or resisters, they tend to ignore the potential of employees' contribution. Lack of opportunity to participate in decision making and low employee involvement in the organization can damage employee morale and motivation. When opportunities for employees are not available, over time, they will become less motivated and less committed to the organization and its strategy. It is worth mentioning here that the Fourth Workplace Employee Relations Survey (1998) based on 3,000 workplaces, found that a group of HR practices—training, teamworking, supervisors trained in employee relations matters, and problem solving groups—were statistically associated with each other, which can be construed as positive evidence for an HRM approach to employee participation and involvement in decision making.[50] Chapters 5, 6, 7, and 8 have all presented theories and proposals for effective HRM on topics partially addressed in the guidelines on managing change discussed in this chapter—for example: facilitating employability, enabling career development, improving the motivational content of work, maintaining equitable pay arrangements, ensuring supportive performance management, and fostering a culture of learning and employee development. The frameworks on change covered in this chapter were intended by their originators to be short statements of principles and thus are unable to attend in depth to many critical issues that arise during organizational change. Therefore, managers and HR practitioners who attempt to apply the frameworks and guidelines presented in this chapter without insight into their limitations run the risk of over-simplifying and underestimating a variety of factors that contribute to effective HRM during the management of change. However, one important advantage of the frameworks and literature reviewed in this chapter is that, overall, they encourage management to assume personal responsibility and accountability for managing change; and they attach high priority to the need for managers to be clear about both the *direction* and *process* of organizational change.

---

**BOX 9.2**

## Case Study—Fairbank Centre

Fairbank Centre was opened in 1965 to provide a varied programme of entertainment events for the citizens of Fordingham in the 'swinging sixties'. Situated in the heart of a wealthy provincial county, the Centre became a focus of activity in the new town with little direct competition in the region. It had the full support of both local people and the borough council, who enjoyed its high profile as a centre for civic functions and prestigious orchestral concerts.

Fairbank had good occupancy rates throughout the 1970s, providing a venue for pop groups and high-quality orchestras. Problems began to arise in the early 1980s when competition intensified, occupancy rates began to drop, and the local authority became less supportive of utilizing the venue and meeting the rising costs. With the introduction of compulsory competitive tendering (CCT) for a range of local government services, Fairbank diversified its business. Duncan Arnold, the general manager, led the organization into new ventures, including exhibitions, conferences, private hire, and weddings; however, little business planning or marketing was undertaken and the business was generated in an *ad hoc* and reactive manner.

Arnold was very aware of the deteriorating performance of Fairbank, having managed the organization since its heyday in the 1960s and 1970s. He was an actor by profession and a sociable man with an outgoing personality, but was nearing retirement age and did not possess the motivation or experience to turn the organization around. Fairbank had been subject to CCT for catering, cleaning, and portering services, but following the success of the in-house bid there was no substantial change in working practices or performance.

The organization drifted during the 1980s and failed to adapt to change in the entertainment industry. It had spread into a range of activities, several of which were not making a profit. The income of the Centre improved during the boom years of the mid-to-late 1980s, but by the end of the decade, with the onset of the national recession, the organization again fell into crisis. A review was undertaken by the Director of Community and Leisure and it was agreed that the Fairbank Centre had a continuing role to play in the market as a service provider, but that it must become more commercially viable.

A new general manager, Anne Roberts, was appointed. She had had a career in the leisure and retail industries. Roberts undertook an audit of the venue and analysed its structure, operations, culture, and resources. Shortly after commencing the audit, Roberts appointed a marketing manager who had experience in conference and exhibitions work and a professional qualification from the Chartered Institute of Marketing. He was the first full-time marketing manager for Fairbank Centre and shared Roberts' enthusiasm for its business potential.

A marketing plan was developed and each of the core areas of business identified and their markets targeted and segmented. It was agreed by the senior management that Fairbank would become a focal point for business conferences and events and that the private-hire business would be expanded.

These services were planned to generate income, a proportion being used to assist the promotion of an enhanced and competitive entertainment programme. Having developed a clear vision of the way forward, Roberts acknowledged that her top-down, directive management style would be successful only in the early stages of the process of change. In fact, over an 18-month period, a number of management initiatives were successfully implemented, but through discussion and consultation with employees.

Following an employee conference, the first ever to be held, and open group discussions using a firm of local HR consultants as external facilitators, a new corporate strategy was devised and documented. The organization was restructured into business areas and service teams. The service contract was revised and was re-tendered. New systems, targets, and controls were established. A new corporate identity was adopted using a local PR and advertising firm, and the first up-to-date and networked IT system was installed by the borough's outsourced IT services provider.

Income generated from two profitable education and IT conferences held during Roberts' first two years at Fairbank Centre provided the much-needed revenue for reinvestment. The IT conference was first identified by one of the junior employees as something that Fairbank could do every bit as well as the conference organizers based in London. By offering a location near London, well-connected with the motorway and rail links, Roberts and her marketing manager successfully undercut the existing conference providers. Fairbank Centre was upgraded at a cost of £500,000 for refurbishment and infrastructure improvements. The building was improved to provide customers, visitors, and promoters with facilities that were modern and practical. The investment raised the profile of the venue in the minds of two important stakeholders, the borough council and the local business community.

After the first eighteen months of Roberts' general management, resistance to change was still evident amongst some of the employees and local councillors. A small group of senior employees still possessed a strong power base from which to influence particularly the longer-serving employees of the Fairbank Centre. Their shared belief was that the change was temporary and could be 'sat out'. This blockage to change was tackled by holding team-building sessions outside the workplace and following them up with identification of training needs and subsequent development activity. Personal management support was given to those experiencing greatest difficulty in adapting to the new way of doing things. Some of the councillors were uncomfortable with Roberts' strategy of going down the commercial road, partly because it involved a loss of special privileges. However, in business terms, Fairbank survived its internal differences and the local politics, returning impressive business results during the period 1993–5.

Occupancy rates rose 37% with 400 events being held each year. Market share was up by 16% and costs down by 19%. The budget was balanced and a profit on subsidy achieved. Since 1995, Fairbank has consolidated the change in employee attitudes as well as behaviour, and better teamwork is evident throughout. As for the customer, market research surveys show an improvement in the Centre's reputation.

*Case Study Activity*

1  Write a set of ten OHP transparencies analysing the process of change at the Fairbank Centre in terms of the three stages of change described by Lewin (recognizing the need for change, change, and habituating the change).

2  Analyse the implementation of change at the Fairbank Centre using Todd Jick's ten commandments (discussed in Section 4 of this chapter) or Kotter's eight-stage framework (see Fig. 9.6 below).

# Study Questions

1   Why is an understanding of the external environment and organizational culture important for achieving major organizational change?

2   Describe two different examples of excellent companies. In what respects and to what degree do their cultures differ?[51]

3   Identify a major organizational change and conduct a force field analysis by drawing up a list of the forces driving the organization towards its goal and a list of those forces that are restraining management from achieving their goal.

4   In what ways can individuals resist organizational change and how in your view should this resistance by managed?

5   Compare and contrast Todd Jick's ten commandments (see Section 4 of this chapter) with the guidelines from either Patrick Dawson's processual approach to organizational change or Kotter's eight-stage process, both reproduced below.:

## Patrick Dawson, 'Organizational Change: A Processual Approach'

 (1)  maintain an overview of the dynamic and long-term process of change, and appreciate that major change takes time;
 (2)  recognize that the transition process is unlikely to be marked by a line of continual improvement from beginning to end;
 (3)  be aware of and understand the context in which change takes place;
 (4)  ensure that change strategies are culturally sensitive and do not underestimate the strength of existing cultures;
 (5)  consider the value of having a champion of change;
 (6)  affirm that the substance of the change is fully understood;
 (7)  train staff in the use of new equipment, techniques or procedures;
 (8)  ensure senior management commitment and support;
 (9)  develop a committed and local management team;
(10)  ensure that supervisors are part of major change programmes;
(11)  gain trade union support;
(12)  spend time developing good employee relations;
(13)  clearly communicate the intentions of change to employees;
(14)  provide appropriate funding arrangements;
(15)  take a total organizational approach to managing transitions.

*Source*: Dawson, P., *Organizational Change: A Processual Approach* (1994), chapter 10, 'Conclusion: Managing transitions in modern organizations', p. 179.

# John Kotter, 'Leading Change'

---

**1 Establishing a sense of urgency**

- Examining the market and competitive realities
- Identifying and discussing crises, potential crises, or major opportunities

---

**2 Creating the guiding coalition**

- Putting together a group with enough power to lead the change
- Getting the group to work together like a team

---

**3 Developing a vision and strategy**

- Creating a vision to help direct the change effort
- Developing strategies for achieving that vision

---

**4 Communicating the change vision**

- Using every vehicle possible constantly to communicate the new vision and strategies
- Having the guiding coalition model the behaviour expected of employees

---

**5 Empowering broad-based action**

- Getting rid of obstacles
- Changing systems or structures that undermine the change vision
- Encouraging risk taking and non-traditional ideas, activities, and actions

---

**6 Generating short-term wins**

- Planning for visible improvements in performance, or 'wins'
- Creating those wins
- Visibly recognizing and rewarding people who made the wins possible

---

**7 Consolidating gains and producing more change**

- Using increased credibility to change all systems, structures, and policies that don't fit together and don't fit the transformation vision
- Hiring, promoting, and developing people who can implement the change vision
- Reinvigorating the process with new projects, themes, and change agents

---

**8 Anchoring new approaches in the culture**

- Creating better performance through customer- and productivity-oriented behaviour, more and better leadership, and more effective management
- Articulating the connections between new behaviours and organizational success
- Developing means to ensure leadership development and succession

---

**Figure 9.6  The eight-stage process of creating major change**

*Source*: Reprinted by permission of Harvard Business School Press. From *Leading Change* by J. P. Kotter, Boston, MA 1996, p. 21. Copyright © 1996 by the President and Fellows of Harvard College; all rights reserved.

# Further Reading

Dawson, P., *Organizational Change: A Processual Approach* (London: Paul Chapman Publishing Ltd, 1994).

Deal, T. E., and Kennedy, A., *Corporate Cultures: The Rites and Rituals of Corporate Life* (London: Penguin Books, 1982).

Kotter, J. P., *Leading Change* (Boston, MA: Harvard Business School Press, 1996).

Whittington, R., McNulty, T., and Whipp, R., 'Market-driven change in professional services: problems and processes', *Journal of Management Studies* (1994), 31, 6, November, pp. 829–45.

# Notes

1. Parry, C., overhead projector transparencies on 'UK experience of public sector change' (London (Whitehall): Public Information Services, Cabinet Office, 1998).
2. Chandler, A. D., *Strategy and Structure: Chapters in the History of the American Industrial Enterprise* (Cambridge, MA: MIT Press, 1962).
3. Pugh, D., 'The measurement of organisation structures: does context determine form?', *Organisational Dynamics* (1973), Spring, pp. 19–34.
4. Deming, W. E., *Quality, Productivity and Competitive Position*, (Cambridge, MA: MIT Press, 1982); Juran, J. M., Sedler, L. A., and Gryna, Jr, F. M. (eds.), *Quality Control Handbook*, 2nd edn. (New York: McGraw-Hill, 1962).
5. Starkey, K. and McKinlay, A., *Strategy and the Human Resource: Ford and the Search for Competitive Advantage* (Oxford: Blackwell, 1993).
6. Greiner, L. E., 'Evolution and revolution as organisations grow', *Harvard Business Review* (1972), No. 72407, July–August, pp. 37–46.
7. Schein, E. H., *Organizational Culture and Leadership*, 2nd edn. (San Francisco: Jossey-Bass, 1992), p. 12.
8. Deal, T. E. and Kennedy, A. A., *Corporate Cultures—the Rites and Rituals of Corporate Life* (London: Penguin, 1982).
9. Ibid., pp. 159–61.
10. Pettigrew, A. M., *The Awakening Giant: Continuity and Change in ICI* (Oxford: Blackwell, 1985).
11. Peters, T. J. and Waterman, R. H., *In Search of Excellence: Lessons from America's Best Run Companies* (New York: Harper & Row, 1982).
12. They were employed by organizations such as McKinsey and Harvard.
13. Wilson, D. C., *A Strategy of Change: Concepts and Controversies in the Management of Change* (London: Routledge, 1992), p. 75.
14. Guest, D. E., 'Right enough to be dangerously wrong: an analysis of the In Search of Excellence phenomenon' in G. Salaman, S. Cameron, H. Hamblin, P. Iles, C. Mabey and K. Thompson (eds.), *Human Resource Strategies* (London: Sage, 1992), pp. 5–19.

15. Based on Peters and Waterman, *In Search of Excellence*, pp. 14–16.

16. Legge, K., *Human Resource Management: Rhetorics and Realities* (London: Macmillan, 1995), pp. 79–80.

17. *Video Arts* (1985), 'Excellent Companies' video cassette tape. A more recent example of similar rhetoric emphasizing the central role of people in organizations is Gary Hamel's remark during his address at the October 1998 Institute of Personnel and Development Conference (Harrogate): Hamel said, 'I look on HR as much more valuable compatriots in helping companies prepare for the future than financial or strategic planners.'

18. Watson, T. J., *In Search of Management—Culture, Chaos and Control in Managerial Work* (London: Routledge, 1995); Hope, V. and Hendry, J., 'Corporate cultural change—is it relevant for the organisations of the 1990s?', *Human Resource Management* (1992) 5, 4, pp. 61–73.

19. Derivatives of Lewin's ideas are often evident on OHP transparencies and Powerpoint slides.

20. Lewin, K., 'Frontiers in group dynamics', *Human Relations* (1947), 1, pp. 5–42; Lewin, K., *Field Theory in Social Science* (New York: Harper, 1951).

21. Pettigrew, *The Awakening Giant* (1985) (n. 10 above); Pettigrew, A. and Whipp, R., *Managing Change for Competitive Success* (Oxford: Blackwell, 1991).

22. Lewin, 'Frontiers in group dynamics', and *Field Theory in Social Science*.

23. Lewin, K., *A Dynamic Theory of Personality: Selected Papers* (New York: McGraw-Hill, 1935). Lewin was one of the well-known Gestalt psychologists who emigrated from Germany to the USA following Adolf Hitler's rise to power during the 1930s.

24. Handy, C., *Understanding Organizations*, 4th edn. (New York: Penguin, 1993); Argyris, C. Review essay: 'First and Second-order Errors in Managing Strategic Change: the Role of Organizational Defensive Routines', in A. M. Pettigrew, *The Management of Strategic Change* (Oxford: Basil Blackwell, 1988).

25. Whittington, R., McNulty, T., and Whipp, R., 'Market-driven change in professional services: problems and processes', *Journal of Management Studies* (1994), 31, 6, November, pp. 829–45.

26. Morris, T. J. and Pinnington, A. H., 'Promotion to partner in professional firms', *Human Relations* (1998), Vol. 51, No. 1, pp. 3–24.

27. Handy, *Understanding Organizations* (1993).

28. Ibid.

29. Ibid.

30. Cooper, C. and White, B., 'Organisational behaviour', in S. Tyson (ed.), *Strategic prospects for HRM* (London: Institute of Personnel and Development 1995), pp. 112–45, at p. 120.

31. Reger, R. K., Gustafson, L. T., Demarie, S. M., and Mullane, J. V., 'Reframing the organisation: why implementing total quality is easier said than done', *Academy of Management Review* (1994), 19, 3, pp. 565–84.

32. Hill, S., 'Why quality circles failed but total quality management might succeed', *British Journal of Industrial Relations* (1991), December, Vol. 29, pp. 541–68; Kerfoot, D. and Knights, D., 'Empowering the quality worker? The seduction and contradiction of the total quality phenomenon', in A. Wilkinson and H. Wilmott, *Making Quality Critical: New Perspectives on Organizational Change* (London: Routledge, 1995), pp. 219–39; Pinnington, A. H. and Hammersley, G. C., 'Quality circles under the new deal at Land Rover', *Employee Relations* (1997), Vol. 19, No. 5, pp. 415–29.

33. Burns, R., *Managing People in Changing Times: Coping with Change in the Workplace—a Practical Guide* (London: Allen & Unwin, 1993), p. iv.

34. Ibid., p. 56.

35. Tyson, S. (ed.), *The Practice of Human Resource Strategy* (London: Pitman, 1997); Nadler, D. A. and Tushman, M. L., 'Organisational frame bending: principles for managing reorientation.' *The Academy of Management, Executive Magazine* (1989) 3, 3, pp. 194–204.

36. Jick, T., 'Implementing Change', Harvard Business School Teaching Case, No. 9 (1991), 491–114, pp. 1–12.

37. Ibid., p. 10.

38. Ibid., p. 4.

39. Ibid., p. 8.

40. Welch, J. F., 'A matter of exchange rates', *Wall Street Journal* (1994), 21 June, p. 23; also quoted in R. S. Schuler and M. Huselid, 'HR strategy in the United States', in S. Tyson (ed.), *The Practice of Human Resource Strategy* (London: Pitman, 1997), pp. 174–202, at p. 174.

41. Dawson, P., *Organisational Change: a Processual Approach* (London: Paul Chapman, 1994), pp. 180–2; Kotter, J. P., *A Force for Change: How Leadership Differs from Management* (New York: The Free Press, 1990).

42. Mueller, F., 'Societal Effect, Organisational Effect and Globalisation', *Organisation Studies* (1994), 15, 3, pp. 407–28; Mueller, F., 'Strategic Human Resource Management and the Resource-Based View of the Firm: Toward a Conceptual Integration', Aston University Business School Working Paper (1994); Mueller, F., 'Human Resources as Strategic Assets: An Evolutionary Resource-Based Theory', *Journal of Management Studies* (1996), 33, 6, November, pp. 757–86; Kamoche, K., 'The Integration–Differentiation Puzzle: A Resource-Capability Perspective in International HRM', *International Journal of Human Resource Management* (1996), 7, 1, pp. 230–44; Kamoche, K., 'Strategic Human Resource Management Within a Resource-Capability View of the Firm', *Journal of Management Studies* (1996), March, 33, 2, pp. 213–33; Kamoche, K., 'Knowledge Creation and Learning in International HRM', *International Journal of Human Resource Management* (1997), 8, 2, April, pp. 213–25.

43. Bae, J., Chen, S. J., and Lawler, J. J., 'Variations in human resource management in Asian countries: MNC home-country and host-country effects', *International Journal of Human Resource Management* (1998), 9, 4, August, pp. 653–70 (see pp. 667–8).

44. Webb, M. and Palmer, G., 'Evading surveillance and making time: an ethnographic view of the Japanese factory floor in Britain', *British Journal of Industrial Relations* (1998), 36, 4, December, pp. 611–27 (see p. 611); Delbridge, R., 'Surviving JIT: Control and Resistance in a Japanese Transplant', *Journal of Management Studies* (1995), 32, 6, November, pp. 803–17 (see p. 803).

45. Tayeb, M., 'Transfer of HRM practices across cultures: an American company in Scotland', *International Journal of Human Resource Management* (1998), 9, 2, April, pp. 332–58 (see p. 353).

46. Marchington and Wilkinson, in M. Marchington and A. Wilkinson, *Core Personnel and Development* (London: Institute of Personnel and Development 1996), call it 'personnel and development' rather than HRM. This different nomenclature acknowledges the role of the professional Institute of Personnel and Development and underlines their preference to remain open-minded to the potential for improved contribution by unions in joint regulation of the employment relationship.

47. Mayo, A., 'Economic Indicators of Human Resource Management', in S. Tyson (ed.), *Strategic Prospects for HRM* (London: Institute of Personnel and Development, 1995), pp. 229–65; Tyson, S. and Fell, A., *Evaluating the Personnel Function* (London: Hutchinson, 1986).

48. Watson, T. J., *The Personnel Managers: A Study in the Sociology of Work and Industry* (London: Routledge & Kegan Paul, 1977); Legge, K., *Power, Innovation and Problem-Solving in Personnel Management* (London: McGraw-Hill, 1978).

49. Tyson, S. and Fell, A., 'Looking Ahead', in S. Tyson (ed.), *Strategic Prospects for HRM* (London: Institute of Personnel and Development, 1995), pp. 266–89.

50. Cully, *People Management* (1998), 4, 21, 29 October, p. 71. Marchington, M., Wilkinson, A., Ackers, P., and Goodman, J., *New Developments in Employee Involvement*, Employment Department Research Paper. Series No. 2, 1992.

51. The interested reader should obtain the 'Excellent Companies' video distributed by Video Arts (previously a Melrose film) for more information on how these attributes work in practice. The video concentrates almost exclusively on the positive features and you will need to talk to people who have first-hand experience of the companies to get a balanced picture. Alternatively, if primary data collection is not feasible, you may wish to undertake research by consulting informative secondary materials (books, articles, newspapers, and magazines). The 'excellent companies' (said to have sound performance and possess the eight traits) were: Bechtel, Boeing, Caterpillar Tractor, Dana, Delta Airlines, Digital Equipment, Emerson Electric, Fluor, Hewlett-Packard, IBM, Johnson & Johnson, McDonald's, Procter & Gamble, and 3M.

# Part IV

# Future Developments

Chapter 10

# Internationalization

## Chapter Contents

# Introduction

I N Chapter 2, key recent developments in the environment of HRM were established. One key development in the 1980s and 1990s has been the internationalization of economic activity, which has increased competitive pressures on firms. One consequence of this was identified in Chapter 4, namely that firms were less able to 'take wages out of competition' through joining together with other firms in order to deal with trade unions. Thus, internationalization undermined multi-employer bargaining. In this chapter we examine the role of internationalization in the way firms manage their employees in more detail. In particular, we examine the way in which multi-national companies act as bearers of national systems of HRM to the countries in which they operate.

# 1 Evidence of Internationalization

O VER recent decades economic activity has become increasingly internationalized in a number of ways. International trade has consistently grown at a faster rate than output, resulting in a greater proportion of economic activity being subject to competitive pressures from overseas. In addition, huge sums of money can be transferred across countries almost instantaneously, partly because of the abolition of restrictions on capital movements between developed economies and partly because of developments in information technology. A further aspect of internationalization, and one with arguably the greatest impact for HRM, is the growth of multinational companies (MNCs).

The activities of MNCs have grown substantially throughout the post-war period and particularly rapidly in the 1980s and 1990s. Indeed, this growth has led to intra-enterprise trade within MNCs (that is, sales from one part of an MNC to another) constituting the largest single source of international economic exchange. One in five workers in the developed economies is employed by MNCs; this figure doubles once those working for firms that are dependent on MNCs are included. Moreover, MNCs account for two-thirds of trade in manufacturing within countries in the Organization for Economic Cooperation and Development (OECD). Table 10.1 charts the growth of the operations of MNCs.

Some observers refer to this increasing internationalization as constituting a 'globalization' of economic activity. Writers such as Kenichi Ohmae and Robert Reich argue

**TABLE 10.1**

**The growth of MNCs: outward stock of investments by MNCs (billions of US dollars)**

| 1967 | 1973 | 1980 | 1988 | 1995 |
|------|------|------|------|------|
| 112  | 211  | 551  | 1,141 | 2,730 |

*Source*: United Nations, *World Investment Report* (New York: UN, 1997). Statistics used with the permission of the United Nations Conference on Trade and Development, Geneva.

that globalization has led to a convergence in business organization and practices between countries.[1] Nationally distinct economic and industrial policies are being eroded by the influence of the international financial markets and, in Europe, by the Maastricht criteria for the single currency.[2] Moreover, the increasing ease with which capital can move across borders and the reduction in the cost and increase in the speed of international communications has led Ohmae to claim that the world has become 'borderless'.

The 'globalization' thesis sees MNCs as playing a central role in the process of the development of the borderless world. From this point of view, MNCs are seen as having spread their activities widely across the globe, freeing themselves from reliance on the country in which they originated. Moreover, senior management teams in these 'global' companies comprise managers from many different countries, while their finances are raised from around the world. In essence, MNCs that have globalized owe allegiance to no one country over another and, hence, are becoming 'stateless'. One implication of this is that the companies' strategies and orientation will be shaped less by the characteristics of particular countries and more by 'global' economic and technological forces.

The globalization thesis has recently been called into question, however, for two reasons. The first is that the proponents of globalization ignore the continued distinctiveness of 'national business systems'.[3] It is argued that the nature of the law, institutions, and cultures continue to differ between countries and that the interrelationships between these factors combine to produce nationally distinct forms of business organization in general and of labour management in particular. Writing in this vein, Porter has stressed how the competitive advantage of nations arises out of the characteristics of firms' national resource base.[4] Relatedly, other writers have stressed the dominance of particular national systems. This theme is clearly evident in consideration of the dominance of the Japanese economy and the pressures for the diffusion of Japanese practices to other countries:

Writers such as Elger and Smith (1994) have emphasized that international competition is rooted in the specific arrangements of national systems, and that national economies compete to impose their version of economic development. The competitive advantage of a particular version of capitalism creates strong pressures for its dissemination, a process in which MNCs are key protagonists. Thus Japanese MNCs, as representatives of the currently 'hegemonic' capitalist power, are seen as transmission belts for the business and work organization practices of Japanese capitalism.[5]

The second criticism of the globalization thesis centres on the rarity—some would say complete absence—of MNCs that can genuinely be described as 'global' or 'stateless'. Two recent surveys of MNCs testify to this rarity. Hirst and Thompson show that, despite the talk of globalization, MNCs continue to hold the majority of their assets and sell the majority of their goods in the country in which they originated. The authors concluded that 'the home oriented nature of MNC activity along all dimensions looked at seems overwhelming'.[6] In the same vein, Ruigrok and van Tulder demonstrate that of the largest 100 MNCs in the world, none can justifiably be characterized as being global in nature.[7] In addition to supporting the above findings on the concentration in the home country of the activities of MNCs, the authors also showed that MNCs employ the majority of their workforces in the home country; that the shares of MNCs are bought and sold overwhelmingly in the home country; and that the management boards of MNCs are generally dominated by nationals of the home country (see Table 10.2). In sum, MNCs are deeply rooted in the cultures and institutions of the country in which they originated and, hence, they should be seen not as 'global' firms but as 'national firms with international operations'.[8]

The reliance by MNCs on their home countries for finance means that the pressures on MNCs vary according to their country of origin because the nature of financial institutions differs between countries. Generally, MNCs from America and Britain face pressures to satisfy shareholders, who are the dominant stakeholders in these systems. Shares can be bought and sold relatively easily and, hence, companies can also be taken over relatively easily (as we saw in Chapter 2). This poses a threat to an existing managerial team, who may be replaced if the company changes hands; in order to prevent takeover, management face pressure to maximize profitability in the short term in order to raise the share price and pay out large dividends to shareholders. Consequently, managerial objectives centre on the short term; planning for the long term is difficult for firms from these systems. In contrast, MNCs from continental Europe and Japan are not subject to such short-term pressures. Shareholdings are held

---

**TABLE 10.2**

**Characteristics of the 100 largest MNCs**

|  | More than 50% foreign | Less than 50% foreign | No data |
|---|---|---|---|
| Distribution of assets | 36 | 46 | 18 |
| Composition of management board | 8 | 92 | 0 |

*Source*: United Nations, *World Investment Report*, 1998, New York: UN (Statistics used with the permission of the United Nations Conference on Trade and Development, Geneva); Ruigrot, W. and van Tulder, R., 1996. *The Logic of International Relations*, London: Routledge.

by stable and interlinked networks of individuals, families, and institutions who tend to be committed to the company for a long period. Hostile takeovers of the sort that pose a threat to existing managerial teams are rare in these systems. A key consequence of this is that managers are able to plan ahead and pursue long-term goals with a greater degree of freedom.[9] Overall, therefore, we might expect MNCs from America and Britain to be subject to short-term pressures more so than MNCs from continental Europe and Japan.

The domination of management boards by nationals of the home country also gives rise to variations between MNCs from different countries. Educational and training systems, religions, and social values differ significantly, of course, from one country to another; as a result the priorities and values of senior managers also differ. This means that MNCs have distinctively national characteristics that shape many of their key decisions, including location, strategy, and management style. The following section investigates how national variations in MNCs affect employment practice.

# 2 Implications of National Identity in MNCs for HRM

THERE are good reasons for believing that MNCs will be an important channel through which employment practices are diffused across borders. The MNC is a relatively effective mechanism for transferring knowledge across borders.[10] As Capelli and McElrath argue, much of the context within which managers operate is similar in different parts of an MNC; organizational structures and, to some extent, managerial goals and corporate cultures have common aspects throughout an MNC.[11] One important implication of MNCs retaining such strong roots in the home country, therefore, is that this is likely to influence their approach to the management of labour in their overseas subsidiaries. That is, many MNCs will seek to manage their subsidiaries as a cultural extension of the parent company and, therefore, will adopt employment practices overseas that are characteristic of the country of origin. Since the environment of HRM varies between countries, the multinational can be seen as a mechanism through which the ideology and practices of different versions of HRM can be diffused across borders.

Indeed, there is considerable evidence that MNCs have acted as innovators to host countries in diffusing across borders practices that are characteristic of the home country. Interest in the diffusion of practices across countries has often centred on American MNCs, recently because of their role as bearers of HRM. American-style HRM centres on Quality of Working Life programmes, which stress employee involvement in production-related decisions and the importance of integrating HRM policy goals with one another and with business goals. Guest notes, as we recall from Chapter 1, that models of HRM were first developed in US universities, particularly Harvard,[12] and the most widely cited exemplars of the model were mainly US companies such as IBM and Kodak.[13] The values of HRM are compatible, according to Guest, with aspects of American culture, such as individualism and charismatic leadership, and also sat comfortably with the political context of the 1980s, which saw revived interest in the 'American Dream'—the ability of individuals to be successful through hard work and self-improvement. The perceived success of HRM practices in delivering employee commitment to quality creates interest in the diffusion of these practices across borders. Moreover, there is some evidence that American MNCs have diffused such practices to their overseas subsidiaries.[14]

Generally, the literature shows US firms to be more highly centralized in their decision making on IR issues than are MNCs from other countries. In addition, American MNCs use more formalized systems of control than other MNCs do, such as written policies and direct reporting.[15] A key implication is that US MNCs are likely to have diffused their practices to their overseas subsidiaries. Several studies suggest that US MNCs exhibit lower levels of union membership and recognition than local firms do, especially among white-collar workers.[16] Although this finding is not universal, it does suggest that a practice of avoiding unions, present in the majority of firms in the USA, has been diffused to the overseas subsidiaries of some US MNCs. Moreover, where they do recognize unions, many US MNCs pursue collective bargaining practices characteristic of the USA, such as fixed-term agreements, single-employer (especially plant) negotiations, and productivity bargaining.[17] There is also some evidence that US MNCs have tried to diffuse other employment practices that are characteristic of HRM, such as job enlargement, semi-autonomous work teams, and performance-related pay.[18]

The attention of researchers recently has centred on the role of Japanese MNCs in diffusing practices across borders. The interest has been in the extent to which MNCs from Japan have diffused the techniques of lean production and the associated HRM practices to their overseas subsidiaries. Lean production stresses the benefits management can gain from changing the organization of production, arguing that these are at least as great as those to be realized through technical innovation. Hence, the emphasis has been on the reduction of inventory through 'just-in-time' (JIT) production and 'getting it right first time' to eliminate defects and waste through 'total quality management' (TQM).[19] A central element of lean production, therefore, is the focus on the social relations in production. The attempt to reduce waste and defects requires worker commitment to these goals; lean production is associated with a set of HRM practices designed to elicit the necessary commitment. These include job rotation, teamwork, a single status for blue- and white-collar workers, and employee involvement through means such as quality circles and team briefings.

Indeed, research demonstrates that the attempt by Japanese MNCs to export these practices is widespread. In reviewing the literature, Ferner stresses 'the strong but informal centralized nature of their foreign operations, highly reliant on establishing an international network of Japanese expatriate managers'.[20] While this degree of centralization has not led to a wholesale diffusion of Japanese practices to their overseas subsidiaries, many Japanese-style practices have been diffused to their overseas plants, albeit often in amended form. The preference of Japanese MNCs for single-union deals can be seen as an attempt to recreate Japanese company union structures in a different context.[21] There is also evidence to suggest that Japanese firms commonly diffuse to their overseas subsidiaries other IR practices that are characteristic of Japan, such as quality circles, single status, teamworking, job rotation, functional flexibility, and attempts to generate a strong company culture through recruitment and training.[22] Perhaps most significantly, Japanese MNCs commonly implement lean production in their overseas subsidiaries: 'the extent of teamwork and employee involvement in quality circles and the like might vary greatly, but the more basic tenets of JIT/TQC production such as waste elimination, continuous improvement, and fault tracing are pursued relentlessly whether it be in autos in the USA or electronics in Malaysia'.[23]

A small amount of research exists on the behaviour of European MNCs in their overseas subsidiaries. This research suggests that MNCs from Europe are more decentralized than American and Japanese MNCs.[24] The available studies on German MNCs confirm this; there has been little attempt to diffuse to their UK subsidiaries characteristically German practices such as works councils,[25] while the same seems to hold for German firms in the USA.[26] Part of the explanation for this finding may lie in the constraints on the diffusion of employment practices that characteristics of host countries present, something considered in the following section.

# 3   Constraints from Host Countries

THUS differences in MNCs according to their country of origin arise out of differences in 'national business systems'. These differences lead to the diffusion of employment practices across borders, with MNCs acting as carriers of practices characteristic of the country of origin. However, this diffusion of practices is also constrained by these differences in national business systems. As Whitley puts it:

The extent to which such a transfer of business system characteristics to host economies occurs does, of course, depend on the openness of dominant institutions in those economies to novel forms of economic organization and the relative strength of business systems in them. The more open and pluralistic an economy is, the more likely it will be to accept (or at least acquiesce in) the transplanting of new firm–market relationships. Conversely, where institutions are cohesive, integrated and have generated a distinctive business system, it is more likely that MNCs will have to adapt their mode of operation to the prevailing pattern.[27]

One element of national business systems that constrains diffusion specifically in relation to HRM is the nature of the legal framework for employment. In all countries the law stipulates how certain aspects of the employment relationship are conducted, but this varies between countries. Thus in many countries representative structures are enshrined in law, whereas in others they are left to the 'voluntary' negotiation of management and trade unions. German and Austrian works councils are examples of the former, while Britain is an example of the latter.[28] Redundancy provisions also differ between countries in terms of the amount of compensation due and the amount of notice required. Management may also find that law constrains its freedom to organize production and work, since in some countries the law regulates levels of pay according to job classifications: Coller describes how the *ordenanza laboral* in Spain impeded attempts by a food MNC to diffuse a practice of job enlargement that operated in its British plant.[29] These legal differences constrain the freedom of MNCs to diffuse practices across their sites between countries.

The nature of labour market institutions can also constrain cross-border diffusion. Where trade unions are strong, an MNC may feel that granting recognition is unavoidable, or at least that not doing so would be very costly. Participating in collective bargaining may constrain the range of choices an MNC has concerning elements of industrial relations such as pay determination and consultation.[30] The nature of a country's educational and training institutions may also constrain the range of choices that management in an MNC face, since an MNC wishing to diffuse practices requiring high levels of skill may find it impractical to do so in countries where employees do not have the necessary skills. Humphrey notes how Japanese electronics companies in Brazil could only diffuse partial versions of Total Quality Control because the available employees did not possess adequate numeracy skills and were not able to perform the required range of tasks.[31] A number of studies detail the success of the German training system in producing a highly skilled workforce; arguably, practices such as functional flexibility, which operates relatively easily in Germany, will be more problematic in other countries where the workforce is not as highly skilled.[32]

A further factor that constrains cross-national diffusion is cultural differences between countries that result in practices that are generally accepted in some countries being less acceptable in others. Evans *et al.* argue that corporate culture within an MNC can help in the diffusion of practices across borders through the forging of shared understandings and values.[33] However, one of the best-known works in this respect, Hofstede's study of IBM, found significant cultural differences between IBM's plants in different countries despite this company's attempts to forge a strong corporate culture.[34] One implication is that continuing differences in national cultures constrain the ability of an MNC to diffuse practices across countries. Performance-related pay is an example of a practice that operates more easily in some cultures than in others: while it is generally accepted in Anglo-Saxon business cultures, it is less widely accepted in France, Germany, or Italy, where there is resistance to the idea 'that individual members of the group should excel in a way that reveals the shortcomings of others'.[35]

These cross-national differences, then, result in MNCs facing constraints in the extent to which they are able to diffuse practices across borders and, further, the strength of these constraints varies from country to country. In Whitley's terms, some national business systems are more open to novel forms of business organization than are others.[36] There is more scope for MNCs to diffuse practices to countries characterized by a 'permissive' legal framework and weak labour market institutions than there is for them to diffuse practices to more regulated countries. As we have seen, in many continental European countries statutory provisions exist for union recognition, employee representation, and redundancy provision, whereas these provisions are much weaker in Britain. Furthermore, MNCs experience less difficulty in diffusing practices between plants that are characterized by similar national cultures than between plants in quite different cultures.

The strength of these constraints also varies according to different employment matters, being stronger in some areas and weaker in others. Typically, pay determination, union recognition, consultative structures, and redundancy provisions are regulated to a greater extent by the law and labour market institutions than are direct employee involvement practices, work organization, and management development.[37] Further, some aspects of IR are dependent upon extra-firm supportive structures while others can operate independently of such structures and are, hence, more easily diffused. The training practices found in German firms, as we have seen, are embedded in a distinctive training infrastructure which would make it difficult for a firm in Britain to emulate the approach.[38] Another example concerns teamworking. In German and British plants of the same company, German team members have been found to be more positive about teamwork than their British counterparts. Attitude to teamwork appears to be influenced by the national institutional structure of employee relations, the traditional British adversarial system having negative effects on worker participation and team contribution.[39] On the other hand, direct employee involvement practices are less dependent on the existence of extra-firm supportive structures and, hence, there is more scope for their diffusion.

Even in those areas of employment where management face constraints in diffusing practices across borders, however, they may be able to diffuse modified versions of practices that operate in other countries. The degree to which teamwork involving functional flexibility can be diffused across borders will be constrained by the skill mix of the workforce and by the willingness of employees to adapt to a practice they are unused to (see Chapter 9 on organizational change). But these constraints do not completely remove the scope for diffusion. Humphrey's study of Japanese transplants in Brazil, mentioned above, found that the low skill and educational level of Brazilian workers constrained the diffusion of TQC, but the constraints still permitted an amended version of the practice to be diffused.[40] Therefore, it is likely that in many cases the process of diffusion will involve some modification of practices in order to fit the new environment.

Moreover, the constraints facing MNCs presented by cross-national differences should not be treated as fixed. Rather, they are subject to the influence of powerful MNCs. Thus MNCs may use their political power to influence governments into amending labour laws. In addition, they generally have more scope for avoiding union recognition than do 'domestic' firms, or for pioneering new collective bargaining practices. Japanese MNCs in the UK, particularly those in Wales and Telford, are examples of this: many have pursued an 'enclave' strategy in which their operations are established on a greenfield site and the workforce is largely young, often female, and has little history of trade unionism.[41] In these circumstances the constraints on management in diffusing practices posed by cross-national diffusion are minimized and managerial prerogative maximized.[42] Writing in this vein, Morris and Wilkinson argue that differences in the systems of political economy, education, industrial relations, and culture all constrain what Japanese companies attempt to export to their overseas subsidiaries but that 'the export of practices has been able to occur in spite of very different institutional environments in different countries around the world, and that successful transfer depends more on the establishment of managerial prerogatives than an amenable societal culture'.[43]

# Summary

THE chapter began by noting the growth in the size and scope of MNCs, one of the key forces behind the internationalization of economic activity. Despite the current vogue for talk of globalization, however, we have seen that most MNCs retain a very strong focus in their countries of origin and that this gives them distinctive national characteristics. A key implication of this is that MNCs are likely to bring employment practices characteristic of their home country—especially those concerning HRM—to countries in which they have subsidiaries.

The review of the evidence showed this to be the case. Many American and Japanese firms have been active in implementing in their UK subsidiaries practices that are characteristic of their home countries. In the case of American MNCs these took the form of performance-related pay and job enlargement practices; for Japanese firms they comprised the HRM practices accompanying lean production, such as teamwork, employee involvement, and single status. However, there are significant constraints to the ease with which MNCs can diffuse practices across borders. Legal frameworks, labour market institutions, and national cultures all differ from one country to another and constrain the ability of MNCs to transfer practices. Thus the nature and extent of diffusion of HRM practices depends on the interplay of these influences.

---

BOX 10.9

## Case Study—Tomakuri

Tomakuri, a Japanese MNC, set up a plant in Britain in the late 1980s. The company manufactures electronic goods such as cameras and photocopiers. Tomakuri holds the majority of its assets, employs the majority of its workers, and raises the majority of its finance in Japan; further, its managerial board is composed entirely of Japanese nationals. In this respect the company is typical of almost all MNCs in that it retains a very strong base in the country of origin, giving it distinctive national characteristics.

This Japanese influence is clearly visible in its UK plant, which was set up as a greenfield site. Many of the senior managerial positions in the plant were filled by Japanese expatriate managers, whose brief was to ensure that the plant adopted many of the characteristics of Tomakuri's domestic operations that the management at HQ felt were responsible for the company's success. Uppermost amongst these were aspects of lean production. Thus the plant operated on a 'just-in-time' basis and employed other manufacturing practices associated with lean production, such as cellular working. These were linked to many Japanese-style HRM practices being employed at the plant, of which there was also evidence. The workforce was broken down into teams that shared responsibility for the quality and output of products from their particular stages of the production process. These teams were kept informed about developments in the plant through a daily system of team briefings and were also expected to meet regularly to discuss problems that were affecting their work. There was also a policy of single status at the plant: all employees, including managers, were to wear the same uniform, eat in the same canteen, and have the opportunity to join the company pension scheme. The plant is non-union, management having repeatedly resisted calls from unions to grant them recognition.

Managers in the plant were keen to portray this diffusion as a success story, painting a largely harmonious picture of relationships between managers and staff at the plant. Research into the attitudes of employees, however, leads us to call into question this positive picture. There were aspects of the Japanese-style practices that employees largely supported. For example, 82% of employees saw problem-solving groups as 'a good thing' and 58% said there was a fairly strong or very strong 'sense of teamwork'. However, employees also expressed dissatisfaction with many elements of their working lives. Three-quarters of them, for instance, said that they were working harder than they were three years ago. Moreover, only 3% of employees said that there was complete trust between management and employees, and only another 16% that there was trust most of the time.

The research demonstrated that there are constraints to the way that practices can be lifted from one system and diffused to another. In this case, cultural factors appeared to constrain the implementation of the Japanese practices. A number of other sources suggest that creating high-trust relationships between management and the workforce is always problematic and that the introduction of Japanese practices rarely transforms these relations. This is very largely because of underlying tensions in the employment relationship and, more specifically, because employees in Britain are not used to the pressures and expectations made of them under this style of management. The resulting managerial style can be seen as a hybrid, reflecting the competing influences of the Japanese parent company and the British employees' attitudes and values.

*Note*: We are grateful to Chris Rees for letting us use information which he gathered from the same company during a different research project.

*Case Study Activity*

Discuss which aspects of HRM Japanese companies are likely to find relatively easy to implement in Britain and which they are likely to find more difficult.

# Study Questions

1   Why has there been a growth in the activities of multinational companies?

2   In what ways are multinationals, even very large ones, influenced by the country in which they originated?

3   Of the largest one hundred multinationals in the world, twenty-eight are American, eleven are Japanese, and ten are German. Why are these three countries the base for so many MNCs?

4   You have just obtained a job as HR manager in the British subsidiary of a Japanese electronics company. What differences might you detect from your previous job in a comparable British firm?

5   How does the legal, institutional, and cultural framework of host countries constrain the approach of a multinational to the management of people?

# Further Reading

Ferner, A., 'Country of Origin Effects and HRM in Multinational Companies', *Human Resource Management Journal* (1997), 7, 1, pp. 19–37.

Marginson, P. and Sisson, K., 'The Structure of Transnational Capital in Europe: the Emerging Euro-Company and its Implications for Industrial Relations', in Hyman, R. and Ferner, A. (eds.), *New Frontiers in European Industrial Relations* (Oxford: Blackwell, 1994).

Morris, J. and Wilkinson, B., 'The Transfer of Japanese Management to Alien Institutional Environments', *Journal of Management Studies* (1995), 32, 6, pp. 719–30.

Ruigrok, W. and Van Tulder, R., *The Logic of International Restructuring* (London: Routledge, 1996).

# Notes

1.  Ohmae, K., *The Borderless World* (London: Collins, 1990); Reich, R., 'Who Is Us?', *Harvard Business Review* (1990), Jan–Feb, 53–64.

2.  Mueller, F., 'Societal Effect, Organisational Effect and Globalisation', *Organisation Studies* (1994), 15, 3, pp. 407–28.

3. Whitley, R. (ed.), *European Business Systems: Firms and Markets in their National Contexts* (London: Sage, 1992).

4. Porter, M., *The Competitive Advantage of Nations* (New York: Free Press, 1990).

5. Ferner, A., 'Country of Origin Effects and HRM in Multinational Companies', *Human Resource Management Journal* (1997), 7, 1, pp. 19-37.

6. Hirst, P. and Thompson, G., *Globalisation in Question* (Cambridge: Polity, 1996), p. 95.

7. Ruigrok, W. and Van Tulder, R., *The Logic of International Restructuring* (London: Routledge, 1996).

8. Hu, Y., 'Global or Stateless Corporations are National Firms with International Operations', *California Management Review* (1992), 34, 2, pp. 107-26.

9. Whitley, R. (ed.), *European Business Systems: Firms and Markets in their National Contexts* (London: Sage, 1992); Whittington, R., *What is Strategy—and Does it Matter?* (London: Routledge, 1993).

10. Bartlett, C. and Ghoshal, S., *Managing across Borders* (London: Hutchinson, 1989).

11. Capelli, P. and McElrath, R., 'The Transfer of Employment Practices through Multinationals', paper presented to the Third Bargaining Group Conference, University of California, Berkeley, 1992.

12. Guest, D., 'Human Resource Management and the American Dream', *Journal of Management Studies* (1990), 27, 4, pp. 377-97.

13. Peters, T. and Waterman, R., *In Search of Excellence* (New York: Harper and Row, 1982).

14. Ferner, A., 'Country of Origin Effects and HRM in Multinational Companies', *Human Resource Management Journal* (1997), 7, 1, pp. 19-37.

15. Ibid.

16. Buckley, P. and Enderwick, P., *The Industrial Relations Practices of Foreign-Owned Firms in Britain* (London: Macmillan, 1985).

17. Ibid.

18. Beaumont, P. and Townley, B., 'Non-Union American Plants in Britain: Their Employment Practices', *Relationnes Industrielles* (1985), 40, 4, pp. 810-25.

19. Schoenberger, R., *World Class Manufacturing* (New York: The Free Press, 1986).

20. Ferner, A., 'Country of Origin Effects and HRM in Multinational Companies', *Human Resource Management Journal* (1997), 7, 1, pp. 19-37.

21. Oliver, N. and Wilkinson, B., *The Japanization of British Industry: New Developments in the 1990s* (Oxford: Basil Blackwell, 1992).

22. Ibid.

23. Morris, J. and Wilkinson, B., 'The Transfer of Japanese Management to Alien Institutional Environments', *Journal of Management Studies* (1995), 32, 6, pp. 719-30.

24. Bartlett, C. and Ghoshal, S., *Managing across Borders* (London: Hutchinson, 1989).

25. Beaumont, P., Cressey, P., and Jakobsen, P., 'Key Industrial Relations: West German Subsidiaries in Britain', *Employee Relations* (1990), 12, 6, pp. 3-6.

26. Rosenzweig, P. and Nohria, N., 'Influences on Human Resource Management Practices in Multinational Corporations', *Journal of International Business Studies* (1994), 25, 2, pp. 229-51.

27. Whitley, R. (ed.), *European Business Systems: Firms and Markets in their National Contexts* (London: Sage, 1992), p. 277.

28. Ferner, A. and Hyman, R., *Changing Industrial Relations in Europe* (Oxford: Blackwell, 1998).

29. Coller, X., 'Managing Flexibility in the Food Industry: A Cross-National Comparative Case Study of European Multinational Companies', *European Journal of Industrial Relations* (1996), 2, 2, pp. 153-72.

30. Ferner, A., 'Multinational Companies and Human Resource Management: An Overview of Research Issues', *Human Resource Management Journal* (1994), 4, 3, pp. 79-102.

31. Humphrey, J., 'The Adoption of Japanese Management Techniques in Brazilian Industry', *Journal of Management Studies* (1995), 32, 6, pp. 767-88.

32. See, for example, Streeck, W., 'Skills and the Limits of Neo-Liberalism', *Work, Employment and Society* (1989), 3, 2, pp. 89-104; Steedman, H. and Wagner, K., 'Productivity, Machinery and Skills: Clothing Manufacture in Britain and Germany', *National Institute Economic Review* (1989), 128, May, pp. 40-57.

33. Evans, P., Doz, Y., and Laurent, A. (eds.), *Human Resource Management in International Firms* (London: Macmillan, 1989).

34. Hofstede, G., *Culture's Consequences* (Beverly Hills: Sage, 1980).

35. Lorenz, C., 'Learning to Live with a Cultural Mix', *Financial Times*, 23 April 1993.

36. Whitley, R. (ed.), *European Business Systems: Firms and Markets in their National Contexts* (London: Sage, 1992).

37. Ferner, 'Multinational Companies and Human Resource Management' (1994) (n. 30 above).

38. Lane, C., 'Industrial Order and the Transformation of Industrial Relations: Britain, Germany and France Compared', in R. Hyman and A. Ferner (eds.), *New Frontiers in European Industrial Relations* (Oxford: Blackwell, 1994).

39. Murakami, T., 'The formation of teams: a British and German comparison', *International Journal of Human Resource Management* (1998), 9, 5, October, pp. 800-17 (see pp. 814-15).

40. Humphrey, 'The Adoption of Japanese Management Techniques in Brazilian Industry', (1995) (n. 31 above).

41. Wilkinson, B., Morris, J., and Munday, M., 'Japan in Wales: a New IR', *Industrial Relations Journal* (1993), 24, 4, pp. 273-83.

42. Dedoussis, V., 'Simply a Question of Cultural Barriers? The Search for New Perspectives in the Transfer of Japanese Management Practices', *Journal of Management Studies* (1995), 32, 6, pp. 731-45.

43. Morris, J. and Wilkinson, B., 'The Transfer of Japanese Management to Alien Institutional Environments', *Journal of Management Studies* (1995), 32, 6, pp. 719-30.

# Chapter 11
# Conclusion: Future Developments

THIS book has investigated the meaning of human resource management and has reviewed the evidence concerning its practice. In this final section, we briefly review key elements of HRM and consider potential lines of development in the future.

At the beginning of the book we introduced and discussed different models of HRM. There continue to be differences of opinion on what constitutes HRM and disagreement on how far it is a welcome and progressive philosophy and approach. Indeed, many of those who wrote radical critiques of personnel management and HRM in the 1980s and 1990s continue to draw attention to HRM's contradictions, and some have become more rather than less critical of its role in work, organizations, and society. To quote one example of this scepticism of the benefits of HRM:

The unctuous rhetorical blandishments of Human Resource Management (HRM) coexist successfully with the harsh legitimations of Business Process Reengineering (BPR), while there is no inconsistency in simultaneously promoting teamwork, delayering, commitment, flexibility, loyalty, individualism, greed, empowerment and surveillance.[1]

So HRM continues to have strong critics, but it also has its advocates. Research on different attitudes towards HRM found that the groups who believe in it most strongly are professional practitioners and members of the Institute of Personnel and Development.[2] Marchington and Wilkinson, in their book published by the IPD, propose that one way forward for organizations is to adopt a 'best practice' model of personnel and development, but at the same time they caution against over-optimism, noting that genuine pursuit of best practice will require people to be 'deviant innovators' rather than 'conformist innovators'.[3] These terms were originally used by Karen Legge over twenty years ago to characterize different roles of the personnel management function.[4] If Marchington and Wilkinson's recommendation is to be followed, then innovation will have to be against the grain of what is traditionally expected in organizations and it will require the courage and persistence of a significant group of innovators, which, in practice, seems improbable given the fact that both the HR and the personnel professional have generally been more acceptable in the conformist innovator role.[5]

Some recent research on HRM does provide evidence for a link between coherent HR practice and superior organizational performance. As was mentioned in Chapter 7, research conducted during the 1990s has found that HRM policies and practices can have a significant influence on company performance. Mark Huselid's study of approximately 1,000 US firms has moved the 'HRM and performance' debate forward by uncovering empirical evidence that HRM practices have affected employee turnover, employee productivity, and corporate and financial performance.[6] Brian Becker and Barry Gerhart's review of the recent conceptual and empirical research concludes that human resources are most influential when the HR system has high internal and external fit (with internal fit, components of HRM complement and support each other; with external fit, there is a consistent match with the developmental stage and the strategy of the organization). They claim that HR must be properly aligned if it is to solve business problems and support operational and strategic initiatives. HR managers are at a crossroads, they argue: either they take up the challenge and stimulate improved HRM, resulting in added value for their companies, or the HR function will be outsourced by disenchanted senior managers with the result that achieving strategic goals through human resources will become all the harder.[7]

While it is apparent that there is no universal agreement on what HRM is in theory or in practice, it is clear that the models introduced in Chapter 1 share some common features. First, all of the models emphasize the importance of managing labour in a 'strategic' way. That is, they stress the need to integrate the management of people with the long-term goals of the business. A second common feature amongst the models is that they are based on a unitarist ideology, which plays down the potential for conflict within organizations and instead stresses common interests between management and employees. Third, advocates of HRM are optimistic about the social consequences for employees, as well as for managers, of an organization adopting HRM. In particular, they stress the opportunities that HRM offers for employees to develop their skills and contribute to decision making.

One theme of this book has been that, while there has been considerable interest in HRM amongst practitioners, the evidence suggests that it has not taken root in as coherent a way as might appear at first sight. Many of the practices associated with HRM—such as sophisticated recruitment and selection, performance-related pay, teamwork, and employee involvement—have undoubtedly become more widespread. Furthermore, other developments, such as the growth of training initiatives and the decline in collective representation, are consistent with a move towards HRM. However, while the significance of these developments should not be denied, the evidence does not suggest that HRM in Britain has been implemented in a strategic way; neither has it substantially changed managerial ideology, nor has it always had beneficial consequences for employees.

In part, HRM in practice in Britain reflects actual tensions and contradictions within the models of HRM. For example, two practices commonly considered to be components of the HRM approach are teamwork and pay linked to individual performance. It is clear that these two practices may on occasion be in tension with one another, and an employee may be more concerned with maximizing his or her own performance and contingent rewards than with meeting the complete range of goals of the team. As we have shown, particularly in Chapter 2, there are also potential tensions and contradictions between HRM and its environment. National institutions and culture both affect the implementation of HRM. It seems that a number of the key elements of the British environment therefore are likely to continue in the future to be inimical to HRM.

The pragmatic way that HRM has been implemented in the UK is partly explained by the difficulties involved in changing the deeply embedded ideologies of managers. Many British managers, for example, have been reluctant to accord genuine influence to employees in decision making, believing decision making on key issues to be the preserve of managers alone, and it will take more than textbooks on HRM such as this one to persuade them otherwise. Perhaps, most importantly, the pragmatic and piecemeal way in which HRM has been implemented owes much to the uncertainties of the environment in which organizations operate. For most firms the last twenty years has been a period of rapid technological change, while it has also been characterized by significant turbulence in the international economy—the two oil shocks in the 1970s, two deep recessions, and, most recently, a series of financial crises in different parts of the world. This turbulence and uncertainty in the environment make a strategic approach on the part of firms more difficult and in Britain these difficulties are amplified by characteristic features of the British economic system, particularly the way in which firms are financed and governed, which create a preoccupation with short-term considerations.

Innumerable initiatives have been pursued and new practices established that have been in part a consequence of the rise of interest in HRM. Moreover, many of these initiatives and practices appear to have delivered some limited benefits for managers and, in some cases, for employees too. Overall, though, we have sought to show the inherent problems and difficulties management and employees experience in pursuing HRM, while not wishing to deny that there is much of significance in HRM. Storey said that there were signs that HRM has attained a secure foothold and offers some important intellectual and practical developments in, for example, resource-based competitiveness, core competences and the learning organization. But he warns that the future prospects of strategic HRM are not strong in companies organized into devolved business units where line managers are continuously subject to stringent short-term profit targets and expected to treat human assets primarily as a cost.[8]

What, then, of the future? A detailed analysis of what may happen in the first decade of the twenty-first century and beyond lies outside the scope of a short concluding chapter, but we would like to highlight two important developments. The first of these concerns the emergence of 'social partnership'. In many ways social partnership has much in common with HRM; it is being touted as a new approach to the management of people that promises benefits for both management and employees. As with HRM, there is some difficulty in defining exactly what it is, though a common element appears to be a recognition by both managers and employees that, as well as there being some areas where their interests diverge, there are also many areas where mutual benefits can be achieved through co-operation. In the organizations that claim to have adopted a social partnership approach a common feature has been a promin-ent role for trade unions, a key difference from HRM. In organizations like Blue Circle and Tesco, for example, social partnership deals have involved new agreements between management and unions. It is too soon to predict how widespread social partnership deals will become, but one factor that may encourage their spread is the Labour government's legislation concerning trade union recognition; in the future, wherever a majority of a workforce want to be represented by a trade union, manage-ment must formally recognize the union. This may persuade some managers that avoiding unions is impossible and that, given that they must deal with a union, a social partnership approach is preferable to an adversarial one.

The second development likely to be influential on British firms is European integra-tion. The completion of the Single European Market and, more recently, the process of European Monetary Union are key factors for many British organizations, increasing the degree of competition within Europe. If Britain joins the single currency, as seems increasingly likely, the greater ease with which the prices of goods and services in different parts of Europe can be compared will present new opportunities and chal-lenges to firms in Britain. Moreover, a further part of European integration concerns employment policy. The Social Chapter of the EU is producing a growing number of regulations that affect the way employers in Britain manage their workforces in rela-tion to, for example, working time, representation, and equal opportunities. It seems inevitable that the competitive pressures associated with European integration and the EU's influence over employment policy will grow in the coming years.

# Notes

1. Keenoy, T., Oswick, C., and Grant, D., 'Organizational Discourses: Text and Context', *Organization* (1997), 4, 1, pp. 147–57 (see p. 147).
2. Grant, D. and Oswick, C., 'Of believers, atheists and agnostics: practitioner views on HRM', *Industrial Relations Journal* (1998), 29, 3, pp. 178–93.
3. Marchington, M. and Wilkinson, A., *Core Personnel and Development* (London: Institute of Personnel and Development, 1996).
4. Legge, K., *Power, Innovation and Problem Solving in Personnel Management* (London: McGraw-Hill, 1978).
5. Marchington and Wilkinson, *Core Personnel and Development*, p. 411.
6. Huselid, M. A., 'The Impact of Human Resource Management Practices on Turnover, Productivity, and Corporate Financial Performance', *Academy of Management Journal* (1995), 38, 3, pp. 635–72 (see p. 635).
7. Becker, B. and Gerhart, B., 'The Impact of Human Resource Management on Organizational Performance: Progress and Prospects', *Academy of Management Journal* (1996), 39, 4, pp. 779–801 (see pp. 797–8).
8. Storey, J., *Human Resource Management: a Critical Text* (London: Routledge, 1995), pp. 383–5.

# Appendix

# Dictionary of Terms

## Agency

The freedom to act from choice and with individual responsibility. Agency results wherever individuals have the ability to act on their intentions. Agency is their capability to behave according to individual choice. Whenever individuals have choice over how to behave, they should assume that moral judgements may reasonably be made by others about their actions.

## Agency Theory

Agency theory addresses how owners of capital and businesses control the management of their enterprises. The theory says that owners (principals) must control and give incentives to managers (agents) so as to ensure that agents' behaviour is consistent with the principals' interests. Agency theory has been dominant in the financial economics literature during recent years.[1]

## Annual/Annualized Hours

Under this arrangement, employees are contracted to work an agreed number of hours per year, with working time schedules (including holidays) determined at the beginning of 12-month cycles. Annual hours contracts are typically one of two main types (though in practice many contain mixtures of the two): (1) where variability of weekly hours is detailed in agreements such that work periods are longer at busy periods and shorter during slacker times; and (2) where the number of shifts rostered in the annual hours schedule is less than the agreed annual working time, with the difference comprising non-rostered work time, during which employees are effectively 'on-call' and can be brought in to work to cover unforeseen circumstances.[2]

## Atypical Working

Work that is not full-time employment involving attendance in the workplace. 'Atypical working (part-time, temporary and home-work) is disproportionately performed by women.'[3]

## Behaviour Modification

Behaviour modification is concerned with changing behaviour through rewards. The original term for behaviour modification is 'operant conditioning', which comes from reinforcement theory. Robert Vecchio argues that expectancy theory of motivation and reinforcement theory are similar theories of motivation and rewards.[4]

## Casual Contract

Casual contracts are non-standard employment contracts that do not include full-time and part-time employees who are covered by more extensive employment protection legislation. Temporary and fixed-term working are typical casual contracts of employment.[5]

The paradigm case for casual employment is, of course, that of temporary employees or those on fixed-term contracts. As shown earlier, although their numbers have increased in absolute terms the number of temporary workers in the UK remains much lower than the number of part-time employees or self-employed people. Most of the growth in temporary work has been in areas which have long relied on this form of support, for example secretarial, clerical and nursing. The evidence that the UK is moving towards a more casual pattern of employment is at best inconclusive.[6]

## Centralization

The degree to which the authority to make certain decisions is located at the top of the management hierarchy.[7]

## Collectivism/ist

A collectivist approach is characterized by an emphasis on the needs of the group. Collectivism is the opposite of individualism. Within collectivist approaches, there are different motivational bases for working collectively.[8] See 'Individualism/ist' below.

## Collectivist National Culture

Geert Hofstede defined national collectivist cultures as comprising in-groups (relatives, clan, organizations) and out-groups. Members of the in-group expect to be looked after and, in exchange, they offer loyalty to the group. The collectivist culture exhibits some of the following features:

In society, people are born into extended families or clans who protect them in exchange for loyalty.
'We' consciousness holds sway.
Identity is based in the social system.
There is emotional dependence of the individual on organizations and institutions.
The involvement with organizations is moral.
The emphasis is on belonging to organizations; membership is the ideal.
Private life is invaded by organizations and clans to which one belongs; opinions are predetermined.
Expertise, order, duty, and security are provided by organization or clan.
Friendships are predetermined by stable social relationships, but there is a need for prestige within these relationships.
Belief is placed in group decisions.
Value standards differ for in-groups and out-groups (particularism).[9]

See 'Individualist National Culture' below.

## Configuration

The 'shape' of the organization's role structure, for example, whether the management chain of command is long or short, whether superiors have a limited span of control (relatively few subordinates) or a broad span of control (a relatively large number of subordinates), and whether there is a large or small percentage of specialized or support personnel. 'Configuration' is a blanket term used to cover all three variables.[10]

## Content Theories

Content theories of motivation focus on what motivates behaviour. Maslow's frequently cited Hierarchy of Needs is a content theory.[11] See 'Process Theories' below.

## Descriptive

Descriptive models of HRM describe what HRM is, and try to reflect exactly what has happened or is happening when it is implemented. Karen Legge subdivides descriptive models of HRM into two types: descriptive-functional and descriptive-behavioural. Descriptive-functional models state what *is* rather than what *should be* the function of HRM. Descriptive-behavioural models state more precisely what are the actual behaviours of specialists and managers engaged in HRM activities.[12] See 'Prescriptive' below.

## Distributive Justice

Distributive justice is the fairness of judgements made about an individual or individuals. It is an important concept in pay bargaining and equity theory of motivation.[13]

## Diversification Strategy

Diversification is an organization's expansion into new products, services, and markets. The growth is managed by dividing the company into separate business units. It has become less common for companies to grow by unrelated diversification and rather to seek diversification that exploits interrelationships between, for example, tangible similarities in product technology or intangible similarities in skills and services.[14]

## External Labour Market

The external labour market consists of human resources not employed directly by the organization. It comprises different groups of employees who, according to their occupational group and the economic demand for their labour, experience different degrees of bargaining power and of the value of their labour input. Recruitment of individuals direct from the external labour market rather than development of employees in the internal labour market has been a common approach by small and medium-sized UK businesses. The external labour market is used by the organization as a source of temporary employment including both primary workers (such as individuals with high skills, the self-employed, and subcontractors) and secondary workers (typically individuals with low-level skills and other less essential groups). Workers on the external labour market and from the primary group may find themselves in a relatively powerful bargaining position.[15]

The more highly skilled workers may be in great demand, and may choose to remain outside of mainstream organisational life in order to maintain greater control over their own lives, as well as earn larger amounts of money for their efforts. Obviously, some of the more successful consultants would fall into this category, as would other individuals whose skills are in demand (e.g. information technology specialists).[16]

See 'Internal labour market' below.

## Extrinsic Rewards

Extrinsic rewards are rewards that do not come as an inherent part of performing the work itself. Workers perform the job in order to gain some external desired commodity. Examples of extrinsic rewards are pay, bonuses, overtime pay, paid holiday time, membership in pension or other financial schemes, and prizes and awards. See 'Intrinsic Rewards' below.

## Fixed-term Contract

A fixed-term contract is 'non-permanent' employment. The number of fixed-term contracts grew less dramatically during the 1980s and early 1990s in other parts of Europe than it did within the UK. Brewster gives what he calls 'five main advantages in short-term contracts' to managers and employers:

First, managers frequently have little idea how long demand for certain goods or services will last or whether further work will accrue. Second, they know that some jobs only involve a short period of time (seasonal work, housebuilding, etc.). Third, in many cases the costs of short-term recruitment will be less since less care may be needed in selection, temporary employees will require less, and sometimes zero, administration for sickness or pension schemes, etc. Fourth, short-term appointments may be an answer to an immediate problem where skills are otherwise unavailable. In these, and a number of less important ways, short-term employment is extremely flexible. In most cases, crucially, the complications involved in terminating long-term contracts are absent: it is easy to dispense with the services of these employees.[17]

## Flexibility (Psychological Contract)

Psychological contracts are resistant to change. Flexibility can therefore be hard to achieve in practice whenever it means breaking with what was previous custom and practice.[18]

## Formalization

The degree to which instructions, procedures, etc., are written down.[19]

## Hard HRM

Hard HRM focuses on managing human resources in line with business strategy and on treating people primarily as an economic resource.

The 'hard' model stresses HRM's focus on the crucial importance of the close integration of human resources policies, systems and activities with business strategy, on such HR systems being used 'to drive the strategic objectives of the organization', as Fombrun *et al*. (1987) put it . . . In essence, then, the 'hard' model emphasizes the 'quantitative, calculative and business strategic aspects of managing the headcount resource in as "rational" a way as for any other economic factor' (Storey, 1987). Its focus is ultimately *human resource management*.[20]

See 'Soft HRM' below.

## Hygiene Factors

Herzberg developed a two-factor theory of motivation from his studies of job satisfaction. Interviewees who took part in the study were asked to describe job-related events in which their satisfaction had improved or declined. The hygiene factors included job security, company policies, interpersonal relations, and working conditions. They could not motivate a worker to achieve higher levels of performance, but could create great dissatisfaction when not attended to.[21]

## Individualism/ist

An individualist approach is characterized by an emphasis on the needs of individuals. Individualism is the opposite of collectivism (see separate entry above). Storey and Bacon propose criteria contrasting individualism with collectivism. Where individualism is high, industrial relations will be oriented towards non-unionism, the work organization will place high importance on autonomy, and the division of labour will be high. The employment contract will be tailored to individual terms and conditions, and rewards will be according to individual skills and performance. Job security and career planning will be low, as will individuals' identification with collective myths, symbols, and values.[22] Karen Legge argues that 'soft' HRM is torn between promoting the contrasting ethics of individualism and collectivism.[23]

## Individualist National Culture

Geert Hofstede defined national individualist cultures as comprising a loosely knit social framework. People are expected to take care of themselves and their immediate family members. The individualist culture exhibits some of the following features:

In society, everybody is supposed to take care of himself/herself and his/her immediate family.
'I' consciousness holds sway.
Identity is based in the individual.
There is emotional independence of the individual from organizations or institutions.
The involvement with organizations is calculative.
The emphasis is on individual initiative and achievement; leadership is the ideal.
Everybody has a right to a private life and opinion.
Autonomy, variety, pleasure, and individual financial security are sought in the system.
The need is for specific friendships.
Belief is placed in individual decisions.
Value standards should apply to all (universalism).[24]

See 'Collectivist National Culture' above.

## Instrumental/ist

To behave in an instrumental way is to act in order to achieve outcomes rather than doing something for the sake of it or for some higher-order purpose. To treat people instrumentally is to treat them as means to achieving ends rather than treating them as ends in themselves. Vroom's theory of motivation includes instrumentality, by which, according to Vroom, work-related outcomes have valence for individuals. Valence is an expected level of satisfaction and/or dissatisfaction. Motivation is influenced, Vroom says, by the extent to which the individual perceives that the outcomes of his or her actions will be a means to (that is, instrumental in) achieving satisfaction.[25]

## Internal Labour Market

The internal labour market consists of human resources that are employed by the organization, in contrast to the external labour market (see separate entry above), which comprises human resources outside the organization's employ. The value of human resources on the internal labour market depends partly on how easy they are to replace by similar labour from the external labour market. Organizations often recognize the different economic values attached to distinct occupational groups. Development of the internal labour market is evident particularly in lifetime employment systems, which are typical of large Japanese corporations. However, even in organizations that practise lifetime employment, the internal labour market is most often segmented into different groups of employees. Primary and secondary groups of workers and different associated approaches to the management and planning of the employment relationship are evident in corporations in the East and the West.[26]

## Intrinsic Rewards

Intrinsic rewards are those rewards employees gain simply by performing the work itself, such as self-esteem, pride, a sense of challenge, or enjoyment.

Intrinsically motivated behavior is operationally defined as choice behavior which is exhibited for no apparent external reward. The psychological basis of this is in people's need to be competent and self-determining . . . In other words, people behave in ways which they think allow them to feel competent and self-determining in relation to their environment.[27]

See 'Extrinsic Rewards' above.

## Just-In-Time (JIT)

Just-in-time production produces goods as and when the market requires them. Its operation usually requires sustaining multiple dependency relationships between organizations, systems, and employees.

There are a number of critical elements to JIT production. Given, that, ideally, products are produced at a rate perfectly matched to market demand, at least one of two conditions is implied if production is to be performed at the last minute. Either demand is uniform—or at least predictable—and so plans can be made in advance, or the production process itself must be inherently very responsive . . .[28]

## Managerialism/ist

An approach to the planning, organization, control, and administration of work that gives the concerns and interests of managers priority to such an extent that it sometimes will exclude legitimate issues facing other stakeholders. HRM is said to be more managerialist than personnel management is because it emphasizes the role of managers over and above the role of personnel or HR specialists. Barbara Townley distinguishes HRM from personnel management on the basis of the former being more managerialist than the latter:

A primary distinction is the separation of planning or directive roles ('human resource management') from an essentially secondary information control function ('personnel management or administration'). The latter is regarded as an aid for management designed to enhance rational decision-making. HRM is promoted as a central organizational concern, associated with a long-term perspective, and strategic integration with business planning. Emphasis is placed on the role of employees as a valued resource, an ethos informing organizational culture and corporate goals. HRM stresses coherence in employee relations policies to ensure a strategic response for competitive advantage. Much more managerialist in focus, HRM is an area of senior management responsibility and line management implementation. HRM is now very closely tied with the strategic management and the leadership literature, and from this adopts the themes of the importance of planning and the imposition of control over change in an era of uncertainty . . .[29]

## Matrix Management

Matrix management is based on a structure that involves dual lines of authority combining functional and product organization.[30]

## Motivator/Motivating Factors

Herzberg developed a two-factor theory of motivation from his studies of job satisfaction. Interviewees who took part in the study were asked to describe job-related events in which their satisfaction had improved or declined. Work satisfaction seemed to improve according to the content of the job.

The satisfiers usually pertained to the content of the job and included such factors as career advancement, recognition, sense of responsibility, and feelings of achievement.[31]

## Need Theories

Need satisfaction models of motivation assume that people have basic, stable, relatively unchanging needs that must be attended to and managed in the workplace. This assumption is helpful only in situations where individuals' needs are stable.[32]

## Normative

Normative approaches reflect or establish standard ways of behaving. These values or norms set expectations for individuals and groups. Models of 'hard' HRM by Fombrun, Tichy, and Devanna (1984) and 'soft' HRM by Beer, Spector, Lawrence, Quinn Mills, and Walton (1984) and by Guest (1997) are all examples of normative models.[33]

## Organizational Behaviour (OB)

Stephen Robbins defines organizational behaviour (OB) in the following way:

Organizational behavior . . . is a field of study that investigates the impact that individuals, groups, and structure have on behavior within organizations for the purpose of applying such knowledge toward improving an organization's effectiveness. That's a lot of words, so let's break it down.

Organizational behavior is a field of study. That statement means that it is a distinct area of expertise with a common body of knowledge. What does it study? It studies three determinants of behavior in organizations: individuals, groups, and structure. In addition, OB applies the knowledge gained about individuals, groups, and the effect of structure on behavior in order to make organizations work more effectively.

To sum up our definition, OB is concerned with the study of what people do in an organization and how that behavior affects the performance of the organization. And because OB is specifically concerned with employment-related situations, you should not be surprised to find that it emphasizes behavior as related to jobs, work, absenteeism, employment turnover, productivity, human performance, and management.

There is increasing agreement as to the components or topics that constitute the subject area of OB. Although there is still considerable debate as to the relative importance of each, there appears to be general agreement that OB includes the core topics of motivation, leader behavior and power, interpersonal communication, group structure and processes, learning, attitude development and perception, change processes, conflict, work design, and work stress.[34]

## Organization Development (OD)

OD is the name given to planned change interventions that are intended to improve organizational effectiveness and employee well-being.

This improvement to the way an organisation functions is carried out with the help of a 'change agent' (internal or external consultant) who assists the organisation in defining a given problem, gathering data, discussing the implications of the data, and recommending action. Interventions may focus on the interpersonal behaviour of individuals, groups and/or wider structural and technical improvements . . .[35]

## Pluralist

Pluralist perspectives assume organizations are composed of coalitions of interest groups that possess potential for conflict.[36] See 'Unitarist/Unitary' below.

## Power Distance

Power distance is the extent to which power is distributed unevenly amongst members of a group or organization. Some national cultures accept large power distance while others value small power distance.

Small Power Distance

Inequality in society should be minimized.
All people should be interdependent.
Hierarchy means an inequality of roles, established for convenience.
Superiors consider subordinates to be 'people like me'.
Subordinates consider superiors to be 'people like me'.
Superiors are accessible.
The use of power should be legitimate and is subject to the judgement as to whether it is good or evil.
All should have equal rights.
Those in power should try to look less powerful than they are.

The system is to blame.

The way to change a social system is to redistribute power.

People at various power levels feel less threatened and more prepared to trust people.

Latent harmony exists between the powerful and the powerless.

Cooperation among the powerless can be based on solidarity.

Large Power Distance

There should be an order of inequality in this world in which everybody has a rightful place; high and low are protected by this order.

A few people should be independent; most should be dependent.

Hierarchy means existential inequality.

Superiors consider subordinates to be a different kind of people.

Subordinates consider superiors as a different kind of people.

Superiors are inaccessible.

Power is a basic fact of society that antedates good or evil. Its legitimacy is irrelevant.

Power-holders are entitled to privileges.

Those in power should try to look as powerful as possible.

The underdog is to blame.

The way to change a social system is to dethrone those in power.

Other people are a potential threat to one's power and can rarely be trusted.

Latent conflict exists between the powerful and the powerless.

Cooperation among the powerless is difficult to attain because of their low-faith-in-people norm.[37]

## Prescriptive

Prescriptive models of HRM are designed to authoritatively impose on others what should be the case and what should be done. Prescriptive research-based models make hypothetical claims that if certain pre-conditions are met then outcomes that are specified within the model will be achieved. The advantage of prescriptive models of HRM according to some researchers is that they are more open to scientific test than are descriptive or critical models. David Guest's model of HRM is prescriptive and proposes that when policies and practices are established in a way that is consistent with the model and integrated with the business strategy, this will lead to desirable outcomes for HRM, people, and the organization.[38] See 'Descriptive' above.

## Process Theories

Process theories of motivation concentrate on how rewards control behaviour.

These theories focus on the dynamics, or process aspects, of work motivation. Expectancy, equity, reinforcement, and social learning theories are examples of process theories.[39]

See 'Content Theories' above.

## Relational

A relational contract of employment is one that is long-term, such as those associated with lifetime employment systems and clan-based organizations. More permanent contracts of employment are predicted by Williamson to be preferable where there is high uncertainty in terms of monitoring productivity and quality, high frequency of exchange, and asset specificity.[40]

## Social Learning Theory

Social learning theories of motivation link social expectations, behaviour, and rewards.[41]

People develop expectations about their capacity to behave in certain ways and the probability that their behavior will result in rewards. When a person meets a standard of behavior, that person rewards himself or herself with increased personal satisfaction and enhanced self-image.[42]

## Soft HRM

Soft HRM focuses on developing employees' skills and achieving employee commitment and trust.

In contrast [to hard HRM; see separate entry above], the soft 'developmental humanism' model, while still emphasizing the importance of integrating HR policies with business objectives, sees this as involving treating employees as valued assets, a source of competitive advantage through their commitment, adaptability and high quality (of skills, performance and so on) . . . Employees are proactive rather than passive inputs into productive processes; they are capable of 'development', worthy of 'trust' and 'collaboration', to be achieved through 'participation' and 'informed choice' . . . The stress is therefore on generating commitment via 'communication, motivation and leadership' . . . If employees' commitment will yield 'better economic performance', it is also sought as a route to 'greater human development' . . . In this model, then, the focus is on HR policies to deliver 'resourceful' humans . . . on *human resource* management.[43]

## Specialization

The degree to which an organization's activities are divided into specialized roles.[44]

## Standardization

The degree to which an organization lays down standard rules and procedures.[45]

## Strategic Business Units (SBUs)

Individual units within an organization, each emphasizing a key competitive area of business. The organization structure comprises businesses defined according to key points of competitive leverage.[46]

## Temporary Contract

Employment on a temporary contract is a form of 'non-standard employment' that has been rising in the UK during the 1990s, but it is not yet clear whether this is evidence for long-term change in the proportion of total employment that is temporary work.

Since 1984, temporary jobs have increased by almost 31 per cent, compared to a 0.5 per cent increase in permanent jobs. Between 1984 and 1991 the proportion of temporary workers in the labour force changed little, remaining at around 5 per cent. Since 1992, however, there has been a significant increase in the incidence of temporary working—in the order of 30 per cent between spring 1992 and spring 1996. By spring 1996 there were around 1.6 million temporary workers in Britain, representing over 7 per cent of the workforce. In absolute terms most of this increase has come from the more widespread use of fixed-term contracts. In percentage terms, however, agency temping shows the most dramatic increases—rising by 148 per cent over this period, followed by fixed-term contracts, which rose by 39 per cent.

What are the characteristics of temporary working? LFS [Labour Force Survey] figures (spring 1996) show that over half of all temporary employees (51 per cent) are on fixed-term contracts. This is followed by casual work (20 per cent), agency temping (13 per cent), 'other' (10 per cent) and seasonal work (5 per cent). Women are more likely to hold temporary jobs than men are . . .[47]

## Total Quality Control (TQC)

A quality assurance system in which quality is considered the responsibility of all employees in the organization. Products and services are planned and produced in response to customer requirements by using integrated, efficient work systems.

. . . [T]he total quality concept (also referred to as company-wide quality control) is frequently assumed to be Japanese in origin. In fact, the idea may be traced to an American, J. M. Juran, a specialist in quality control who was invited to Japan in 1954 by a branch of JUSE (the Japanese Union of Scientists and Engineers). Juran's philosophy was that quality control should be conducted as an integral part of management control, in contrast with the traditional situation in which responsibility for product quality was vested in the hands of a quality control department, which acted as a 'policeman' to production. Between 1955 and 1960, these ideas spawned the company-wide quality control movement . . .[48]

## Total Quality Management (TQM)

Total Quality Management aims to ensure quality for the customer through the rigorous application of principles and practices of quality management. TQM must be part of the organization culture and have a fundamental influence on human resource management policies if it is to be effective. TQM, therefore, has implications for how human resources are organized and managed.

Interestingly, some of the most advanced philosophies of quality management (such as TQM) tend to focus, like HRM, as much if not more on the quality of managers and managerial performance as on that of non-management employees . . . They are also strongly associated with the redesign of organization structures, 'delayering' of extended management hierarchies and a redefinition of middle and junior management roles.[49]

## Transactional

A transactional relationship is one focused on a short-term exchange between two parties. Transaction cost economists are interested in how contracts can maximize efficiency. A market-based contract is transactional and fixed-term. In recent years employers have experimented more with transactional contracts of employment.[50]

### Unitarist/Unitary

Unitarist perspectives assume an identity of interest between management and employees.

In contrast [to the pluralist perspective; see separate entry above], the unitary perspective asserts that top management presides over a unified authority and loyalty structure based on the common interests and values shared by all members of the organization. There is thus no rational basis for conflict between management and employees, and trade union organization is viewed as unnecessary or illegitimate. It follows that conflictual industrial relations can be explained only by past or present management failings, such as poor communications, or by the actions of irrational or subversive trade unions in exploiting them. In the latter circumstances, the reassertion of management prerogative would be justified through the imposition of economic or legal sanctions on unions.[51]

# Notes

1. Hill, C. W. L. and Jones, T. M., 'Stakeholder-Agency Theory', *Journal of Management Studies* (1992), 29, 2, March, pp. 131–54.
2. Blyton, P., 'Working Hours', in K. Sisson, *Personnel Management: A Comprehensive Guide to Theory & Practice in Britain*, 2nd edn. (Oxford: Blackwell, 1994), pp. 495–526, at pp. 515–6.
3. Dickens, L., 'Wasted Resources? Equal Opportunities in Employment', in Sisson, *Personnel Management* (1994), pp. 253–97, at p. 271.
4. Vecchio, R. P., *Organizational Behavior*, 3rd edn. (Fort Worth, TX: The Dryden Press, 1995).
5. Emmot, M. and Hutchinson, S., 'Employment Flexibility: Threat or Promise', in P. Sparrow and M. Marchington (eds.), *Human Resource Management: The New Agenda* (London: Financial Times, Pitman Publishing, 1998), pp. 229–44.
6. Ibid., pp. 240–1.
7. Pugh, D. S., 'The Measurement of Organization Structures: Does Context Determine Form?', in D. S. Pugh (ed.), *Organization Theory: Selected Readings*, 3rd edition. (London: Penguin Books, 1990), p. 46.
8. Eby, L. T. and Dobbins, G. H., 'Collectivistic Orientation in Teams: An Individual and Group-Level Analysis', *Journal of Organizational Behavior* (1997), Vol. 18, p. 277.
9. Hofstede, G., 'Motivation, Leadership and Organization: Do American Theories Apply Abroad?' *Organizational Dynamics* (1980), summer, p. 48.
10. Pugh, 'The Measurement of Organization Structures', (n. 7 above), p. 46.
11. Maslow, A. H., 'A Theory of Human Motivation', *Psychological Review* (1943), 50, pp. 370–96.
12. Legge, K., *Human Resource Management: Rhetorics and Realities* (Basingstoke: Macmillan Business, 1995), pp. 4–6.
13. Vecchio, R. P., *Organizational Behavior* (1995), p. 201.
14. Porter, M., *Competitive Advantage: Creating and Sustaining Superior Performance* (New York: Macmillan, The Free Press, 1985), p. 378.
15. Loveridge, R. and Mok, A., *Theories of Labour Market Segmentation: A Critique* (The Hague: Martinus Nijhoff, 1979), p. 123.
16. Marchington, M. and Wilkinson, A., *Core Personnel and Development* (London: Institute of Personnel and Development, 1996), p. 29.
17. Brewster, C., 'Flexible Working in Europe: Extent, Growth and the Challenge for HRM', in P. Sparrow and M. Marchington (eds.), *Human Resource Management: The New Agenda* (1998), p. 252.
18. Gomez-Mejia, L. R., Balkin, D. B., and Cardy, R., *Managing Human Resources* (Englewood Cliffs, NJ: Prentice-Hall, 1995), p. 396.
19. Pugh, 'The Measurement of Organization Structures' (1990), (n. 7 above), p. 46.

20. Legge, K., 'HRM: Rhetoric, Reality and Hidden Agendas', in J. Storey (ed.), *Human Resource Management: A Critical Text* (London: Routledge, 1995), pp. 34–5.
21. Vecchio, *Organizational Behavior* (1995), p. 191.
22. Storey, J. and Bacon, N., with J. Edmonds and P. Wyatt, 'The "New Agenda" and Human Resource Management: A Roundtable Discussion with John Edmonds', *Human Resource Management Journal* (1993), 4, 1, pp. 63–70.
23. Legge, *Human Resource Management* (1995) (n. 12 above), pp. 130–1.
24. Hofstede, 'Motivation, Leadership and Organization' (1980) (n. 9 above), p. 48.
25. Vroom, V. H. and Deci, E. L. (eds.), *Management and Motivation*, 2nd edn. (London: Penguin, 1992), p. 92.
26. Bratton, J. and Gold, J., *Human Resource Management: Theory and Practice* (Basingstoke: Macmillan, 1994), pp. 133–4.
27. Shapira, Z., 'Expectancy Determinants of Intrinsically Motivated Behavior', abridged from the *Journal of Personality and Social Psychology* (1976), Vol. 34, pp. 235–44, in V. H. Vroom and E. L. Deci, *Management and Motivation*, 2nd edn. (London: Penguin Books, 1992), p. 106.
28. Oliver, N. and Wilkinson, B., *The Japanization of British Industry*, 2nd edn. (Oxford: Blackwell, 1992), pp. 25–6.
29. Townley, B., *Reframing Human Resource Management: Power, Ethics and the Subject at Work* (London: Sage, 1994), pp. 14–15.
30. Robbins, S. P., *Organizational Behavior: Concepts, Controversies, Applications*, 8th edn. (Upper Saddle River, NJ: Prentice Hall, 1998), pp. 490–1.
31. Vecchio, *Organizational Behavior* (1998), p. 191.
32. Salancik, G. R. and Pfeffer, J., 'An Examination of Need-Satisfaction Models of Job Attitudes', abridged from G. R. Salancik and J. Pfeffer, 'An Examination of Need-Satisfaction Models of Job Attitudes', *Administrative Science Quarterly* (1977), Vol. 22, pp. 427–56, in V. H. Vroom, and E. L. Deci, *Management and Motivation*, 2nd edn. (London: Penguin, 1992), p. 206.
33. Legge, *Human Resource Management* (1995) (n. 12 above), pp. 64–5.
34. Robbins, *Organizational Behavior* (1998) (n. 30 above), pp. 7–9.
35. Inns, D., 'Organisation Development as a Journey', in C. Oswick and D. Grant (eds.), *Organisation Development: Metaphorical Explorations* (London: Pitman Publishing 1996), pp. 21–2.
36. Clark, J. and Winchester, D., 'Management and Trade Unions', in K. Sisson (ed.), *Personnel Management: A Comprehensive Guide to Theory & Practice in Britain* (1994), p. 695.
37. Hofstede, 'Motivation, Leadership and Organization' (1980) (n. 9 above), p. 46.
38. Guest, D. E., 'Human Resource Management and Industrial Relations', *Journal of Management Studies* (1987), 24, 5, pp. 503–21.
39. Vecchio, *Organizational Behavior* (1995) (n. 4 above), p. 204.
40. Williamson, O. E., *Markets and Hierarchies: Analysis and Anti-trust Implications* (New York: The Free Press, 1975).
41. Bandura, A., 'Self-Efficacy: Toward a Unifying Theory of Behavioral Change', abridged from A. Bandura, 'Self-Efficacy: Toward a Unifying Theory of Behavioral Change', *Psychological Review* (1977), Vol. 84, pp. 191–215, in V. H. Vroom, and E. L. Deci, *Management and Motivation*, 2nd edn. (London: Penguin, 1992), pp. 78–89.
42. Vecchio, *Organizational Behavior* (1995) (n. 4 above), p. 207.
43. Legge, 'HRM: Rhetoric, Reality and Hidden Agendas' (1995) (n. 2 above), p. 35.
44. Pugh, 'The Measurement of Organization Structures' (1990) (n. 7 above), p. 46.
45. Ibid.
46. Goold, M. and Campbell, A., *Strategies and Styles: The Role of the Centre in Managing Diversified Corporations* (Oxford: Blackwell Business, 1987), p. 180.
47. Emmot, M. and Hutchinson, S., 'Employment Flexibility: Threat or Promise?', in P. Sparrow and M. Marchington (eds.), *Human Resource Management: The New Agenda* (1998), p. 234.
48. Oliver and Wilkinson, *The Japanization of British Industry* (1992) (n. 28 above), pp. 20–1.

49. Clark, J., 'Personnel Management, Human Resource Management and Technical Change', in J. Clark (ed.), *Human Resource Management and Technical Change* (London: Sage, 1993), p. 5.

50. Guest, D. E., 'Beyond HRM: Commitment and the Contract Culture', in P. Sparrow and M. Marchington, *Human Resource Management: The New Agenda* (1998), pp. 31–57.

51. Clark, J., and Winchester, D., 'Management and Trade Unions', in K. Sisson, *Personnel Management: A Comprehensive Guide to Theory and Practice in Britain* (1994), pp. 695–6.

# Bibliography

Adams, J. S., 'Toward an understanding of inequity', *Journal of Abnormal and Social Psychology* (1963), 67, pp. 422–36.

—— 'Inequity in social exchange', in L. Berkowitz (ed.), *Advances in Experimental Social Psychology*, Vol. 2 (New York: Academic Press, 1965).

Alberga, T., Tyson, S., and Parsons, D., 'An Evaluation of the Investors in People Standard', *Human Resource Management Journal* (1997), 7, 2, pp. 47–60.

Alderfer, C. P., *Existence, Relatedness and Growth* (New York: Free Press, 1972).

Anderman, S., 'Unfair Dismissal and Redundancy', in R. Lewis (ed.), *Labour Law in Britain* (Oxford: Blackwell, 1986).

Anderson, G., 'Performance appraisal', in B. Towers (ed.), *The Handbook of Human Resource Management*, 2nd edn. (Oxford: Blackwell, 1992), pp. 196–222.

Argyris, C., Review essay: 'First- and Second-order Errors in Managing Strategic Change: the Role of Organizational Defensive Routines', in A. M. Pettigrew (ed.), *The Management of Strategic Change* (Oxford: Basil Blackwell, 1988).

—— 'Skilled incompetence', in K. Starkey (ed.), *How Organizations Learn* (London: Thomson Business Press, 1996), pp. 82–91.

—— and Schon, D. A., *Organizational Learning: A Theory of Action Perspective* (Reading, MA: Addison Wesley, 1978).

Armstrong, M., *A Handbook of Personnel Management Practice*, 6th edn. (London: Kogan Page, 1996).

—— *Employee Reward* (London: Institute of Personnel and Development, 1996).

—— and Murlis, H., *Reward Management*, 3rd edn. (London: Kogan Page, 1994).

Arulampalam, W., and Booth, A. L., 'Training and Labour Market Flexibility: Is there a Trade-off?', *British Journal of Industrial Relations* (1998), 36, 4, December, pp. 521–36.

Ashton, D. and Felstead, A., 'Training and development', in J. Storey, *Human Resource Management: A Critical Text* (London: Routledge, 1995), pp. 234–53.

Baddon, L., Hunter, L., Hyman, J., Leopold, J., and Ramsay, H., *A Critical Analysis of Profit-sharing and Employee Share Ownership* (London: Routledge, 1989).

Bae, J., Chen, S. J., and Lawler, J. J. 'Variations in human resource management in Asian countries: MNC home-country and host-country effects', *International Journal of Human Resource Management* (1997), 8, 2, April, pp. 213–25.

Bakan, I., 'The effect of profit sharing and share option schemes on employee job attitudes', unpublished PhD thesis, Coventry University, June 1999.

Bandura, A., *Social Learning Theory* (Englewood Cliffs, NJ: Prentice Hall, 1977).

—— 'Self-efficacy: toward a unifying theory of behavioral change', *Psychological Review* (1977), 84, pp. 191–215.

Baron, A. and Armstrong, M., 'Out of the tick box', *People Management* (1998), 4, 15, 23 July, 1998, p. 38

——, and Janman, K. 'Fairness in the Assessment Centre', in C. L. Cooper and I. T. Robertson, *International Review of Industrial and Organizational Psychology*, vol. II (Chichester: John Wiley, 1996), pp. 61–114.

Bartlett, C. and Ghoshal, S., *Managing across Borders* (London: Hutchinson, 1989).

Beardwell, I and Holden, L., *Human Resource Management: A Contemporary Perspective*, 2nd edn. (London: Financial Times, Pitman Publishing, 1997).

Beaumont, P., *Human Resource Management: Key Concepts and Skills* (London: Sage, 1993).

——, and Townley, B., 'Non-Union American Plants in Britain: Their Employment Practices', *Relationnes Industrielles* (1985), 40, 4, pp. 810–25.

—— Cressey, P. and Jakobsen, P., 'Key Industrial Relations: West German Subsidiaries in Britain', *Employee Relations* (1990), 12, 6, pp. 3–6.

Becker, B. and Gerhart, B., 'The Impact of Human Resource Management on Organizational Performance: Progress and Prospects', *Academy of Management Journal* (1996), 39, 4, pp. 779–801.

Beer, M. and Spector, B., 'Corporate wide transformations in human resource management', in R. E. Walton and P. R. Lawrence (eds.), *Human Resource Management—Trends and Challenges* (Boston: Harvard Business School Press, 1985), pp. 219–53.

—— —— Lawrence, P. R., Quinn Mills, D., and Walton, R. E., *Managing Human Assets: The Groundbreaking Harvard Business School Program* (New York: The Free Press, 1984).

Berne, E., *Transactional Analysis in Psychotherapy* (New York: Grove Press, 1961).

—— *Games People Play: the Psychology of Human Relationships* (New York: Grove Press, 1964).

Bloom, B. S. (ed.), *Taxonomy of Educational Objectives, the Classification of Educational Goals*, by a committee of college and university examiners (New York: David McKay Co., 1956).

Blyton, P., 'Working Hours', in K. Sisson (ed.), *Personnel Management: A Comprehensive Guide to Theory and Practice in Britain*, 2nd edn. (Oxford: Blackwell Business, 1994).

—— and Turnbull, P. (eds.), *Reassessing Human Resource Management* (London: Sage, 1992).

—— —— *The Dynamics of Employee Relations* (Basingstoke: Macmillan, 1998).

Boam, R. and Sparrow, P., *Designing and Achieving Competency: A Competency-Based Approach to Developing People and Organizations* (Maidenhead: McGraw-Hill, 1992).

Bournois, F., *La Gestion des Cadres en Europe (Personnel Management in Europe)* (Paris: Editions Eyrolles, 1991).

Boyatzis, R., *The Competent Manager: A Model for Effective Managers* (New York: Wiley, 1982).

Boydell, T. H., *A Guide to the Identification of Training Needs* (London: British Association for Commercial and Industrial Education, fourth impression, 1990).

—— and Leary, M., *Identifying Training Needs* (London: IPD, 1996).

Bramham, J., *Human Resource Planning*, 2nd edn. (London: Institute of Personnel and Development, 1994).

Bratton, J. and Gold, J., *Human Resource Management: Theory and Practice*, 1st edn. (London: Macmillan, 1994), 2nd edn. (London: Macmillan, 1999).

Brewster, C., 'Flexible working in Europe: extent, growth and the challenge for HRM', in P. Sparrow and M. Marchington (eds.), *Human Resource Management: The New Agenda*, (London: Financial Times, Pitman Publishing, 1998). pp. 245–58.

——, 'HRM: the European Dimension', in J. Storey (ed.), *Human Resource Management: a Critical Text* (London: Routledge, 1995), pp. 309–31.

—— 'National cultures and international management', in S. Tyson (ed.), *Strategic Prospects for HRM* (London: Institute of Personnel and Development, 1995).

—— and Bournois, F., 'A European Perspective on Human Resource Management', *Personnel Review* (1991), 20, 6, pp. 4–13.

—— and Hegewisch, A. (eds.), *Policy and Practice in European Human Resource Management: The Price Waterhouse Cranfield Survey* (London: Routledge, 1994).

Brown, W., Marginson, P., and Walsh, J., 'Management: Pay Determination and Collective Bargaining', in P. Edwards (ed.), *Industrial Relations: Theory and Practice in Britain* (Oxford: Blackwell, 1995), pp. 123–50.

Browne, J., 'Unleashing the power of learning: an interview with BP's Chief Executive John Browne', *Harvard Business Review* (1997), September–October, pp. 147–68, reprint number, 97507.

Buchanan, D. A., 'Principles and practice in work design', in K. Sisson (ed.), *Personnel Management: A Comprehensive Guide to Theory and Practice in Britain*, 2nd edn. (Oxford: Blackwell, 1994), pp. 85–116.

Buckley, P. and Enderwick, P., *The Industrial Relations Practices of Foreign-Owned Firms in Britain* (London: Macmillan, 1985).

Burns, R., *Managing People in Changing Times: Coping with Change in the Workplace—a Practical Guide* (London: Allen & Unwin, 1993).

Burrell, G. and Morgan, G., *Sociological Paradigms and Organizational Analysis* (London: Heinemann, 1979).

Capelli, P. and McElrath, R., 'The Transfer of Employment Practices through Multinationals', paper presented to Third Bargaining Group Conference, University of California, Berkeley, 1992.

Chandler, A. D., *Strategy and Structure: Chapters in the History of the American Industrial Enterprise* (Cambridge, MA: MIT Press, 1962).

Clark, I., 'Competitive Pressures and Engineering Process Plant Contracting', *Human Resource Management Journal* (1998), 8, 2, pp. 14–28.

Clark, I. and Winchester, D., 'Management and Trade Unions' in K. Sisson (ed.), *Personnel Management: A Comprehensive Guide to Theory and Practice in Britain* (1994), pp. 694–723.

Clark, J., 'Personnel Management, Human Resource Management and Technical Change', in J. Clark (ed.), *Human Resource Management and Technical Change* (London: Sage, 1993), pp. 1–19.

Clegg, H., *The Changing System of Industrial Relations in Great Britain* (Oxford: Blackwell, 1979).

Cockerill, A., 'The kind of competence for rapid change', *Personnel Management* (1989), 21, 9, September, pp. 532–56.

—— 'Managerial competence as a determinant of organizational performance', unpublished PhD thesis (University of London, London Business School, 1990).

Cole, G. A., *Personnel Management*, 3rd edn. (London: DP Publications, 1993).

Coller, X., 'Managing Flexibility in the Food Industry: A Cross-National Comparative Case Study of European Multinational Companies', *European Journal of Industrial Relations* (1996), 2, 2, pp. 153–72.

Colling, T. and Ferner, A., 'Privatization and Marketization', in P. Edwards (ed.), *Industrial Relations: Theory and Practice in Britain* (Oxford: Blackwell, 1995), pp. 491–514.

—— and Dickens, L., 'Selling the Case for Gender Equality: Deregulation and Equality Bargaining', *British Journal of Industrial Relations*, (1998), 36, 3, pp. 389–411.

—— Commission on Public Policy and British Business, *Promoting Prosperity: A Business Agenda for Britain*, Vintage, 1997.

Connock, S., *HR Vision: Managing a Quality Workforce* (London: Institute of Personnel Management, 1991).

Constable, J. and McCormick, R., *The Making of British Managers* (London: British Institute of Management, 1987).

Cooper, C. and White, B., 'Organisational behaviour', in S. Tyson (ed.), *Strategic Prospects for HRM* (London: IPD, 1995), pp. 112–45.

Cowling, A. and James, P., *The Essence of Personnel Management and Industrial Relations* (London: Prentice Hall, 1994).

Crystal, G. S., *In Search of Excess: the Overcompensation of American Executives* (New York: W. W. Norton, 1991).

Cully, M., et al., 'Fourth Workplace Employee Relations Survey', *People Management* (1998), 4, 21, 29 October, p. 71.

Curnow, B. and McLean F. J., *Third Age Careers* (London: Gower Press, 1994).

Daniel, W. and Millward, N., *Workplace Industrial Relations in Britain* (London: Heinemann, 1983).

Davis, J. H., Schoorman, F. D., and Donaldson, L., 'Toward a stewardship theory of management', *Academy of Management Review* (1997), 22, 1, pp. 20–47.

Dawson, P., *Organisational Change: A Processual Approach* (London: Paul Chapman, 1994).

De Cock, C., and Hipkin, I., 'TQM and BPR: Beyond the Beyond Myth', *Journal of Management Studies* (1997), 34, 5, September, pp. 659–75.

Deakin and Morris, *Labour Law* (London: Butterworths, 1998).

Deal, T. E. and Kennedy, A., *Corporate Cultures* (Reading, MA: Addison-Wesley, 1982).

—— —— *Corporate Cultures—The Rites and Rituals of Corporate Life* (London: Penguin, 1982).

Dedoussis, V., 'Simply a Question of Cultural Barriers? The Search for New Perspectives in the Transfer of Japanese Management Practices', *Journal of Management Studies* (1995), 32, 6, pp. 731–45.

Delbridge, R. 'Surviving JIT: Control and Resistance in a Japanese Transplant', *Journal of Management Studies* (1995) 32, 6 November, pp. 803–17.

Deming, W. E., *Quality, Productivity and Competitive Position* (Cambridge, MA: MIT Press, 1982).

Department of Employment, *Glossary of Training Terms*, 2nd edn. (London: HMSO, 1978).

—— 'Employment for the 1990s', Cm 540 (London: HMSO, 1989).

Devanna, M. A., Fombrun, C. J., and Tichy, N. M., 'A Framework for Strategic Human Resource Management', in C. J. Fombrun, N. M. Tichy, and M. A. Devanna, *Strategic Human Resource Management* (New York: John Wiley & Sons, 1984), pp. 33–51.

Dibella, A. J., Nevis, E. C., and Gould, J. M., 'Understanding organizational learning capability', *Journal of Management Studies* (1996), 33, 3, May, pp. 361–79.

Dickens, L., 'Anti-Discrimination Legislation: Exploring and Examining the Impact on Women's Employment', in W. McCarthy (ed.), *Legal Intervention in Industrial Relations: Gains and Losses* (Oxford: Blackwell, 1992).

—— 'Wasted Resources? Equal Opportunities in Employment', in K. Sisson (ed.), *Personnel Management: A Comprehensive Guide to Theory and Practice in Britain*, 2nd edn. (Oxford: Blackwell, 1994), pp. 495–526.

—— 'Comparative Systems of Unjust Dismissal: The British Case', *Annals of the American Academy of Political and Social Sciences* (November, 1994).

—— 'What HRM Means for Gender Equality', *Human Resource Management Journal* (1998), 8, 1, pp. 23–40.

—— and Hall, M., 'The State: Labour Law and Industrial Relations', in P. Edwards (ed.), *Industrial Relations: Theory and Practice in Britain* (Oxford: Blackwell, 1995), pp. 255–303.

—— Jones, M., Weekes, B., and Hart, M., *Dismissed: A Study of Unfair Dismissal and the Industrial Tribunal System* (Oxford: Blackwell, 1985).

Dickerson, A., Gibson, H., and Tsakalotos, E., *The Impact of Acquisitions on Company Performance: Evidence from a Large Panel of UK Firms* (Canterbury: University of Kent Press, 1995).

Dixon, N. M., *The Organizational Learning Cycle: How We Can Learn Collectively* (Maidenhead: McGraw-Hill, 1994).

Doherty, N., 'Downsizing', in S. Tyson (ed.), *The Practice of Human Resource Strategy* (Financial Times, Pitman Publishing, 1997).

Donaldson, L. and Davis, J. H., 'CEO Governance and Shareholder Returns: Agency Theory or Stewardship Theory', Paper presented at the annual meeting of the Academy of Management, Washington, DC, 1989.

—— —— 'Stewardship Theory or Agency Theory: CEO Governance and Shareholder Returns', *Australian Journal of Management* (1991), 16, pp. 49–64.

Dowling, B. and Richardson, R., 'Evaluating Performance-Related Pay for Managers in the National Health Service', *International Journal of Human Resource Management* (1997), 8, 3, June, pp. 348–66.

DTI, *Annual Report* (London: DTI, 1997).

Donovan Commission, *Royal Commission on Trade Union and Employers Associations* (London: HMSO, 1968), p. 1.

Dunn, S., Richardson, R., and Dewe, P., 'The impact of employee share ownership on worker attitudes: a longitudinal case study', *Human Resource Management Journal* (1991), 1, 3, Spring, pp. 1–17.

Ebadan, G. and Winstanley, D., 'Downsizing, Delayering and Careers—The Survivor's Perspective', *Human Resource Management Journal* (1997), 7, 1, pp. 79–91.

Eby, L. T. and Dobbins, G. H. 'Collectivist orientation in Teams: An Individual and Group-Level Analysis', *Journal of Organizational Behaviour* (1997), vol. 18, p. 227.

Edwards, P., 'The Employment Relationship', in P. Edwards (ed.), *Industrial Relations: Theory and Practice in Britain* (Oxford: Blackwell, 1995).

Emmot, M. and Hutchinson, S. 'Employment Flexibility: Threat or Promise', in P. Sparrow and M. Marchington (eds.), *Human Resource Management: The New Agenda* (London: Financial Times, Pitman Publishing, 1998), pp. 229–44.

*Employment Gazette*, various issues.

Estes, W. K., 'Reinforcement in human behavior', *American Scientist* (1972), 60, pp. 723–9.

Evans, P., Doz, Y., and Laurent, A., (eds.), *Human Resource Management in International Firms* (London: Macmillan, 1989).

Evenden, R., 'The strategic management of recruitment and selection', in R. Harrison, *Human Resource Management: Issues and Strategies* (Wokingham, England: Addison-Wesley, 1993).

Feldman, D. C. and Kim, S., 'Acceptance of buyout offers in the face of downsizing: empirical evidence from the Korean electronics industry. Study of a major Korean electronics company', *International Journal of Human Resource Management*, 9, 6, December, pp. 1008–25.

Feltham, R., 'Using Competencies in Selection and Recruitment', in R. Boam and P. Sparrow, *Designing and Achieving Competency: A Competency-Based Approach to Developing People and Organizations*, (Maidenhead: McGraw-Hill, 1992), pp. 89–103.

Ference, T. P., Stoner, J. A. F., and Warren, K. E., 'Managing the career plateau', in R. Katz (ed.), *Managing Professionals in Innovative Organizations* (Cambridge, MA: Ballinger Publishing Company, Harper & Row, 1988).

Ferner, A., 'Multinational Companies and Human Resource Management: An Overview of Research Issues', *Human Resource Management Journal* (1994), 4, 3, pp. 79–102.

—— 'Country of Origin Effects and HRM in Multinational Companies', *Human Resource Management Journal* (1997), 7, 1, pp. 19–37.

—— and Hyman, R. (eds.), *Changing Industrial Relations in Europe* (Oxford: Blackwell, 1998).

Filella, J., 'Is there a Latin Model in the Management of Human Resources?', *Personnel Review* (1991), 20, 6, pp. 15–24.

Finegold, D., 'The implications of training in Britain for the analysis of Britain's skill problem: how much do employers spend on training?', *Human Resource Management Journal* (1991), 2, 1, Autumn, pp. 110–15.

—— and Sostice, D., 'The failure of training in Britain: analysis and prescription', *Oxford Review of Economic Policy* (1988), 4, 5, Autumn, pp. 41–53.

Fletcher, C., *People Management* (1998), 4, 23, 26 November, p. 40.

—— and Anderson, N., 'A superficial assessment', *People Management* (1998), 4, 10, 14 May, p. 44.

—— and Williams, R., 'The route to performance management', *Personnel Management* (1992), October, pp. 42–7.

Fombrun, C. J., Tichy, N. M., and Devanna, M. A., *Strategic Human Resource Management* (New York: John Wiley & Sons, 1984).

Foot, M. and Hook, C., *Introducing Human Resource Management* (London: Longman Publishing, 1996).

Franks, J. and Mayer, C., 'Do Hostile Take-overs Improve Performance?', *Business Strategy Review* (1996), 7, 4, pp. 1–6.

Freeman, R., 'The Limits to Wage Flexibility in Curing Unemployment', *Oxford Review of Economic Policy* (1995), 11, 1, pp. 63–72.

—— 'Does Globalisation Threaten Low-Skilled Western Workers?', in J. Philpott (ed.), *Working for Full Employment* (London: Routledge, 1997), pp. 132–50.

French, J. L., 'Employee perspectives on stock ownership: financial investment or mechanism of control?', *Academy of Management Review* (1987), 12, pp. 427–35.

Gagné, R. M., *Essentials of Learning for Instruction* (Illinois, The Dryden Press: Holt, Rinehart and Winston, 1975).

Galbraith, J. R. *Organization Design* (Reading, MA: Addison-Wesley, 1978).

—— 'Designing the innovating organization', in K. Starkey, *How Organizations Learn* (Thomson International Business Press, 1996), pp. 156–81.

—— and Nathanson, D., *Strategy Formulation: Analytical Concepts* (St. Paul, MN: West Publishing Company, 1978).

Garrahan, P. and Stewart, P., *The Nissan Enigma: Flexibility at Work in a Local Economy* (London: Mansell, 1992).

Gilman, M., *Performance Related Pay in Practice: Organization and Effect* (PhD Thesis: University of Warwick, 1998).

Gomez-Mejia, L. R. and Balkin, D. B., *Compensation, Organisational Strategy, and Firm Performance* (Cincinnati, Southwestern Publishing, 1992).

—— —— and Cardy, R., *Managing Human Resources* (Englewood Cliffs, N.J.: Prentice-Hall) 1995.

Goold, M. and Campbell, A., *Strategies and Styles: The Role of the Centre in Managing Diversified Corporations* (Oxford: Blackwell Business, 1987).

Gospel, H., 'The Revival of Apprenticeship Training in Britain?', *British Journal of Industrial Relations* (1998), 36, 3, September, pp. 435–57.

Gowler, D., Legge, K. and Clegg, C., *Case Studies in Organizational Behaviour and Human Resource Management*, 2nd edn. (London: Paul Chapman Publishing, 1993).

Grant, D. and Oswick, C., 'Of believers, atheists and agnostics: practitioner views on HRM', *Industrial Relations Journal* (1998), 29, 3, pp. 178–93.

Greiner, L. E., 'Evolution and revolution as organisations grow', *Harvard Business Review* (1972), No. 72407, July–August, pp. 37–46.

Grewal, H., *A Guide to the Sex Discrimination Act* (London: Macdonald, 1990).

Grint, K., 'What's wrong with performance appraisals? A critique and a suggestion', *Human Resource Management Journal* (1993), 3, 3, pp. 61–77.

Guest, D. E., 'Personnel and HRM: Can You Tell the Difference?', *Personnel Management* (1987).

—— 'Human Resource Management and Industrial Relations', *Journal of Management Studies* (1987), 24, 5, pp. 503–21.

—— 'Human Resource Management and the American Dream', *Journal of Management Studies* (1990), 27, 4, pp. 378–97.

—— 'Right enough to be dangerously wrong: an analysis of the In Search of Excellence phenomenon', in G. Salaman *et al.*, *Human Resource Strategies* (London: Sage, 1992), pp. 5–19.

—— 'Human Resource Management, Trade Unions and Industrial Relations', in J. Storey (ed.), *Human Resource Management: A Critical Text* (London: Routledge, 1995), pp. 110–41.

—— 'Human Resource Management and Performance: a Review and Research Agenda', *The International Journal of Human Resource Management* (1997), 8, 3, June, pp. 263–76.

—— 'Beyond HRM: Commitment and the Contract Culture', in P. Sparrow and M. Marchington (eds.), *Human Resource Management: The New Agenda* (London: Financial Times, Pitman Publishing, 1998), pp. 37–51.

—— *People Management*, 4, 21, 29 October, 1998, pp. 64–5.

—— *People Management*, 4, 24, 10 December 1998, p. 14

Guirdham, M., *Interpersonal Skills at Work* (London: Prentice Hall, 1990).

Hackman, J. R. and Oldham, G. R., 'Motivation through the design of work: test of a theory', *Organizational Behavior and Human Performance* (1976), 16, pp. 250–79.

—— —— *Work Redesign* (Reading, MA: Addison-Wesley, 1980).

Hall, D. T., 'Human resource development and organizational effectiveness', in C. J. Fombrun, N. M. Tichy, and M. A. Devanna, *Strategic Human Resource Management* (New York: John Wiley and Sons, 1984), pp. 159–81.

Hall, L. and Torrington, D., 'Letting Go or Holding On—The Devolution of Operational Personnel Activities', *Human Resource Management Journal* (1998), 8, 1, pp. 41–55.

Hall, M. and Sisson, K., *Coming to Terms with the EU Working Time Directive* (London: IRS, 1997).

Handy, C. B., *The Making of Managers* (London: MSC/NEDO/BIM, 1987).

Handy, C. J., *Understanding Organizations*, 4th edn. (London: Penguin, 1993).

Hanson, C. and Mather, G., *Striking Out Strikes* (London: IEA, 1988).

Harrison, R., *Employee Development* (London: IPD, 1992).

—— *Human Resource Management: Issues and Strategies* (Wokingham: Addison-Wesley, 1993).

Hatch, M. J., *Organization Theory: Modern, Symbolic and Postmodern Perspectives* (Oxford: Oxford University Press, 1997).

Hendry, C. and Jenkins, R., 'Psychological Contracts and New Deals', *Human Resource Management Journal* (1997), 7, 1, pp. 38–44.

Hepple, R., 'The Rise and Fall of Unfair Dismissal', in W. McCarthy (ed.), *Legal Intervention in Industrial Relations: Gains and Losses* (Oxford: Blackwell, 1992).

Herriot, P., 'The Management of Careers', in S. Tyson (ed.), *Strategic Prospects for HRM* (London: Institute of Personnel and Development, 1995), pp. 184–205.

—— 'The Role of the HRM Function in Building a New Proposition for Staff', in P. Sparrow and M. Marchington (eds.), *Human Resource Management: The New Agenda* (London: Financial Times, Pitman Publishing, 1998), pp. 106–16.

—— and Pemberton, C., *New Deals: the Revolution in Managerial Careers* (Chichester: John Wiley & Sons, 1995).

Herzberg, F., 'One more time: how do you motivate employees?', *Harvard Business Review* (1968), 46, 1, pp. 53–62.

Hill, C. W. L. and Jones, T. M., 'Stakeholder-Agency Theory', *Journal of Management Studies* (1992), 29, 2, March, pp. 131–54.

Hill, S., 'Why quality circles failed but total quality management might succeed', *British Journal of Industrial Relations* (1991), December, vol. 29, pp. 541–68.

Hodgkinson, G. P. and Payne, R. L., Short research note: 'Graduate Selection in Three European Countries', *Journal of Occupational Organizational Psychology* (1998), 71, pp. 359–65.

—— Daley, N., and Payne, R. L., *International Journal of Manpower* (1995), 16, 8, pp. 59–76.

—— Snell, S., Daley, N., and Payne, R. L., 'A Comparative Study of Knowledge of Changing Demographic Trends and the Importance of HRM Practices in Three European Countries', *International Journal of Selection and Assessment* (1996), 4, 4, October, pp. 184–94.

Hofstede, G., *Culture's Consequences: International Differences in Work Related Values* (Beverly Hills: Sage, 1980).

—— 'Motivation, Leadership and Organization: Do American Theories Apply Abroad?', *Organizational Dynamics* (1980), summer, p. 48.

—— *Cultures and Organisations: Software of the Mind* (London: McGraw-Hill, 1991).

Honey, P. and Mumford, A., *The Manual of Learning Styles*, 1st edn. (Maidenhead: Peter Honey, 1981), 2nd edn. (1992).

Hope, V. and Hendry, J., 'Corporate cultural change—is it relevant for the organisations of the 1990s?', *Human Resource Management Journal* (1992), 5, 4, pp. 61–73.

Hope-Hailey, V., Gratton, L., McGovern, P., Stiles, P., and Truss, C., 'A Chameleon Function? HRM in the 90s', *Human Resource Management Journal* (1997), 7, 2, pp. 5–18.

Hu, Y., 'Global or Stateless Corporations are National Firms with International Operations', *California Management Review* (1992), 34, 2, pp. 107–26.

Hughes, E. C., 'Institutional Office and the Person', *American Journal of Sociology* (1937), 43, pp. 404–13.

Humphrey, J., 'The Adoption of Japanese Management Techniques in Brazilian Industry', *Journal of Management Studies* (1985), 32, 6, pp. 767–88.

Huselid, M. A., 'The Impact of Human Resource Management Practices on Turnover, Productivity, and Corporate Financial Performance', *Academy of Management Journal* (1995), 38, 3, pp. 635–72.

Hutton, W., *The State We're In* (London: Jonathan Cape, 1996).

Hyman, R., 'The Historical Evolution of British Industrial Relations', in P. Edwards (ed.), *Industrial Relations: Theory and Practice in Britain* (Oxford: Blackwell, 1995), pp. 27–49.

Iles, P. and Salaman, G., 'Recruitment, Selection and Assessment', in J. Storey (ed.), *Human Resource Management* (London: Routledge, 1995), pp. 203–33.

Industrial Relations Review and Report, 'Recruitment and Training Abroad. The Labour Market in France', No. 500, November 1991.

Institute of Personnel Management, *Statement on Human Resource Planning* (London: IPM, 1992).

Inns, D., 'Organisation Development as a journey', in C. Oswick and D. Grant (eds.), *Organization Development: Metaphorical Explorations* (London: Pitman, 1996), pp. 20–34.

Jaques, E., *Equitable Payment* (New York: Wiley, 1961).

Jarvis, V. and Prais, S., 'Two Nations of Shopkeepers: Training for Retailing in Britain and France', *National Institute Economic Review* (1989), May, pp. 58–74.

Jenkins, A., 'The French Experience of Flexibility: Lessons for British HRM', in P. Sparrow and M. Marchington (eds.), *Human Resource Management* (London: Pitman Publishing, Financial Times, 1998), pp. 259–71.

Jick, T., 'Implementing change', Harvard Business School: Teaching Case No. 9 (1991), 491–514.

Jones, P. J., 'Outdoor management development: a journey to the centre of the metaphor', in C. Oswick and D. Grant, *Organization Development: Metaphorical Explorations*, (London: Pitman Publishing, 1996), pp. 209–25.

Juran, J. M., Sedler, L. A., and Gryna, F. M. Jr. (eds.), *Quality Control Handbook*, 2nd edn. (New York: McGraw-Hill, 1962).

Kamoche, K., 'The Integration–Differentiation Puzzle: A Resource-Capability Perspective in International HRM', *International Journal of Human Resource Management* (1996), 7, 1, pp. 230–44.

—— 'Strategic Human Resource Management Within A Resource-Capability View of the Firm', *Journal of Management Studies* (1996), March, 33, 2, pp. 213–33.

—— 'Knowledge Creation And Learning In International HRM', *International Journal of Human Resource Management* (1997), 8, 2, April, pp. 213–25.

Kandola, R. and Pearn, M., 'Identifying Competences', in R. Boam and P. Sparrow, *Designing and Achieving Competency: A Competency-Based Approach to Developing People and Organizations* (Maidenhead: McGraw-Hill, 1992), pp. 31–49.

Kanter, R. M., *The Change Masters: Corporate Entrepreneurs at Work* (London: Allen & Unwin, 1984).

Kaplan, R. S. and Norton, D. P., 'Begin by linking measurements to strategy', *Harvard Business Review* (1993), September–October, pp. 134–42.

Keenoy, T., 'HRM: Rhetoric, Reality and Contradiction', *International Journal of Human Resource Management* (1990), 1, 3, pp. 363–84.

—— 'HRM: a Case of the Wolf in Sheep's Clothing?' *Personnel Review* (1990), 19, 2, pp. 3–9.

—— and Anthony, P., 'Human Resource Management: Metaphor, Meaning and Morality', in P. Blyton and P. Turnbull (eds.), *Reassessing Human Resource Management* (London: Sage, 1992), pp. 233–55.

—— Oswick, C., and Grant, D., 'Organizational Discourses: Text and Context', *Organization* (1997), 4, 1, pp. 147–57.

Keep, E., 'Vocational education and training for the young', in K. Sisson (ed.), *Personnel Management: a Comprehensive Guide to Theory and Practice in Britain* (Oxford: Blackwell, 1994), pp. 299–333.

—— 'Missing links', *People Management* (1999), 5, 2, 28 January, p. 35.

—— and Mayhew, K., 'Training Policy for Competitiveness', in H. Metcalf (ed.), *Future Skill Demand and Supply* (London: PSI, 1995).

—— and Rainbird, H., 'Training', in P. Edwards (ed.), *Industrial Relations: Theory and Practice in Britain* (Oxford: Blackwell, 1995).

—— 'Performance pay', in K. Sisson (ed.), *Personnel Management: A Comprehensive Guide to Theory and Practice in Britain*, 2nd edn. (Oxford: Blackwell, 1994).

Kerfoot, D. and Knights, D., 'Empowering the quality worker? The seduction and contradiction of the total quality phenomenon', in A. Wilkinson and H. Wilmott, *Making Quality Critical: New Perspectives on Organizational Change* (London: Routledge, 1995) pp. 219–39.

Kessler, I., 'Reward Systems', in J. Storey (ed.), *Human Resource Management: A Critical Text* (London: Routledge, 1995), pp. 254–79.

Kets de Vries, M. F. R. and Balazs, K., 'The Downside of Downsizing', *Human Relations* (1997), 50, 1, pp. 11–50.

Kinnie, N. and Lowe, D., 'Performance related pay on the shopfloor', *Personnel Management* (1990), November, pp. 45–9.

—— and Purcell, J., 'Teamworking', *People Management* (1998), 4, 9, 30 April, p. 35.

Klein, K. J., 'Employee stock ownership and employee attitudes: a test of three models', *Journal of Applied Psychology Monograph* (1987), 72, 2, pp. 319–32.

Knights, D. and McCabe, D., 'How Would You Measure Something Like That?: Quality in a Retail Bank', *Journal of Management Studies* (1997), 34, 3, May, pp. 371–88.

—— —— 'The Times they are a Changin'? Transformative Organizational Innovations in Financial Services in the UK', *International Journal of Human Resource Management* (1998), 9, 1, February, pp. 168–84.

Kochan, T. A., Katz, H. C., and McKersie, R. B., *The Transformation of American Industrial Relations*, 1st edn. (New York: Basic Books, 1986).

—— —— —— *The Transformation of American Industrial Relations*, 2nd edn. (New York: Cornell University Press, 1994).

—— and Osterman, P., *The Mutual Gains Enterprise: Forging a Winning Partnership among Labor, Management and Government* (Boston, MA: Harvard Business School Press, 1994).

Kolb, D. A., *Individual Learning Styles and the Learning Process* (MIT Sloan School Working Paper No. 535–71, 1971).

—— *Experiential Learning* (Englewood Cliff, NJ: Prentice-Hall, 1984).

—— 'Management and the learning process', in K. Starkey, *How Organizations Learn* (London: International Thomson Business Press, 1996), pp. 270–87.

—— Rubin, I. M. and McIntyre, J. M., *Organizational Psychology: An Experiential Approach* (Englewood Cliffs, NJ: Prentice-Hall, 1974).

Kotter, J. P., *The General Managers* (New York: Free Press, 1982).

—— *A Force for Change: How Leadership Differs from Management* (New York: The Free Press, 1990).

—— *Leading Change* (Boston, MA: Harvard Business School Press, 1996).

Landy, F. J. and Becker, W. S., 'Motivation theory reconsidered', in L. L. Cummings and B. M. Staw (eds.), *Research in Organizational Behaviour*, Vol. 9 (Greenwich, CT: JAI Press, 1987).

—— 'Industrial Order and the Transformation of Industrial Relations: Britain, Germany and France Compared', in R. Hyman and A. Ferner (eds.), *New Frontiers in European Industrial Relations* (Oxford: Blackwell, 1994).

Latham, G. P. and Locke, E. A., 'Goal setting: a motivational technique that works', *Organizational Dynamics* (1979), 8, 2, pp. 68–80.

Lawler, E. E. III, 'The strategic design of reward systems', in C. Fombrun, N. M. Tichy, and M. A. Devanna, *Strategic Human Resource Management* (New York: John Wiley & Sons, 1984), pp. 127–47.

Leat, M., *Human Resource Issues of the European Union* (London: Financial Times, Pitman Publishing, 1998).

Legge, K., *Power, Innovation and Problem Solving in Personnel Management* (London: McGraw-Hill, 1978).

—— 'Human Resource Management—A Critical Analysis', in J. Storey (ed.), *New Perspectives on Human Resource Management* (London: Routledge, 1989), pp. 19–40.

—— *Human Resource Management: Rhetorics and Realities* (Basingstoke: Macmillan, 1995).

—— 'HRM: Rhetoric, Reality and Hidden Agendas', in J. Storey (ed.), *Human Resource Management: A Critical Text* (London: Routledge, 1995), pp. 33–59.

Lewin, K., *A Dynamic Theory of Personality: Selected Papers* (New York: McGraw-Hill, 1935).

—— 'Frontiers in group dynamics', *Human Relations* (1947), 1, pp. 5–42.

—— *Field Theory in Social Science* (New York: Harper, 1951).

Lewis, P., 'Managing Performance-Related Pay based on Evidence from the Financial Services Sector', *Human Resource Management Journal* (1998), 8, 2, pp. 66–77.

Long, R., 'The effects of employee ownership on organizational identification, employee job attitudes, and organizational performance: a tentative framework and empirical findings', *Human Relations* (1978), 31, 1, pp. 29–48.

Lorenz, C., 'Learning to Live with a Cultural Mix', *Financial Times*, 23 April, 1993.

Loveridge, R. and Mok, A., *Theories of Labour Market Segmentation: A Critique* (The Hague: Martinus Nijhoff, 1979).

Lyon, P., Hallier, J., and Glover, I., 'Divestment or Investment? The Contradiction of HRM in Relation to Older Employees', *Human Resource Management Journal* (1998), 8, 1, pp. 56–66.

MacDuffie, J. P., 'Human Resource Bundles and Manufacturing Performance: Flexible Productions in the World Auto Industry', *Industrial Relations and Labor Review* (1995), 48, pp. 97–221.

Management Charter Initiative (MCI) (1997) Management standards information pack. MCI, Russell Square House, 10–12 Russell Square, London WC1B 5BZ.

Mangham, I. and Silver, M. S., *Management Training: Context and Practice* (London: ESRC, 1986).

Marchington, M. and Wilkinson, A., *Core Personnel and Development* (London: IPD, 1996).

—— —— Ackers, P., and Goodman, J., *New Developments in Employee Involvement*, Employment Department Research Paper, Series No. 2, 1992.

Marginson, P. *et al.*, *Beyond the Workplace: Managing Industrial Relations in the Multi-Establishment Enterprise* (Oxford: Blackwell, 1988).

—— Armstrong, P., Edwards, P., Purcell, J. with Hubbard, N., *Warwick Papers in Industrial Relations*, No. 45, December, 1993.

—— and Sisson, K., 'The Structure of Transnational Capital in Europe: The Emerging Euro-Company and its Implications for Industrial Relations', in R. Hyman and A. Ferner (eds.), *New Frontiers in European Industrial Relations* (Oxford: Blackwell, 1994), pp. 15–51.

Marsden, D. and Richardson, R., 'Performing for pay? The effects of "merit pay" on motivation in a public service', *British Journal of Industrial Relations* (1994), 32, 2, June, pp. 243–62.

Martin, G., Staines, H., and Pate, J., 'Linking Job Security and Career Development in a New Psychological Contract', *Human Resource Management Journal* (1998), 8, 3, pp. 20–40.

Maslow, A. H., 'A Theory of Human Motivation', *Psychological Review* (1943), 50, pp. 370–96.

Mayo, A., 'Economic Indicators of Human Resource Management', in S. Tyson (ed.), *Strategic Prospects for HRM* (London: Institute of Personnel and Development 1995), pp. 229–65.

Mayo, E., *The Human Problems of an Industrial Civilisation* (New York: Macmillan, 1933).

McClelland, D. C., *The Achieving Society* (Princeton, NJ: Van Nostrand, 1961).

McGovern, P., *HRM, Technical Workers and the Multinational Corporation* (London: Routledge, 1998).

—— Gratton, L., Hope-Hailey, V., and Stiles, P., 'Human Resource Management on the Line?', *Human Resource Management Journal* (1997), 7, 4, pp. 12–29.

McGregor, D., *The Human Side of Enterprise* (New York: Harper Row, 1960).

McKenna, E. and Beech, N., *The Essence of Human Resource Management* (London: Prentice Hall, 1995).

Megginson, D. and Pedler, M., *Self-development: a Facilitator's Guide* (Maidenhead: McGraw-Hill, 1992).

Miller, E., 'Strategic staffing', in C. Fombrun, N. M. Tichy, and M. A. Devanna, *Strategic Human Resource Management* (New York: John Wiley & Sons, 1984).

Millward, N., *The New Industrial Relations?* (London: PSI, 1994).

—— Stevens, M., Smart, D., and Hawes, W., *Workplace Industrial Relations in Transition* (Aldershot: Dartmouth, 1992).

Mintzberg, H., 'Crafting Strategy', *Harvard Business Review* (1987), July–August, pp. 65–75.

Morgan, G., *Riding the Waves of Change: Developing Managerial Competencies for a Turbulent World* (San Francisco, CA: Jossey-Bass Inc, 1988).

Morris, J. and Wilkinson, B., 'The Transfer of Japanese Management to Alien Institutional Environments', *Journal of Management Studies* (1995), 32, 6, pp. 719–30.

Morris, T. J. and Pinnington, A. H., 'Promotion to partner in professional firms', *Human Relations* (1998), 51, 1, pp. 3–24.

—— and Pinnington, A. H., 'Evaluating Strategic fit in professional service firms', *Human Resource Management Journal* (1998), Vol. 8, No. 4, pp. 1–12.

Mueller, F., 'Societal Effect, Organisational Effect and Globalisation', *Organisation Studies* (1994), 15, 3, pp. 407–28.

—— 'Strategic Human Resource Management And The Resource-Based View Of The Firm: Toward A Conceptual Integration', *Aston University Business School Working Paper* (1994).

—— 'Human Resources As Strategic Assets: An Evolutionary Resource-Based Theory', *Journal of Management Studies* (1996), 33, 6, November, pp. 757–86.

Mumford, A., 'Individual and Organizational Learning: the Pursuit of Change', in *Managing Learning* (London, The Open University: Routledge, 1994).

—— Honey, P., and Robinson, G., *Director's Development Guidebook* (London: Institute of Directors and Employment Department, 1991).

Murakami, T., 'The formation of teams: a British and German comparison', *International Journal of Human Resource Management* (1998), 9, 5, October, pp. 800–17.

Nadler, D. A. and Tushman, M. L., 'Organisational frame bending: principles for managing reorientation', *The Academy of Management Executive Magazine* (1989), 3, 3, pp. 194–204

Newell, S., and Rice, C., 'Assessment, Selection and Evaluation: Problems and Pitfalls', in J. Leopold, L. Harris, and T. Watson, *Strategic Human Resourcing: Principles, Perspectives and Practices* (London: Financial Times, Pitman Publishing, 1999), pp. 129–65.

Office for National Statistics, *Labour Market Trends* (London: ONS, 1998).

Ohmae, K. *The Borderless World* (London: Collins, 1990).

Oliver, N., 'Work rewards, work values and organizational commitment in an employee owned firm: evidence from the UK', *Human Relations* (1990), 43, 6, pp. 513–26.

—— and Wilkinson, B., *The Japanization of British Industry* (Oxford: Blackwell, 1988).

—— —— *The Japanization of British Industry: New Developments in the 1990s* (Oxford: Blackwell, 1992).

Ouchi, W., *Theory Z* (Reading, MA: Addison-Wesley, 1981).

Parker, S. K. and Wall, T. D., 'Job Design and Modern Manufacturing', in P. Warr (ed.), *Psychology and Work*, 4th edn. (London: Penguin, 1996).

Parry, C., 'Overhead projector transparencies on UK experience of public sector change' (London [Whitehall]: Public Information Services, Cabinet Office, 1998).

Pedler, M., Burgoyne, J., and Boydell, T., *The Learning Company: A Strategy for Sustainable Development* (Maidenhead: McGraw-Hill, 1991).

*People Management*, 4, 15, 23 July, 1998.

*People Management*, 4, 16, 13 August, 1998.

—— 4, 19, 1 October, 1998.

—— 4, 24, 10 December, 1998.

—— 4, 25, 24 December, 1998.

—— 5, 1, 14 January, 1999.

—— 5, 2, 28 January, 1999.

Perls, F. S., Hefferline, R., and Goodman, P., *Gestalt Therapy: Excitement and Growth in the Human Personality* (Harmondsworth: Penguin (reprinted), 1977).

Peters, T. J. and Waterman, R. H. Jr., *In Search of Excellence: Lessons from America's Best Run Companies* (New York: Harper and Row, 1982).

Pettigrew, A. M., *The Politics of Organisational Decision Making* (London: Tavistock, 1973).

—— *The Awakening Giant: Continuity and Change in ICI* (Oxford: Blackwell, 1985).

—— and Whipp, R., *Managing Change for Competitive Success* (Oxford: Blackwell, 1991).

Pfeffer, J., *Competitive Advantage through People* (Boston, MA: Harvard Business School Press, 1994).

Pinder, C. C., 'Valence-Instrumentality-Expectancy Theory', in V. H. Vroom and E. L. Deci (eds.), *Management and Motivation* 2nd edn. (Harmondsworth: Penguin Books, 1992).

Pinnington, A. H., 'The formative evaluation of interactive video', unpublished PhD thesis (Henley Management College and Brunel University, Uxbridge, 1990).

—— and Hammersley, G. C., 'Quality circles under the new deal at Land Rover', *Employee Relations* (1997), Vol. 19, No. 5, pp. 415–29.

Pitt, G., *Employment Law* (London: Sweet and Maxwell, 1995).

Poole, M. and Jenkins, G., 'How employees respond to profit sharing', *Personnel Management* (1988), July, p. 33.

—— —— 'Developments in Human Resource Management in Manufacturing in Modern Britain', *International Journal of Human Resource Management* (1997), 8, 6, December, pp. 841–56.

Porter, L. W. and Lawler III, E. E., *Managerial Attitudes and Performance* (Homewood, IL: Irwin-Dorsey, 1968).

Porter, M., *Competitive Advantage: Creating and Sustaining Superior Performance* (New York: Macmillan, The Free Press, 1985)).

Porter, M., *The Competitive Advantage of Nations* (New York: Free Press, 1990).

Prahalad, C. and Hamel, G., 'The core competence of the corporation', *Harvard Business Review* (1990), May–June, pp. 79–91.

Pugh, D. S., 'The Measurement of Organisation Structures: Does Context Determine Form?', *Organisational Dynamics* (1973), Spring, pp. 19–34 in D. S. Pugh (ed.) *Organization Theory: Selected Readings*, 3rd edn. (London: Penguin Books, 1990) pp. 44–63.

Pugh, D. S., 'The Measurement of Organization Structures: Does Context Determine Form?', in D. S. Pugh (ed.), *Organization Theory: Selected Readings*, 3rd edn (London: Penguin Books, 1990).

Purcell, J. and Gray, A., 'Corporate personnel departments and the management of industrial relations: two cases in ambiguity', *Journal of Management Studies* (1986), 23, 2, pp. 205–23.

Redman, T. and Keithley, D., 'Downsizing goes East? Employment restructuring in post-Socialist Poland', *International Journal of Human Resource Management* (1998), 9, 2, April, p. 274–95.

Reger, R. K., Gustafson, L. T., Demarie, S. M., and Mullane, J. V., 'Reframing the organisation: why implementing total quality is easier said than done', *Academy of Management Review* (1994), 19, 3, pp. 565–84.

Reich, R., 'Who Is Us?', *Harvard Business Review* (1990), Jan–Feb, pp. 53–64.

Revans, R., *Action Learning* (London: Blond & Briggs, 1980).

—— *The ABC of Action Learning* (London: Chartwell-Bratt, 1983).

Reynolds, A. and Iwinski, T., *Multimedia Training: Developing Technology-based Systems* (New York: McGraw-Hill, 1996).

Robbins, S. P., *Organizational Behaviour: Concepts, Controversies, Applications* (Upper Saddle River, NJ: Prentice-Hall, 1998).

Robertson, I. T., Iles, P. A., Gratton, L., and Sharpley, D., 'The Psychological Impact of Selection Procedures on Candidates', *Human Relations* (1991), 44, 9, pp. 963–82.

Rogers, C., *On Becoming a Person: a Therapist's View of Psychotherapy* (London: Constable, 1961).

Romiszowski, A. J., *Producing Instructional Systems* (London: Kogan Page, 1986).

Rosenzweig, P. and Nohria, N., 'Influences on Human Resource Management Practices in Multinational Corporations', *Journal of International Business Studies* (1994), 25, 2, 229–51.

Rothwell, S., 'Human Resource Planning', in J. Storey (ed.), *Human Resource Management: A Critical Text* (London: Routledge, 1995), pp. 167–202.

Rowntree, D., *Exploring Open and Distance Learning* (London: Kogan Page, 1992).

*Royal Commission on Trade Unions and Employers' Associations Report* (Donovan Commission) (HMSO: London, 1968).

Ruigrok, W. and Van Tulder, R., *The Logic of International Restructuring* (London: Routledge, 1996).

Salancik, G. R., and Pfeffer, J., 'An Examination of Need Satisfaction Models of Job Attitudes', *Administrative Science Quarterly* (1977), 22, pp. 427–56.

Schein, E. H., *Career Dynamics: Matching Individual and Organisational Needs* (Reading, MA: Addison-Wesley, 1978).

—— 'How "career anchors" hold executives to their career paths', in R. Katz (ed.), *Managing Professionals in Innovative Organizations* (Cambridge, MA: Ballinger Publishing Company, Harper & Row, 1988), pp. 487–97.

—— *Organizational Culture and Leadership*, 2nd edn. (San Francisco: Jossey-Bass, 1992).

Schoenberger, R., *World Class Manufacturing* (New York: The Free Press, 1986).

Schroder, H. M., *Managerial Competence: The Key to Excellence* (Iowa: Kendall Hunt, 1989).

Schuler, R. S. and Huselid, M., 'HR strategy in the United States', in S. Tyson (ed.), *The Practice of Human Resource Strategy*. (London: Pitman, 1997).

—— and Jackson, S. E., *Human Resource Management: Positioning for the 21st Century*, 6th edn. (Minneapolis, St. Paul: West Publishing Company, 1996), pp. 137–41.

—— —— 'Linking Competitive Strategies with Human Resource Management Practices', *Academy of Management Executive* (1987), 1, 3, pp. 207–19.

Scullion, H., 'International HRM', in J. Storey (ed.), *Human Resource Management: A Critical Text* (London: Routledge, 1995), pp. 352–82.

Senge, P., *The Fifth Discipline: The Art and Practice of the Learning Organization* (New York: Doubleday/Currency, 1990).

Senge, P., 'The Leader's New Work: Building Learning Organizations', in K. Starkey, *How Organizations Learn* (London: International Thomson Business Press, 1996), pp. 288–315.

Shackleton, V. and Newell, S., 'European management selection methods: A comparison of five countries', *International Journal of Selection and Assessment* (1994), 2, pp. 91–102.

Shapira, Z., 'Expectancy Determinants of Intrinsically Motivated Behavior', abridged from the *Journal of Personality and Social Psychology* (1976), Vol. 34, pp. 235–44 in V. H. Vroom and E. L. Deci, *Management and Motivation*, 2nd edn (London: Penguin Books, 1992).

Sisson, K., *The Management of Collective Bargaining: An International Comparison* (Oxford: Blackwell, 1987).

—— 'In Search of HRM', *British Journal of Industrial Relations* (1993), 31, 2, pp. 201–10.

—— (ed.), *Personnel Management: A Comprehensive Guide to Theory and Practice in Britain*, 2nd edn. (Oxford: Blackwell Business, 1994).

—— and Marginson, P., 'Management: Systems, Structures and Strategy', in P. Edwards (ed.), *Industrial Relations: Theory and Practice in Britain* (Oxford: Blackwell, 1995), pp. 89–122.

Snape, E., Thompson, D., Yan, F. K., and Redman, T., 'Performance appraisal and culture: practice and attitudes in Hong Kong and Great Britain', *International Journal of Human Resource Management* (1998), 9, 5, October, pp. 841–61.

Sparrow, P., 'New Organisational Forms, Processes, Jobs and Psychological Contracts: Resolving the HRM Issues', in P. Sparrow and M. Marchington (eds.), *Human Resource Management: The New Agenda* (London: Financial Times, Pitman Publishing, 1998), pp. 117–41.

—— and Hiltrop, J.-M., *European Human Resource Management in Transition* (Hemel Hempstead: Prentice-Hall, 1994).

—— and Marchington, M., 'Re-engaging the HRM Function', in P. Sparrow and M. Marchington (eds.), *Human Resource Management: The New Agenda* (London: Pitman Publishing, The Financial Times, 1998), pp. 296–313.

—— (eds.), *Human Resource Management: The New Agenda* (London: Financial Times, Pitman Publishing, 1998).

Starkey, K., *How Organizations Learn* (London: International Thomson Business Press, 1996).

—— and McKinlay, A., *Strategy and the Human Resource: Ford and the Search for Competitive Advantage* (Oxford: Blackwell, 1993).

—— —— 'Product Development in Ford of Europe: Undoing the Past/Learning the Future', in K. Starkey (ed.), *How Organizations Learn* (London: International Thomson Business Press, 1996), pp. 214–29.

Steedman, H. and Wagner, K., 'Productivity, Machinery and Skills: Clothing Manufacture in Britain and Germany', *National Institute Economic Review* (1989), 128, May.

Stiles, P., Gratton, L., Truss, C., Hope-Hailey, V., and McGovern, P., 'Performance Management and the Psychological Contract', *Human Resource Management Journal* (1997), 7, 1, pp. 57–66.

Storey, J., 'Developments in the management of human resources: an interim report', *Warwick Papers in International Relations* (University of Warwick, November, 1987).

—— *New Perspectives on Human Resource Management*, 2nd edn. (London: Routledge, 1991).

—— *Developments in the Management of Human Resources* (Oxford: Blackwell, 1992).

—— (ed.), *Human Resource Management: a Critical Text* (London: Routledge, 1995).

—— and Bacon, N., with J. Edmonds and P. Wyatt, 'The "New Agenda" and Human Resources Management: A Roundtable Discussion with John Edmonds', *Human Resource Management Journal* (1993), 4, 1, pp. 63–70.

—— and Sisson, K., *Managing Human Resources and Industrial Relations* (Milton Keynes: Open University Press, 1993).

Streeck, W., 'Skills and the Limits of neo-Liberalism', *Work, Employment and Society* (1989), 3, 2, pp. 89–104.

Summerfield, J. and van Oudtshoorn, L., *Counselling in the Workplace* (London: IPD, 1995).

Swabe, A. I. R., 'Performance-related pay: a case study', *Employee Relations* (1989), Vol. 11, No. 2, pp. 17–23.

Tayeb, M., 'Transfer of HRM practices across cultures: An American company in Scotland', *International Journal of Human Resource Management* (1998), 9, 2, April, pp. 332–58.

Taylor, P. and Walker, A., 'Policies and Practices Towards Older Workers: A Framework For Comparative Research', *Human Resource Management Journal* (1998), 8, 3, pp. 61–76.

Terry, M., 'Trade Unions: Shop Stewards and the Workplace', in P. Edwards (ed.), *Industrial Relations: Theory and Practice in Britain* (Oxford: Blackwell, 1995).

Torrington, D. and Chee Huat, T., *Human Resource Management for South-east Asia* (London: Prentice-Hall International (UK) Ltd, 1994).

—— and Hall, L., *Personnel Management: HRM in Action*, 3rd edn. (Hemel Hempstead: Prentice Hall, 1995).

Towers, B., *The Handbook of Human Resource Management*, 2nd edn. (Oxford: Blackwell, 1992).

Townley, B., 'Selection and Appraisal: Reconstituting "Social Relations"?', in J. Storey (ed.), *New Perspectives on Human Resource Management* (London: Routledge, 1991), pp. 92–108.

—— *Reframing Resource Management: Power, Ethics, and the Subject at Work* (London: Sage), 1994.

Trist, E. L. and Bamforth, K. W., 'Some social and psychological consequences of the longwall method of coal-getting', *Human Relations* (1951), 4, pp. 3–38.

—— Higgin, C. W., Murray, H., and Pollock, A. M., *Organizational Choice* (London: Tavistock Institute, 1963).

Trompenaars, F., *Riding the Waves of Culture* (London: Economist Books, 1993).

Truss, C., Gratton, L., Hope-Hailey, V., McGovern, P., and Stiles, P., 'Soft and Hard Models of Human Resource Management: A Reappraisal', *Journal of Management Studies* (1997), 34, 1, January, pp. 53–73.

Tyson, S. (ed.), *The Practice of Human Resource Strategy* (London: Financial Times, Pitman Publishing, 1997).

—— and Fell, A., *Evaluating the Personnel Function* (London: Hutchinson, 1986).

—— —— 'Looking Ahead'. in S. Tyson (ed.), *Strategic Propsects for HRM* (London, Institute of Personnel and Development, 1995), pp. 266–89.

United Nations, *World Investment Report* (New York: United Nations, 1998).

Vecchio, R. P., *Organisational Behavior*, 3rd edn. (Orlando, FL: The Dryden Press, 1995).

Vroom, V. H., *Work and Motivation* (New York: Wiley, 1964).

—— and Deci, E. L., (eds.), *Management and Motivation*, 2nd edn. (Harmondsworth: Penguin Books, 1992).

Waddington, J. and Whitston, C., 'Trade Unions: Growth, Structure and Policy', in P. Edwards (ed.), *Industrial Relations: Theory and Practice in Britain* (Oxford: Blackwell, 1995).

Walton, R. E., 'Toward a Strategy of Eliciting Employee Commitment Based on Policies of Mutuality', in R. E. Walton and P. R. Lawrence (eds.), *Human Resource Management—Trends and Challenges* (Boston: Harvard Business School Press, 1985), pp. 35–65.

—— 'From control to commitment in the workplace', *Harvard Business Review* (1985), 63, 2, pp. 77–84.

Watson, T. J., *The Personnel Managers: A Study in the Sociology of Work and Industry* (London: Routledge, and Kegan Paul, 1977).

—— *Management, Organization and Employment Strategy: New Directions in Theory and Practice* (London: Routledge and Kegan Paul, 1986).

—— *In Search of Management—Culture, Chaos and Control in Managerial Work* (London: Routledge, 1994).

Webb, J., 'The open door? Women and equal opportunity at ComCo (North)', in D. Gowler, K. Legge and C. Clegg, *Case Studies in Organizational Behaviour and Human Resource Management*, 2nd edn. (London: Paul Chapman Publishing, 1993), pp. 92–105.

—— and Palmer, G., 'Evading surveillance and making time: an ethnographic view of the factory floor in Britain', *British Journal of Industrial Relations* (1998), 36, 4, December, pp. 611–627.

Welch, J. F., 'A matter of exchange rates', *Wall Street Journal* (1994), 21 June, p. 23.

West, M. A., Borril, C. S. and Unsworth, K. L., 'Team effectiveness in organizations', in C. L. Cooper and I. T. Robertson (eds.), *International Review of Industrial and Organizational Psychology*, Vol. 13, (Chichester, John Wiley, 1998), pp. 1–48 at p. 32.

Whitley, R. (ed.), *European Business Systems: Firms and Markets in their National Contexts* (London: Sage, 1992).

Whittington, R., *What is Strategy—and Does it Matter?* (London: Routledge, 1993).

—— McNulty, T. and Whipp, R., 'Market-driven change in professional services: problems and processes', *Journal of Management Studies* (1994), 31, 6, November, pp. 829–45.

Wickens, P. D., *The Road to Nissan* (London: Macmillan, 1987).

Wilkinson, B., Morris, J. and Munday, M., 'Japan in Wales: a New IR', *Industrial Relations Journal* (1993), 24, 4, pp. 273–83.

Williams, S., 'Strategy and objectives', in F. Neale (ed.), *The Handbook of Performance Management* (London: Institute of Personnel Management, 1992), pp. 7–24.

Williamson, D. E., *Markets and Hierachies: Analysis and Anti-trust Implications* (New York: The Free Press, 1975).

Wilson, D. C., *A Strategy of Change: Concepts and Controversies in the Management of Change* (London: Routledge, 1992).

Wilson, F. M., *Organizational Behaviour and Gender* (Maidenhead: McGraw-Hill, 1995).

Womack, J. P., Jones, D. T., and Roos, D., *The Machine that Changed the World: The Triumph of Lean Production* (New York: Rawson, Macmillan, 1990).

Wood, S. and Albanese, M., 'Can We Speak of a High Commitment Management on the Shop Floor?', *Journal of Management Studies* (1995), 32, 2, pp. 1–33.

Woodruffe, C., 'What is meant by a competency', in R. Boam, and P. Sparrow, *Designing and Achieving Competency: A Competency-Based Approach to Developing People and Organizations*, (Maidenhead: McGraw-Hill, 1992), pp. 16–30.

Wright and Storey 'Recruitment and Selection' in I. Beardwell and L. Holden, *Human Resource Management: a Contemporary Perspective*, 2nd edn. (London: Financial Times, Pitman Publishing, 1997), 210–76.

# Index